"This book makes an important and highly valuable contribution to a renewed interest and multifaceted debate on justice seeking in the legally plural contexts of African postcolonies and beyond. It does so through a complex and very nuanced study of legal proceedings in Botswana that have played out in different customary and state courts as well as religious fora over the past 50 years. Written by renowned and long-established experts in the field with an exceptional depth of personal experience of the local dynamics and complexities, the book makes an important theoretical case for combining jurisprudential debates on public ethics with a study of living laws within the normative pluralities characterising not only the postcolony, but increasingly also the world at large."

Olaf Zenker, Chair of Social and Cultural Anthropology at the Martin-Luther-University, Halle-Wittenberg, Germany

African Customary Justice

This book presents an important ethnographic and theoretical advance in legal anthropological scholarship by interrogating customary law, customary courts, and legal pluralism in sub-Saharan Africa. It highlights the vitality and continued relevance of customary justice at a time when customary courts have waned or even disappeared in many postcolonial African nations.

Taking Botswana as a case study from in-depth fieldwork over a fifty-year period, the book shows, the 'customary' is robustly enduring, central to settling interpersonal disputes, and constitutive of the local as well as the national public ethics. Customary law continues to be constitutionally protected, authorised by the country's past as an authentic, viable legacy, from the British colonial period of indirect rule to the postcolonial state's present development as a highly bureaucratised democracy. Along with a theoretical overview of the underlying issues for the anthropology and sociology of law, the book documents customary law as living law in the context of legal pluralism. It takes a legal realist approach and highlights the need to pay close attention to the lived experience of justice and its role in the production of legal subjectivities.

The book will be valuable to Africanists but also, more broadly, to social scientists, social historians and socio-legal scholars with interests in law and social change, public ethics and personal morality, and the intersection of politics and judicial decision making.

Pnina Werbner is Professor Emerita of Social Anthropology, Keele University, UK. She has published extensively on Law and Anthropology.

Richard Werbner is Professor Emeritus in African Anthropology, Honorary Research Professor in Visual Anthropology, the University of Manchester, sometime Senior Post-Doctoral Fellow, Smithsonian Institution, Senior Fellow (National Humanities Center), Overseas Professor (National Museum of Ethnology, Osaka). He has recently given the Elliot P. Skinner Memorial Lecture for the Association for Africanist Anthropology, the Royal African Society Lecture, and the Jackman Lectures.

Cultural Diversity and Law

Around the world, most states are faced with difficult issues arising out of cultural diversity in their territories. Within the legal field, such issues span across matters of private law through to public and constitutional law. At international level too there is now considerable jurisprudence regarding ethnic, religious and cultural diversity. In addition, there are several layers of legal control – from communal and religious regulation to state and international regulation. This multiplicity of norm setting has been variously termed legal pluralism, inter-legality or inter-normativity, and provides a fascinating lens for academic analysis that links up to cultural diversity in new and interesting ways. The umbrella of cultural diversity encompasses various population groups throughout the world ranging from national, ethnic to religious or indigenous groupings. This series particularly welcomes work that is of comparative interest, concerning various state jurisdictions as well as different population groups.

Series Editor:
Prakash Shah, School of Law, Queen Mary University of London, UK

Also in the series

Law, Cultural Diversity, and Criminal Defense
Craig L. Carr and Lisa Johnson

Culture and the Judiciary
The Anthropologist Judge
Ilenia Ruggiu

African Customary Justice
Living Law, Legal Pluralism, and Public Ethics
Richard Werbner and Pnina Webrner

For more information about this series, please visit:
https://www.routledge.com/Cultural-Diversity-and-Law/book-series/CULTDIV

African Customary Justice

Living Law, Legal Pluralism, and Public Ethics

Pnina Werbner and Richard Werbner

Routledge
Taylor & Francis Group
LONDON AND NEW YORK

First published 2022
by Routledge
2 Park Square, Milton Park, Abingdon, Oxon OX14 4RN

and by Routledge
605 Third Avenue, New York, NY 10158

Routledge is an imprint of the Taylor & Francis Group, an informa business

British Library Cataloguing-in-Publication Data
A catalogue record for this book is available from the British Library

Library of Congress Cataloging-in-Publication Data
A catalog record has been requested for this book

ISBN: 978-1-032-14943-1 (hbk)
ISBN: 978-1-032-14946-2 (pbk)
ISBN: 978-1-003-24188-1 (ebk)

DOI: 10.4324/9781003241881

Typeset in Galliard
by Deanta Global Publishing Services, Chennai, India

In memory of Ontlogetse Mafoko,
and dedicated to our wonderful research assistants
Disikalala Sebata Gaseitsiwe, Gaseitsiwe Gaseitsiwe. Njebe Molefhe
Gabanakgosi, and Queen Gaseitsiwe

Figure 0.1 Moremi's newly built court.

Contents

Figures

Acknowledgements

This book is a product of almost 50 years of research. Our fieldwork in Moremi village began when Richard Werbner made a brief reconnaissance visit to Tswapong Hills in Botswana's Central District in 1971. In 1972–73, supported by a research grant awarded to him by the Social Science Research Council, UK, we arrived for a year's fieldwork and made our home in the village of Moremi, or Goo-Moremi as it is now gazetted. We are indebted to the people of Moremi who continued to welcome us so hospitably throughout our research in the village until our last visit in 2018.

The main customary law cases presented here were recorded by us and, with the help of our research assistants, transcribed in Tswana, and then translated into English. We dedicate this book to these assistants, and hope they will enjoy it as a testament to their remarkable dedication, cultural insight, and tireless collaboration. We are deeply grateful to Ontlogetse Mafoko who helped introduce us to the village; to Sebata, Gaseitsiwe, and Queen, all from the Gaseitsiwe family, and finally, to Njebe Molefhe Gabanakgosi. The family became our main hosts on our later visits; Gaseitsiwe lent us the one-room thatched house or hut he had built when he was a young labour migrant before he built his own substantial homestead nearby; and we lived there for most of our later fieldwork trips. Queen translated many of the later recordings and the customary court records. Days Lengonapelo and finally, his son, Tshito Days, also took a great interest in our research and generously supported us throughout it.

We are especially grateful to Professor Bojosi Otlhogile of the University of Botswana for his invaluable advice on the changes that have occurred in customary law in Botswana and for his meticulous comments on different chapters of the book. We are ourselves responsible, of course, for the text, as it stands. Our visits to Botswana's capital gave us the chance to discuss our work in progress with friends and colleagues at the University of Botswana. At the risk of singling too few out, we want to offer our special thanks to Phineas and Pauline Makepe, Richard and Rosina Mannathoko, Changu Mannathoko, Joy and Mphapi Phumapi, Pinky and Mbiganyi Charles Tibone, and John Makgala. Lesedi Leepile, and Kagiso Senthufhe of the Ministry of Local Government and Land Development were immensely helpful and supportive throughout the later part of the research.

Over the years, research funding was awarded from different bodies including the Hayter fund of the University of Manchester; the Social Science Research Council, UK; the Economic and Social Research Council UK; and the Nuffield Foundation. Most recently, between 2015 and 2017, the research was funded in an Emeritus Fellowship granted to Pnina by the Leverhulme Trust on the topic of 'The Changing Kgotla: The Transformation of Customary Courts in Village Botswana' (Ref. EM-2015-014). The authors wish to express their gratitude to all these research bodies for their assistance and particularly to the Leverhulme Trust for its generous support.

Earlier versions of various chapters were presented at the universities of Manchester, Keele, London (S.O.A.S.), Wales (Swansea), and Botswana, at the EASA biannual conference in a session on Law and Emotion, and at the Satterthwaite Colloquium. We wish to thank participants in all these events for their excellent comments. Chapters 7, 8, 9, and 10 draw extensively on Werbner and Werbner (2018, 2019, 2020a, and 2020b). The map of Tswapong (Figure 2.1) is printed courtesy of Pnina Motzafi-Haller (2002).

1 Introduction

Living law, chiefship and legal pluralism in Botswana

The entanglement of the law in everyday life and common-sense assumptions is as true of legal practice in modern courts as it is in customary courts in Africa. This book responds to a movement in legal scholarship towards a new legal realism and the comparative critical study of social and cultural change in the quest for justice. We carry our response forward with a whole range of cases, from suits over communal affairs, governance, and criminal justice to personal disputes over divorce, adultery, inheritance, and insult. Our aim is to bring the strengths of ethnography to bear upon this movement and on the growing socio-legal interest in living law.

The documentation, offered in depth and with due care for the people's own ideas and their vernacular terms, shows the case-by-case deployment of forensic reason in argumentation. It is a range of cases that extends across a breadth of legal pluralism, including state and non-state authorities, in complex, often-reviewed processes of decision-making. Foregrounded in our analysis of these cases is the semi-autonomy of customary courts, their flexibility, and their resilience as popular deliberative forums.

Our approach, with critical attention to issues of proportionality and the fit between punishment and crime, such as in excessive sentences for cattle rustling, does not disregard wrongs in law enforcement, but we focus on the regard by the people themselves for the courts' respect for honesty and fairness, equity, and due process. Hence, our accounts of how people argue and decide or even fail fully to decide their cases disclose the bearing of public ethics and personal morality as well as lawfare and politics in the quest for justice.

We pursue throughout the book the implications of our cases for a growing and interdisciplinary literature on postcolonial transformations in the quest for justice. In its heyday, the study of customary law in Africa, particularly during the colonial period, engaged some of the most prominent anthropologists of the twentieth century. The renewed interest in this topic, after a hiatus of almost 50 years, has occurred particularly in the post-apartheid era, and especially in studies by socio-legal scholars and a younger generation of anthropologists. There has been a vast outpouring of articles on living law, mainly in South Africa, indicative of the great interest in the topic.

DOI: 10.4324/9781003241881-1

Our book engages with these studies as it also picks up an interrupted conversation on law and ethics, legal pluralism and communal law, and collective identity and village chiefship as these are played out in the postcolonial era.[1] According to the recent South African Law Commission, living law 'rests squarely on the existing and generally accepted social practices of a community' and is thus 'imprecise, flexible, and liable to constant and subtle change' (Oomen 2005: 200–201). Accordingly, our approach is ethnographic, closely informed by first-hand fieldwork among people we have come to know well and who have come to know us well over many years, in particular during our research in Botswana and, since 1972, primarily in Moremi, a small village in the country's Central District. We focus our ethnography on customary law as living law, responsive to change. Among reasons for this focus, the most compelling is the continuing importance of customary law as it is negotiated and renegotiated in the everyday lives of villagers in Moremi and its neighbours. They are powerfully aware of uncertainties in a changing wider world and yet they ground most of their arguments, though not all, of course, on premises of tradition and culturally received procedure. We show that customary law in the context of political and structural flux is negotiated and processual (Oomen 2005: 203).

A key impetus for the book has been the striking fact, noted by Fombad (2004: 167), that, at a time when the 'role of customary courts in the legal systems of many African countries is on the wane', customary courts in Botswana 'have shown a remarkable resilience and, arguably, have reacted rather robustly to the contact and interaction with modern statutory courts, so that their role in the settlement of disputes has come to surpass even that of the modern courts' (ibid.).

At the same time, as we show in Chapter 9, procedural changes introduced by the state threaten the civic, participatory nature of customary courts, whereas, against that, the Court of Appeal attempts to preserve the (semi-) autonomy of customary courts.

Much has been written about the public sphere as a deliberative forum (Werbner 2004). The village customary court we consider, known as the *kgotla*, is viewed by many scholars as a precursor of democracy, and the tradition of deliberation in court is seen to underpin the successful upholding of democracy since independence in 1966 (Molutsi and Holm 1990). But what exactly is the *kgotla* today?

1 Among relevant works, Sapignoli (2018) on Botswana, Johnson (2018) on Malawi, Oomen (2005: 200 *et passim*) and Himonga and Moore (2015) on South Africa, and Zenker and Hoehne (2018) on sub-Saharan Africa stand out; also illuminating are Comaroff (2018) on chiefship in Africa, Johnson and Karekwaivanane (2018) on justice in Africa, Faulk and Brunnegger (2016), and Brunnegger (2019), both on justice more widely, beyond Africa. At the same time there is, particularly for Africa, a remarkable dearth of in-depth contemporary monographs/ethnographies on legal pluralism, customary law, courts, and chiefship, with the important exceptions of Ntsebeza (2005)'s historical monograph, Sapignoli (2018), and Johnson (2018).

The present book analyses the *kgotla* in the light of socio-legal and anthropological, legal scholarship on colonial and postcolonial customary law. We argue that earlier studies, which raised questions of legal pluralism and customary law as an evolving, living law, require further consideration in the context of a postcolonial country's present development as a highly bureaucratised democracy. Of course, much of the bureaucratic practice, apparently swelling in increasing complexity and an avalanche of paperwork, is beyond our present scope.

Three major themes are entangled in the contemporary scholarly debate: customary law as generative of and responsive to 'living law' in the face of radical political and legal change; legal pluralism; and the 'paradox' of chiefship as a viable institution in African democracies.

Recently, there has been a significantly renewed interest in the anthropology of justice (see Clarke 2019; Faulk and Brunnegger 2016; Sapignoli 2018: 9), not as an abstract, philosophical concept but as embodied practice – an ethnographically embedded sense of rightful entitlements and practice. Faulk and Brunnegger argue that 'an anthropology of justice needs to pay close attention to the lived experience of justice and its role in the production of legal subjectivities' (2016: 9). Such legal subjectivities, we show, range from the collective and communal to the individual, as subjects negotiate among themselves and with ruling, powerful outsiders. When it comes to customary courts, however, a neglected theme at the heart of an anthropology of justice is that of the experiential and intellectual dimensions of ethics and morality as they relate to and are applied to the law by local actors. This is the issue we turn to first.

Ethics and customary law: a forgotten topic in legal anthropology?

When anthropology writ large rejected the focus on morality that emerged within legal anthropology in the 1950s, the discipline effectively ruptured a fruitful conversation just started with socio-legal scholars. It is remarkable that, outside of legal anthropology, there has only recently been a renewed disciplinary interest in local notions of ethics and moral conduct, mostly within studies of ritual and religion (e.g., Lambek 2003; Mahmood 2005; Robbins 2013, R. Werbner 2015, 2019),[2] and almost entirely focused on personal ethics. This is exemplified in the contention of Laidlaw (2002) that, despite anthropology's indebtedness to Durkheim, it has, surprisingly, produced 'no sustained field of enquiry and debate' on ethics and morality, no 'connected history'. Other than a nod to Malinowski's *Crime and Custom in Savage Society* (1926), Laidlaw omits legal anthropology from his

2 Against claims by these authors, questions of ethics were never really absent from discussions of religion. With regard to law, Clifford Geertz, writing from a sharply cultural relativist perspective, stressed that indigenous cultural notions of justice were incommensurable, so unique as to make it impossible to draw sociological (as against intercultural) comparisons across societies (1983).

overview, and focuses instead on agency and freedom as theorised, not by anthropologists, but by philosophers – Kant, Nietzsche, and Foucault. Issues of legal public ethics and morality remained relatively untouched in this renewed discussion, until the recent interest in public ethics in state bureaucracies (Bierschenck and Olivier der Sardan 2014; Eckert 2021) and the recent rise of an anthropology of human rights, engaged with wider interdisciplinary debates but without attending to earlier disciplinary considerations of ethics in dispute settlement.[3] One has to go back to the work of Max Gluckman on judicial decision-making among the Barotse of Northern Rhodesia (now Zambia) to find a clearly laid-out, foundational anthropological analysis of the morality and ethics of law in non-Western societies.

Whereas this earlier generation of legal anthropologists, led by Gluckman, carried on an interdisciplinary conversation on judicial moral reasoning, their fellow anthropologists dismissed them for being 'ethnocentric', and the discussion was summarily abandoned. As a result, with the few exceptions highlighted below, neither discipline – anthropology nor socio-legal studies – has appreciated the other's cognate work about the ethics and morality of the law. In the present book, we try to show, however, that such comparisons can – and did – contribute to the development of shared interdisciplinary theoretical insights across legal anthropology and socio-legal studies, regarding the morality and rationality of the law, and, more specifically, morally grounded judicial reasoning. We illustrate this here first with an overview of debates in legal anthropology before turning to the deployment of moral reasoning in Botswana's modern-day courts.

Although Gluckman did not identify himself explicitly with any school of thought, his debates with a range of jurists make it clear that he is a post-Legal Realist critic,[4] and his writings constitute a precursor of discussions on morality and law in the works of Ronald Dworkin and others. He follows Llewellyn and Hoebel's Realist view, expressed in *The Cheyenne Way*, that 'the safest main road into the discovery of law' was 'through the study of disputes or "trouble cases"' because 'not only the making of new law [but] the effect of old … shine clear through the crucible of conflict' (Ubink 2011: 86).

Gluckman accepted the Realists' view that the law allows, indeed requires, wide latitude for interpretation. For any case, facts must be assembled and judged as they occur in particular social situations, in accord with a variety of sometimes conflicting rules. As he says, 'Judicial decision supplements legislation. Through the 'reasonable standards' they [the Barotse] maintain their traditional laws and traditional morals, and yet cope with the effects of the introduction of Christianity and schools, labour for whites and money and trade-goods, new

3 On the whole, anthropologists have approached human rights with caution, as in Wilson's highly sceptical and critical analysis of the Truth and Reconciliation Commission in the post-apartheid era in South Africa (2001), or Englund's (2006) trenchant critique of human rights NGOs' poor record in defence of employee labour rights *vis-à-vis* employers in Malawi, despite a raft of recent progressive liberal legislation there.

4 The 'post' refers to his additional stress on ambiguity in language and the flexibility of terms and concepts, an issue taken up by later legal scholars.

skills, changes in every aspect of Barotse life' (1963: 192). In deploying notions of reasonable behaviour or the 'reasonable man,' he says, 'Social principles and prejudices, customs and habits, group interests, and individual experiences are absorbed to relate the fixed rules of law to the changing variety of life. But the law aims at justice, and the idea of a reasonable man implies an upright man' (ibid.).

Law is thus marked by an essential 'indeterminacy,' allowing for 'judicial discretion,' a starting point for Gluckman's analysis, as it was for the Realists (see ibid.: 198). Indeterminacy implies, as the American Appeal Court Judge Benjamin Cardozo argued, that the law is a malleable instrument that allows judges to mould amorphous words like 'reasonable care', 'unreasonable restraint of trade', and 'due process', to justify any outcome they desire. To avoid the potential for legal arbitrariness, Realists such as Cardozo advocated that all judges must interpret the law to advance the welfare of society. Thus, some Realists, it has been argued, turned Bentham's philosophy on its head, arguing that the law should serve the interests of the most fragile members of society, enacting legislation to protect certain vulnerable classes of employees, particularly women and children, from harsh working conditions. This strand of Realism came to be known as 'sociological jurisprudence,' according to which judges used their own sense of fairness and ethical sensibility in passing judgement.[5]

As Gluckman acknowledges, Barotse judges' notions of reasonableness were inevitably influenced by their biases, stereotypes, and prejudices, and rooted in their day-to-day experiences. But the important point he makes is that, in passing judgement, judges drew on notions of equity, fairness, and reasonableness. They saw their task as a moral or ethical one – 'so-and-so did this, and it was immoral' (1967 [1955]: 196). Necessarily, therefore, he says, 'the *kuta* [Barotse court] ends up by trying to protect the ethical code, *even if it is against the application of the letter of the law*' (ibid.: 196–97, emphasis added).

Referring to Cardozo, Gluckman proposes that Barotse judges, too, 'employ his so-called 'method of sociology', by which they import equity, social welfare, and public policy into their applications of the law. They are able to do so because the main certainty of the law consists in certain general principles, the constituent concepts of which are 'flexible' – as is the law itself, right and duty, good evidence, negligence, reasonableness' (1967 [1955]: 24).[6] In their judgements, Barotse courts are dominated by ideas of ethics, justice, and equity (ibid.: 256–67). These ideas 'influence their total evaluation of evidence' (Gluckman 1963: 197). They call these principles 'laws of God,' the equivalent of English natural justice (ibid.). Hence, Barotse courts of law are also courts of morality (ibid.:

5 For a review of the moral dimensions of legal realism, see Dagan (2005). See also West's *Encyclopedia of American Law* entry for 'Legal Realism,' at: http://www.answers.com/topic/legal-realism. Tamanaha (2009: 734) considers the movement's historical antecedents. For a critical historical review, see Horwitz (1992: 169–92).

6 Gluckman engages primarily with Cardozo (1928). He also argues in *The Judicial Process* (1967) against the Realist sceptic Jerome Frank (1930). Later, he engaged the Realists as a movement more generally (Gluckman 1973).

194). Although they do not enforce very high ethical standards beyond the legal demand for reasonableness, they proclaim these higher standards publicly in their judgements (ibid.: 192).

Where Gluckman parts with Cardozo is regarding the sources of legal indeterminacy. Indeterminacy stems not merely from legal gaps or contradictions, he contends, but from the intrinsically flexible nature of certain overarching concepts, such as fairness (1967: 337–38). Drawing on legal semantic theory, he suggests, 'The most important legal concepts have to cover the widest range of rules and processes' (ibid.: 341), and therefore legal concepts and ethical principles should be conceived of as arranged hierarchically. This allows them to 'absorb, and be permeated by, the ever varied and changing exigencies of life' (ibid.: 355). Although Gluckman did not highlight this in *The Judicial Process among the Barotse*, a key building block of Legal Realism was the attention to social 'situations' (Tamanaha 2009: 754), which itself became a central concept in Gluckman's extensive *oeuvre*.[7]

Against charges by Bohannan (1957; 1969) and others (e.g., Conley and O'Barr 2004: 209–12) that *The Judicial Process* was ethnocentric, a major strength of the book is its attention to indigenous concepts of justice, fairness, and equity. Among these, the notion of 'rights', *liswanelo*, matches the cognate Tswana notion of *ditshwanelo*, meaning both rights and obligations (Gluckman 1967: 166; Schapera 1955 [1938]: 35–36).

Against those who seek to posit an epistemic break to the modern (or colonial) period, we concur with Ajantha Subramanian's view about 'the inadequacy of treating rights as simply a by-product of Western modernity or colonial governmentality.' Instead, Subramanian says about the Indian fishermen she studied, 'Rights claims are embedded in dense histories of struggle and, in this sense, are not distinct from other cultural expressions of relationality and obligation' (2009: 20–21). In a similar vein, we suggest that ideas about rights and equity were already embedded in the discourse of the Barotse *kuta*, as in the Tswana *kgotla*, even before the advent of British colonialism and the introduction in postcolonial Botswana of statutory, modern courts.[8] The fundamental notion of *tshiamo*,

7 Gluckman discussed the place of legal case studies *versus* rules in the Realists' and his own work (1973). In a masterly tribute to E. Adamson Hoebel, he argued that a combination of both is essential in the 'triad of case-rule-praxis' (ibid.: 617). By then, Gluckman was clearly aware of Dworkin's work (ibid.: 616).

8 In trying to argue that Barotse legal concepts were imposed by the British, who 'needed native courts', Conley and O'Barr (2004: 209–10) err in conflating the very different modes through which state and stateless societies were incorporated into the colonial state. They fail to see that indigenous, hierarchical Barotse courts (*kuta*), like Tswana courts (*kgotla*), preceded colonial indirect rule and thus differed radically from the stateless Tiv 'government' courts that were a British invention. Prins, for example, while he mentions debates in the Barotse *kuta* only in passing, tells us that 'white power never attained a high intensity in Prins' (1980: 2). Schapera wrote that 'apart from certain changes regarded as essential, there has been as little interference as possible with the traditional forms of government and jurisdiction' (1955: 39–40).

of 'fairness' and 'justice', as we shall see here, is still used by Tswana judges in the modern, postcolonial era, and is an everyday concept pervasive in all areas of social life.

Gluckman's analysis linked Barotse jurisprudence to a major jurisprudential intellectual legal movement that questioned the certainty of law, and introduced questions of ethics, everyday life, and historical change into legal anthropology. Yet, innovative and bold as his analysis was, it was never fully taken up by his fellow anthropologists, and it certainly did not lay the foundation for an anthropology of ethics and morality. Instead, it was dismissed as Anglocentric and vague, and much of the legal anthropology that soon followed stressed not morality but manipulation, individual strategising, and the notion that, pragmatically, in most societies studied by anthropologists, power trumps law (see Moore 2001), although this begs the question of why people bother to go to law at all.[9] Moore defends Gluckman on the grounds that, in the colonial context, with its racist assumptions about primitive irrationality, his intent was 'political': 'Gluckman wanted to show that indigenous African legal systems and practices were as rational in the Weberian sense as Western ones' (ibid.: 98). But Moore fails to acknowledge that, in addition to demonstrating that they were rational, Gluckman was just as concerned to show that 'African legal systems and practices' were morally and ethically grounded, much like their Western counterparts. Gluckman argued that, for the Barotse, morality and rationality were inextricably linked.

The reasonable man and the whole edifice of ethics and morality associated with that concept and others like it (fairness, equity, justice, uprightness) thus virtually vanished from anthropology, having been greeted with scepticism, never fully understood, and often taken as a substantive description of a type of person rather than as a principle of practical ethical judgement.[10] As Epstein admitted, 'It is plain that the notion of the reasonable man has not had the impact that Gluckman clearly hoped it would have' (1973: 644). To rescue the term, Epstein suggested that it needed to be located in the opposition between rules and standards. In legal theory, standards are much wider and more indeterminate than rules, and require judges to use their discretion in deciding whether an act is reasonable and thus acceptable (see Kaplow 1992; Korobkin 2000). As a result, cases concerning standards are often unpredictable. Epstein echoes Gluckman in arguing that the value of the reasonable man concept lies in explaining how judges adapt the law under changing circumstances (1973: 654–55).

9 The term 'power' here refers to litigants' alleged ability to influence the outcome of a dispute through superior support mobilisation or connections to decision makers, rather than necessarily through the threat of violence or persuasive argumentation alone.

10 This is evident, most recently, in an article by Maurer (2005), which poses the reasonable man as being opposed to the economic man, a clear misunderstanding of the highly abstract notion of reasonableness as applied to particular situations, informing judicial reasoning.

This is only a partial reading of Gluckman, however. Beyond referring to 'normative' standards, there is little in Epstein's critical evaluation that shows that what is at issue is not merely judges' practical evaluation of reasonable behaviour or expectation, but also the wider issue of interpersonal ethics and morality in highly politicised contexts. Conservative readings and an inability or unwillingness to raise comparison to a more abstract level or to consider the complex intangibles of ethics in a social context have thus arguably led generations of legal anthropologists into a blocked *cul-de-sac*.[11]

This rupture has persisted in research on customary courts in post-colonial states, such as Botswana. For example, challenging the discrete autonomy of customary law or courts, legal anthropologists John Comaroff and Simon Roberts (1981) influentially shifted the terms of the debate – a move importantly paralleling, in some ways, the move in Critical Legal Studies – to stress that everyday rules, norms, and customs, beyond formal courts, were all mobilised in legal argumentation. They thus denied the separation between law, custom, and politics typical of what they termed the 'rule-centred' paradigm adopted, in their view, by Gluckman and others (ibid.: 8). The 'processual' paradigm they recommended instead, and a landmark in its time, consisted of an unsystematic 'loosely constructed repertoire' (ibid.: 18) of rules, habits, and norms, often contradictory or ambiguous, that enables litigants to formulate multiple interpretations ('paradigms') in their defence, as they engage in negotiations, alliance-making, and individual political manoeuvrings. This whole range of customary rules, norms, and values, they said, is constantly being constructed and reconstituted (ibid.: 20). Accordingly, the two Tswana groups they studied, the Kgatla and the Tshidi-Barolong, possessed no indigenous 'laws' that could determine dispute outcomes in any predictable fashion (ibid.: 14–15, 18).

There is a major fallacy in this contrast, and it is one that, given its contemporary influence as a bold departure, now needs careful rethinking. The fallacy lies in the authors' implicit definition of the 'rule-centred' paradigm in legal positivist, objectivist, formalist *pre-Realist* (and hence pre-Gluckman) terms; essentially, 'rule-centred' posits, for a straw man to be dismissed, an inert body of definitive law (see Dagan 2005: 55–56; Hunt 1986: 4). In rejecting this so-called rule-centred approach, Comaroff and Roberts also denied a privileged place to judges and judicial reasoning (ibid.: 14). Even further, we argue, in order to re-open more of the neglected interest in work by Schapera and Gluckman, they failed to consider the possibility that customary court decisions are embedded in considerations of equity that also inform wider ideological, critical movements and processes of judicial innovation, and legal reform. Their very own data show that, contrary to this denial, chiefly Tswana tribal 'innovators' have historically had the capacity to introduce legal judgements in response not only to changing circumstances

11 As Gluckman himself commented, 'I cannot help feeling that it is lamentable that so-called 'legal anthropologists' should be so ignorant of those [American Realist] jurisprudential controversies' (1973: 616).

or norms (Schapera 1970) but also changing notions of equity and fairness. In particular, Comaroff and Roberts themselves reported that the chief presiding over the Kgatla court at the time of Roberts' research, Linchwe II, decided, in the face of widespread opposition, on an equitable distribution of inheritance on the grounds that, in his words, 'In recent times, eldest sons had shown a tendency to "eat up" the heritable cattle themselves (at the expense of their younger siblings). … In these circumstances it seemed pointless, *indeed unfair,* to perpetuate such an inappropriate norm' (Comaroff and Roberts 1981: 80, emphasis added; also 179–83).

This is the only mention of the principle of 'fairness' in Comaroff and Roberts' entire monograph, and it is notable that it appears to describe judicial reasoning. Remarkably for a rich study that situates political manoeuvring at the heart of dispute settlement (see, for example, ibid.: 211), Comaroff and Roberts' *Rules and Processes* fails to recognise the way the Kgatla chiefly Customary Court of Appeal (the highest in the tribe) repeatedly awarded women in divorce cases generous property settlements, even when their marital status was relatively ambiguous (e.g., ibid.: 149, 155, 164, also 181). The question of why the interests of the weaker party (women) had increasingly come to be protected by the Kgatla court is mentioned (ibid.: 183) but left untheorised. Here our critical assessment, acknowledging the landmark importance Comaroff and Roberts' work had in its time, points to a challenge recognised and beginning to be addressed in later ethnography.

The contrast with the neighbouring Kwena tribe, studied by Anne Griffiths (1997), is stark. Among the Kwena, the customary tribal court of appeal repeatedly sought to reconcile marriage partners even when this clearly went against women's welfare; where divorce seemed inevitable, judges awarded women little or no property settlement. We find a hint of the possible reason for the contrast with the Kgatla in the few occasions on which the Kgatla judge, Chief Linchwe II, who had presided over the court studied by Comaroff and Roberts, was called in to adjudicate Kwena disputes. Chief Linchwe tended to protect women's interests. In one case, as Griffiths points out explicitly, the chief as judge 'based his argument on notions of fairness', arguing, 'A woman should not go back to her parents with nothing at all … . We found that it was a reasonable share because she is also entitled to a better [decent] life' (ibid.: 199).

Chief Linchwe's equitable division of the matrimonial property in one case 'astounded' the local Kwena headmen ('It was the talk of Molepolole for weeks afterward'), who told Griffiths that his verdict 'was not based on the 'old traditional Tswana ways of doing things; it is done according to modern ideas'' (ibid.: 200). Griffiths remarks that Linchwe had 'made his own mark on chiefship' (ibid.). In the verdict cited above, Linchwe referred explicitly to 'the hard rule of common law and equity' (ibid.: 202). Griffiths highlights these cases to support her more general argument:

> In Botswana, it is clear that any analysis of law must incorporate the legal system as a whole and that any attempts to focus on customary and common

> law as discrete entities that stand apart from one another cannot be sustained. Earlier ethnographies of law, including those written in the postcolonial period (Comaroff and Roberts 1981; Kuper 1970), failed to address the national legal context, thereby limiting their study of village life to certain forms of local ordering divorced from the broader national dimension and their relationship with the state.
>
> (Griffiths 1997: 208)

The other side of this interpenetration of different legal domains is, Griffiths suggests, that 'social understandings, expectations, and values permeate law – regardless of whether law is located in the customary or Western setting' (ibid.). Following this line of reasoning, this book demonstrates that widely held moral and ethical notions of fairness, equity, and reasonableness permeate legal decision-making in the postcolonies, such as Botswana, across customary, common, and administrative law.[12]

The relative autonomy of the law, whether customary or modern, is key to understanding historical trends in Botswana's legislative and social reform.[13] A limitation of studies such as *Rules and Processes*, which deny any separation between the law or legal institutions and everyday norms, is their inability to trace trajectories of legal reform or innovation over time, apart from changing normativities.[14] In many postcolonies, including Botswana, feminists have campaigned for legal reform of women's rights in marriage and divorce settlement, and their ideas about equitable property distribution have consequently also entered the customary courts, as we show in this book, as well as leading to a series of reforms of statutory law.

Significantly, Chief Linchwe II, a reformist judge, became president of the Botswana Customary Court of Appeal, the highest customary court in the land. In a series of our conversations with another member of that court, Phineas Makepe, we found that, although in 2000, Makepe dismissed the idea that customary law could be reformed since it was 'unwritten', in 2005 he told us that when it comes to divorce, 'In the customary court we follow the principle of division of property. This is a new practice influenced by wider practice. The Customary Court of Appeal has accepted the principle of division of the

12 Changes to the law and its jurisdiction can be experienced by ordinary people to be threatening and confusing, as in the case of land law reforms introduced in Botswana with the creation of land boards (Werbner 1980).

13 On the relative autonomy of courts more generally, see Tomlins (2007). Tomlins argues that the autonomy of courts is always 'relational' to some other entity (e.g., 'society'). Arguing for the relative autonomy of customary courts in Tanzania, Sally Falk Moore speaks of their 'semi-autonomy' (1978: 54–81). Admittedly, Comaroff could well offer a rejoinder, in terms of the relativity of 'semi-autonomy', to part of our critique of his work with Roberts. We would agree that the interrelation of statutory and customary courts is now more strikingly evident than it was earlier in their period of fieldwork, and certainly in the time of Schapera's and Gluckman's research.

property [in the case of divorce]. In 1997 it was there and was confirmed by the High Court'. He explained further, 'When it comes to natural justice, the question is, according to whom? When it comes to me, Phineas, as a judge, it must be my understanding of natural justice. I am a Western-educated man, baptised in the Catholic Church, and these influence my idea of natural justice' (17 August 2005). The Tswana chief of the Customary Court of Appeal in Tswapong North told us that customary courts had 'always' practised an equitable division of property in cases of divorce. In fact, he claimed, *statutory* or common law had learnt from and borrowed its current reforms from customary law.

Despite the pervasive folk mythology, then, that customary law never changes, it seems evident, as Griffiths argues, that, in postcolonial Botswana, different legal institutional domains are infused with ideas about equity, reasonableness, and fairness. Here post-independence legal complexity is further complicated by the nature of the judiciary, which includes a number of expatriate commonwealth judges. This commonwealth recruitment perhaps explains the incorporation of legal doctrines such as judicial review from English administrative law. Public law in these postcolonies, as in many others, is modelled on English law, including English administrative law, even though the country's common law is based on South Africa's Roman-Dutch law.

To sum up the argument so far, then, our purpose in tracing a genealogy of legal anthropological engagements with notions of morality has been to recuperate an earlier conversation between legal anthropologists and legal scholars on the place of morality in legal judgements.

'Living law', the new legal realism, and legal pluralism

In his review article on Legal Realism (2008–9), Brian Tamanaha highlights the way that Realists managed two opposing tendencies – on the one hand, towards flexible, innovative, manipulation of the rules and, on the other hand, towards their fixed stability:

> The term *realism*, as it is used in this Article, has two integrally conjoined aspects – a sceptical aspect and a rule-bound aspect. Realism refers to an awareness of the flaws, limitations, and openness of law – an awareness that judges must sometimes make choices, that they can manipulate legal rules and precedents, and that they can be influenced by their political and moral views and by their personal biases (the sceptical aspect). But realism about law and judging also conditions this more sceptical awareness with the understanding that legal rules nonetheless can work; that judges can abide by and apply the law; that there are practice-related, social, and institutional factors that constrain judges; and that judges can render generally predictable, legally based decisions (the rule-bound aspect). A realistic view holds that the rule-bound aspect of judging can function reliably notwithstanding the challenges presented by the scepticism-inducing side, although this is an

> achievement that must be earned, is never perfectly achieved, and is never guaranteed.
>
> (2008–9: 732)

As we have seen, Gluckman argued similarly that customary law – and indeed all law – is *intrinsically* uncertain while being *at the same time* certain. This apparently paradoxical feature of law derives from the flexibility and elasticity of overarching legal concepts, which open specific cases to interpretation and reinterpretation in the light of changing circumstances and prevailing moral ideas on the one hand, along with a body of rules currently believed to be binding by members of a society (Gluckman 1955.67; cf. in particular Chapter VI, pp. 291–326; see also Schapera 1983). In the case of customary law, although these seemingly certain rules are unwritten, they are 'hallowed' by a strong faith in their antiquity (ibid.: 352).

Although he does not label himself a Realist, Gluckman by his own admission sees his work as aligned with that of American Realists, above all Cardozo, but others as well – Holmes, Gray, Frank, Llewellyn, Pound (1955/67: 327). In line with these legal scholars, he makes clear repeatedly, as we saw above, that the legal principles that animate judicial decision-making are ethical and moral principles, though these are often unstated by judges. Instead, they use the notion of reasonableness or uprightness. In Setswana, the equivalent notion is *tshiamo*, righteousness, justness, justice, or equity. A further fundamental Tswana legal notion is that of 'rights' or 'duties', *ditshwanelo*. These overarching concepts are broad enough to be adapted to changing circumstances so that the law can be applied to new contexts while seemingly remaining the same.

As both Gluckman and Schapera agree, 'law' in the case of customary law is a concept not easily defined. The Tswana expression, *mekgwa le milao*, customs and laws, is broadly used to apply to regular rules of conduct and is invoked by judges in customary courts. Unlike law (*milao*), however, custom (for example, politesse, or ritual taboos), while regularly practised, is not usually subject to legal sanctions (cf. Schapera 1983: 36). The further argument is between those who wish to restrict 'law' to societies with courts or extend the concept to cover all rules of conduct. As Schapera notes, however:

> This controversy need not detain us here; for the Tswana, like ourselves, have attained a stage of legal development where certain rules of conduct can, in the last resort, be enforced by the material power of compulsion vested in tribal courts. ... The rules of conduct distinguished from the rest by this ultimate sanction of judicial enforcement may for all practical purposes be regarded as the 'laws' of the Tswana.
>
> (1983: 37)

Gluckman disagrees, accepting that societies without established judicial fora can also have 'laws'. He enumerates various meanings of the law – for example, the Lozi distinguish between laws of God (scientific laws) and laws of humankind, as well as laws of nations in the case of interethnic disputes. In the light of this multiplicity, Gluckman confesses that he

> 'wishes to avoid becoming entangled in the disputation that has accumulated around the word 'law'. Much of this disputation has concerned the definition of 'law', and the relation between law as a body of enacted or customary rules recognised by a community as binding, and law as a series of decisions by judges in particular cases'
>
> (1955/67: 226)

Law is a multiple concept with many meanings and referents (ibid.). For the purposes of our analysis in this book, however, we follow Gluckman and Schapera in defining law in two main senses: as a *corpus juris*, a body of rules (subject to interpretation and reinterpretation), and as *adjudication*, or legal rulings in courts (see 1955/67: 227).

The New Legal Realist approach which we adopt in this book balances legal scepticism regarding the fixity of the law with the view that, at any one time, most customary law is grasped by local people as 'hallowed' by tradition, to be followed by customary courts and those who attend them.[14] We thus reject a legal-formalist or positivist view of customary law as fixed and subject to codification. As we shall see, this was an approach taken by colonial, and especially the apartheid, regime. But by the same token, we reject analyses of customary law that regard it as infinitely malleable and manipulable, subject to the interests of powerful players at the expense of the weak and vulnerable. That customary law is contested does raise the question of who has more power to define it, of course; and our account examines continuing uncertainties in the answers to this question (on definitive power in South Africa, see Oomen 2005:88).

The current 'living law' debate starts from the understanding that, rather than being fixed and unchanging, customary laws are responsive to current conditions and are interpreted according to particular cases and social situations. This approach is particularly significant in the South African post-apartheid context in which the Constitutional Court is being called upon repeatedly to consider the validity of certain customary laws. Clearly, the Court operates with the view of 'living customary law' as opposed to 'official customary law' (Nlhapo 2017: 12). But in ascertaining what customary law is, the Court must 'have regard for the spirit, purport, and objects of the Bill of Rights' (ibid.: 13), which guarantees cultural rights, while at the same time attempting to ascertain the content of customary law as it currently stands. Historically, the apartheid regime engaged a vast army of ethnologists, mainly Afrikaners, to codify the customary laws of different ethnic groups, but these written codes are now questionable; they cannot be regarded as simply valid or safe in the rapidly changing contexts of post-apartheid South Africa, if they ever were. As many commentators have noted,

14 An example is the changing acceptable standards of property settlements in cases of divorce.

they were 'distorted' by their mode of collection to favour chiefly and patriarchal interpretations of the law.

Beyond South Africa, in Botswana the 'living law' debate has surfaced only once, in the Court of Appeal in 2013 (see Chapter 8). With no Constitutional Court equivalent to South Africa's, and no recent codification since Isaac Schapera's masterly 1948 *Handbook of Tswana Law and Custom*, in Botswana, customary judges have, on the whole, interpreted the law according to changing ideas about gender and generation, but without always explicitly referring to these changes. It is these interpretations, as we shall see, which are considered by the Customary Court of Appeal.

Our New Legal Realist approach in this book thus follows the definition of customary law as made up of a *corpus juris* and legal rulings in court. It is the latter that reflect changing customary law as living law. But this assumes that some customary laws are at any one time relatively fixed. Against Comaroff and Roberts (1981), Hund argues that law and custom are not endlessly manipulable (Hund 1998: 431). Comaroff and Roberts' extreme legal scepticism leads Hund to the (logical) conclusion that Tswana seem to have 'less "law" than is found in some other customary societies' (ibid.: 433). This is, of course, absurd: with its hierarchy of customary appeal courts and the lengthy debates in court hearings, as we show in this book, Tswana customary law is a firmly established legal corpus, determined not merely by the power and influence of litigants but by considerations of justice and equity. The continuous dialectic is between established rules and new moral, political, and economic circumstances. Because customary law is relatively established at any one time, it is possible to recognise historical changes that occur in response to changing ethical and moral ideas permeating the wider society, and often in response to statutory law. This leads us to the question of *legal pluralism.*

As Watson (1993) and others have argued, legal comparisons are always 'perilous', and particularly so when the comparison is between customary judicial processes in past African tribal courts and modern-day customary or statutory African courts. Comparison is valuable nonetheless for illuminating commonalities across differences. The cases outlined here disclose that, in order to justify ethically or morally 'fair' judgements, customary judges must first mobilise the full intricacy of the law in rational argumentation. To be seen to be fair, in other words, a judgement must be seen to be based on 'objective' legal facts and edicts set out logically and coherently. Rationality and morality are thus two faces of a single coin.

Legal Pluralism, like customary 'law', is beset by definitional conundrums. Even within a single society there are many sub-fields of law, and, in this sense, law is plural even in Western societies (see, for example, Merry 1988; Benda-Beckman 2002). For our purposes here, however, our focus is on the dialogical encounter between two legal fields in postcolonial societies: traditional 'customary' law and statutory law. In a suggestive article, Diala draws on Moore's analysis of the 'semi-autonomous field' (Moore 1973) to propose that 'state law and customary law may not just be semi-autonomous social fields, but could, in some cases, be a *single social field*' (Diala 2017: 151, emphasis added). This is a valuable insight. It fails to recognise, however, that 'living' law – though not named as such – was a feature of Gluckman's early neo-Realist approach to customary law as 'process'. Diala is right, however, as we saw above, that, in contemporary South Africa, 'the forces that drive living law's emergence' are 'the interaction of state law with customary law' (ibid.). This points to an important feature of current customary law in postcolonial states; whereas, in the past, although Lozi or Tswana judges did take account of the colonial state's legal interventions related to customary law, on the whole, they were left to adapt customary law to current conditions autonomously, without state intervention. These days, by contrast, Tswana judges in customary courts are far more aware of changing normative-cum-legal standards in the wider society, in particular regarding gender and generation and, as we show in this book, they respond to these despite the fact that, in their postcolonial state, customary law is not only unwritten but is constitutionally independent of state law.[15]

Our aim in this book is to analyse the dialogical relationship between customary law and statutory law, not as mediated by a statutory constitutional court, as in South Africa, but as influenced by changing ethical standards and notions of equity and justice among villagers and in the wider society.

Traditional leadership, public ethics, village factionalism

Chiefship has been the subject of renewed scholarly interest as chiefs have resurfaced in many parts of Africa as political players on the postcolonial stage (van Niewaal and van Dijk 1999). Abolished in many African states after independence, they have gradually been reinstated and have acquired wealth, status, and political influence. The story varies across sub-Saharan Africa (see Comaroff and Comaroff 2018). For our purpose here, the contrast between chiefship in Botswana and neighbouring South Africa is the most stark. At independence in South Africa, in 1994, it was intended to grant chiefs symbolic status. As Lungisile Ntsebeza says, the position of the ANC towards traditional authorities 'has always been ambivalent' (2005: 258). The party never had a stronghold in rural areas (ibid.: 260). By 1993, it was clear that the association of African chiefs from the apartheid Bantustan era, CONTRALESA, 'rejected the ANC's vision that the institution of chieftainship be a ceremonial and advisory body' (ibid.: 269). Instead, they demanded to be the primary level of government in rural areas. They were supported by the Zulu Inkatha threats of secession.

The result was, essentially, that the separate 'homelands' policy of the apartheid era, with its arbitrarily appointed and autocratic chiefs, was *reincorporated* into the new South Africa. Indeed, the 2003 Act 'recognises Tribal Authorities which were established in the apartheid era and in terms of the 1951 Bantu

15 On 'living law' in the South African context see, in addition to the above, discussions by Claassens and Budlender (2013), Himonga and Bosch (2000), and Diala (2017).

Authorities Act' (ibid.: 285). A further strengthening of the chiefs' influence was in granting them authority over the allocation of land and the right to the income from mineral resources. They resisted any attempts to subject them to a system that would make them 'more representative and accountable to their communities' (ibid.: 280) and they opposed all 'new democratic structures', including the separation of powers and the introduction of alternative structures (ibid.: 281). In addition, traditional authorities in South Africa are granted huge annual stipends. Not all chiefs in the new South Africa are equally wealthy, as Cook (2018) shows in a brilliant essay. But nearly all are perceived to be autocratic and non-accountable.

The story of chiefship in Botswana has been remarkably – and radically – different from that of chiefship in South Africa. At independence, Botswana was one of the poorest countries in Africa. Diamonds had yet to be discovered in large numbers. Seretse Khama, the founding father of the nation, renounced his right to the paramount chieftaincy of the Bamangwato tribe, the largest in Botswana, to become Botswana's first president in 1966. This set the tone for further reforms to the chiefship. Botswana was to be a modern democracy. First, chiefs were to be civil servants, non-partisan, and prohibited from participating in politics; second, minerals were legally defined as the property of the nation, irrespective of where they were found; thirdly, not chiefs but elected representatives would rule at local government level in elected district councils; and finally, chiefs were deprived of one of their main sources of power: control over the land. As Richard Werbner (1980: 137) explains:

> The dominant reading, widely held in Botswana among leading politicians, senior civil servants and prominent entrepreneurs, that a re-organisation of the political control and public administration of land tenure was an essential part of development from the many tribes of the colonial Protectorate to the one democratic nation under an elected government. … an end had to be put to certain powers of paramount tribal rulers or, as denounced by the ruling party's 1969 election manifesto, 'the arbitrary decisions of the Chiefs'.
> (Masire 1969: 14)

The Tribal Land Act (1968), as described in the 1969 ruling party manifesto, was meant to ensure that

> all tribesmen … will no longer be subjected to the whims of a chief whose decisions on land matters may be affected by all kinds of considerations which have nothing to do with the interests of the farmer or the nation.
> (ibid.)

The Tribal Land Act was meant to support 'progressive farmers' (ibid.: 138).

Although chiefs and headmen have a measure of influence – they sit *ex officio* on the tribal land boards that were created following the Act – and despite many implementation hurdles and unforeseen consequences (see R. Werbner 1977), land in Botswana is now no longer the preserve of chiefdoms. Citizens are entitled to apply for land in the communal areas anywhere in the country, and, especially in the per-urban areas near the capital city, Gaborone, there is both much diversity in landholders' origins and much controversy over control on behalf of local villagers in the face of heavy external demand. At the same time, chiefs still preside as judges over customary courts and are endowed with much respect and prestige, symbolically and ceremonially, as we show in this book. Village chiefs or headmen continue to exercise much control over the public arena in small villages like Moremi.

The House of Chiefs, *Ntlo ya Dikgosi*, was established as a purely advisory council, although it does debate issues relating to the customary law, tribal administration, and constitutional amendment. The House has been expanded so it now includes eight hereditary chiefs and 22 indirectly elected members who serve five-year terms. Of these indirectly elected members, four are chosen from sub-chiefdoms and five are appointed by the president (on chiefship and the politics of recognition, see Werbner 2002c).

Thus, we see how the Botswana Democratic Party took the path that the ANC failed to take for reasons of *realpolitik* (van Kessel and Oomen 1997). The results are evident: Botswana is truly a democracy for all its citizens, who are not subject to the arbitrary 'whims' of autocratic non-appointed and unelected local leaders and who can all share in the mineral wealth of the nation. Even recent attempts by the son of Seretse Khama, Ian, a 'royal' who was president for ten years from April 2008 to April 2018, to secure special privileges after he retired, have come up against the democratic institutions of the state (Ditsheko 2019; Werbner 2020: 308).

The book is divided into two parts. Part one, following this introduction, is devoted to the issue of public ethics and legal pluralism as manifested in village conflicts over a period of some 50 years. Part two of the book is devoted to an analysis of legal subjectivities, ethics, and legal pluralism, particularly as it relates to changing notions of gender and generation. The concluding chapter of the book reviews a series of questions which are central to the research on customary law. Many of these revolve around disputes arising in domestic life (marriage, divorce, adultery, insult, and inheritance). Others revolve around disputes in which passionate attachment to identity (the politics of memory, honour, 'nature' and religion) are revealed. Throughout the book we have argued that, above all, it is through an in-depth analysis of these customary court hearings that we can achieve an understanding of how customary law evolves over time, and how the legal issues at stake are embedded in wider legal developments in Southern Africa. Furthermore, the cases reveal the complexity of legal pluralism in a postcolonial state in which statutory law only partially and selectively encompasses customary law. Our conclusion highlights the need for more comparative research and raises questions of legal consciousness, decision-making, and procedures in the understanding of customary law courts as 'courts of equity', in the words of a Court of Appeal judge. Throughout the book, our aim has been to show how customary judges and courts respond to changing notions of equity, justice, and fairness, on the one hand, and how chiefs-as-judges are held to account, on the other hand.

By way of introduction, we want to provide a basic view of Moremi, the village at the centre of our fieldwork (for videos of Moremi, see R. Werbner 2005, 2007, 2014, 2018b, and for videos of the nearby town, Palapye, R. Werbner 2014). Moremi village, located along the Lotsane River, north of Tswapong Hills and 60 km east of the railway town Palapye, is a small village with an extensive cultivation area to the north and east and pastures to the west and south, covering altogether an area of about 400 km^2, stretching all the way to the Hills. The cultivation area is shared with villagers living in nearby Matolwane's Moremi and Matoposane wards. Matolwane (now officially known as Lesenepola) has a bigger population than Moremi.

The owner of two permanently flowing sacred springs (*Mannonye* and *Mutodi*) and centre of the secret ancestral cult of the drum (*Komana*, *Sedimo*, the court of divinity), Moremi is widely regarded as genealogically senior among the Tswapong Hills villages which claim to be ethnically Pedi, with ancient origins in the Transvaal. In recent years, both *Mannonye*, with its chain of waterfalls and pools, and the *Sedimo* cult have become well known throughout Botswana, with the old abandoned village site near the spring being nominated as a heritage site, now with a lodge and restaurant, and a stream of visitors and supplicants arriving to be treated by the cult.

Nearly all Moremi villagers claim to belong to what we call a supertribe, Tswapong. Isaac Schapera described its composition as diverse: 'The tribe called Tswapong is really a collection of several groups named generally after the hills in which they live' (Schapera 1952,185). Included are Pedi along with a good number of smaller tribes. As Pnina Motzafi-Heller notes, 'Those who are often considered to be the original inhabitants of the hills are known as Bapedi, and their histories of migration into the region and splitting once they settled continue to be a subject of intense public debate' (Motzafi-Haller 2002, 5). Linguistically, a dialect called Tswapong and related to Pedi, was commonly spoken by Moremi elders in the past, though now under the influence of schooling, most villagers speak standard Tswana. If outside the village, they speak with a Tswapong accent, they risk being regarded as hillbillies. All the same, assertion of Tswapong cultural identity is now being expressed through Tswapong Cultural Society for the whole of Tswapong North region, which we discuss in Chapter 3.

One register of migration history is kept by Moremi villagers in their division of the village into three main wards, each with its own headman. The first is that of the original Pedi immigrant to the Hills, the ward of Moremi, which is the ward of the village chief and his agnates. The second, Mogoma, also of Pedi origin, stands *vis-a-vis* Moremi ward in a relation of perpetual kinship, as 'mothers' brothers'.They constitute the dominant lineage in neighbouring Malaka. Finally, there is the ward of strangers, Mapaka, which includes, among others, a few villagers of Kalanga origin and one large extended family said to be originally 'Matabele'.

When we began our fieldwork in 1972, labour migration was mainly seasonal, with annual trips for men to work in the South African mines. Since independence and the rapid urbanisation of the capital, Gaborone, as well as the new copper mining town of Selibe-Phikwe, nearer Moremi, the shift has been remarkable. It has not only drawn Moremi villagers, men and women, to work in Botswana, in the city and towns, including the nearby railway town, Palapye, but they also straddle town and country by having multiple residences, one in the village and another one in their own houses, distant from Moremi. Moremi's continued pull as a community is, nevertheless, so great that many of the youth who grew up in the distant urban centres still continue to regard Moremi as their home village. The adult town–country straddlers themselves often maintain their claims to plots of land and inheritance of residential sites, as we document in court cases, and they show their village and kinship loyalties in faithful attendance at funerals and family rituals, including even, among some Christians, sacrifices and offerings at the *Sedimo* cult.

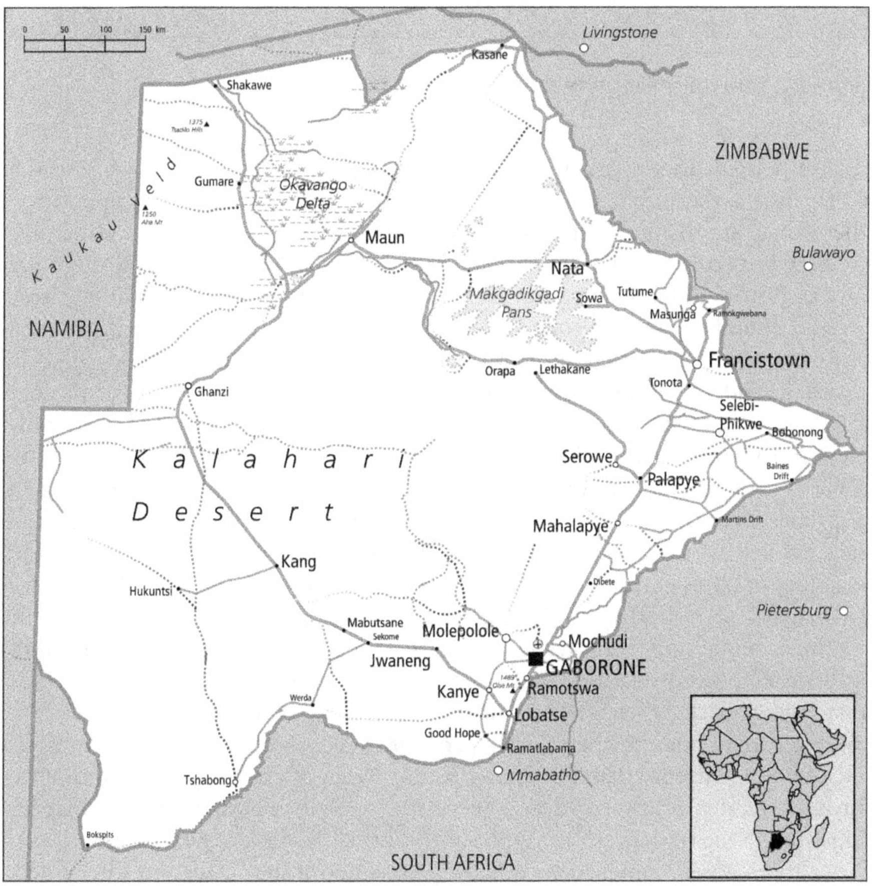

Figure 1.1 Map of Botswana.

Figure 1.2 Moremi village view towards the Tswapong Hills.

What is perhaps most striking, looking back over the 50 years of our research in Moremi, is the public appearance of a substantial move towards prosperity. Where once stood mud huts, many in disrepair or even abandoned under the threat of forced removal from the village, as discussed in Chapter 2, there are now big houses of brick and concrete. Some are smartly tiled, others have corrugated roofs and a few, flush toilets, electricity, and phones. We ourselves installed solar power in the thatched hut lent us very generously by Gaseitsiwe Moatlhodi, our friend and sometime research assistant. Building a house for an old mother or father is evidence straddlers proudly display, or at least signal, of still truly belonging to the village. Where once there was no major public investment in village development, now government employment is considerable, with jobs in the primary school, the village court, and the clinic, and various public works and roads, as well as at the tourist lodge, which has become communally owned and managed, in co-operation with the government. Village poverty is still harsh for too many villagers in Moremi. But with better integration into the wide economy and the national opportunities for higher education, often taken up with funding from employed relatives, has come increased social mobility, and for a few outstanding villagers, top careers in the civil service, their own investments in new enterprises, and the chance to become private consultants, city or town landlords, or new entrepreneurs, with inside knowledge of government departments. Through all this transformation, the village court has itself thrived, hence its resilience is a major concern throughout this book. But as the next chapter documents, there was a moment when the very existence of the village was threatened.

Part I

Public ethics and legal pluralism

2 Looking back

Small-man politics and the rule of law[1]

Preamble: looking back

As we shall see in the following chapters, the village split in 1971 continued to be recalled and to impact on *kgotla* debates and village politics for years to come. The politics of memory made the split an integral part of the present. Although still a small village of between 500 and 600 residents, since the split Moremi village has grown and prospered: it is now reached by a tarred road from Palapye and Selibe Pikwe and boasts a purpose-built primary school with teachers' quarters, a clinic, piped running water, and most recently, electricity and telephone. It is reachable by one of the mobile phone networks.

When we first returned to the village in 2000, after a gap of 22 years, we followed the signs to Moremi and arrived at a settlement with white houses and gleaming red roofs that was nothing like the scattered thatched huts lacking even fences that we had left behind. Only after a young boy pointed us to the house of the village chief, Days Mapulane, did we begin to believe that this was indeed Moremi village. Over the years since we had left, the Village Development Committee and the government between them had built many of the red-roofed houses for public use, and some houses were built by villagers who had prospered in the meanwhile, mainly through labour migration. The newly built, elegant village *kgotla* was now a court of record with a court clerk, a police station, a secretary, a bailiff, and other government officials. After many delays, 'development' had indeed reached the village.

Development included the building of a lodge near the spring at Mannonye and the fencing of a large area around it, barring access to the spring for villagers' cattle, although a water trough for cattle was provided outside the fence. Diviners too were prohibited from digging up roots near the sacred spring and

1 This Chapter was originally published by Richard Werbner and appeared as 'Small Man Politics and the Rule of Law: Centre–Periphery Relations in East-Central', *Journal of African Law* 21, 1, Essays in Honour of Isaac Schapera (Spring, 1977), pp. 24–39. Pnina Werbner accompanied Richard to the field. We have added some comments and modifications but otherwise the original remains unchanged.

DOI: 10.4324/9781003241881-2

women from picking wild fruit like morula. Ownership of the lodge was thus in some ways contested, though officially, the Ministry of Environment, Wildlife and Tourism 'recognised' the area and its two springs as 'belonging' to the village through a CBO (Community-Based Organisation). Nonetheless, the personal involvement of the Khamas, Ian and his brother Tshekedi, until recently Minister of Tourism, in the project meant that the 'chiefs from Serowe' still seemed to have their eye on Moremi's permanent springs, much as was feared in the early 1970s, as we show below. In the meanwhile, the lodge provided employment and an annual bursary to the village. In 2018, the lodge opened a restaurant and facilities for a conference centre. Streams of visitors arrived to see the 'sacred' spring of Mannonye, the abode of the ancestral *badimo*, mainly on day trips, with a few venturing up through the series of waterfall cascades to see the Cape vultures nesting on the hills above. The two zebras and several waterbucks recently purchased by the lodge remained almost entirely invisible.

The following analysis, originally published by Richard Werbner (1977), describes the background and events leading to the village split and explains the continued involvement of villagers now living in neighbouring Matolwane in the affairs of Moremi village and their sense of entitlement to be consulted and make decisions even though they did not live there, that we record in subsequent chapters. Two issues animate the discussion: the first relates to factional politics in small villages, the second to the propensity of citizens to use judicial review to challenge government and local government decisions in the courts, in this particular case through the customary courts of appeal.

In advance of the discussion below, it needs to be pointed out that the events leading to the village split took place at the cusp of a major transformation in chiefly power and authority in Botswana though, as we point out, this was not entirely clear to the village actors fighting their displacement.

In defence of citizenship

Factional politics appear to have been an endemic feature of Tswana politics, even before independence, and certainly after it (Makgala 2006). Botswana thus seemed to conform to a familiar stereotype overrunning much of the anthropological literature on political and economic development in new nations, which drew on transactional theory. In this transactional model, brokers and big men captured the stage, and their chains and alliances, their manipulations and calculations, their political games as men in the middle of centre–periphery relations loomed larger than life in the literature. Indeed, it came almost to be a matter of faith in certain studies of new African nations, especially studies influenced by work on India, to regard political questions within the frame of a patronage model, since it was taken for granted that transactions between patrons and clients or 'friends of friends' control the stuff of politics, the decisions about who gets what, when, and how.

How and why the rule of law is upheld during those periods of major change in government that came immediately before and after independence remained a largely neglected question.[2] Yet, in a new nation, citizens may also take political action through appeals to ministers, courts, tribunals, or commissions of enquiry and thus subject decisions by the local government to judicial review and sometimes revision by the central government. The outcome need not be a foregone conclusion, because the hearings may pit the interests of the central and the local government against each other. The central government may then have to defend the aggrieved citizen against the local elected officials or civil servants. The point is not that a citizenship model has to be put in the place of the old patronage model. Rather the power of citizens in a new nation *qua* citizens has to be taken as problematic, and their powerlessness without middlemen or brokers cannot be assumed, especially in centre–periphery relations.

A further challenge for analysis and general theory must also be recognised. The connections between the macropolitics of a nation and the micropolitics of small, remote villages in its hinterland have to be appreciated correctly. False boundaries must not be drawn through the use of nice distinctions, such as between the legal and the political or between politics and administration, which divorce interrelated phenomena from each other. That is why our analysis, based on research in Tswapong villages in Botswana,[3] examines the pragmatics of power relations – transactions and their course – along with the rules and procedures for regulating such relations.

Part of the argument about the types of events that characterise power struggles is based on transactional analyses, particularly by Bailey (1968).[4] It is important, however, to make plain from the start some central yet awkward features of Bailey's approach which have to be rejected here. These have to do with the certainty of rules or values and the view of politics as a big man's game. Bailey's approach assumes that values or rules are shared and clear cut in political contests. Yet in some periods of transition, where conditions of uncertainty arise, people do not agree about all the important rules, even though some people assume that

2 A notable exception to this, for the colonial period, is Fallers (1969, 1977). See also more recent work on African chiefs by Baldwin (2016), which takes up issues of patronage.

3 Richard Werbner carried out his fieldwork among Tswapong of Botswana in 1972-73 for twelve months and made his main centre and home in the village of Moremi, or Goo-Moremi as it is now gazetted. He is indebted to the people of Moremi who welcomed him so hospitably and is grateful also to the University of Manchester for paid leave and the Social Science Research Council for a grant as part of a five-year project, under his direction, on Rural Competition and Social Change in Botswana. He wishes to thank, too, N. J. Mahoney whose research on the village of Bobonong was a part of the SSRC project, who challenged him to rethink his views on the politics of big villages. Earlier versions of the chapter were presented to seminars at Brandeis University, and the Universities of Manchester, Wales (Swansea), and London (S.O.A.S.). He also benefitted from the comments of E. V. Walter, Tim Ingold, David Rheubottom, and Clyde Mitchell, who read the paper and helped him to improve it.

4 For a useful critique of Bailey's approach, see Sydel Silverman, 'Bailey's Politics' (1974), 2, *Journal of Peasant Studies*, 11 1-220. Our argument has also been stimulated by Bruce Kapferer, *Strategy and Transaction in an African Factory*, Manchester, 1972, and in Kapferer (ed.) *Transactional Analysis*, Philadelphia, 1976.

such agreement exists. Moreover, awareness about changes in the rules varies and spreads unevenly among the people actively taking part in politics. Bailey's basic analogy is to a game in which a big man and his team come to grips with their opponents, under the watchful eyes of a referee or referees. The big man appears as the kind of entrepreneur who calculates the best tactics for a pay-off and then rationally manipulates others to achieve this. He is ever ready for the main chance. Here, as Thoden Van Velzen points out, 'The question is not raised what role the unbound weak – those who are neither big man nor followers – play in the political equation' (1973: 596).

In other words, so much attention is paid to teams of leaders and followers that little or no account is given of political moves made by others, such as persons not bound in dependence to any leader. Moreover, leader–follower relations so hypnotise attention that the relations between the followers themselves are largely neglected. Thus, Bailey's approach is inadequate, because it makes the study of factional politics too narrowly a study of the big man's managerial problems; of how he tests, proves, and accumulates his strength. By contrast, our analysis takes account of moves made by persons who are not members of a political team, and we are not concerned exclusively with tactics or manoeuvres which are deliberately calculated. We consider also political moves which are made inadvertently and have unexpected outcomes.

Yet to consider conditions of uncertainty is not to imply a complete lack of continuity. Old policies and longstanding struggles for power are sometimes abandoned when one form of government replaces another. But often people do not disengage themselves from entrenched competition for locally established prizes, despite a re-organisation of government. The more restricted and uneven the spread of knowledge of the re-organisation's critical effects on the redistribution of power, the more an old policy is likely to be retained, even if disguised in a new political rhetoric. During a transition period, a disguised old policy, such as the one we discuss here at length, the centralisation of settlement, provides something quite different from merely another ground for testing strength of support or following. It provides a crucial proving ground for defining the very rules of politics and government. People are compelled to explore the scope of various authorities *vis-a-vis* themselves and each other, while they enter into struggles over how concentrated power is to be. Many of the moves they then make may be inadvertent: they fumble, rather than manipulate, and theirs is not the game of political big men on which Bailey focuses.

Related difficulties follow from the way Bailey develops the game analogy through a distinction between tactics in contests and fights. In contests, antagonists agree on a set of rules for competition and permissible tactics. In fights, they disagree about all this, though they may agree about the prizes for which they compete. Bailey distinguishes also between two kinds of events characteristic of a contest, i.e., (1) 'confrontation' and (2) 'encounter'. In a confrontation, antagonists challenge one another directly; they mutually communicate messages about their own strength, assert claims and make demands, but they achieve no decisive victory, and for each side the outcome is immediately inconclusive. The encounter goes a stage further and has a decisive conclusion with a victor and a vanquished.

This distinction as it stands does not highlight an important aspect of certain political events in small village contests; namely, their indirectness or obliqueness: the political messages are sometimes ambiguous to the contestants themselves. To grasp this, a concept is needed that refers to events in which one side makes a bid for support or asserts claims without being openly contradicted or directly opposed, at least not immediately. Antagonists do not come to grips with one another, and thus they produce dubious messages about their strength of support or no messages at all about this. We refer to this kind of event as a *blind probe* and mean to emphasise that the blindness is not a deliberate or calculated device in that those who start the probe or bid through it do seek unambiguous support.

In Tswapong villages, perhaps the most common example of a blind probe occurs at a partial assembly. It is a partial assembly because supporters of one side come to a public meeting of the village apart from their known opponents but along with other villagers, who are independent of a recognised leader, uncommitted or somewhat unclearly committed to a cause or a side. Issues raised then may be rehashed at a later meeting, when another side prevails in another partial assembly, and meetings may take place repeatedly without a direct confrontation or a decisive encounter. We argue that blind probes are at once an expression of ambiguity in political support and also a factor contributing to instability in such support. Blind probes have further implications which we discuss later when we examine the details of an actual sequence of events in certain Tswapong villages.

Our discussion illuminates a long-term policy of district or local government and its implications for change in small villages during a period of postcolonial re-organisation of government in the Central District of Botswana and, indeed, throughout the country.[5] It is a policy of concentration of settlement and centralisation. Similar policies are not rare in other parts of Africa. But the presence among Tswana of big villages as an indigenous, or at least long-established, model, is rare in other African countries, and thus the study of this case provides a key extreme for the understanding of fairly general processes which link the micropolitics of a small village with the macropolitics of its district and nation. Here we draw our main evidence from an attempt to group together four small villages in Tswapong Hills of Botswana's largest and perhaps administratively most unwieldy district.

From the local government's viewpoint, the four Tswapong villages seemed especially suited for this policy of centralisation, because the government had so far spent little on any development at the villages' old sites and had provided only one village with any facilities, namely a school and an engine-driven pump with a water tank. Though it was hardly adequate for the domestic needs of one small village, re-siting it and the school was the foundation to be provided for

5 The seminal account of tribal political organisation in this district under the Protectorate is I. Schapera, 'The Political Organisation of the Ngwato of the Bechuanaland Protectorate', in M. Fortes and E. E. Evans-Pritchard (eds.), *African Political Systems*, Oxford, 1940a.

the new big village. The local government's objective was a big village with a population of about 1400 and an area of somewhat under 200 square miles. The policy of centralisation was a prevailing concern long before independence, when it took on a fresh momentum and was reformulated in a new language of national 'development'. The policy had various advantages for the district's local government. Welfare services would be less costly; savings could be made on roads and water supplies; fewer schools could serve more people; and other economies of scale could be achieved. Moreover, the new centres would be less isolated, with more frequent transport and quicker communication. The old centres in small villages were often located, as in Moremi, at sites convenient for permanent water supplies from a spring or river but somewhat inaccessible for lorries because of rocks or dunes. Administratively, in the new centralised village, it would be easier to reach people, to get them to participate in village assemblies, and to mobilise them for development projects, public works, and co-operative societies.

In part also, the change might be acceptable as not being a radical transformation. For the small village has been, in certain respects and somewhat superficially, like the large one in form: each small village has had its own headquarters, and administrative and residential centre, and its own component wards (or administrative divisions) and localities which, extending irrespective of administrative divisions, are named expanses of land around well-known landmarks where recognisable sets of neighbours live. Moreover, in both kinds of village, somewhat distinct localities have been found: some localities cover areas primarily of pasture around cattle posts along with scattered gardens, while other localities cover cultivation areas, known as the 'lands', with homesteads where, for most of the year, people live and keep some of their stock in nearby pens.

Existing big villages, with well over a thousand people, were comparatively rare in the Central District, and indeed throughout Botswana, in 1972. Apart from the district capital, Serowe, with about 15,000 people at the time, they represented less than a quarter of the district's *de facto* population. Yet the big villages were, and are, prestigious, even in the eyes of people in small villages, and they are considered to have stronger, more effective village leadership. They were taken to be a model towards which the small village should aspire. Despite widespread, popular acceptance of this, the centralisation policy met resistance; it was largely unsuccessful, and it had consequences contrary to those planned or desired.

An economic vicinity

How radical a policy centralisation is depends crucially on the established patterns of transhumance, involving movement to live near fields, in small villages and the actual distribution of these villages, their interdependence or discreteness. That is why, somewhat in advance of our general discussion, a brief sketch of the four Tswapong villages due to be 'centralised', one of them being Moremi, is essential in order to show the inter-village relations that had, in a sense, prepared the groundwork for a centralisation policy. Moreover, for clarity of analysis, a concept must be introduced that refers to an area of relations which the villagers themselves are aware of but do not explicitly recognise or label as such and is thus unlike an administrative or social division of a higher order than the village itself. This concept is the 'economic vicinity', and it refers to a continuous area of production and land use formed by zones which may be somewhat indefinite in their limits.

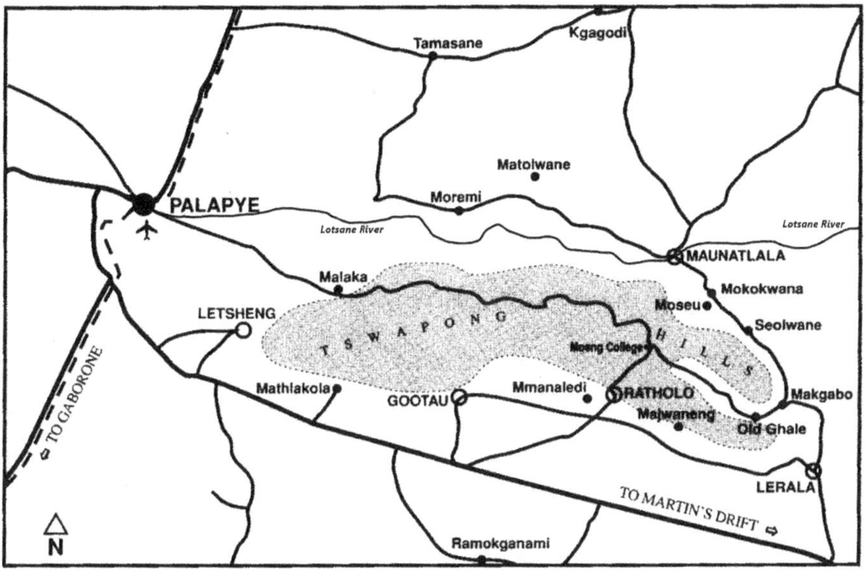

Figure 2.1 Map of the Tswapong Hills and their surrounding villages.

The four Tswapong villages belong to a single economic vicinity. Across their territories run zones which make the villages economically interdependent. All four villages are contiguous, and, in a central part where all their territories meet, adjacent fields are cultivated by some members of each village, to some extent overriding the boundaries of different villages and mixing together villagers who have different origins. Some of these neighbours are somewhat estranged from their home villages; they no longer have a hut or other residence at their village's centre and have thus separated themselves, to a degree, from many of their home villagers. Yet, far-reaching as this separation is, it is not a total break in co-operation, since, at the height of the cold dry season or in a severe drought, they may have to resort to the use of permanent water supplies near their village's centre.

An illustrative example of this was the case of Moreetsi, a senior agnate, first-born son to a senior brother of the headman Days (see Genealogy 1). We find Moreetsi in Chapters 4 and 9 as an active participant in Moremi village politics, who felt entitled to have a say on who should be the next headman or where the *Komana*, the sacred cult of the drum, should be located. Yet Moreetsi had never lived in the present site of Moremi village near the Lotsane river, where most residents had moved from the spring at Mannonye. He had remained living in the 'lands' area and moved directly from there to Matolwane, the new centralised village, like many other senior agnates in Moremi ward. In Matolwane, he became ward headman and continued to be actively involved, as we shall see, in the *Komana*.

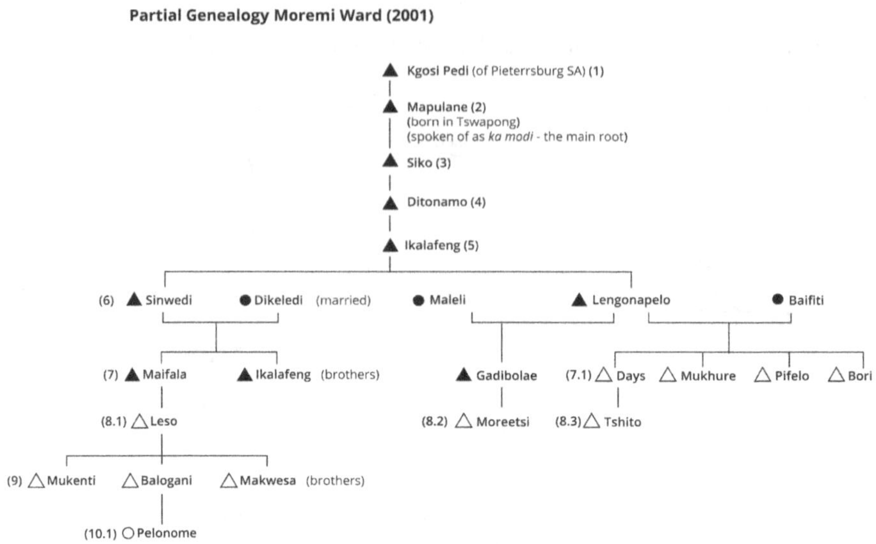

Figure 2.2 Partial Genealogy of the senior Moremi ward.

For those amongst the villagers who had cattle, the prevailing pattern of transhumance has been between a cattle post in one secondary yet seasonally critical locality, where they usually have some home villagers as neighbours, and a peripheral locality where they maintain their permanent residence, cultivate and herd their large and small stock – cattle, goats, sheep – together or nearby for all but a few months after the harvest at the height of the cold dry season.

It follows from this pattern of transhumance that for most of the year some members of each village have more day-to-day contact and involvement with neighbours from different villages than with fellow villagers living in more remote localities. Economically, the villages' interdependence arises from the fact that none has exclusive use and control of all the basic natural resources it needs, primarily its water supplies. The Lotsane river that runs through them all has water near or on the surface for only a small part of the year. The two parent villages (Moremi to the west and Lesenepole to the east) from which the smaller villages (Matoposane and Raphiri, both to the north) developed, both as offshoots of Moremi,[6] have exclusive, permanent water supplies near the centre of each – a resource which is highly prized and jealously guarded. The

6 We have kept the villages' own names and not used a pseudonym, because they are readily recognisable due to Moremi's unique cult of the *Komana*. In the original article, Werbner referred to the three other nearby villages geographically in relation to the new central village as East, North, and South. Because of the events that follow in Chapter 11, we have now identified them by their real names.

smallest villages also have springs of their own, though not reliable, permanent ones like the others. Each village, parent or offshoot, shares access to some pans or springs in localities on their peripheries. Clearly, both interdependence and jealously guarded village autonomy work, if sometimes against each other, to make such an economic vicinity; and since the economic vicinity is not simply a village writ large, to transform it into a single village does call for a qualitative change in organisation.

Political information and representation in a wider field

From the start, it is important to recognise that one of the resources drawn on in small village politics is a wide-reaching net of information and rumour. Nothing could be further from the mark than the notion that small villages characteristically lack any wider political awareness. In many small villages, the flow of people to the capital, to Palapye, the nearest railway town, and to other nearby villages is too great for that. Quite the contrary is usually the case. We found that in their meetings the people of small villages drew comparisons between their circumstances and those in other villages, they discussed action taken elsewhere in response to government policies, and they debated with information and rumours collected from the district and sub-district capitals, the sub-chief's headquarters in Palapye, and almost any of several dozen nearby villages. Part of the lobbying which takes place at beer drinks and informal gatherings is the spreading of highly circumstantial and suitably coloured reports of public and private statements attributed to officials and party politicians.

Yet merely to recognise the existence of a far-reaching net of political information and rumour is not enough. The need, perhaps the most essential job in analysis, is to appreciate how continuities as well as discontinuities in power relations locate village politics within a wider political field. However big or small a village may be, it is not to be understood as an isolate; nor, indeed, as the starting point for an analysis, and thus our account starts from an appreciation of a wider political field and continues to give it full weight in analysis.

One obvious key to this wider political field is the kind of representation that villagers have in their district's highest political body, the local government's District Council. In 1971, villagers elected one councillor to the District Council which controlled, among other things, the allocation of funds for local works, such as schools and water pumps. The district was and still is so vast, however, that each of the 31 councillors (at the time) had to have a constituency covering at least the equivalent of a rather big village. Moreover, since the district votes overwhelmingly for the ruling National Botswana Democratic Party (BDP), the choice of councillor is largely a matter of nomination which an inner circle of the party determines with regards to public and party interests, that can have relatively little to do with particular small villages.

A brief profile of a councillor, the one representing the set of small villages whose centralisation we discuss in a full case history later, is a useful illustration of political representation in the district. Perhaps most crucial for an indication of what this councillor represents politically is his membership of an entrepreneurial elite based at the district capital, Serowe. His interests, like those of others in this elite, spread across villages and widely separated areas of the district, even apart from his constituency. Besides keeping his permanent residence at the capital, the councillor has his herds at cattle posts remote from each other and from the area, also outside his constituency, where he hires workers to cultivate land with his tractor. With his own lorry, he is able to make frequent trips to buy and sell stock, to take a prominent part in council debates and decision making at the regional capital, to visit widely in his constituency, and to manage his distant areas of production. What he does not do is take a leading part in his constituency's small village assemblies, the *kgotlas*, and he rarely addresses them except when he accompanies the member of parliament or a government official or when he has a special mission to inform villagers about new council policies. He acts far more as a channel for the capital to communicate with the small villages than the other way round.

As for the four small villages which are the subject of our main case history, they total fewer in population than a quarter of their councillor's constituency of about 6,000 people. Furthermore, they are, in various senses, of secondary importance for him politically. Within the constituency his main bases are elsewhere. One is in a village near one of his several cattle posts. Another is in a village where he managed a store, at the time of his first election, and it was from this village that he extended credit widely in times of shortage, on behalf of the European storeowner, and bought cattle over much of what became his constituency. Moreover, his main core of support was among Kalanga like himself, ethnically distinct from most of the people in his constituency and in the four small villages who are mainly Tswapong in origin, with the exception of Lesenepole. Throughout his constituency this councillor devoted much time and effort to mobilising support for the council's policy of centralisation.

Paradoxical as it may seem, the alliance on which the councillor relied most heavily for support in favour of the council's centralisation policy is with the 'Tribal Authority' or acting chief and head of the tribal court, who, in 1971, was Rasebolai Kgamane (see Gillet 1973:184).[7] However, this is perhaps more ironic than paradoxical, viewed historically. Especially in the period of self-government before independence and immediately after it, leading party politicians anticipated a struggle in their campaign to transfer power from tribal rulers to an elected, national, and local government. At that time "The Tribal Authority" was also the District Council chairman. Thus, one important factor in this councillor's nomination initially, according to a high-ranking party official, was his reputation for being outspoken and ready to oppose tribal rulers and men of hereditary rank

7 Rasebolai, an 'authoritarian conservative', was appointed in 1971 by President Seretse Khama to quell factional quarrels in the Khama family. He had been Tribal Authority under the British in 1953 and a Sergeant Major in the High Commission Territories Pioneer Corps. He was described by Moremi villagers as *bogale* – fierce, angry.

at the capital. Nevertheless, since such men at the capital also had grounds for backing a policy of centralisation, which they had themselves initiated long before independence, they were a highly valuable resource for the councillor in dealing with resistance in the small villages.

In effect, what had been a campaign by the district capital's tribal rulers became a campaign by their successors. Elected politicians and tribal rulers became allies as men in the capital opposed to decentralisation in the hinterland, and they co-operated to promote centralisation. In particular, this councillor, who appreciated how critical a resource the hierarchical relations in tribal administration and their sanctions could be, used them – almost successfully – to win a decisive victory in an encounter with the villagers. Further implications of this will become clearer later in the course of our account of the villagers' politics over an eight-year period. But first certain qualitative differences between big and small villages must be understood.

Political pluralism *versus* the concentration of power

More than a change in the mode of settlement is at issue in the grouping together of small villages to make big ones. The distribution of power is crucially at stake. In a small village, the concentration of power within some centrally based elite tends to be avoided, and the village's location away from the centre tends to make it more autonomous. In a big village the opposite is usual, and members of various elites based in the big village's headquarters tend to be dominant, both politically and commercially. The small village's centre provides less of a power base. It usually contains homes for less than the majority of the village's population, homes normally lived in for a relatively short period, at the height of the dry season, and then not in every year. Here the concentration of power is avoided partly at the price of instability in the support for various leaders. The village chief's own family group, on which he is immediately dependent, need not be numerous or prosperous, and is often relatively weak compared to some other family groups. He must therefore rely on support from other leaders who readily recombine to resist the emergence of one among them as dominant.

The village assembly, the *kgotla*, often becomes a setting for the politics of obstruction when issues of communal concern are raised. As leaders realign, they resort to tactics which compel compromise. Rather than engaging in encounters which would be decisive, they stall and delay or boycott the village assembly, complaining later that they were not consulted and never gave their consent.[8] In effect, they withhold from the village assembly the power to take certain communal decisions, perhaps most crucially any decision about re-siting the village centre, as in the present case.

8 A comparable situation is reported for the small village of Kgalagadi in western Botswana by Kuper (1972, 1975a, 1975b). See also Walter (1969: 65).

Similarly, in a small village's location away from the centre, just as at the centre, a kind of political pluralism prevails at the expense of the concentration of power. Each locality has a plurality of leaders or men of influence, rather than a single one, and no leader or coalition dominates the locality as a whole. Primarily, a leader is the head of a family group which is prominent enough to be a major focus of relationships within, if not always outside, a locality in that his group and many of the others around it are bound to each other through marriage. The leader's supporters may be under obligation to him because of personal transactions, gifts or loans of land and livestock, and various services, including defence in disputes. The political pluralism is all the more diffuse, because some of the people in a locality are independents, neither themselves men of influence nor leaders, nor their followers.

In certain key respects, then, power relations tend to vary from small to big villages. In small villages, the concentration of power is avoided, the lack of a monopoly of any scarce and critical resource is sustained, and the spread of a leader's interests, as well as his web of social relationships, is narrowly restricted. One way that such a monopoly might be secured within a locality, even in a small village, is through ownership of a government-drilled deep well and pump, since regulations aimed at pasture control require a five-mile distance between wells. A man could thus come to be in control of the only permanent water supply in his locality, a monopoly which might be critical, depending on the availability of grazing. A small village may have men rich enough to afford this, but in the villagers we have been dealing with here, none, at the time, had made the investment and only one said he planned to do so, whereas such monopolies are found in some big villages (see Tordoff 1974). A locality leader's base of influence in a small village does usually extend beyond his own locality to another where he has a personal foothold, perhaps a temporary home or a seasonal post for his cattle. However, in a big village, members of an elite, who may grow crops in several different localities and have homes and stock posts in various others, are able to spread their influence much more widely and diversify their relationships. By contrast, a small village's locality leaders are so limited that none can become like a spider at the heart of a web of marital and other ties that catches up even a few of his village's localities.

Local political history and a history of local politics

This is best exemplified in a case study. The probes, confrontations, and encounters through which politics proceeded in Moremi village in 1964–72 can best be illuminated through an account of an actual sequence of events. The sequence we report here took place over an eight-year period, including the year of our fieldwork among Tswapong in 1972–73. Besides drawing on our own observations, therefore, we have had to reconstruct a history from the memories of virtually all the main participants and from the rather scant contemporary documentation in participants' letters, court transcripts, and other government records. We do not feel at all confident that there is only a single history of these events. Too much remains a matter of controversy for that, particularly because participants tended to recall events selectively and on certain issues flatly contradicted each other according to their current positions.

We must stress, moreover, that controversy over the past was not limited to interviews with us. Beliefs, or at least statements about what had actually happened, were resources frequently and extensively marshalled at public meetings in the *kgotla*; leaders repeatedly tried to justify or excuse their actions and were subject to attempts to hold them accountable historically. The public use of local history in all its intricate elaboration was also a means to resist encroachment by government and party officials who might otherwise have focused debates in assemblies on the current merits of a policy, without much regard for questions of who had taken which stand in the past.[9] Indeed, exasperation with the villagers' historical tactics led their newly elected member of parliament, then the Minister of Local Government and Lands, to try to forestall them, somewhat unsuccessfully, when the centralisation issue was raised on his first visit to his constituency. Despite his insistence that he already knew and thus did not have to hear again recitals of what had been said at the courts of the present Palapye sub-chief, Majashango, and the court of Rasebolai, the Serowe acting chief, he found himself having to hear these discursive historical complaints.

To turn now to an account of the sequence of events, it is convenient for purposes of exposition, though not necessary for analysis, to begin with a change from one major phase to the next. At first, decisive encounters took place, and were expected to do so, within the framework of tribal arbitration; villagers came to courts and brought complaints to higher customary courts as adversaries, which superior tribal rulers, the sub-chief and acting chief, decided judicially. The courts were expected to give binding decisions on political issues treated as legal issues. This was a form of judicial review in the customary courts, in which citizens challenge central or local government decisions. It presaged later cases of judicial review in Botswana, which almost universally took place in statutory courts.[10]

Following the court hearings, in the next and more experimental phase, which began barely a few months before our fieldwork, no encounters occurred. Instead, probes and confrontations went beyond the framework of tribal arbitration, and contests verged on fights with increased uncertainty about permissible tactics and their consequences. Moreover, some of the ground rules of political competition were in question. The change was dependent on those

9 Richard Werbner develops related points about the politics of history under colonial rule in Werbner (1969). See also Colson (1974: 80) and Comaroff (1978).

10 Richard Werbner has discussed judicial review in Botswana in relation to the Chiefship law case (R. Werbner 2004: 60–62, 194–95). Famous other instances of judicial review in Botswana, all of which were heard in the High Court and Court of Appeal, were the Unity Dow case, the CKGR San case (Sapignali 2018), and the Manual Workers Union unofficial strike case (for a discussion, see P. Werbner 2014a).

national processes which drastically reduced or at least redefined one sphere of decision making – that controlled by hereditary or tribal rulers – and, at the same time, greatly expanded another sphere: this was the sphere which elected leaders and civil servants had to divide among themselves. Nevertheless, local resources and restraints were critical for determining the pace and, to a significant extent, the direction of the change.

At the beginning of the first phase, consent for centralisation was sought, though not unambiguously gained, from the authorities then governing in the four villages. Who these authorities were and how they were consulted was a matter of controversy, although it is clear that there was general agreement about a primary rule for proper consultation. No one, not even the Councillor, considered that consent had to be given then or later by an elected village development committee and its chairman. Under the agreed rule, such a decision had to be made, initially, by the village chief with his senior agnates (*borrangwane*, father's brothers) at a moot (*morero*). Eventually, their decision would have to have the backing of a consensus in the *kgotla,* the village assembly, to be effective. Moreover, it was understood that genealogical seniority made one village chief fit to be the spokesman for the rest in making the joint request for centralisation. This was Leso Maifala, the chief of Moremi, universally acknowledged to be the parent village not merely of the four villages but of all Tswapong, a standing which gave the chief ritual importance and a measure of respect, though not control, in other villages. In pragmatic terms, as his opponents were quick to point out, his very weakness, poverty, and lack of a large, prosperous family group of his own made him a useful frontman for other, more powerful men, though one given to vacillation between powerful opponents.

Ambiguity about the consent of village authorities was at once a product and a factor in the development of struggles between those in control of a village centre and dissidents from a locality at the village's periphery. According to Moremi's village chief himself, he took the key initiative, without having the centralisation of four villages as his objective. Witnesses, including opponents of his, agree that he first approached the acting chief merely to provide a well to meet the water shortage in the 'lands', the area where Moremi had many of its cultivation fields adjacent to residents from the four other villages. The chief hoped eventually to move the village's centre to the well, because the existing centre of Moremi village, on the sandy slope of the Lotsane river, had proved to be poorly sited for access by lorries. ('This is a place not fit even for camels,' was the favourite shout of one of the village's veterans of the North African campaign in World War II.)

In response to a plea by Rasebolai, the acting chief in Serowe, for small villages to come together, the village chief then favoured a new site close to a boundary with Moremi's somewhat smaller offshoot, Matoposane. The senior agnates who urged the headman to this choice were dissidents already living near the proposed site, so-called 'jackals' living permanently outside the main village. They were the ones who were to authorise a move without consulting any of their agnates with homes at Moremi's village centre. The choice was a compromise acceptable to Matoposane: it had long resisted pressure by district officials to get it to re-join Moremi, but this proposal meant remaining an autonomous community politically while sharing a joint centre at the boundary with its parent village.

Before this compromise was agreed upon with the district officials, however, a further development which completely transformed it extended the political field to include two more villages. Senior agnates from another parent village, who were also living nearby and away from their own centre, made a takeover bid through a proposal to group together their village, Lesenepole, and an off-shoot, Raphiri, along with the other two. The timing was opportune for these dissidents: one of them, while still away from his village centre, had recently become acting village chief when the Lesenepole chief died leaving a son who was a minor. These dissidents' proposal was a bid not merely to wrest control of their own village's centre, but potentially to dominate the new one in the planned big village, since the only school, pump, and water tank were to come from Lesenepole and they counted among their number the only entrepreneur rich, experienced, and well-connected enough to establish a major store in the joint centre.

At this point, despite the fact that the request was not authorised by any agnate representing the villagers in any of the centres, apart from that of Matoposane, the Councillor could and did claim that the villages' proper authorities asked for centralisation. Later, both in court and in interviews, he maintained this claim by arguing that Moremi's village chief called him to a moot along with the chief's two most senior agnates (he omitted to say that both were dissidents living permanently in the lands) and put the request on behalf of the four villages. The agreement which was made and then recorded in a letter to the council chairman, Rasebolai, the acting chief, did not immediately become an issue in a confrontation, since it was not regarded as public knowledge until it was announced by Leso Maifala, Moremi village chief, to the *kgotla*, when a government crew arrived to drill for water.

This announcement started the first of a series of confrontations, culminating in an encounter at the acting chief's customary appeal court in Serowe, the tribal and district capital. No one is recalled to have come to the village chief's defence in the assembly – he himself pleaded that he was drunk when he consented to the move. In an effort to nullify the agreement, the villagers carried their complaint forward to the sub-chief's court in Palapye. The trial was brought by a delegation which represented an overwhelming majority of the villagers and included the village chief's deputy, Days Mapulane, other agnates, and locality leaders (see Genealogy 1). The Palapye sub-chief himself summoned representatives of the other villages. Afterwards, Moremi delegation took the trial's outcome to be their victory, although it actually postponed a decisive encounter.

Figure 2.3 Chief Days Lengonapelo.

In upholding the rule about consultation of agnates, the sub-chief rebuked Leso, Moremi village chief, and cautioned him to go back and make the decision about moving in a moot with his 'father's brothers', which Moremi delegation took to mean those governing from the village's centre. This outcome won the villagers time, but it did not allow them to stall forever, since drought brought on a new crisis. Relief rations had to be allocated during the drought. As new resources, they were a critical prize. The winning of important political advantages depended on decisions about how and where to allocate the rations. The government was committed to a programme of food for work on communal projects such as road or school building. In the case of the four villages, this posed a dilemma. If each village were to receive food separately and do a project for its own centre, then the policy of centralisation would suffer a setback; the permanent amenities villagers built could be used as justifications for not moving to a joint centre, and the district council might be saddled with more costly schools serving too few to be economic. On the other hand, if all the villages were to work and be fed together at this time, they would suffer great hardship in that permanent water supplies had yet to be installed at the joint centre and this was at a considerable distance from the residences of many of the villagers.

Nevertheless, villagers claim that the Councillor tried to make the food-for-work programme suit the centralisation policy, with the co-operation of the acting village chief of Lesenepole, who was to have the distribution storehouse near him and, in effect, under his charge. The successful tactic of Moremi delegation, led by Days, the deputy village chief of Moremi, was again to turn to the Palapye sub-chief, this time to use him against the Councillor and to ask him to intercede on Moremi's behalf on humanitarian grounds.

Even before they won control of their own relief rations, the villagers lost little time and began to work together with great zeal. Indeed, so much so that when the village oracle, the *Komana*, spoke in a communal ritual, it complained that the ancestral spirits were getting restless because of the fires constantly burning through the night to bake bricks. From the core of recalcitrant dissidents, including the village chief's two most senior agnates, a very few worked only to build the new joint centre. The rest of the villagers united overwhelmingly to defend and improve their centre by the Lotsane river through building a storehouse and a primary school.

Victory was theirs, but it was, they came to realise bitterly, a Pyrrhic victory, which cost too highly not merely in materials but in organisational resources also; as a long-term consequence, their village development committee was stultified. Indeed, at the time of our fieldwork some five years later we found the village at an impasse and the classrooms and many other huts in ruins or abandoned. The villagers had not anticipated the Council's counteraction. They did manage to raise their own funds to hire a teacher when the Council refused to supply one, contrary to a promise often repeated, they claimed, by visiting ministers and members of parliament, that they needed only to build classrooms and teachers would be provided. However, they were unable to keep any teacher for long, when the Councillor made an effective threat of prosecution for running an unaccredited, private school.

Blocked in their efforts to develop their own centre, Moremi villagers resorted to stalling tactics which delayed a decisive encounter for several years. In the meantime, a minority from Lesenepole and virtually the whole of Matoposane, in the midst of whose land the joint centre was sited, gave it their whole-hearted support by building huts and classrooms around the pump and tank transferred from the old Lesenepole site. Messages went back and forth, and a succession of acting chiefs went to the new joint centre to call all the villages to come together, in vain. At last, the Councillor, backed by the acting chief Rasebolai in Serowe, decided to prosecute them in the customary court of the Tribal Authority for disobedience to a lawful order, or as categorised in the court record's description of the case, 'Disobedient Lawful'.

Disobedient Lawful

'Disobedient Lawful' – the odd sting of truth in this was due to the fact, which Moremi villagers crucially did not realise, that their action, while disobedient, ***was lawful.*** For the whole trial was a bluff, and the Serowe Tribal Authority and the Councillor, though not the villagers, knew it. Here the full extent of the political field had to be concealed from the villagers. It was crucial, if this encounter were to be decisive, that the villagers' belief in the authority and sanctions of the tribal court could be used as a local resource against them. They were actually in a far stronger position than they realised, because national legislation, whose implications they did not recognise, had already transferred from the Tribal Authority to a Land Board powers over settlement and land tenure. As we were told by a member of parliament on a private visit to Moremi from his nearby constituency,

> In the old days, Rasebolai (the acting chief) would have ordered the people to move, and if they refused, he would simply have had their huts knocked down. Now there is no question of this. Rasebolai has to persuade them. They might be persuaded partly out of respect for him and partly they might believe that he has the power to get them removed, even though he does not have this power.

This member of parliament also told us that he did not agree with Rasebolai that villages ought to be concentrated, but we failed to determine whether he eventually aided or abetted the villagers' resistance. In the trial, the Councillor opened the prosecution, prominent villagers from Lesenepole and Moremi replied and were cross-examined, and finally Rasebolai, the Serowe acting chief, passed his memorable sentence, repeatedly cited in subsequent years: 'If you do not remove [to the joint centre] by the end of November [in six weeks' time] I will put each and every one of you in prison!'

Only the briefest account of the trial can be given here, but this point must be stressed: it was a kind of encounter in which an attempt was made, unsuccessfully, to bring in an appeal to an authority transcending the participants' and the court's own. While Kgosi Leso, the village chief of Moremi, admitted his guilt in going back on his word which he had given with his two most senior agnates, he argued in defence that this was due not simply to the people's refusal but also to objections voiced by the ancestral spirits who speak in the secretive, communal cult, *Komana*. His second-in-command in the cult, one of the senior agnates and dissidents living permanently in the 'lands' (and described by villagers as jackals, *phokojwe,* wild animals), denied this, despite the village chief's insistence that the agnate was absent from the ritual at the time.

Briefly, then, the villagers' opposition crumbled rapidly; the chiefly bluff worked, at first and the villagers, accepting defeat, returned home to build the new centre in compliance with the court order, since no one questioned the legality of the proceedings. Nevertheless, decisive as this was at the time, it could not remain so or conclude the struggle, for at least two important reasons. First, resentment against what many villagers considered oppression and intimidation did not need much to be kindled into further disobedience, so long as the sanctions could be dodged. Second, and perhaps most critically, the most sensitive question, a political one, was left unresolved, indeed was unresolvable by the court. Who was to dominate the new centre?

The encounter in court between the villagers and the district officials had to lead to a direct confrontation testing the strength of leaders from different villages. It was the official view that each of the villages was to be an equal, with its own leaders and control of its own resources, but this view was a political fiction which served but did not deter the rivals from different villages who competed for leadership of the new village as a whole. No doubt the official view would have had a different force had the district government had the personnel and resources to direct a planned change very closely. As it was, much had to be left to the *ad hoc* arrangements of the villagers themselves.

By the time of the trial, command of the living space around the school had already been taken on behalf of Lesenepole by its acting village chief. Rather than concede this critical advantage, as other Moremi villagers urged in divinatory seances, Days Mapulane, a rich and powerful rival, the deputy chief of Moremi, made a challenge. He hired a tractor and labour, at considerable cost, to move his hut poles and wire fence to a site at the very centre of the new village, close to the school. In response, a sign of a gun was left inscribed on a nearby tree, implying a clear threat of violence; the fence was cut into, and Lesenepole's acting chief himself trespassed and dug a hole in Moremi's deputy chief's yard.

All of this provoked a further *kgotla* trial, this time by the Palapye sub-chief and a representative of the district commissioner, for trespass, damage, and alleged sorcery. Its outcome was, in effect, a defeat for Days, the deputy chief of Moremi, and his supporters, though the Palapye sub-chief tried to reach a compromise between the two sides. Lesenepole villagers were forbidden to drive Days away, but he was allowed to remain on their terms, as a stranger in their midst, blocked from drawing his supporters around him in the area nearest the school, and without compensation for the damage.

From legal challenges to expanding the political field

A major change from a phase of legal and political contest to one of experiment resulted from this encounter. The terms meant paying too high a price for compliance with the Serowe acting chief Rasebolai's earlier order; the moral and pragmatic grounds for disobedience and resistance were greatly enhanced, and the villagers gained time to resort to new tactics.

Defeat taught the deputy village chief of Moremi and his supporters a crucial lesson: that they could not win against their opponents or defend various resources and their autonomy so long as they confined their actions to a local political field within the district and particularly within the tribal courts. A basic ground rule of their politics was also in question, i.e., the one that required those making an appeal to be forwarded along a chain of authorities by the authorities themselves.

The villagers' image of their national government was crucial here, since they were confident that as loyal citizens they could appeal to the head of their country or his immediate delegate and expect a just response. We quote at some length from an interview with the deputy headman, because his remarks highlight the image of national government which helped to strengthen the villagers' resistance to district policy:

> Our ruler is not like [some unknown rulers] in countries which we don't know. Our ruler was born like Jesus Christ. In his mind and in his feelings, he is the spirit of this country, he is not jealous and does not want a person to be anxious. The ministers are the hands and the ears of the president. They are supposed to take the people's complaints and carry them to the president. He must realise that his people are being reduced in cooking like grilled caterpillars. When my people wanted to go by train to Seretse [the president], I told them to wait, I would write; and someone gave me the minister's address.

Writing on the assumption that consent, rather than coercion, was the basis of government, Days began his letter to the minister by asking whether 'it was according to law that people should be told to [move] from a village they like without any reasonable ground for removing them?' The full text of the letter read:

> We, the people of Moremi in Tswapong greet you. Our master, we are reminding you that we once wrote you a letter talking of our being removed from our village, Moremi. We are being removed to the desert where a borehole is dug, the water of which is not fit for people as it is very, very salty. ... Our master, here in Moremi are two springs with pools and pools of water. We are surprised that we are to leave them without being told about the fault of the place where our village is. But since long ago, we have never been troubled by water here. As I write, the people are truly refusing to go to the place we do not like. This, they consider to be the ultimate oppression (*patiko*) of being removed to the desert and made to abandon the springs. You, of the rule by people, I am Days Mapulane, Go-Moremi.
>
> (19 August 1972)

In response, the ministry sent a district officer who investigated the complaints about 'ultimate oppression' and unpalatable and inadequate water at the new joint centre. The latter complaint, was, in his view, 'just a camouflage'. 'The Moremi residents have some other complaints beside water and they are not prepared to say them out'.

No one did say what was repeatedly said in private conversation, namely, that it was a scheme of the Councillor and his friends at the capital, including the Bamangwato chiefs, to take over the village's springs for their own cattle posts and great herds through moving the villagers to the joint centre seven miles away. But strong objection was also voiced by several villagers to being under another village, Lesenepole; an objection which the district officer somehow did not report. His recommendation was for a decision to be taken 'collectively' by the local member of parliament (i.e., his minister), the Councillor, the Tribal Authority, the Council Secretary, and the District Commissioner after they all met with the four villages.

The consequent visit by the minister, the Councillor, and a district officer was understood by most villagers to be a triumph for their campaign of resistance. Their consent was essential, the minister confirmed, and no one would be moved against his will, but they should accept progress and development, i.e., the new joint centre, otherwise tomorrow their children would stand over their graves and spit on them, saying, you held us back. The outcome was, as a personal triumph, greatest for Days, the deputy village chief. In years to come, as we shall see throughout this book, the village prospered. Not long after the split, after the discovery of diamonds, the government adopted a policy of funding schools and other amenities in villages of over 500 persons. The threat of no development turned out to be an empty threat.

Hereditary office and political opposition

As the case illustrates, hereditary village chiefship remained at the nub of struggles for leadership in each of the small villages that we observed, although, since independence, a village committee[11] and chairman were elected under local government regulations. Such village chiefship, like the village itself, is considered to be the property of a body of agnates, in some senses the acknowledged 'owners' of the village. Only if the most senior among them are consulted, and consent on behalf of the others, can certain decisions, such as re-siting the village centre, be taken legitimately. The headman's close agnates, however, are not merely sharers in village authority, they are also rivals for power and office, the headman's own and his appointed deputy's.

Significantly, it is a rivalry which was highly visible in the case of Moremi, with a clear expression in space. The areas at the centre and periphery of the village have a distinct political value. In opposition to the village chief or his deputy, dissidents among the close agnates had withdrawn from residence at the centre, without abandoning the village completely, and made their permanent home in a locality at the periphery of the village. Perhaps more than other villagers, such dissidents had special interests in capturing the centre of the village by shifting its site closer to themselves. This is why dissidents represented a ready core of supporters, sometimes virtually the only ones, for a government policy of grouping villages together at a new site, especially one in the common area on the periphery of several villages and thus closer to themselves.

In inter-village politics the effectiveness of dissidents is rather limited. Similar interests lead dissidents from different villages to co-operate with each other up to a point, but we found that these interests were not enough to make them allies committed to each other through marriage between them. Instead, the lack of lasting, publicly binding ties made their co-operation a matter of *ad hoc* mutual convenience. It also meant that each set of dissidents, while pressing for

11 For a general account of village development committees in Botswana, see Wass (1969: 4), Vengroff (1974: 33) and Tordoff (1974: 298).

the same policy, largely operated without much backing from outside the village, except from the local government itself, and, as we have seen, from the district councillor.[12]

Dissidents gathered around them their own close relatives, affines, and cognates, who formed a core of supporters against the village chief or his deputy in control at the centre. They boycotted the village assembly when it met at the centre, but they sometimes dominated it, when it met occasionally during the growing season near the arable fields in a peripheral locality. The dissidents continued to be politically influential in the village, because they usually invested more heavily in their relationships with fellow villagers than in those with nearby outsiders from other villages at the periphery. Most often, they and their fellow villagers turned to each other primarily, rather than to the outsiders nearby, when they arranged for co-operative labour, such as ploughing partnerships and work bees, when they made gift exchanges or stock loans, when they held moots for disputes, performed domestic rituals, or gave feasts, and bought, sold, and drank their beer. The village was no less multi-purpose for them because of their dissent, but their involvement, while concentrated primarily on fellow villagers, was somewhat selective and did separate them from some villagers who they sought to avoid.

Whereas a qualitative difference in the concentration of power marks the change from a small to a big village, their forms of local administration appear similar, at least superficially. The basic units of administration are wards, each of which has a hereditary head. Every villager must belong to one ward, usually his father's, unless he is an immigrant without a locally represented ward, in which case he may be affiliated to one, perhaps another relative's, at the discretion of the village chief. Villagers conceive of a ward as being founded with a legal and spatial estate of its own; initially its land, including a quarter within the permanent residential centre, is allocated by the ward head. As they speak of it, the present often represented a confused or disorderly departure from an ideal which was 'the way of old'. Wards in both big and small villages often lack any clear territorial or residential definition. Their members are intermingled, though not evenly dispersed, so that members of a particular ward may outnumber others and be somewhat more numerous in part of a locality. Sometimes, in the past a ward head controlled the allocation of a large tract considered to be the fallow of his father and predecessor, but often he had no such tract where most of his ward's members lived or cultivated.

In 1971, insofar as the granting of land was managed at all and was not a matter of self-allocation by neighbours, it was usually done by other locality leaders, themselves not being ward heads. Thus, though every ward head had authority delegated from the village chief to decide members' disputes in the first instance,

12 The Councillor was a close affine of the acting head of Lesenepole, once himself a dissident living away from his village's centre, and the affinal relationship was important not only for their alliance but also for the campaign of the Councillor's enemies to discredit his efforts.

the power to grant or re-allocate land rarely underwrote this authority. Without a centrally based elite, the village headman whose delegates were weak was all the more dependent on the relative strength of his own family group.

Conclusion

In Richard Werbner's contribution to the special issue of the *Journal of African Law*, dedicated to Professor Isaac Schapera, he took up a discussion which Schapera had advanced on the basis of his long observation of tribal government and politics in Botswana during the Protectorate era, in which he suggested that the following was a trend in the area he knew so well:

> increased power is always checked and balanced by increased responsibility: the more powerful a government becomes, the more numerous and elaborate are the devices by means of which subjects can protect themselves against misrule and oppression.
>
> (Schapera 1956: 22)

Our analysis in this chapter traced a continuous course of political action through tribal courts, administrative tribunals, and other meetings with civil servants and elected officials, from district councillor to the Minister of Local Government and Lands. We distinguish different types of events – blind probes, confrontations, and encounters – in order to illuminate the factional and citizens' power struggles that were triggered by a policy for the centralisation of small villages in the Central District of Botswana. The sequence we have analysed shows how blind probes recur repeatedly under conditions of uncertainty, without necessarily leading to any decisive conclusion in an encounter. Although we take account of bids for support based on transactions over goods and services, we have also tried to establish where the power of citizens *qua* citizens and their claims to rights enters into the political equation. Protection against misrule and oppression can never be automatic, a matter of necessary constitutional devices only. Hence the study of small-man politics in a developing postcolonial nation provides a much-needed approach to the understanding of political pluralism and, indeed, its opposite, the concentration or even monopolisation of power.

3 Tlholego

Nature, culture, destiny, chiefship, and the moral economy

Tlholego

Tlholego, a polysemic term referring, at its simplest, to nature, the non-human environment, denotes, more profoundly, a subject's essential nature and hence history, destiny, and culture. It is deployed in a variety of meanings among Tswapong, who claim descent from Pedi in the Transvaal.

In much argument in Tswapong customary courts, *tlholego* is implicit. Sometimes, however, as in the non-justiciable court case we analysed in Chapter 2, people invoke it explicitly, when they reason during a hearing and appeal to a fundamental principle. In preparation for our analysis of this case, we unpack the broad significance which Tswapong give *tlholego.*

The importance of this step in our ethnography is that it provides a basis for appreciating traditional deliberation and the division of decision-making in a dual court system, the customary court and *Kgotla ya Sedimo,* the court of divinity. Although we sometimes call the latter the 'cult of sedimo', having primarily in mind its ritual and sacred initiation, Tswapong usually call it a court, or, for short, *Sedimo*, Divinity. Their usage foregrounds *kgotla,* their traditional and communal forum. *Kgotla*, whether only for the living or with the dead also, is a forum in the same fenced-off central place, dedicated to deliberation and chiefly authority. The difference is that, unlike the open and more transparent customary court, *Sedimo*, being much heard but little seen by the public, is secretive and esoteric with its oracular cult for initiates. Yet what both courts hold beyond question is their shared axiom of *tlholego*: hence, we introduce it first.

Later, in Chapter 4, we examine how, in a customary court hearing, villagers deliberate over a disturbance in the usually taken-for-granted balance between the two courts. For our comparative interest in the seeking of customary justice, the villagers' predicament is all the more significant, for this reason. In the face of a challenge to how the courts' relative power and authority is to be defined and sustained, the reaching of a resolution is uneasy, as we shall see – especially because the case is known to be unprecedented and the cause in dispute, not a matter fit for judicial decision in a customary court.

In the present chapter, we first consider *tlholego* as a critical attribution of Tswapong personhood and subjectivity, basing our account on *Divination's*

DOI: 10.4324/9781003241881-3

Grasp (Werbner 2015). In the second part of the chapter, moving away from the individual subject of *tlholego,* we turn to an analysis of *tlholego* as a force in the collective history and future destiny of Moremi. While Moremi claims to be the senior among the villages dotted around Tswapong Hills, it is one of the smallest (see Map 2). Tswapong Hills range east–west from the border with South Africa, and rise to an elevation of 300–400 metres above the plateau in the vicinity of Moremi. They are home to wildlife, from the relatively rare Cape vultures to leopards and hyenas, kudu and baboons, and are cut in places by deep gorges enclosing waterfalls and permanent springs. Village life, however, proceeds at the foothills, facing the hills at some distance, and more attuned to the bellowing of cattle, the bleating of goats, and the morning chorus of crowing roosters.

As *Divination's Grasp* documents, there are significant links among *tlholego,* 'the character or nature of a person, nature' (the dictionary definition), to 'creation' (*tlholega*), fate or destiny (*thlolelo*), and, more indirectly, to portending an evil omen (*tlholetswe*). *Tlholego* as 'nature' refers to origins and authenticity: to whom one 'really' is (R. Werbner 2015: 241).

Tlholego is invoked most frequently and explicitly by Moremi's guardians of culture and tradition. Among these select individuals, the diviner Morebodi figures prominently in *Divination's Grasp.* Morebodi declared '*tlholego* is your very parents'; it is life itself, created for people by their parents (ibid.). It follows that uncovering *tlholego*, as a diviner does, calls for 'aesthetic renewal', 'in effect, re-creation' (ibid.); of 'ordered creation' or 'nature'. Morebodi believed that Tswapong were denying *tlholego,* which meant that they 'no longer knew or respected their nature and their origins' (ibid.: 242); not only were they 'estranged from their own culture' but from their very selves (ibid.). He blamed much of this on 'Europeans' who had caused people to exchange their own ancestral divinities (*badimo*) for European ones (ibid.: 243), in particular, for a 'white' Jesus. Indeed, he insisted that 'those who know not the *badimo* are despised, because they do not know their *tlholego*' (ibid.: 244). During divination, Morebodi found this to be true in the case of the ethnographer's assistant Njebe, whose grandfather was a well-known diviner. Njebe's abandoning of his alleged inherited vocation as a diviner, his *tlholego,* had cast him into shadow and darkness (*sefifi)* and rendered him impotent, revealed Morebodi.

Morebodi's finding about *badimo,* the ancestral spirits, foregrounded the collective nature of *tlholego* and its deep connection not only to history, but to nature, since the *badimo* in Moremi village are said to dwell in the pools of Mannonye, the permanent spring flowing through Moremi Gorge in the hills. The spirits have to be asked to come to the village, when there is a need for healing or to beseech for rain. Then, summoning the spirits to the village court is the work of members of the cult of *sedimo,* the oracle of divinity, otherwise called *komana*, the drumming of the secrets. Morebodi was a very active member of the cult, as well as, very controversially, one who called on the spirits in his individual healing practice as a diviner in his own hut.

As a collectivity, the *badimo* include all the ancestors, from the eponymous Mapulane, the first named ancestor of Pedi, who migrated to Tswapong Hills

Figure 3.1 Moremi Gorge waterfall and pool.

from the Transvaal. Originally, the ancestors of the current villagers settled at Mannonye, beside the hills, deploying hoe agriculture in the heavy black basalt soil, but, when ploughs were introduced, they moved across the Lotsane River to live closer to the sandy red soil more suitable for ploughing. They stayed close enough to a second spring, Mothodi, not far from the hills, where they drew water for drinking and domestic use, and also watered their cattle.

Thlolego: cultural and economic capital

When we first arrived in Moremi, in 1971, the village – a small, isolated place reachable only by 4-wheel drive vehicles, along a virtually impassable 10-km sandy road, was being subjected to pressure from the Central District Council and the tribal authorities. As we saw in Chapter 2, they demanded that villagers had to move into a centralised village, Matolwane, which would join together Moremi with three other small villages. Shortly before our return in 1972, the acting village chief, Days Lengonapelo, it will be recalled, had moved to the centralised village for a few days. Then he went back to Moremi, having realised that he and the whole of Moremi would be marginalised in the new central village. Despite enormous pressure from the authorities to resettle, and despite even threats to bring in the army, Days dug in his heels heroically. Appealing over the heads of the District and tribal authorities, he wrote a letter, as we saw in Chapter 2, to the Minister, complaining of being 'oppressed' in the newly independent nation. He seized on the democratic promise of citizenship for all – we are all Batswana – to assert the right of his community to live in their own place, where they belong, and not to be resettled by force against their will. They were not to be driven and dispossessed, as if merely subjects and inferiors, Tswapong, under the arbitrary rule of their masters, Tswana, at tribal headquarters.

It was said that the senior (but no longer acting) village chief, Leso Maifala, had sold the village for a pot of beer. He was too weak (and poor) to stand up to the District and tribal authorities. A perception of *tlholego* was striking in the villagers' understanding of what motivated the authorities' drive for resettlement and centralisation. Their true motive, perceived Days, an affluent diviner even before becoming village chief, was to possess Moremi's two permanent springs. The tribal authorities had had their greedy eyes on the springs from time immemorial. Moreover, while the water of Moremi springs was sweet, the water from the borehole dug at the new centralised village was 'salty' (*letswai*) or chalky, in other words, undrinkable. Not only that – the *badimo* were complaining at being dislodged from the pools of Mannonye. As head of the court of *sedimo*, the younger brother of the village chief had held night vigils in which these complaints were heard. These night vigils were attended by all the senior members of Moremi's chiefly and cognate wards, including several initiates who were living permanently at their 'lands', close to the new village, and were inclined to move there.

The recalcitrant villagers, who refused to move to the centralised village, were threatened with six months in jail by the authorities and later warned that, if they did not move, they would never have a school or any other facilities, such as a clinic. The new centralised village was about 10 km away and children would have to walk to school there. They would never, ever, get 'development'!

Of course, those posing threats reckoned without *tlholego*. The destiny of the village, as it turned out, would not be decided in remote government or tribal offices but by the village's historical distinction as the most senior among all Tswapong. Or so villagers now believe, as we recount more fully below.

It must also be said that there is a perceived aura around Tswana chiefs. Insofar as they are perceived to have power and authority, it is taken as if this too emanated from their own *tlholego*, their intrinsic nature. Even as their authority and power have waned in modern Botswana, a vestige of this prestigious inner nature has persisted as perceived and experienced charisma. In October 1972, we asked Moremi's chief, Days, why he had appealed to Minister Kgabo after the Acting Paramount Chief at the tribal headquarters, Serowe, judged that rebels who refused to move to the new centralised village of Matolwane would be imprisoned.[1] Days answered,

> Kgabo is the hand of the Great Lion (i.e., the President). Masire (the Vice-President) and those (others) are the ears of the President. They are supposed to take the complaints of people and carry them to the President. He must see that his people are being reduced in cooking like *pane* (Mapane caterpillars). We knew that by writing to Kgabo it can reach the President. We didn't know his address [but] we are his people, (we) are all the people of the President.

1 Case No CRB 286/71, 21 October 1971, Serowe, presided over by R.G. Kgamane.

Even though President Seretse Khama had abdicated his paramount chiefship, he was still a 'great lion', the protector of his people, his *tlholego* undimmed by secular office.

Though only dimly guessed at by local villagers in 1972, however, the power and authority of paramount chiefs in Botswana were already in decline in the face of progressive democratic forces, in policy initiatives led by the President. The 1969 Election Manifesto of the Botswana Democratic Party, the ruling party, underlined these developments. Firstly, mineral rights had been nationalised, with the agreement of tribal authorities, to 'prevent inequality' throughout the nation (BDP Manifesto 1969: 51); secondly, the Tribal Land Act was passed so that people would 'no longer be subject to the whims of a chief whose decisions on land matters may be affected by all kinds of considerations which have nothing to do with the interests of the farmer or the nation' (ibid.: 14); thirdly, elected District Councils had replaced the 'traditional functions of the old tribal administration', with the *kgotla* no longer being a 'sounding board' for chiefs (ibid.: 12). Chiefs, defined as civil servants, were not permitted to enter politics and had to resign the chiefship if they wished to do so. In 1969, however, chiefs were still ex-officio District Council Chairmen and Chief Executives of the Council (ibid.: 13). Land Boards were not yet operational.

Explicitly intended to undermine the power and authority of chiefship in Botswana, these progressive democratic reforms remain in stark contrast to the evolution of chiefship in post-apartheid South Africa. There, such reforms were never achieved: tribal groups still own mineral rights, chiefs retain the right to allocate land, and can still be part of the decision-making process, or even the main decision maker in rural areas (see Oomen 2005). Some appear to be endowed with immense and autocratic power, only partly circumscribed by the Constitutional Court. The comparison of the South African system with that in Botswana is instructive to achieve an understanding of the differences between chiefship in different African countries (see Comaroff and Comaroff 2018, and a fuller list of recent studies in our Conclusion).

In Botswana, in 1972, when the struggle over village centralisation took place, many of the reforms envisaged by the ruling party had yet to be implemented. A series of public *kgotla* meetings took place, as we saw, in various towns – Maunatlala, Palapye, and Serowe – to discuss removal to a central village. Above all, what Moremi villagers stressed in these fora was the lack of public consultation: a village cannot be forced to move without consultation and the agreement of the village elders, they argued. Moremi's chief Leso had never consulted them nor sought their agreement on the removal. Despite this basic conviction, they admitted to feeling powerless in the face of the intimidation and threats by the tribal authorities. These left them speechless and some submitted.[2] Others repeatedly fought for what they declared to be justice and did not simply give in, as we record in detail in Chapter 10.

2 The image of lorries carrying people away from their natal homes is a sadly familiar one in Botswana. Sapignoli similarly describes the removal of Basarwa from the Central Kalahari Game Reserve (CKGR), and their fight for justice (Sapignoli 2018).

By 1999, when we returned to Moremi, the village had its own primary school and clinic. By 2016, it was reached by a tarred road, the clinic was being upgraded, the village had reticulated water, a telephone line, a viable mobile connection, and electricity (just arrived). The *kgotla* had become a court of record, with a well-designed and carefully constructed new court building and its own police outpost, bailiff, and court clerk.

Although it was still a small village, with about 500 to 600 residents, according to the most recent census in 2011, Moremi had also become the communal owner of Moremi Lodge and Moremi Gorge, a popular tourist attraction jointly managed with the Ministry of Tourism. The gorge, nationally publicised and renowned as the site of the sacred spring of the ancestors, with its cascading pools, had now been made accessible to visitors. Visitors who climbed to the very top of the gorge could see the nests of Cape vultures, a magnificent, rare bird found in only one other place in Botswana.[3] The whole area, reaching into the hills, was now fenced as a mini-reserve, with cattle excluded and villagers only allowed in with a special permit. The fencing was controversial. Nevertheless, there were plans to bring in wildlife – there were already some zebra and waterbuck. The President himself at the time (also the Ngwato tribe's hereditary paramount chief), a frequent visitor to the lodge, was friendly with the current village chief, Tshito, Days' son, and formerly a major in the regiment of the President when the latter was an army commander.

Early on, before the fencing and the building of the lodge, we visited Mannonye with one of the village elders. As we passed by a giant rock in the middle of the stream leading to the waterfall, the elder pointed it out and told us the amazing, miraculous story of how the rock got there as a landmark and memorial. It happened, he said, the night of the death of Seretse Khama, the designated tribal paramount chief before he abdicated to become a politician, president, and founder of the nation. At first, there was a terrible roaring sound, heard all the way to the village, and then the rock fell into the water. In this way was proved *tlholego*, the close connection in origins and destiny between the ultimate owner of the tribal land, the Ngwato paramount chief, and Moremi, the senior village among Tswapong.

True, the *badimo* were said not to be very happy with the recent developments, especially the electrified fence, but the lodge and gorge provided employment for local village people, most of them young, and the Ministry paid an annual subvention of some 200,000 pula (about £13,500) to the whole village, a large sum by local standards. In the meanwhile, it had also turned out that the chalky water in the centralised village was indeed undrinkable, as Moremi villagers had claimed all along. Sweet water had to be piped to the new village from Moremi's Mannonye and Mothodi springs. (More recently, the drinking water at Moremi village itself had begun to be pumped from the new Lostsane Dam at Maunatlala, a village some 20 km away as the crow flies, to the disapproval of the *badimo*, we were told.)

3 For ecstatic reviews by tourists to the gorge, who comment both on its natural beauty and sanctity, see https://www.tripadvisor.co.uk/Hotel_Review-g1379986-d7040750-Reviews-Goo_Moremi_Gorge-Palapye_Central_District.html#/media/7040750/421741751:p/?albumid=101&type=0&category=101

By refusing to move to the centralised village, Moremi had defended its *tlholego*, its symbolic and cultural capital, and was now converting this into economic capital. As Botswana prospered after the diamond-based boom, heritage, tourism and reputation, *seriti* or *tlotlo*, became commodifiable assets. The government wanted to 'diversify' the economy, especially through tourism, and to alleviate poverty by providing new sources of employment. Moremi had developed a brand name, with the spring, its waterfalls, and pools appearing periodically on the weather forecast of Botswana Television (BTV). Truckloads of foreign and local tourists could be seen making their way to the sacred spring. Some stayed the night, either at the lodge or the adjacent camping site. Many trekked into the hills, scaling the cascading pools of the gorge, led by a villager guide.

Tlholego contested: cultural performance

Tlholego can, of course, be contested. This was evident in the lead-up to the ceremony of *molelo wa kgolagana* – the 'roving torch of unity'– marking the 50th anniversary of Botswanan independence. The torch had been carried throughout Botswana and was due to arrive at the capital in August 2016 for the Independence celebrations. Moremi was honoured with the 'visit' of the torch overnight, and it was rumoured that the President might actually turn up for the celebrations. The cultural preparations for the arrival of the torch included choirs, dancers, poets, and feasting.

Figure 3.2 The roving torch arriving at Moremi.

One part of the planned programme was a visit to the apical ancestor Mapulane's grave, said to be located near the hills. The grave of Sinwedi, another ancestor, was already there, within the fenced space of Moremi Gorge. Mapulane's grave, it turned out, however, was unknown and had to be 'located'. An expedition set off to find the grave and mark it (or identify it) by a large rock near the Mapulane Gorge, not far from Mannonye. The invention of tradition in this case was led by another guardian of culture, Mashate Busang, an ex-teacher who was also, at the time, chair of Moremi–Mannonye Community Trust. The grave was rather inaccessible without a journey in a four-wheel drive vehicle. The upshot was that the President did not turn up, but the preparation of the grave hinted at the extent to which *tlholego* opened the gates to poetic elaboration, much as we saw it do for Morebodi. Mashate Busang admitted that visiting graves was a new thing, inspired by the setting-up of the Trust and the need to show visitors the importance of the ancestors. It still needed to be developed.

Explaining this to us, Mashate said that *tlholego* referred to who you are, the way you were born and the way you were brought up, influenced by the environment in which you live. It involves the things that control your life and have influenced you. Asked if it was individual or communal, he replied that,

> There is always one *tlholego*, one culture. By *tlholego*, we mean culture. Culture is something we all as a community are following. This is how we believe. This is how we were brought up. It is different when you consider different communities. There is the *tlholego* of the BaPedi people (Tswapong) and the *tlholego* of the Bamangwato people (the dominant tribe in the Central District). And, all in one, there must be something in common, embracing all these people so that they can all unify and think 'we are Batswana'. That one thing that is common to us all – that we are all Batswana, even though we have different cultures within.

When we then asked him if he could have his own *tlholego*, he said he could not. 'The *tlholego* I will have will be the one within my community'. Moreover, he said, 'the way you were brought up does not only concern where you come from; it also **embraces** where you are going in life. It will keep on like that until infinity'.

But who decides your *tlholego* – is it God?

'[No.] Your *tlholego* is decided by your nature … And we believe also that every time spiritually you are there, God is on top of you, keeping you alive, keeping you safe, and all that. That is the spiritual way of thinking about things'.

So, can you change your *tlholego*?

'There is no how you can change it. That was there from whomever created it'.

So Moremi being the highest village, is that *tlholego*?

'Moremi, irrespective of it being small, by nature, we know, these people came here first, and they are the ones who are responsible for Tswapong here'. Standing against Mashate, the chair of the Trust, another guardian of culture and *tlholego* was a woman, Paulina, who used to practise traditional midwifery before her services were dispensed with, after the advent of a maternity ward at the hospital in neighbouring Palapye. Paulina was also knowledgeable about Tswapong *mothei* girls' puberty ritual in its full symbolic elaboration. She was related matrilaterally to the old chief, Leso Maifala, who was known to be buried in the *kgotla*'s cattle enclosure, under an ancient tree. As a young girl, her mother had 'lent' Paulina to Leso's wife, her sister, to help with household chores, and she was clearly attached to the old chief. She condemned the expedition to find Mapulane's grave and had spent time cleaning Leso's grave. That, too, should be visited, she claimed. Leso, however, was a politically contentious figure during his lifetime, the target of repeated attacks by Days, then the soon-to-be late father of the present village chief. As far as we know, no-one visited Leso's grave, though it was very near all the festivities. Indeed, grave visitation is not customary among Tswapong. We can see, then, that, in memory, *tlholego*, remained a source of division in Moremi.

Asked what *tlholego* means, Paulina said, *ngwao* (culture and tradition). On further probing, she added ancestral origins – Mapulane – and so on. She said Moremi was a place of *tlholego*, *thata* (totally)! It was first among all the villages, it had the *komana*, though nowadays that wasn't given the respect it once had. She said 'everyone' was dead and she named all the late seniors in the *komana*.

The crowning proof that Moremi was widely recognised as a village of *tlholego*, of authentic tradition, was the choice of the village as the site for the 'Cultural Day' celebrations organised by Tswapong Cultural Society for the whole of Tswapong North region. Preparations for this involved cultural performances, including that of the *mothei*, the puberty ritual dance. The regional organiser claimed that uniquely Tswapong songs and stick dances were performed. We see here *tlholego* writ large, for how Tswapong as a tribe, now an ethnic group, felt to be incorporated, historically against their will, by the Ngwato.

Tlholego as nature

Tlholego can simply mean 'nature', but more often in the sense of pristine nature, unspoiled[4] by human intervention. This was made evident in the lengthy presentation by a consultant sent from the Ministry of Tourism to explain to the gathered Moremi villagers about 'Phase II' of the development of the lodge in 2017. The plan was to include a restaurant, conference facilities, and more accommodation. In the course of his explanation, the consultant used *tlholego* in a taken-for-granted way to refer to nature, the natural environment. 'Nature' had to be looked after, *babalela* (taken care of), *sireleditse* (conserved), *somarelwe* (preserved, conserved). Then, there were the cultural traces, the archaeology in

4 In a rare mention of the term *tlholego*, Booyens found, in a survey of illness causality made by a Tswana-speaking group in a black township in western Transvaal, that illnesses were thought to be either 'personalistic' (sorcery, ancestral wrath) or 'naturalistic' (*tlholego*) 'from God'. The latter were usually not a cause of worry.

Moremi Gorge, for example, where there were remains of clay pots (*dipatsana*) embedded in rock. *Ditso* or *ngwao* (culture, origins) was contrasted with *dithlolego* (natural things). Soil erosion had to be guarded against. The fencing had to be extended into the hills because people were hunting kudu and other antelopes. To prevent this and preserve nature was the 'responsibility' (*boikarabelo, marapo*) of the village Trust, a contract (*mokwalo*), reflecting, he claimed, 'fundamental law' (*molao motheo*, the Constitution). Mashate, too, acknowledged the many meanings of *tlholego*. Pointing to a tree, he said that that too was *tlholego* because 'God has created this' (*thlodilwe – se thlodilwe ke modimo*).

The speech represented a clear instance of how ordinary villagers were being educated, indeed socialised, into an international discourse of conservation: the idea that Moremi Gorge, once used productively for crop growing and later for cattle herding, now had to be guarded *against* domestic animals for the sake of the natural environment. If villagers went along with this discourse, it was only because the projected development promised work, and work was badly needed in Moremi village, especially for young people. At the same time, villagers continued to grieve at the loss brought about by the electrified gorge fence, which prevented them from grazing their animals in the lush grass of the Mothodi spring during the dry season. The hoped-for prize, in the shape of 'tourists' (*bajanala*) flocking to the gorge, was recognised, however. Moreover, villagers took for granted that it was right that tourists should *want* to see the gorge with its sacred spring – this was a site of high value, a sacred site, defended by them from the Ngwato tribal chiefs and, more recently, from a commercial firm which for a while took over the management of Moremi Gorge. The gorge was, finally, owned by the villagers – it was their *tlholego*, whether in the shape of culture or nature.

But too much *tlholego* can also be mocked as oppressive, it seems. This was satirised by the new Moremi Choir, recently formed by a nephew of both Morebodi and Paulina. He wrote the choir songs, expressing an iconoclastic vision and making fun of tourists, the gorge, and even the chief. One of the songs, 'We can see the path to Mannonye', speaks of the 'birds of tourism' (referring presumably to the Cape vultures) and the 'hills of tourism', reducing both to consumer items, no longer the sacred landscape of *tlholego*.

To sum up the discussion so far, *tlholego* is a very special term in Tswapong and Tswana lexicons: it is nature, it is culture, it is history, it is ancestrality, it is the creation of an ineffable 'God' above. These notions are all intermeshed, inseparable, just as the lives of villagers are inextricably interlinked with each other, past and future. *Tlholego* invokes reputation, dignity, and respect. As an expansive term, it allows for, indeed demands, poetic creativity, in the name of immutable tradition. It also allows for compromise, for the sake of employment.

As an active, moving term that does something, *tlholego* has historical force in the sense that it can affect events in the here and now. Even further, we suggest that, much like symbolic or cultural capital, *tlholego* is an idea that underpins an ineffable truth and moves people to action. It invokes an imagined reality, a moral universe, the world as it should be because it is, already, essentially there. For Moremi village, this has meant resisting bullying by outsiders, but readily taking from the same outsiders, in rather surprising and unexpected ways sometimes, the support needed to build a viable village community in modern Botswana.

Chiefship and waning of chiefly authority in modern Botswana

The demand by the public for serious consultation in court during the 1970s is not reflected in current practice. The *kgotla*, once esteemed as a public forum for such consultation, has in recent years become more an assembly for the dissemination of news from either the district or the central government. It is also a forum for planning events and electing new village committees such as the Village Development Committee (VDC). It is rarely a forum for debate or genuine consultation.

What the *kgotla* has remained throughout is being a court of customary law and a forum for the symbolic enactment of chiefly charisma. During recent Independence celebrations, this was evident in the ceremonial arrival of the roving torch, *molelo wa kgolagano*, to Moremi *kgotla*, as we recorded in our notes for the occasion:

When the torch, carried from the crossroads, arrived at Moremi, it was passed on to the chief who was sitting behind a table in the *kgotla* on a ceremonial throne. The main torch was lit. The chief was flanked by army and police personnel, the deputy District Commissioner (DC) from Palapye (a woman), and all the *dikgosana*, the deputy headmen. The head of a local church led the first prayer. The masters of ceremonies were a young man and a woman from the village who had arrived that day from Palapye. There was a printed programme. The chair of the Village Development Committee made a short speech. The chief then spoke solemnly and magisterially, ending his speech by evoking cries of '*pula*' (rain). The ceremony opened with all the participants singing the national anthem. There were flags adorning the stage.

The ceremony was followed by abundant food, singing, dancing, and music playing. The male elders sat around a fire with the headman until late at night, chatting and telling stories.

The symbolic centrality or *tlholego* of the village chief, the most senior in Tswapong Hills, was enhanced by the arrival of the torch, which eventually reached the capital, Gaborone. Moremi was clearly recognised as a significant place on the national map.

Tlholego and the current power of chiefs

Despite the loss of most of their formal and political power, chiefs in Botswana retain enormous respect and, often, much of their chiefly charisma. Although they must resign if they want to enter politics, in exceptional cases chiefs who enter politics preserve this charismatic aura. The most extreme example is that of Seretse Khama's son, Ian, who, unlike his father, refused to abdicate. Ian Khama, successor to the Ngwato paramount chiefship and ex-commander of the Botswana Defence Forces, was selected by the Botswana Democratic Party as their Presidential candidate, in good measure because he was perceived to have an immense appeal to rural constituents. He insisted on keeping his chiefship as a condition of accepting the party's nomination. During his time in office as president, some credited Khama with bringing rain to Botswana, and we ourselves witnessed his boast during the ceremonial opening of the Maunatlala Dam that, from being empty, dams across the country were now full to capacity. Whenever a dam he referred to had reached 99% capacity, his announcement was greeted with loud ululations from the audience (Maunatlala Lotsane Dam opening, 7 April 2016).

But the Khama chiefly family's entanglement with Moremi village goes much deeper and continues to this day. Khama's dedication to wildlife conservation found its local expression in his love of Moremi Gorge and its Cape vultures. Once Moremi Gorge lodge was built, he would arrive there by helicopter, bypassing the village. Tshito, Moremi's current chief and Khama's former regimental sergeant major, remained in contact with him. For villagers, however, this connection was understood not to be unequivocally positive; it was also somewhat suspect. Recall the fears, expressed by Tshito's father Days and the villagers of Moremi in 1972, that the real reason for their removal to a centralised village was dispossession: the Serowe chiefs had their eyes on the village springs. This seemed to be coming true with the fencing of the area around the gorge and the removal of villagers and their cattle from it, all in the name of conservation.

Figure 3.3 Chief Tshito Days Lingonapelo with Mogoma ward head.

Such dispossession was made, despite the fact that the key tourist attractions – the gorge with its sacred spring and Cape vultures – were not threatened by the presence of Moremi villagers. The tourism and wildlife department insisted on fencing off a vast area around the two springs, the gorge and the hills, and prohibiting villagers from entering the enclosure. Experts insisted that there had been erosion, which threatened the Ministry of Tourism's long-term plan to introduce wildlife into the area. Mannonye, the ancestral home of Moremi, was now no longer owned by the village but by the nation as a whole. Although there was a village CBO (Community Based Organisation), Moremi–Mannonye Conservation Trust, which controlled tourism to the gorge, operating in partnership with the Ministry. At one point, it did seem that the village had lost control entirely, because the gorge management was handed over to a private company for 20 years. Luckily for the village, the company made no profit. In a conversation in April 2016, chief Tshito explained to us that, while the lodge was losing money, the Ministry of Tourism was paying the company 60,000 pula per annum. The situation was untenable, and the gorge reverted back to the Ministry.

With personal as well as chiefly stakes in all this were the Khamas, not only Ian but his brother, Tshekedi, then Minister of the Environment, Wildlife, and Tourism. They were well known for acquiring huge shares in the tourism industry. Would Moremi Gorge be added to their portfolio? In the meantime, the Ministry was paying the village 200,000 pula per annum, and in 2016, this was the third year of these payments. Chief Tshito told us he hoped to use the money for village development and was looking around for a project. Both the VDC and CBO were suspected, in the village, of corruption; they were often highly politicised. Nevertheless, the lodge project continued to Phase II, the building of a restaurant, conference facilities, and more accommodation.

In June 2017, Air Botswana's inflight magazine Peolwane had a lead article, 'Haven in the Hills'. It confirmed the close link between the lodge project and the Khama chiefly family. Spread across the middle pages of the article were coloured pictures of the two brothers, Ian and Tshekedi, shaking hands in one photograph, and looking over the Mannonye wilderness in the second. The President had himself launched the opening of the expanded lodge. The article described this hidden treasure:

> Nestled in the Tswapong Hills in eastern Botswana, the Goo-Moremi Gorge is a sacred place of great spiritual significance to many Batswana, rich in history and natural beauty, and a perfect destination for exploration and relaxation. A community-run resort at the Gorge was recently officially opened.
> (Mogame 2017: 14)

The article conjures up the 'mysticism surrounding Goo-Moremi Gorge', 'the traditional belief that nothing happens unless it is approved by *badimo* (ancestral spirits)'. It appeals to the attraction not of the primitive but of the glories of exotic and mysterious tradition: 'Elaborate sacrifices and sacred festivities often are performed by the *komana* (an intermediary who communicates with the ancestors)'. (ibid.: 16). The then Minister of the Environment, Natural Resources, Conservation, and Tourism, the Honourable Tshekedi Khama, was said in the article to have handed over 'the keys of the resort to President Khama – and the people of Botswana – [at] this historic moment' (ibid.: 19). Among the lessons learnt, he said, was that 'there is no such thing as primitive beliefs' (ibid.: 19). Notably, the village chief attended the ceremony. The article further informed the reader of the 'medicinal qualities' of the water 'inter-connecting' past and present, nature and humankind, earth and spirit (ibid.: 20).

Conclusion

Here, then, is *tlholego*, now captured for international tourism. The message of this chapter is not, however, to make the fairly obvious point that heritage sites can be successfully commodified (see Mbaiwa 2011). Rather, we have been arguing here for quite a different point. The villagers had a deep attachment to their springs and the ancestral cult of the *badimo*, the cult of their forefathers and mothers, and of the Pedi ancestors who founded the village and all the other Tswapong villages in the hills. This deep attachment was critical in the villagers' battle in 1972 to save the village from extinction in the face of external pressures from Serowe, the District capital, by tribal chiefs and District Council officials. It was an attachment having perceptions of *tlholego*, and thus the symbolic and cultural capital they possessed, despite their poverty – all this inspired the villagers' resistance, and endowed them with the confidence and willpower to stand up to more powerful adversaries.

The arrival of the lodge was beneficial in some ways: it provided waged work, mainly unskilled, to women as cleaners and to men as porters and night watchmen; and more skilled work to administrators, nature guides, cooks, builders, drivers, and technicians. There were very few other sources of income in the village. But the huge, fenced, so-called conservation area had deprived the village of clear ownership of their ancestral lands and excluded villagers from it. Could they ever claim it back? Or would it be taken away from them permanently? These were unanswered questions, as was the question of who really was in control. This was an issue that animated the dispute at the heart of the next chapter, Chapter 4.

4 The oracular court of *Sedimo vs.* the customary court

An unprecedented hearing

The *non-justiciable*, a cause beyond the rightful jurisdiction of any court, loomed large and was troublesome at a hearing held in 2001 in the court at Matolwane, which then served as the customary court of record for nearby Moremi also. The court hearing was a bitter exposure of irresolvable and extremely dangerous quarrels and infighting among leading members of the chiefly descent group spanning the two villages, one faction against another. The rift was disruptive and deeply shameful. It stopped the two factions from working together to perform their oracular consultations and rituals at the *Kgotla ya Sedimo*, the court of divinity. Absent was the essential goodwill, kinship amity, and mutual understanding vital to achieving communal protection or to meeting the personal needs of supplicants from a wide region. The risk, when responsible members of the chiefly descent group could no longer *rerisana*, talk things over and peacefully consult each other, was perceived to be cosmic. The deeply held conviction was, and is, that a disturbance in the moral order was also a cosmic disturbance; above all, it held back the rain, a shared good vital for everyone. This meant that the ancestral wrath of *badimo,* aroused over public disorder, undermined nature, the very nature of chiefship and the village itself – it could not work together as one, a single, whole community.

Attending to the non-justiciable by a hearing in the customary court regarding the affairs and infighting of the court of divinity was a transgression. Significantly, it was a transgression not merely in terms of jurisdiction but, perhaps even more profoundly and disturbingly, in the interpretive mode of understanding social life.

What belonged to each court was a proper interpretive project of its own. Essential for the customary court was the project of forensic reason with fact finding, usually in much circumstantial detail, and, even when pursued with emotion and passion, intended to be a work in cogent argument, in accusation, defence, and judgement, among the living about rights and wrongs. The interested parties had the right to speak of and for themselves, given the burden of proof with testimony and visible, material evidence to be presented to the court. It asked them to elucidate (*tlhalosa*, explain) their case, to speak in their own voice, from their disparate viewpoints, on the way to the discovery of forensic knowledge as emergent truth-in-court.

DOI: 10.4324/9781003241881-4

By contrast, there was and is no expectation of such reasoned argument in the court of divinity. Here, one cannot speak for oneself or in one's own voice; fault finding prevails without contentious fact finding, and knowledge disclosed is ever and always declared to be the foreknowledge of the ancestors. They are the unseen ones, from whom the truth cannot be hidden – they see all. The oracular consultation with them emerges through ritual collaboration among initiated peers, in drumming, singing, and in the esoteric sounding of ancestral voices which call for inspired interpretation.

It would be a mistake to consider such oracular consultation to be the end of the matter, as if it were the last word. If that were so, then there would be a radical difference between the court of divinity and the customary court in relation to social life as an ongoing process of consultation, of *rerisana*, talking things over. That would be to say that, whereas the customary moots and the customary and appeal courts afford drawn-out discussion, often probing back and forth, between venues, the court of divinity would be a court of last resort, without any expansion in the direction of the continuing quest for *tlhalosa*, explanation, especially of the significance of suffering and affliction. Instead, what has been very important about the court of divinity has been its actual service and guidance for a great flow of *rerisana*, well beyond its vigils and Moremi itself. The interpreted sounds of the ancestral voice inform the supplicant which way to go, north or south, east or west, for divination, and which kind of diviner to find. In effect, the court of divinity has enabled a whole flow of consultations by supplicants travelling with the court's amulets worn, under the protection of the court and the ancestors, as passports for safe passage, sometimes on long and difficult journeys,

What the ancestral inspiration during a vigil actually means should properly be known by a good measure of consensus and shared understanding, led by the first among the peers, the keeper of the secrets and the ritual paraphernalia. There is no judge; the declared outcome is valid only when it is perceived to be out of anyone's hands. The finding of supplicants' moral faults and blame proceeds in the court itself without any comeback, counterproof, or challenge from the accused supplicants, and they are not innocent until proven guilty. They are guilty, astray from their duty to the ancestors, until they make redemptive offerings and sacrifice. Needing to be heard and met are the demands inspired by the dead and to fail to meet them is to place oneself in grave, possibly mortal peril. Hence, to place the causes of the court of divinity before the consideration of the customary court is to collapse inspiration with the burden of reason, is in effect tantamount to asserting the authority and judgement of the living over that of the ancestors. It is transgressive action deeply problematic for conflict resolution, particularly given the irresolvable tension between each of the proceedings which constitute the *kgotla* as a whole, the proceedings of the court of divinity, and the customary court proceedings.

But what kind of hearing, given this transgression and the mix of political, moral, and cosmic concerns, was the one in Matolwane? Was it a trial? A trial is a *tsheko*, having a case prosecuted in court under a chief's jurisdiction. At the very start, the hearing was declared to be a *kgang* (a debate, a matter of contention) by

Mokgobelelo, the village chief of Matolwane and president of the court. For him, the hearing was an occasion for getting people to stop treating each other badly and to be reconciled. It was not for deciding a legal issue, and he found himself floundering in the effort to make sense of overly detailed stories of disrespect and mischievous meddling in order to sort out the esoteric and mysterious affairs of an unfamiliar setting. Ignorant of the *Kgotla ya Sedimo* and himself not a Pedi nor a Tswapong but a Ngwato, he was an ethnic stranger and an incomer, who had been appointed to the court at Matolwane by the Customary Court of Appeal at Serowe, the tribal capital. His appointment itself was a way out of an impasse over chiefly succession, which the tribal authorities resolved by the selection of an outsider to be village chief, not a true resolution given the further infighting we discuss in Chapters 5 and 11.

In agreement with his view of the hearing as a debate, Moremi's village chief, Days Lengonapelo confessed, 'Since I was born, I have never heard that this (the *Kgotla ya Sedimo*, the court of divinity) can be brought to trial [*sekwa*]'. 'Now is the time', the presiding chief told everyone, 'that you meet to explain *(tlhalosa)* these complaints of yours, according to which you do not treat each other well'. (See Genealogy 1.) For this concern, Kaisara, a well-respected elder, ironically named after the bellicose Kaiser Wilhelm of the First World War, pleaded as the responsible father's brother of Moreetsi, the main complainant among the senior *Sedimo* members: 'Chief, what we are reporting before you is, as you hear – that we do not have any mutual understanding (*kutlwano*), totally! Now today I pray to God so that when we leave this place this issue should be finished'.

Finished? In this chapter, what will be seen is what held for the moment: that the hearing was clearly rich in the rhetoric of reconciliation, and especially so in the presiding chief's final, pious words for peace, whereas the actual progression of the hearing was murky, for many people full of lies. There seemed to be a tussle, back and forth between aggressively intense shaming with its torrent of circumstantial detail, obscure and hard to clarify or explain, and efforts towards peace-making and calm. But what was the outcome? Was it actually long-term conflict resolution or, temporarily, a mere appearance on the surface of social life, concealing the contention (*kgang*) still beneath it?

The complaints were raised first, *aggressively*, by Moreetsi, Moremi ward head at Matolwane and one of the senior members of *Sedimo*; and secondly, more *calmly* in response, by Mokhure, the *Sedimo* leader. Mokhure impressed us as a very shy, reserved man, a withdrawn ascetic who lived mostly at his cattle post or his fields, not at the village centre. In the hearing there was cross-examination by the presiding chief and others, culminating, as already suggested, in the chief's final, lengthy exhortation for amity, so vital for everyone's good and wellbeing.

The hearing was held on 31 January 2001, at a time of terrible suffering. The rains had failed, and drought had spread across the land. As the sun beat down, the crops shrivelled and, to add to the misery, people were dying of HIV/AIDS (this was just before the introduction of free universal antiretroviral treatment in Botswana).

Figure 4.1 Mokhure, keeper of the court of divinity.

Among Moremi villagers present at the hearing were 14 of the 17 *Sedimo* members, along with Moremi's chief Days and three elderly women from the senior Moremi ward, one close to being 100 years old. Also present were men from Matolwane. Of the 17 *Sedimo* members, 11 lived in Matolwane, and six, including the *Sedimo* leader, in Moremi village. The main complainant, Moreetsi, was the son of a senior brother to Days, and many of those who had settled in Matolwane were his father's younger brothers. Moreetsi was thus genealogically senior to both Days and his full

Figure 4.2 Sedimo Sacrificial hide for amulets of Safe Passage.

brother, Mokhure, the *Sedimo* leader. The presiding chief arranged for all the men present to sit on benches in a semi-circle, very close to him. Because of the scarcity of seating, they did not sit according to their role, with complainants (Matolwane) and defendants (Moremi) on opposing sides, but were mixed together, as some arrived later than others. Days was given a chair and sat beside the Matolwane chief. The ethnographers were given permission to video the proceedings.

The presiding chief, very softly spoken, seemed to be making a careful effort to address people and issues in measured, placatory tones. He was also, however, extremely authoritative, and did not allow Moreetsi, in particular, to be abusive in dismissing or shaming others. What was striking about the meeting was the seriousness with which people discussed matters. The hearing was conducted in great silence, and, although most people were given a say, some people were dominant in the interrogation, including outsiders, not members of the *Sedimo*, who expressed their confusion.

Now and then, Moreetsi would stress his chiefly descent and credentials, going back to Tswapong apical ancestor, Mapulane. He spoke stridently and forcefully, but, according to our research assistant, most people thought he was lying about contentious issues. He made an attempt to accuse Mokhure of taking payments as a diviner, since the *Sedimo* redirects patients to various healers, but this was ruled out of court by Days and others, because it had already been discussed at a previous meeting.

Mokhure was, as usual, very soft-spoken but he stuck to his guns and said quite openly, 'They are lying' (*ba aka*). Kaisara claimed that, though he was also a *Sedimo* member, he had not been 'told' of various contentious issues, and he sounded genuine.

At the heart of the contention in the hearing was the lack of communication and cooperation among *Sedimo* members living in the two villages of Moremi and Matolwane. In an interview after the hearing, the *Sedimo* leader, Mokhure, explained the awesome danger to the court of divinity. First, he stressed his own privileged knowledge of oracular understanding compared to most *Sedimo* members:

> Others do not understand but merely hear. Only very few understand. Some just come for the food and drink. *Tiro ye Sedimo e bokete*, the work of *Sedimo* is heavy (grave), and it needs a person who is reserved, *itshekileng mo moeng* (settled in his soul). *Na, ke taloganya sentle* – me, I comprehend well (the oracular instructions from *badimo*, the ancestral divinities). The others are *balatelela*, they take it carelessly. I fear it. Being the one who goes between the *Sedimo* and the people, I must do it correctly. A curse could come and I would be held accountable because I know.

In Moremi videos, Mokhure reflected further on *Sedimo* and the awesome danger of a breach of *Sedimo* tradition.[1]

1 See R. Werbner (2005, 2007) and *Divination's Grasp* (Werbner 2015) which gives an account of Morebodi, a Moremi maverick religious innovator and his *Sedimo* hymns, making Mokhure grieve.

There are five *Sedimo* members, an inner circle sometimes known as the Assembly (*phutego*, in the hearing the presiding chief, spoke of 'the committee') who can interpret the oracle, but they rarely attend. They only come in times of real difficulty. Initiates of *Sedimo* are recognised as being gifted by divinities in different ways. Some are better as drummers, others as chanters or interpreters and messengers of the ancients, speaking in their reedy tones.

Sedimo, divinity, or to give its full name, *Kgotla ya Sedimo*, the court of the divinity, is also called *mophaso*, after its main ritual, or *Komana*, usually translated as secrets. This is a Tswapong version of *ngoma*, a word for drum in many Bantu languages and a cult name known in one form or another across a vast stretch of Africa from Tanzania to the Congo to South Africa (Janzen 1992; Reis, van Dijk and Spierenburg 2000). In all these cults, as in *Sedimo* itself, drums are beaten for healing practice, often having a calling voice and a responding chorus in communication with the dead about affliction, including occult attacks in witchcraft or sorcery.

By way of introduction, some brief comments on *mophaso* are also useful. Because people speak of *mophaso*, respectfully and in short, for a whole session of *Sedimo*, our comments will serve also to give a better sense of what people take for granted in speaking of *mophaso,* namely the accompanying séance and oracular consultation. To appease the *badimo*, the ancestral divinities, supplicants need to perform a *mophaso*, the ritual authorised by *Sedimo*. In the *mophaso*, the supplicants, showing unity in seeking a blessing, blow water and beg named ancestors to cease afflicting their descendants. Afterwards, supplicants share a communion feast. It is before the *mophaso* is performed that the *Sedimo* holds its séance as oracular consultation.

During all-night vigils at the *kgotla*, of intense drumming and singing in call and response, the *badimo* are summoned at the dead of night to heal the living and bring rain to the community. Their arrival, after midnight, is signalled by high-pitched sounds, rumoured to be emanating from a flute made of the bone of a hare, the totemic ancestor of all Pedi. It is thus a voicing that is at once primal and ancestral. The ethereal sounds are understood to be spoken in the tonal, esoteric language of the *badimo*. Somewhat cryptically revealed are faults that have caused suffering, as interpreted by the *phutego*, the assembly of men who are selected and senior members of *Sedimo*, most notably by its leader. These men were said to 'understand' and thus to be profoundly empowered in themselves to interpret the oracle.

The *Sedimo*'s subjective impact as an engagement with divinities is all the more effective because of an innovation Mokhure, the present leader, first took charge of. This is a confidential moment of intimate counselling and moral revelation for the supplicant in the presence of a small congregation, a number of significant others who are usually the closest kin but could be church intimates. After rites at the *kgotla* and *mophaso*, the blowing away of wrath, outside his yard, the leader, or a trusted initiate acting for him, calls the congregation to a special hut. There he or his stand-in rehearses more or less fully the message from *Sedimo*'s oracle. The listeners will have heard the reedy sounds of the dead and the responses of *Sedimo*'s living messengers, but they will not always have understood it well or fully; it can be ambiguous. The leader speaks of himself as 'the keeper of the secrets', *motsware wa diphiri*, 'the messenger of the ancients', *serongwane sa bakgalajwe.*

The counselling may last for as long as two and a half hours, and sometimes elicits intense, dramatic outbursts. These rake up unfulfilled obligations, kinship faults, failures of amity, support, and neglect, even a disregard for what the oracle reveals to be a person's true identity, possibly hidden because of a secret adultery or a bastardising act. Some supplicants are moved to tears; others to passionate expressions of regret and contrition and, more rarely, to angry argument. One such angry supplicant went about protesting that the *Sedimo* messenger, interpreting the reedy tones of divinities, had misheard, when he used a word others took to imply that she was a loose woman, going from man to man, and thus she herself was at fault for her affliction. The counselling session often becomes a moment for bringing much moral pressure to bear, while appeals are made for a change of heart, then of conduct.

Confidential as all this is in the moment, it usually does leak out, and feeds the flow of moral judgements in gossip within villages and across town and country. This, Richard Werbner realised, somewhat to his surprise, after having felt bound by the leader's confidences before discovering that other villagers, also informed about the latest moment, were eager to confide their own moral judgements about the participants' conduct. Most commonly, accompanying the supplicant are at least one or two dozen supporters. A bishop may bring most of his large congregation. It is possible, however, for a supplicant to avoid or limit some of the moral pressure in and from *Sedimo* moments of moral revelation by coming to the *Sedimo* merely with a spouse or one or two relatives. But this is rare; it marks the supplicant as an individual bereft of support, an object of hostility, perhaps of a witchcraft accusation, who is unable or unwilling to mobilise his kin and respond to them with a change of heart, yet still seeks the protection of *Sedimo.*

For an example of the spread of séance gossip, the rival of a rich and leading elder volunteered and relished telling us about this scandal. The rich elder sponsored a session of *Sedimo*, with a big feast. At the *kgotla*, he had to hear that the *badimo* were scolding his children, apart from the two. No good, the oracle said according to the leader's rival, the rest demand money, don't work, and when he doesn't give them money, they tell him that he gives money to all his women, and if he doesn't give to them, they will kill him.

The *Sedimo*'s provision of contact with divinities goes beyond mere communication through an oracle. It constitutes a form of sacred exchange.[2] Hence, perhaps most highly valued by supplicants themselves is the provision of amulets in return for their sacrifice of goats and cattle. With the amulet, a treated piece

2 The importance of sacred exchange in the *Sedimo* is a subject Richard Werbner considers at some length elsewhere (R. Werbner 1989, 2009).

of sacrificial hide, comes protected passage under divine direction, for once the amulet is tied, usually round the neck after an all-night vigil, it is something like a temporary passport. It lasts until it falls off, and, for this time, the supplicant bears the red ochre mark of a person under the special protection of the divinities of the dead. Attack the person and your attack will return back to harm you. In order to secure safe passage, the amulet is treated with a charm against pollution and another charm for surmounting obstacles, for raising up the person with the power of a vine that ascends to the top of the highest tree. This temporary passport is meant to facilitate the supplicant's directed passage to the right doctor or church for further healing and blessing. It is a directed passage in that the oracle indicates the cardinal direction where the right doctor or church can be found. The nodal importance of *Sedimo* comes not from the provision of final intercession with divinities but from its sacred centrality as a cardinal agency for referral to other ritual and healing agencies.

The chief's two beings

Given this preliminary idea of *Sedimo* and the customary court hearing itself – its uneasy mediation in affairs of the court of divinity and its proceeding apart from any usual jurisdiction – a central point has to be considered, at least initially. Chiefship itself needs to be problematised. The reason is not general or true to chiefship throughout Botswana. Special, although not unique, to Tswapong and their tribal fellows, the Pedi of the Transvaal in South Africa, is the problem of what we call 'the chief's two beings'.

There is a duality in such chiefship as a presence. On the one hand, it is personified in the flesh by someone living; on the other, it is spiritually present in the chain of dead chiefs who, by pious welcome or troublesome affliction, still contact the living. Sited in the forecourt of the village, each presence of chiefly being has its central place of power and authority, of deliberation and decision, in its own appropriate *kgotla*. It is, for the living, the village customary court; and for the *badimo*, the divinities of the dead or the ancestral spirits, the *Kgotla ya Sedimo*, the court of divinity (for short the *Sedimo*) in the cult of *Komana* (the drums, the secrets).

What the debate in Matolwane did was unprecedented – to displace from the court of divinity, *Sedimo*, to the customary court issues never before considered there. To document and analyse the significance of that troublesome shift, we begin by describing each of the chief's two beings, and certain problematic relations between them. On this basis, we examine here at some length developments in the court of divinity, with customary court transformations in the chapters that follow. Our aim is to enable the debate to be seen in the light of historic transformations, remarkably extending the regional importance of the *Kgotla ya Sedimo*. Further, in the main body of this chapter, we turn to the *kgang* itself, to show how it dealt with the non-justiciable, how it carried forward unprecedented public wrestling over control and ownership of the court of *Sedimo* and its sacred means of communication, most controversially, its drums.

Our account of the debate foregrounds the values of reconciliation, consultation, cooperation, dialogue, and peace-making, which are the bedrock of decision-making with customary law and the chiefly court ethos in Botswana. The stress on these values is striking in a whole semantic field of cognate words in Tswana, all denoting harmonious cooperation, reconciliation, and dialogue: *agisa* (bring peace) or *agisana* (restore peace); *agisantswe* (to be reconciled), *dumelana* (agree with each other), *kopano* (meet, unite, reconcile), *kopanyo* (reconcile), *kutlwano* (mutual understanding), *kagiso* (peace), *kagisano* (reconciliation), *letlanya* (reconcile, make peace), *tetlanyo* (reconciliation); as well as *puisanyo* (dialogue, communication, negotiation, conversation), *rerisa* (caucusing, consulting), *rerisanya* (sociability, cooperation), *rerisanyo* (join together in consultation), *rerise* (to tell about, discuss), *morero* (moot), *thirisanyo* (cooperation), *tshwaragano/tshwaraganyo* (working together, cooperation, join together), *tumalano/tumelano* (agreement, (in) agreement), and *utlwana* (listen to each other, be of one mind, have understanding). Many of these expressions were used in the course of the hearing. Although the tendency to call for reconciliation in cases of marital dispute is a well-known feature of customary courts, and indeed has been repeatedly subject to feminist critique, in the present case of debate and mediation, we argue, reconciliation, peace, and unity take on *cosmic significance*, a matter of life and death for both individuals and the whole community.

The chief's two beings differ and have been evolving in ways that are important for potential conflict or tension between them. As is well known, the chief of the village customary court is and always has been a hereditary official, who recently succeeded by birth *and* election, as we show in the next chapter, but continues to be appointed ultimately by the government. The chief is a paid civil servant. He holds his office within a hierarchy of tribal administration and with executive responsibility for a village community and its territory, along with its court, and even its agriculture. Later, we discuss more fully in Chapters 5 and 8 the evolution of village chiefship and certain associated shifts. To put it briefly here, at least in Moremi, the office of chiefship has become more bureaucratised and the court itself is liable to be more under the thumb of the chief as presiding officer.

By contrast, no such government appointment or administrative responsibility has come in the court of divinity with being the leader, *moeteledipele* (the one who takes precedence) and *moamogedi*, the host and 'receiver of everyone who comes from elsewhere'. He has not been an executive under the state. Even the chief's trusted and loyal younger brother may act in opposition, making known the discontent of the *badimo* with the chief's practice. Even more, when he has been a senior agnate of the chief, then the *Sedimo* leader has often been an outstanding rival.

The village chief of Moremi has not himself been in charge of the *Sedimo* drums or performances, although usually in the past he has been a *Sedimo* member and, as chief, has had the right to open and close the season for *Sedimo* performances, or, in an emergency, to allow an exceptional performance out of season. The leader of the *Sedimo* has always been a man of chiefly descent, but not a chief. His leadership role, making him the first among equals in the *Sedimo*, has also made him a counterweight and even a focus of opposition, often critical of the chief and his 'frailty in authority' (Gluckman 1960). In many parts of southern Africa, perhaps most prominently in Zimbabwe, a similar counter-position has checked chiefship; a priest or medium, representing autochthonous chiefs of the past and a higher, or at least independent authority, has often been the agent for a critique of current living rulers' power in the light of ancient political tradition.

Shared authority, power-in-common

Members of *Sedimo* have had a basis for a certain equality. It is that of being fellow initiates in the cult of *Komana*, knowing its esoteric mysteries and felt to be empowered by its magic. Hence, again by contrast to the village chief's situation, among the *Sedimo* members courtly authority has been, or at least expected to be, shared and distributed more than has the tendency towards chiefly dominance and executive privilege. Power in *Sedimo* leadership has been intended, ideally, to be what Paul Ricoeur called 'power-in-common', 'the capacity of members of a historical community to exercise in an indivisible manner their desire to live together' (Ricoeur 1992:202).

However, from the time of our early fieldwork in 1971, we found the oracular consultations in *Sedimo* to be much driven by divisive, factional village politics and the disturbing expressions of public disharmony. As we document in Chapter 2 and subsequent chapters, in 1971, just before our arrival at Moremi village for the first time, the tribal administration in Serowe decided on a policy of amalgamating several small Tswapong villages, including Moremi, into that new, larger village of Matolwane, which, the District Council argued, would enjoy the advantage of size for the provision of municipal services. Under threat of force, Moremi villagers first agreed to pull up stakes and move to the new village, before a major rump of rebels and dissidents, led by Days as the acting village chief, returned back to the original village and refused to budge. They declared they were determined to protect their two permanent springs from appropriation by predatory Serowe big men.[3] Days and other villagers argued that the old chief Leso had sold the village out 'for a pot of beer'.

The *Sedimo* leader at that time was Phogole, a senior descendant of Mapulane, but one who lived permanently in the 'bush', not the village, and was thus subject to slander for being like 'a jackal' (*phokoje*). We once attended a *Komana* he convened, unusually, at the village's area of fields. By 2001, like chief Leso, Phogole had died.

Sedimo: scene of factional splits, forum for collegial consensus

Until very recently, there were oracular consultations about personal affliction, but the high point of *Sedimo* was in communal performance, addressing

3 On these events see Chapter 2 and 5, and Werbner 1977.

communal and village concerns. Moral concern was expressed about the consequences for the community of splits and quarrels between the chief and his close relatives, and there were oracular complaints by the *badimo* about abandoning the village site by the river for resettlement in Matolwane, at a site in the bush where the water was too salty, not fit for the *badimo*, to say nothing of people.

The *Sedimo* was itself both a scene of the splits and quarrels and a forum for managing them. It was a collegiate forum, in some ways checking the authority of the chief, and being in a sense a renewal, even a re-incarnation of original chiefship. Kinship with a chief was essential for membership. Members were elected in discussion by consensus, from among the close relatives of past members, such as a son, grandson or sister's son, the will of the members being ratified in oracular consultation with the *badimo*. Each member claimed to be a direct descendant of Mapulane, the original chief and eponymous founding ancestor of Tswapong. Mapulane is believed to have settled besides Moremi village's permanent spring at Mannonye, and it is in the spring's waterfalls and pools, cutting deep through a gorge in the hills, that the ancestral divinities are said to live.

During our second fieldwork in 2000, the *Sedimo* still seemed embroiled in village politics, in struggles between a new chief and a new *Sedimo* leader. The issues had changed as had the opponents and many of the *Sedimo* members. Now pitting the *Sedimo* leader against his own older brother, the chief, was a new struggle over the innermost sanctuary of the sacred centre in the hills at Moremi Gorge, hitherto kept pure for the *badimo*, in the face of a proposal from the Kalahari Conservation Society and the government for a tourist lodge and a wildlife park in the gorge, as discussed in the previous chapter.

Developments in *Sedimo*, its supplicants, and postcolonial society:

More radical change was striking in the *Sedimo* of 2000. The stream of supplicants was far more diverse than in the 1970s. Supplicants came in great numbers with a remarkable boom in all-night vigils, weekend after weekend, throughout the *Sedimo* season, with sessions sometimes held in the same night for more than one patient and their supporting circles of kin and neighbours or church congregations. The schedule was so full that the *Sedimo* leader could hardly find nights for all supplicants, and emergency sessions were sometimes called at very short notice, with the result that supporters, including the ethnographer and his assistant, had to sleep outside even in the most bitterly cold nights, while the *Sedimo* initiates huddled for warmth by the only fire allowed at the forecourt.

It is important for the argument put here to appreciate the fear and awe in which the *Sedimo* has been held. During the nights of drumming when the *badimo* are summoned, a complete curfew was in the past imposed on Moremi village. Music was banned, people were prohibited from moving around on the village paths, and driving vehicles was forbidden in the vicinity of the village. We were told of famous incidents of cars and trucks getting stuck in the sand when they dared break the taboo on movement.

The rituals of the *Komana* cult have been equally fearful, since they have all taken place deep at night, when it has been pitch-dark, with only the sound of drumming or of the oracle's disembodied voice issuing forth through the darkness. Guests would get fleeting glimpses of men's shadowy presences as they danced behind the thick stakes of the *kgotla* enclosure. On two occasions, when we spent the night in our Land Rover with one, then another research assistant from the village, both young men were petrified by the sounds of goats and sheep bleating. They were convinced they were hearing the *badimo*, although these were familiar, unmistakable, everyday pastoral sounds.

The developments we found in *Sedimo* practice during 2000 were the culmination of a gradual transformation. The most striking innovations mainly came gradually during the very late 1970s and mid-1980s. Two related changes affected town and country relations and ethnic difference (Werbner 2002b, 2002c, 2004a). Firstly, there was a shift in the late 1970s and early 1980s from transnational to national labour migration. In the case of Tswapong villagers, overwhelmingly the move was from work by men in the South African mines to work concentrated primarily in the nearby copper town, Selibi-Phikwe, or the trading town, Palapye. Eventually, Tswapong migrants found their way to the capital city, Gaborone, in a movement that included women as well, not only as workers but also as fellow city residents. At first, all were among the lowest-paid workers. Gradually, a few villagers graduated from university, and are now in better-paid jobs, mainly in the civil service.

Home, understood in its most subjectively encompassing commitment, was in the village. Throughout this period, hardly any migrants from Moremi cut themselves off permanently from their fellow villagers and their home village. Nearly all became urban villagers in the sense that they kept one foot in the city or town, and the other in the country, while balancing between them, more or less precariously, and often under pressure to put more weight on one foot than the other.

This straddling has sometimes been more complex. Villagers have taken opportunities to spread themselves by having three or more residences, in the city, a nearby town and also the village. Even more than transnational migration, the national migration of urban villagers was and is a balancing act that calls in new ways for a great deal of social skill and care (Werbner 2002a; Klaits 2010), and yet poses such dilemmas that it leaves many with a sense of unfulfilled obligation, a felt risk to their well-being.

Unfulfilled obligation is the very lifeblood of *Sedimo*. The more it is felt, the more vital *Sedimo* becomes for enabling the conversion of unfulfilled obligation into ritual debt. This is the kind of debt that passes from generation to generation. If never completely payable without a remainder, often even after death, it is reducible through sacrifice and other pious offerings which appease the dead and the living also. 'You have forgotten your forefathers; you must remember them', diviners tell supplicants, directing them to *Sedimo*.

Taken together with the shift from transnational migration, the rapid expansion of the country's first and only city, Gaborone, brought with it considerable reworking of the significance of ethnic difference. As transnational migrants, Tswapong villagers had come to terms with ethnic difference in cities where, outside their own country, they were strangers, not hosts. But once they reached a city in their own country, they met a freshly problematic ambiguity of a distinctively postcolonial kind. Who was the true host? Who really belonged to the city and its environs? Was it only the southern Tswana tribes of this part of the country, or were the immigrants from the north, among them Tswapong villagers, also to be included?

One response to this was an increase in ethnic assertiveness within an intensified process of minoritisation (see Werbner 2004a). Another response was a turn to cognate origins, in an effort to renew contact with remote ancestors, most importantly for Tswapong, the effort by culturally distinct people, such as some Kalanga, to affirm a shared identity, being in origin Pedi from the Transvaal, like Tswapong. Still another response was the attraction to acquire some of what was felt to be the occult power of strangers, especially in its original, authentic source; the more remote, secret, and mysterious that was, somewhere 'out there', the better and the more valuable.

All of this brought pressure to bear on the ethnic closure of *Sedimo* in its old, parochial form. Originally, supplicants were expected to come to *Sedimo* as descendants seeking beneficial communication with the primal Pedi as their own ultimate ancestor, who, in turn, interceded on their behalf with God. Yet, in increasing numbers, supplicants claimed to be driven by their dreams, following the direction of diviners' interpretations, to seek the benefits of *Sedimo*, even if they could trace only vague links to Pedi, or none at all.

No one among the *Sedimo* members wanted to deny the truth of the interpreted dreams by which a stream of non-Pedi supplicants were guided by their own ancestors to *Sedimo*. Acceptance of them as supplicants was at first allowed on the basis of each being a special exception. Eventually, the death of an old *Sedimo* leader allowed the members to choose a new leader, more willing to open out *Sedimo* to all supplicants. Members now talk of the change as if it were something that had to come with the change in making one nation for the whole country. They recite one of the most popular slogans of national unity: *re batho bali bangwe fela*, 'we are one people'. 'We are following the law of the country that says we are one; we are people of the same God, we can't discriminate', they told me.

Seeking to communicate with *badimo* took on a fresh, contemporary force in archaic ritual perceived to be authentic, powerful, and awesome. That communication was held so persuasively that it touched the lives of supplicants, across differences in class, community, and culture. *Sedimo* often moved them deeply. It became a force in the subjection of urban villagers to the demands of their homes in the countryside, because it compelled them to confront their strong sentiments towards highly significant others, including close kin.

There has been a significant transformation in *Sedimo* in recent times. This was not an immediate adaptation to crisis, happening within the very brief period of the AIDS pandemic or merely in response to it. Instead, cumulative innovations prior to the crisis produced a transformation which was then tested and, in the upshot, remarkably consolidated. The transformation came alongside the resettlement struggles and the radical changes in the village's locational politics of place. All of these added to the endemic internal competition for leadership within the village's chiefly lineage and, in parallel, rivalry among *Komana* initiates, who originated primarily from the same chiefly lineage.

Regulating the seasons of *Sedimo,* its location, and agriculture

The intensification in the frequency of séances created a good deal of pressure. Attempts to hold the *Sedimo* at Matolwane had, according to Days, been stopped by the Ngwato chiefs, with a court case going as far as Palapye or Serowe during our absence from the village. There was also a question of where the *letsema*, the ritual opening of the ploughing ceremony in November, should be held. In the past it had always been held at Moremi.

One of the main issues underlying the court hearing in 2001 was the seasonal and agriculturally linked 'closing' and subsequent (possible) '(re)opening' of *Sedimo* for new supplicants. Schapera speaks of three Tswana agricultural ceremonies – the *letsema* (sowing, opening of the ploughing season), *molomo* (first fruits, traditionally ceremoniously 'bitten into' by the chief) and *dikgafela* (harvest) (Schapera 1938: 70; cf. also Schapera 1971). Of these, only the *letsema,* usually taking place in early November after the first rains, seems to have survived as a performed ceremony. The *letsema* at Moremi has been held by the village chief, and it also signals the closing of the *Sedimo* and dispersal of villagers from the main village to the 'lands' for the ploughing season.

In Moremi, the *Sedimo* 'list' of supplicants has usually reopened to new supplicants in the third week of January, the time of the ripening of the first fruits, with a communal *Sedimo* ritual announced by the chief. This, it seems, did not happen in 2001, because of the lack of cooperation between members of the *Sedimo* in Moremi and Matolwane. Or perhaps it had happened. There was some ambiguity surrounding the question of whether the opening had taken place, as we shall see. In the meanwhile, patients were turning up, desperately asking to be treated by the *Sedimo*, but with the list closed, they were being turned away.

The hearing for *Sedimo* in Matolwane's customary court

In response to the presiding chief's opening call for everyone to *tlhalosa*, to make reasonably understood their complaints, the main complainant Moreetsi spoke first. He began by telling of his efforts, in vain, to get Mokhure to co-operate in *Sedimo* for the sake of afflicted supplicants, who wanted *mophaso*, the ritual appeasing the ancestral divinities. According to Moreetsi, some supplicants had come to him first. He found Mokhure absent when needed, not to be reached by letter or even by senior *Sedimo* elders sent as Moreetsi's messengers. Even worse, Mokhure was practising discrimination by serving others, and eventually becoming so recalcitrant that he wouldn't listen even to his own brother, Days, the chief, who pleaded with him to take in the opinions of other *Sedimo* elders.

MOREETSI: Yes, my master, I thank you. I came here to speak of our matter. We went to Moremi, after a person came to us from Lesenepole (the biggest of the four villages now joined together at Matolwane). He told us he was bereaved of five children, and there are three that are ill. But he explained that everywhere he had them examined (*tlhatlhobisang*, examined by divination) it was said that they should be sent to their own place (*isiwe kwa gagabo*, i.e., at the *Sedimo*). I wrote a letter, but I didn't personally deliver it. I sent it to Mokhure. Chief, since we closed the *mophaso*, (the ritual of blowing water for blessing at *Sedimo*) we wondered what should we do? Because this man (the supplicant from Lesenepole), he is losing *setshaba*, people. Our messenger went to Moremi and came back, without seeing this brother (Mokhure). I went there again by lorry to try to see to this matter, I followed this brother and never saw him. Instead, I met with the chief (Days) who told me to bring him (the Lesenepole supplicant) to the chief's place there. We did this, then I returned here (to Matolwane).

A high point in the rest of Moreetsi's troubling and shameful history of Mokhure's faults, his failures to carry out his *Sedimo* duties on behalf of everyone, concerned what Moreetsi spoke of respectfully as the *ngwao*. Literally, *ngwao* means tradition and culture. To respect the *Sedimo*'s esoteric oracular objects as a valued legacy is to speak of them as the *ngwao*. On a visit to Moremi, Moreetsi and other *Sedimo* elders from Matolwane, seeing a lamp burning in the hut for the *ngwao,* went inside, checked, and found the *ngwao* missing. The *ngwao* had secretly been hidden by Mokhure. He alone was in control. When Days pleaded with him to take care and attend to the opinion of other *Sedimo* elders, Mokhure took this pleading as if it challenged his position; he was alleged to say that no one can expel me from the *Sedimo*. But he was not respecting a *morero*, the way of consulting everyone at *Sedimo*.

We can see from this that the moot point at the heart of the matter is control over *Sedimo*. Was it to be from Matolwane by the seniors there or under Mokhure at Moremi? Besides this political issue, there was for the rivals a moral question of respect for personal dignity – each rival complained of being belittled, as if treated like a child and oppressed, not credited with the knowledge, wisdom, and authority of a senior member of *Sedimo,* who has to be consulted

Speaking with the passion of an elder moved to righteous anger, Moreetsi grieved at being belittled as if he were a child and claimed that Mokhure were unable to respect their common descent, to consult, and to seek mutual understanding.

MOREETSI: I am seen as a small child (*ngwana yo monnye*). I am never consulted (*rerisewe*) about this *Komana* (the secret performance of the *Sedimo*). According to long ago (*bogologolo*, in the old days), there was consultation, the old men consulted each other about the *Komana*. They were being men, as if they were born from one person. But with him (Mokhure), though we are born from one person, we totally don't understand one another *(ene ga ke utlawane gothelele le ene)*. I mean, my people, some other things (*dilo tse dingwe*, things that are otherwise, deviant matters) will come out when we are still in this *puo* (talk, matter). But this one will cause people to misunderstand each (*thoka kutlwisisanyo*) and this will destroy everything.

In his anger, Moreetsi overstepped civility. At first, he denied he had any quarrel with Moremi's chief, Days. Then, in a remarkable outburst, he insisted the old women accompanying Days had no place in an affair of *Sedimo*; he abused them as rubbish, and he suddenly blurted out his opinion, significantly not shared by anyone else at the hearing, that 'This is a trial (*tsheko*)'.

MOREETSI: I am saying that I do not have any contention (*kgang*) with Days, and even the other day I spoke thus. He is supposed to bring us together, but only one person refused to come together with us. Like today, I see ordinary folk (*morafe*, the tribe) here and I don't know where they come from. It isn't my custom (*mokgwa*) when I am in a case, I never go around (pointing to Days), collecting rubbish (*gobaka malele*). Here, I do not know where these people come from, and this is a trial (*tsheko*). I speak to those who you see, my father's younger brother (Mokhure).

Moreetsi's remarkable outburst struck a precarious fault line. One of the perceived dangers was a fight, in effect a turn away from peace-making with reconciliation to lawfare and a misuse of the court. Another danger was the undermining of the traditional accommodation, perceived to be sensitive and even awesome, between Moremi's two *kgotlas*, the court of divinity, *Sedimo*, and the customary court. Each danger was explicitly counteracted in turn by persons of authority: on behalf of the court by the presiding chief; on behalf of the complainant's side, by his senior relative, and by Moremi's chief, Days, on behalf of Moremi's two courts, their division of labour and their separation of powers and authority. Each person of authority expressed his moral concern for talking things over, for mutual understanding. It can be seen from this counteraction that the proceedings were highly significant for the people themselves in reaching to achieve care, upholding the common good in a virtuous public sphere.

Immediately, the presiding chief intervened to call Moreetsi back to order, to beg the pardon of the court. It was to restore the understanding that the hearing was of *kgang*, a matter of contention, but not, in Moreetsi's word, a trial (*tsheko*); it was intended for reconciliation.

CHIEF MOKGOBELELA: Let me say, before I go too far, about this matter of contention (*kgang*), let's not descend into pettiness. There are no people, regardless of where they come from, who can be called rubbish. It is a fault to say that kind of thing.

MOREETSI: Yes, on that I ask for pardon *(itshwarelo)*, Chief, I ask for pardon.

CHIEF MOKGOBELELA: When a person has a dispute with another, they can't be just the two of them only, they must be listened to by other people so that they separate them (*ba kaoganya*); to tell them, 'No, you are at fault. And you haven't done anything wrong'. No, I have listened well, my people, these are good words (Moreetsi's apology).

In turn, Moreetsi's senior relative, his father's brother Kaisara, supported the aim of hearing a complaint with reasoned peacemaking, without a fight.

KAISARA: We have no fight, we have a complaint only.

On this agreeable basis, Chief Makgobela turned to Mokhure, for his side of the *kgang*. In his defence, Mokhure not only reconstructed the events and facts, as a history from his point of view, but he also explicitly expanded his argument to a more general plane. He went on to invoke fundamental principles: the idea of law, of rule-governed procedure (*tsamaiso*), and of that highly valued idea which we have elucidated at some length in the previous chapter, namely, *tlholego,* the natural and original way of being, culture and destiny. However misrepresented, all of his conduct in and on behalf of *Sedimo* was actually, according to Mokhure, true to these fundamental principles.

CHIEF MOKGOBELELA: Yes, you can answer for yourself, Mr. Mokhure.

MOKHURE: Thank you, my master. I am ashamed, my parents, about what I hear from Mr. Gadibolae (Moreetsi), the complaint (*ngongora*) he has raised. It shows that he and I, we cannot dwell together nicely (*nnisana sentle*). I recall how he talked regarding the person about whom he said he wrote to the chief (the letter about the Lesenepole supplicant). It was when we were closed, and when we are closed, everything is known (*itsega*), how it should be done according to *tlholego,* the original way and culture. The issue is, Mr. Gadibolae is oppressing me (*gatelela*), He doesn't want me to control anything that I know, because he is the father (*ka ele rre*). The person he is talking about came to me. If he says he never saw me, it is because I stay at the place of our fields, because it is there that I find a living. If he was here (at the court), he would be able to quote me. He came holding a letter like this and he said: 'Sir, here is the letter, I've been sent by Moreetsi'. I said to him: 'My master, the *mophaso* is closed'.

Mokhure then gave in detail his explanation for a misunderstanding. Despite the closure, he had continued to hold a ritual for a man from Malaka village, because he was among those, 'according to the law', still due to be treated, having been on the *Sedimo* list before it was closed. Mokhure had explained this to the disappointed man from Leselepole.

MOKHURE: I told him that there were still those people left, and if I receive you, I will put you in the new list (*palong encha*). Because if I don't do that, I will be committing faults (*diphoso*). When I went home that day of God, I saw the people coming to call me to the chief's place. Truly, I went to the chief's place, I was asked questions and it was found that I refused this person because it was closed. I cannot put him in the list according to the law, when it is closed. I cannot. I remember when I told this, when I was called to the chief's place, I told them what I have done. But the chief went on asking us how we understood each other, until we made peace (*kagiso*), so that we should receive that person. We will make him pass (into the list). I mean, my parents, the truth about this matter is, if the rouser (*motsosa*) of these things is that person (from Lesenepole), I thought that this matter was closed.

When I look at this, my master, he (Moreetsi) just pulls me like a child, who doesn't understand anything. My master, and my parents, I think this matter ended here (when the man was accepted). I heard the summons (*pitso*) (to come to the court) yesterday, when I came from the area of our fields. I stop here, my parents.

Cross-examination followed. The presiding chief directed Mokhure to address the complaint that he was wilful, acting alone secretly with the ritual paraphernalia of *Sedimo*, when he should have been acting in consultation.

CHIEF MOKGOBELELO: But it seems you have forgotten some of the words. It is alleged that you hid (*fitlha*) the *Komana* (the drums, esoteric objects of the oracle) and you were doing this alone (*a le nosi*). You had someone that you were working for (*dirisa*) at that time, the person of Malaka village, at that time. You took it that these people will be two together (done jointly) according to what Moreetsi said now. Now you forgot to answer (this point).

MOKHURE: In other words, it means that, when I was called, I was unaware that this man had been received (for treatment); because I had not put him on the list. (Moreetsi and the elders who came and found the *ngwao* missing) they knew about the one that I treated with (the *ngwao*) because these things are kept at my place. As for those who were closed outside, I had confirmed with them that they will be passed through later on. We had agreed in the assembly (*phutego*) (i.e., before they closed the current list). This assembly knows. It is true, Chief, I speak, I answer well.

CHIEF MOKGOBELELO: Are you saying that the one who had to follow later was there?

MOKHURE: Yes, those who were closed outside, I confirmed with the authorities that when it is closed, there are (still) people on the list, those who should be passed through, and we agreed, and it was with this assembly.

MOREETSI: No, my young brother forgets, he should remind (*ikgagolosa*) himself, when I came, I didn't know that there was a Malaka person who was supposed to enter the *mophaso*.

Moreetsi continued to contest Mokhure's facts and concluded that what he was saying 'was not true'. There was another man involved and being attended for

Sedimo yet not on the list. In reply, Mokhure denied that and insisted that the man came 'because he needed me like he did before. What he was looking for was just between him and me'. In fact, he came to Mokhure in his role as a diviner and healer in his own right, An argument broke out over who had actually come and for what purpose, and in the end Moreetsi remained sceptical, saying, 'I don't know. Maybe others will know. As for me, I just want the truth. Others will know'.

At this point, Days intervened, as much in defence of the separate power and authority, competence, and responsibility of the customary court as in support of his brother, Mokhure. Days spoke to clarify ambiguity about the *Sedimo* season. The *Sedimo* season had indeed been closed, following his holding the *letsema*, the agricultural ceremony marking the opening of the sowing season. But despite having a letter from Moreetsi, he was puzzled about what was wanted from him. Cautious, he felt that as merely the village chief, he should not enter into the awesome matters (*masisi*) of *Sedimo*. Beyond his responsibility and competence, these were about the secret tradition and culture (*ngwao tsa sephiri*), and not something public (*mophatlhalatsa*). Hence, he thought that 'this does not concern me'. He avoided answering Moreetsi's letter. Now he looked forward to the prospect that the words between Moreetsi and Mokhure would be purified. But as a matter of *Sedimo,* it was not a matter for a trial. What had to be understood was how the contention arose. Hence, Days then turned to his brother Mokhure to account for the lack of *kutlwano* between Mokhure and Moreetsi. The two brothers, chief and *Sedimo* leader, then asserted that Mokhure's leadership and appointment was according to rightful procedure (*tsamaiso*). This the chief got Moreetsi, in turn under cross-examination, to confirm.

DAYS: Yes, let me enter between you, my masters, because I hear that you came to me with this letter, the one that Moreetsi talked about of the man from Lesenepole who dwells at Mogapi, as it is alleged (*kaya*). But the Chief and the people here, the *letsema* (and the end of *Sedimo*) was closed, according to law, because it was closed by the chief according to custom. Because I saw that since they all know that the *letsema* is closed, (I wondered) what do they want from me? So, I kept the letter (of Moreetsi on *Sedimo* matters). I didn't answer it, I kept the letter. I don't enter this awesome (*masisi*) work. I am the tree stump of these children as appointed. These words between these men will be cleansed (*tlhapile*).

For the sake of cleansing the words from mean speech, Days appealed for mutual humility (*ikobelana*). The need, he reminded the court, was for answering the question of how and from where came troubles of a kind never ever brought to trial. Days' answer foregrounded the fearful predicament endured by Mokhure, because Matolwane members of *Sedimo* withdrew from consultation, took matters in their own hands without regard for the rightful leadership of *Sedimo*, and readied for ritual by themselves in Matolwane. Days defended his own role, his effort to calm a storm while at the same time trying to avoid meddling in things not his concern. He favoured proof of public unity

– the performance of the ritual for mutual amity and blessing from the *badimo* – but it had to be done by the *Sedimo* seniors, currently at odds with each other, getting together. When they went ahead, without getting together, he warned of the storm, the wind coming as they disgraced themselves

DAYS: Let us not allege that someone has spoken words without regard for how mean (*masesane*, thin) they might be. Let us have humility towards each other (*ikobamelana*) (repeats). Since I was born, I have never heard that this (an affair of *Sedimo*) is brought to trial (*sekwa*). Now what is the trouble? Where did it come from? I know that when *Sedimo* is closed, Mokhure does not have the power (*thata*). No-one has the power. The one who gives himself power, I will be with him (*ke na nae* – in order to punish him), if he doesn't walk in the path (follow the right way of *Sedimo*). I found that there was no consultation (*morero*). Patients are just sent to him (Mokhure) and he keeps on being fearful, because there are no people he can consult with about the secret culture (*ngwao tsa sephiri*). It is not something public (*mophatlhalatsa*).

As I was seated and I thought this does not concern me, those from here (Matolwane) came to us. They found they had already strained (*tlhotlhilwe*) the beer, of the people of Malaka, and the other one was also strained (i.e., of Lesenepole). I was not going to turn them back and say, go and do it at Makwesa's place (in Moremi). I didn't know who took out (*ntshitswe*) these things (the *ngwao*, including the secret drums) from there. I am not the mischief maker (*molothanyi* – stirrer up of strife). To enter into these words, even if they don't concern me (*di sa nkame*). And then, when they came here, I said they should meet (*kopana*), come together, those of here (i.e., Matolwane) and the man, before he came, I found that Mokhure was at odds (*o sele*), and those from here (Matolwane people originally from Moremi) were also at odds. There was no consultation.

At that time, Makwesa (youngest son of the old chief, Leso, and a member of *Sedimo*) was there, coming from Mogapi with the patient. It was in the evening, I told them that, do not create a storm (*go fokwa ke phefo*). When you found this *mophaso* needing to be done, an ox slaughtered, or perhaps a goat, go and take those beers, I said that – and a person's words should be quoted (*etswa*) – gather together (*kopanya*), and put the sticks to sleep (*robaletse dithokwa*, i.e., stay in peace), and bless (*phase*) the people. They were not done (treated?) as you think. They went together, the two women, they followed each other (one from Malaka, one from Lesenepole), they followed each other, and they called them to go and take *majalwa* (beer), and were done at the place where they were supposed to be done (*madirela a one*). That man that came with the ox that he dreamt (*lorisitswe*) of, and he was divined for *(laolwa)*, it was slaughtered.

I said, 'the wind will enter you' (*ka re, le tla itsenya phefo*) (it will bring misunderstanding between you, i.e., members of the *Komana*), you disgrace yourselves (*ikopela*, from 'sing'). I found that if they can do that – if there can be any other reason, I'm not aware of that, and they returned. I heard the voice of Mokhure that his brother's son (Moreetsi) has no *kutlwano*, mutual understanding, with him. Do I hear you well, Mokhure, that you don't have *kutlwano* with him? And why?

MOKHURE: Whatever he does is against procedure (*tsamaiso*), and you'll find that he oppresses me (*oa nkgatelela*).

DAYS: When they say you are the senior (*motona*), where was he when you were appointed *(beilwe)*. Does he know that you are the senior in the *Sedimo*, in the initiation (*bogwera*), does he know?

MOKHURE: I see him as …

DAYS: I'm saying, does he know that you are senior?

MOKHURE: I have no knowledge, my master.

DAYS: I am saying, do you know who is senior in this work, the one who is the leader (*moeteledipele*)?

MOREETSI: It is Mokhure, he was appointed by me.

DAYS: If you appointed him …

CHIEF MOKGOBELELO: I was saying this, chief (Days).

DAYS: No, I stop there, my master.

This left the presiding chief puzzled and having to cross-examine further. He rehearsed Day's account at some length and came to the question of an apparent contradiction. He took Day's story to mean he had resolved the issues in dispute. But if they were resolved, from where came the troubles?

CHIEF MOKGOBELELO: There are some words which have been said to have caused this dispute, regarding this person from Lesenepole, who asked for a *mophaso* because his children were finished (dying), so that he can ask to be blessed (*phaswa*), but it (the list) was closed. When closed, there were other people on the waiting list who wanted to have the blessing performed. Now, he (Moreetsi) was looking at whether someone can be squeezed in (*sukunyediwa*) with those people. Now, he seemed to be baffled (*gakega*), although he had said to close it down, (ordered) by the chief, and that there is no-one who can open beside you (i.e., Days). When he (Moreetsi) wrote the letter, writing it to you, Chief, because he knew that you are the one who has the power to say no or yes, you can enter. He says that when he came to you, you agreed that he can be squeezed in with those of the first (list) because of the problem he has, of his finishing (dying) children. Every year, he buries.

Now, I want to know where it was subverted (*ganefa*), because it came in front of you and you reprimanded (*kgalemela*) for mutual understanding and agreed that they should be treated, mixed together with those (others of Malaka). Now, where does the dispute arise, because this seems to have been reprimanded (and thus resolved).

DAYS: Pardon me, I nearly went astray (*ke ya go sele*). It was not rejected. It was where I met for the first words with the elders (of *Sedimo*) and they met because there was a need for consultation. They could have come to me. I do not have the power to govern (*laolela*) them, unless they ask, with a moot (*morero*). When they met in front of me, I said, 'Go and take that beer and the sacrifice that they brought (from Lesenepole) and put it together with that of the people from Malaka and cease to raise the storm.' I said these words, saying it to Makwesa, who came with this boy from Mogapi where he (Makwesa) stays, where they met. He (the boy) stays (most of the time) at Sefope. This happened, and there were no words (no more quarrelling). If there were any words after the *mophaso*, then I was not there.

MAKWESA: I was supposed to answer because, chief, you have opened a way, and here it is, it is a straight one.

CHIEF: What I need is, what I want to know is, because this man has written a letter and sent it to the chief, and even if it was closed, it was agreed that he be entered with those who were there, when it was closed. There were those who were to be passed through, and he was entered with them, and continued with their work, together. Now, after that, what change (*phetogo*) came and overturned them?

In response, Moreetsi again went over the events, saying that when he got to Moremi, Mokhure was not there. But after hearing all the terrible suffering of the supplicant from Lesenepola, Days had said: 'My brother's child (son), it will be a fault, if we were to refuse these people as they are. It will be a fault even in heaven (*legodimo*). If they die, their blood will be asked from us'. Moreetsi went on to say that 'the beers were different (they were going to be ready on different days for the two patients). When we went there (to Moremi) our beer was supposed to enter its work. We found that Mokhure had hidden the drums. The hiding is not for the first time'. Moreetsi reflected on the old days before Mokhure joined, and the demand Moreetsi had made at an assembly to *restore Sedimo* to leadership by a more senior member of the Lengonapelo line than Mokhure.

MOREETSI: When we left here (Matolwane) with the drums that we kept, going there (to Moremi), the *Komana* was at the chief's place (the old place of Leso, at Moremi). Beating them (the drums, took place) in front of Leso's. This Mokhure, he was not in the *Komana*. Now, one day, he came, I don't know whose ox was slaughtered (to initiate him), but I do know what he did. And he came. And I said, 'My people', talking to this assembly of mine, to our assembly, this *Komana*, we wanted it to be as in the old days (*segologolo*). This *Komana* should go back to the Lengonapelos and go out of here. This man (Mokhure) was to receive the people, it was I who spoke. And this Makwesa (son of the deceased chief, Leso) was there. I said: 'Let it go back to the Lengonapelos'. When I grew up quarrelling, I found that Lengonapelo (Mokhure's father and Moreetsi's father's father) was the receiver (*moamogedi*) of everyone who came from elsewhere (*yo o tswang koo*). It came back. I am the one who brought it back. I said it should come back to my uncle (*Rangwane*, that is, to Mokhure). I found him being an ordinary person (*ele motho fela*). He was an ordinary member of the *Komana* like anyone. I mean, when we talk straight, I don't want to disgrace the child of my father, of my mother, and I don't want anyone to stand for another. We should talk the truth only.

Moreetsi concluded, having piled up further confusing detail, saying that 'I want us to be reconciled (*kopanngwe*) with this person (Mokhure), so that we can be one thing (united, one body) as we were born of one person, Lengonapelo, together'.

As the case continued, the claim was made that the drums were hidden twice, though Days denies remembering they were hidden on the occasion of the patients from Malaka and Lesenepola being treated. To this, one *Sedimo* member from Matolwane, Baruti, intervened to say, 'I don't want to talk of old things'. Then he claimed, confusingly, that the patient had not been treated, the ox was still in the kraal. Baruti could not answer the simple question of how the drums were found:

RAMAGANYA (an outsider): Which way did you find them?
BARUTI: They were found because of the words.
RAMAGANYA: Which say what?
BARUTI: Words which say 'Go and do' (the *mophaso*).

The ensuing cross-examination, led by this outsider, put all the blame on Mokhure who is said to have been admonished publicly by Days. Moreetsi even claimed that Days told Mokhure to 'get out of the *Komana* and let your elder brother (Moreetsi) enter', It was an evidently dubious contention. But Moreetsi insisted also, 'I don't want this person to get out of the *Komana*'. Nevertheless, he suggested Mokhure was at fault and things were being done at Moremi, without members' knowledge and agreement: whereas they at Matolwane know the *Komana* is closed, at Moremi it is open – there is no consultation. 'I don't know anything as a member, not even the other members (know) of the *Komana* (being open)'.

After some more rambling discussion, the chief intervened, still trying to clarify the situation, with answers from Mokhure:

CHIEF MOKGOBELELO: I hear that the *Komana* is closed. Now I hear that it is open, without others knowing.
MOKHURE: That is new to my ears.
CHIEF MOKGOBELELO: It is not open?
MOKHURE: It is not opened. The chief would be in a position to know because he is the one who closed it (Days announced it was closed at the *letsema*, the ceremony starting the sowing season). When the time comes, your honour, I go to him (Days) and say: 'People are troubling me', and it is he (Days) who allows it (to be opened).
CHIEF MOKGOBELELO: Is it true, chief, that it is not opened?
DAYS: It is not opened. It is they who should come to me and say that the time is gone. If they don't come to me, we will enter December (the following

year) without opening it because I don't know how it is done (*ga ke itse jaaka go dirwa*).

MOREETSI: Chief, I don't have a secret. Let it be answered by this man here. I don't talk.

The impasse was obvious. And here another element was introduced, expanding the meaning of 'open' and pinpointing a hidden grievance of Moreetsi and his supporters. They resented a change by Mokhure: the initiation of new members into the *Sedimo*, who were not agnatic relatives. Indeed, it was claimed that the introduction of new members was repeatedly blocked. And then there was the hiding of the drums, allegedly twice. The chief intervened, still worrying about the issue of proper leadership and the hiding of the drums.

CHIEF MOKGOBELELO: About the hiding of the drums. It is the second time that these words are heard as they are, and we don't know what the problem is. Because he (Mokhure) is the leader of the assembly. Now, as he is the one who is doing these things, how does he see things, as he is the one who is supposed to be directing these people? If his colleagues do something wrong, what is he going to tell them? That is the problem he is supposed to think about. You are supposed to think that if a person is the leader of a group, he is not the one who should do wrong things. He is there to direct others when they go wrong in their work. Yes, sir, you wanted to speak?

The chief recognised Morebodi, a *Sedimo* member from Moremi and a new member of the Assembly, who wanted to speak, following the several speakers from Matolwane. Morebodi defended Mokhure who is fearful, even a coward because he bears a heavy responsibility towards the ancestral divinities. Morebodi's point was that to 'fear' is to revere (*sesimoga*). His argument was also that keeping members together under mutual control is hard, and worse still is to breach the secrecy and confidentiality of *Sedimo*. Implied by this is a rebuke of Moreetsi for taking contentious *Sedimo* matters out of its private hut into the public hearing of the customary court. The fault brings in the ignorant to consider what they know nothing about – an obvious, though unnamed, example being the presiding chief himself.

MOREBODI: This man, when we talk things in private, he fears (*o boi*). He is a coward. He fears, this child (Mokhure) has got problems, he is afraid of (*sisimoga*, reveres) the *badimo* because it is difficult to do as you wish without following the laws of *Sedimo*. Now things are happening in the *Sedimo*, I ask the chief of Moremi because this matter is in front of him to work hard to help our leader. It is difficult to take action against others, according to the laws of culture (*tlholego*). They are unable to control each other when they talk, children of the same belly (here referring to Mokhure and Moreetsi).

Mokhure, Morebodi pointed out, is the leader appointed by the *badimo*. When a member of the *Sedimo* makes a mistake, 'We have a house (*ntu*) where we talk *Sedimo* and private matters, not to talk *Sedimo* outside and (allow) entry to people who do not know anything about the *Sedimo* and what is being done'. Nevertheless, given the fact of being on the defence in the midst of this all-too-public hearing, Morebodi was caught in a predicament: to expose and win, or keep secrets secret and lose. He found, despite his insistence on respect for privacy that he had to publicise the matters of private contention.

Over the secretive way of the court of divinity prevailed the public way of the customary court at its own venue. Reasonable as this was in the one court, in the other it was a misuse of court proceedings, otherwise left to consultation with the dead and divinity, rather than the living and cross-examination. A scandal was emerging, about control of the court of divinity. It was different seen from one side or the other. From Moreetsi's perspective, it was a drive to pack the assembly and *Sedimo* as a whole with Mokhure's men. From Mokhure's, it was the demand of *badimo*, as he heard their word, to meet a shortage of *Komana* members at Moremi by opening membership beyond the old limits, and thus fulfil the *tlholego* of *Sedimo*. The immediate outcome was, in effect, a boycott of *Sedimo* by Moreetsi's faction.

The presiding chief pursued more cross-examination, He tried to tease out or make sense of the procedure for initiating new members. After Mokhure responded, saying 'A person is not wanted by Mokhure or Kaisara. He is wanted by the *badimo*', the chief probed him to be more specific about an actual recruit and the selection procedure for his recruitment.

CHIEF MOKGOBELELO: Listen first. You are going too far. The question is the name that just came out now, after he was wanted by the *badimo*, did you call all your *komiti* (in English, for committee, *phutego,* the assembly) members to tell them?

MOKHURE: My master.

CHIEF MOKGOBELELO: Do they know?

MOKHURE: They know well. They refuse, but it is this one who refuses (Moreetsi).

CHIEF MOKGOBELELO: Moreetsi, was he there?

MOKHURE: They are many here who were wanted (by the *badimo*) and he knew. He refused and said, I don't need these people. The question is, when the *badimo* want, as it is in need (*tlhokafaleng*, scarce*),* does he have the power (to block them)? And he will say, I would rather leave and go to my wife's church'. He knows.

Morebodi named two men who were not 'entered' because of Moreetsi and remarked that 'there was a lot of misunderstanding and disagreements with the *badimo* who wanted this child of the people'. One person was entered, during the *letsema*, but the members from Matolwane did not turn up.

MOREBODI, speaking about himself: Like me, I was called hard (*thata*) by the *badimo*, but there was a lot of thorny contention. Here is another one, he is the son of Leso, our elder, brother. This man (Moreetsi) took off his jacket and said, 'If he is entered, I am leaving'.

He continued and addressing Moreetsi directly:

> Son of Gadibolae (Moreetsi), my question was, sir, because these people are wanted by the *badimo* – are you one of the *badimo*? Are you the one who refuses people entry who are wanted by the *badimo*? He said: 'There is no consultation'. I said: 'Who do you consult with? For this person, a consultation was made, and he is wanted by the *badimo*. They are the ones who want him. We, we listen only'. … Now, if you refuse, who are you to refuse the people? Don't you see that you are killing the people (*o bolaa sechaba*) who are wanted by the *badimo*. I mean that this child was entered for this reason. During the *letsema*, before it was closed, they did not come. This '*komiti*' of here, Matolwane, they did not go to Moremi. This child had been called, they know he had been entered. They know well that he is wanted by the *badimo*.

Moreetsi defended himself, saying that 'The *Komana* is entered in order, according to your relatives who once entered. … To initiate (*rupa*), you have to be entered by your fathers'. Of Morebodi, he said he refused him because he was going to stir up fire (*kgotlelela*, defile) the work of *Komana*. He was the one who caused divisions, Moreetsi claimed, counter to the accusation against himself.

It is an irony worth mentioning, although it is somewhat of an aside, that the future contention was so predictable from the past. As Moreetsi predicted, so did Morebodi behave. Morebodi became the maverick mixer of divining and oracular traditions and something of a lone wolf, who broke rules, as a charismatic, to suit his sense of his own spiritual inspiration by the *badimo*. It was much to Mokhure's grief and inability to control.[4] In good measure, what Mokhure himself responded to creatively, on behalf of *Sedimo* as a whole – the pressure for regional expansion and more open inclusion – moved Morebodi, in his self-interest, to meet the boom in his private clients. He found them specially attracted by his practice of bringing together the famously secretive in oracular consultation and the familiar in ways of divining from distant peoples.

To return to the hearing: it was easy for the Matolwane members to deny knowledge of initiates introduced in their absence even though, as Mokhure pointed out, the most recent new member was initiated on the day of the *letsema*, and Moreetsi had been informed of that date and was supposed to attend with the members from Matolwane.

MOKHURE: Even if they say they don't know, I say they (did) know. We look as if we are telling lies when we, we are the place where these things are done.

Finally, Days raised the question whether this issue of initiation was part of the matter raised in the court or had somehow been slipped in midway.

4 For a full account of Morebodi's creative and charismatic innovation, even in *Sedimo* hymns see Werbner 2015.

The chief's summing up: the cosmic imperative of reconciliation

A central value of many legal judgements in the customary court is to achieve reconciliation. As we shall see, this is true in marriage disputes in particular, but also in a range of other interpersonal conflicts. Reconciliation in all these seems to be a pragmatic, secular value, although notions like *kagiso*, peace, may have religious connotations. In the present hearing, however, reconciliation took on cosmic significance, a matter of life and death. This was evident in the presiding chief's final address. It was at once on familiar ground – the due reprimand by authority in resolution of a dispute and the moral sermon common in judgement under parental law – but it was also a conscious entry into *terra incognita,* the wrestling with the non-justiciable in the precarious customary court hearing and the fearful appreciation that chiefly strife and moral disorder entail a spiritual danger – the very livelihood of everyone depended on rain, which the *badimo* withhold in the face of subversive disunity.

The presiding chief began with the courtly expression of humility (*ikoba*). He admitted his and his own court's shortcoming and incapacity. They confronted the work of the *badimo*, which was well beyond their power and authority. Even further, he wanted it to be clearly understood that the proceedings had to be unlike those in an ordinary customary court hearing. This one, engaged with the affairs of *badimo*, was fit for consultation only with the owners of the affairs. It was not to be talked over by the general public, as usual in the open way of the customary court.

Nevertheless, from the opposition and contentious back and forth in the hearing, the chief sought to draw a judicious lesson. He reminded everyone of the good in argument. It was not as if taking sides in debate was, in itself, wrong. In and from the proceedings, there was a lesson on good governance to be taught and learned, the presiding chief conveyed, with good reason. Open disagreement is right. From argument comes truth. 'When people disagree and advise each other to correct their faults, that is where there is good governance'. That said, and momentarily past humility about tradition and the *terra incognita* under the *badimo*, the chief slipped into current common-sense but an untraditional way to settle disagreement: voting and rule by majority. But finally, he came back to the idea of the kind of consultation that is beyond his knowledge and is the responsibility of the *Sedimo* members themselves. 'Start doing well and consulting each other', he admonished in his conclusion.

CHIEF MOKGOBELELO: People of my people, this work of yours, I don't know it. We are about it only, we were afraid of it, we feared it. I once stayed at Moremi, at Sepako's place, I had asked for his old place which had houses. Sepako told me that here in our place if you go during the night, you don't whistle. I stayed with fear only, at that time. Because this work is the work of the *badimo*, the one you come with from long ago with your lives. There are people who talk to them (the *badimo*), not everybody. Me, I take it to be a very sensitive work. It is the one that you are not supposed to do bad things with. Some do as they please, and some do that. This is supposed to be work [in which] you are consulting each other and agreeing well.

I do not know whether these *badimo* of yours never lose their temper, so that they can thrash you and hit you. If I was able to talk to them, I would tell them that they raise a stick so that we would see where you would end. Now, my people, it pains. I do not want to hold this case like other cases, where people come to listen and we say, here is the case. This one, I fear I don't want it to be talked over like this. I want it to be talked by its owners and finish it like that. It makes me fear, to the extent that I think these misunderstandings of yours are the ones that make the sun kill us (*di re bolaisang letsatsi*). This sun will finish the people and everything, but the fault is yours. *Our blood will be asked from you.* You take this work as if it is the work of your homes. You don't take it as the work of the *badimo*, the work of the tribe; the one that we ask every life from, as we know. From them, they tell you as it is that now it will be like this and like this.

When I was a small boy at our place, the other side of the railway (near Serowe), when it was the sun (drought), we knew that Tswapong is where we can flee to. When we did not have ploughing at our place, we knew that at Tswapong we will see something – because they never fail to get something (i.e., rain). Now, if you are doing this, you want us to be the same, and we die all of us. When it is hard, a person runs to his mother and finds life there.

You have your way of praying like that in the Kalanga area.[5] They (Kalanga) have a work like this one. They never come out with nothing in their life (they always reap something). Now you are bringing confusion (*thakathakanyo*), you do as you like. If you were not killing the tribe and you were only killing yourselves, we were going to say, 'The suicide is not wailed for (*moipolai ga a lelelwe*)'. Now you are only proud of answering (arguing in court), you cannot make the rain fall. Do you see what you are doing? *We are dying because of your names.* I don't know whether you see this right. Now we would say, go and sit down, meet and talk, but you refuse. A person will say, I once went to my people, called them, and said: let us sit and talk and they refused me. None of you is saying that. I don't know if all of you are alike (behave in the same way) as Pudulogo (one of the speakers at the hearing) had talked and said that he is also afraid although he is a member of your meeting.

People of my people, *you are doing a painful work, you are killing the land.* If you read the Bible, Ezekiel 3, Ezekiel was a messenger to warn the nation, (counselled) that if he did not warn the nation … when the sword comes to chop and kill them, the blood of these people will be asked from his head.

5 On the regional cult of the High God, Mwali, see Werbner 1989.

> But if he warned them and they became deaf-eared, their blood will be asked from their heads.

So far, it was undoubtedly suited to the hearing's accepted aim that the presiding chief devoted so much of his conclusion to high-minded rhetoric. If some of it was about the unprecedented and the non-justiciable, it all added up to an unsurprising contribution to peace-making through consensus. Yet two sides had come to the hearing at loggerheads. Who was in the right? Was the chief begging this point of contention? Moralising, parental pronouncement, instruction in good governance, all that was proper. Indeed, it was as customary and often as necessary in a trial as in mediation of the kind in progress at the hearing. Necessary but never sufficient in a trial as a *tsheko*: the presiding chief would have to be more decisive to be just and fair. Contrary to that in mediation, there was a better, more suitable alternative – not to say who was in the right, but to be judicious in making the balance between the two sides. Both were in the wrong, both had to change to be in the right, the presiding chief established.

The reprimand for Mokhure was straightforward only on the face of it. Mokhure had to cease being a weak leader, he had 'to stand up', exercise due care, and when need be, turn to the chief to get mutual understanding. However, it could be argued, we suggest, that the strong leadership called for was more the ideal proper for a chief, especially an Ngwato chief, than for a Tswapong first among equals – *moeteledipele* (the one who takes precedence) – as in *Sedimo*. Admittedly, Phogole, an earlier *Sedimo* leader, had a reputation for being far from egalitarian. But this was not exemplary. Hence, though unchallenged, the part of the presiding chief's reprimand directed at Mokhure was somewhat dubious, or at least culturally uninformed. Implicit was a clash between disparate ideals and even premises for two unlike *kgotla*, the court of divinity and the customary court.

For Moreetsi and his faction, the presiding chief's reprimand was simpler, if perhaps again grounded for a Ngwato, in his own common-sense, here of factionalism among chiefly seniors. They had to stop too much seniority in their affairs. As for Mokhure, so too for Moreetsi: the reprimand, if authoritative and suitable in the customary court, was questionable, arguably unsound for *Sedimo*. *Sedimo* concerned the ancestors, immediately the appeal through Lengonapelo, the common ancestor of Mokhure and Moreetsi, who was a past leader of *Sedimo*. To insist on making little of seniority was to go against a fundamental principle. The weight of seniority was all the more grave in Moreetsi's claim, since he spoke with the overwhelming support of most *Sedimo* seniors, and even the presiding chief himself recommended majority rule, here 11 members backing Moreetsi, and merely six for Mokhure. In other words, again we can see a clash of ideals and premises between the two *kgotla*.

As for Days, he too was reprimanded according to customary court ideals, but not in any *kgotla* clash. As a chief, he had to be reminded of his duty to get the truth out of people by talking things through – he had to care and guard (*tlhokomela*) and to protect (*pabalelo*), lest matters get painfully, even disastrously entangled.

CHIEF MOKGOBELELO: Mokhure, you were appointed the leader. If you are the leader, if you are appointed by the *badimo* or by these people (of the *Sedimo*), you are supposed to stand up (show authority). This misunderstanding of these people you should solve. If they don't understand, go to the chief (and tell him): 'When I say let's do like this, they refuse'. The chief will call them, ask for the truth from them. You would have washed your hands (*thapile diata*). Even if they see you are pulling aside, they have the right to call you and advise you. Good government (*puso*) is done that way. You should handle this work with due care (*pabalelo,* protection), knowing that if you make a mistake the people will not be happy.

These birds that you hear crying, they do not talk but they comprehend (*tlhaloganyo*, have understanding). Their life is in rain. *Now when you confuse everything, the badimo will be angry and you will have killed everything.* Forget about saying I am the son of so-and-so, son of so-and-so, in the things of people. Go in the way of your fathers which they left you in. Days, take these people and take care of them (*thokomele*) when you are with them. The chief does not entangle (*tlhakatlhakane*) with people when they tell stories (*polelo*), when they talk their talks, you get out of them and listen to them. So that they will not say that you know that so-and-so talked this or that.

When I go around the village, people are complaining about the sun; they say it is because of this misunderstanding of yours. Go, sit down and consult each other. Even in other meetings, like the VDC (Village Development Committee), or even in the church, when they have visitors they talk. In the church, they talk that we have visitors who are supposed to be received or baptised, so that on the said day anyone who will not afford to come will leave a message.

You should know that when you make mistakes like this, you are making them for the people. You do a thing, call each other, sit and talk. If you don't agree, oppose each other. Normally, a group of people will oppose each other on a matter raised between themselves, until such a time that they agree on something. If you see people in a meeting and they don't disagree, they will end up having no truth. When you disagree, you mean to correct, make the corrections, and do the work. When people disagree and advise each other to correct their faults that is where there is good governance. If you have a disagreement of ideas, you should vote to know the number of the people who agree with the idea and those who disagree with it. Those who are many, you take their idea and use it and work with understanding. That is the way meetings are run. When you disagree and argue, you will see your work going well.

Now, my people, you will cause us pain as you hear some parents saying, it is the first time, they have never seen anything like this, the *Komana* being tried. If that is the case, the *badimo* will never be happy the way you

> do things. Maybe you don't tell us. One of you should tell us that they (the *badimo*) had already told you that, sit and see for yourselves. Anyway, we don't want you to tell us such words. Let them sit in your hearts. Start doing well and consulting each other.
>
> I stop there.

The final comment from many of the people gathered was: 'Thank you, chief. It will rain. It is not going to take more than four days without raining'. As it happened, much to everyone's great and joyful relief, it rained that day, later in the evening.

In February, several weeks after the January hearing, a *Sedimo* elder, John Sebele explained to us why he had avoided the hearing:

> When the case was heard at Matolwane, I didn't go because the *Sedimo* is not prosecuted (tried, *sekwa*). It is only *gakololwa* (a complex term, meaning reminding and recollection). When there is all this mix-up, I am fearfull and I am extra cautious not to get involved. You can't hold a trial over these things of the *Komana*, it carries an affliction (*phepha*, weak with illness, feebleness)'.

For John, the hearing was not at all a good resolution to be favoured or blessed by the *Sedimo*. It was a fearful transgression against *Sedimo*. Wrong and unacceptable in its very procedure, in its mode of understanding, in its intervention into matters only for secret consideration at the court of divinity, the customary court hearing was particularly fearful in provoking retribution beyond the control of the living. John feared still to come from *Sedimo* there would be, for the transgressor and any accomplice, personal affliction, sickness, and suffering.

In accord with that, John explained further, the court of divinity had what should have been followed, rather than the hearing: its own proper procedure for dealing with a member in the wrong. 'If a member does something wrong, the matter is heard among the members themselves, who can fine him a goat and demand a *mophaso*, (the ritual for blowing away and appeasing ancestral wrath). We follow on this path'.

For John, also, the proper mode of understanding in the court of divinity did not entail prosecution or forensic reason as in the customary court, but *gakololwa*, reflection and being reminded, being advised, and counselled so that understanding comes to mind. This properly memorable mode of understanding, as the *Sedimo* leader would warn supplicants, was not comprehension, *italoganya*, making sense by oneself of one's situation. Instead, it was in respectful submission to *Sedimo*, to divinity, and with dependence on authoritative communication with the ancestors, of course, not merely with the living as in the customary court. Coming from an elder living in Matolwane but still in performance at Moremi one of *Sedimo*'s outstanding drummers, John's remarks highlighted the dismay and distress the hearing provoked, and some opposition to it even among Matolwane villagers.

There is an obvious question: how effective was the hearing as an occasion for reconciliation and peace-making? Part of this can be answered briefly here with regard to some accommodation in *Sedimo*. In later chapters, we document and analyse more of the underlying conflict, festering grievances, and factional disputes over the long term. By the time it came for a new season of *Sedimo*, Mokhure told us that he was grieving. People were coming, he said, from all over seeking help, but they were finding that the *Sedimo* had not yet been opened and that he could not help them. First, there had to be unity (*kopano*, an agreeing). He had gone to Days to tell him that nothing had been done about the holding of *mophaso*, and to ask him what he should do about it. For the feast of unity, Mokhure was able to get substantial contributions, from Days, from at least one senior Moremi member of *Sedimo*, and even from Moreetsi. Nevertheless, Days advised Mokhure to wait. He should not just open the *Sedimo* again. He advised him to send a letter. He should only hold the feast when everything was truly ready, after agreement and consultation. Otherwise, he would be blamed. In the upshot, the *Sedimo* was held and included some members from Matolwane. But things did not quite return to evident unity, for some Matolwane members would hold their own vigils in Matolwane, especially during funerals, when the high-pitched sounds of ancestral speech would be interpreted to reveal the cause of death, such as by sorcery.

It can be seen from much of the account in this chapter that, as a *kgotla*, the court of the divinities is a remarkably special forum by contrast with the customary court. Both call for consultation (*rerisana*), foster reflections on good conduct, and bring moral pressure to bear. But whereas secrecy, informing confidences, gossip, and sometimes scandal, is the prized truth of *Sedimo*, it is publicity, open to argument and reasoning with testimony by all, which is the proclaimed virtue of the customary court, and which is also the taken-for-granted basis for its hearing. This difference, as we showed in this chapter, made the use of the customary court for a hearing about *Sedimo* problematic and precarious, and in some respects, unfit for purpose and unsafe.

5 An unburied past

Chiefly succession and the politics of memory

Introduction

Hereditary chiefship in Botswana draws its legitimacy and authority from a perceived genealogical connection to a founding ancestor (see Schapera 1938, Chapter III). The authenticity of chiefship is constituted by 'nature' as 'destiny'. This is captured among Tswapong, as earlier chapters showed, by the notion of *tlholego,* the polysemic term referring at its simplest to the non-human environment, and, more profoundly, denoting a subject's essential nature and hence history, destiny, and culture. In reality, chiefly office is often contested, the centre of passionate factional politics and disputed descent. Legitimacy is never absolute but is always conditional on a past recalled as a swirling series of political manoeuvres, suspicions, jealousies, actions, and counter-actions. This is so even at village level, the topic of the present chapter, and here too chiefship bears the special aura and symbolic power of office, replicated at higher levels of chiefdom.

Botswana has not undergone a process of 'retraditionalisation' evident elsewhere in post-independence Sub-Saharan Africa. In many African countries, chiefship was at first denied and even abolished before rising once again like a phoenix to play a part in contemporary local politics, with chiefs in some countries given greatly enhanced economic or local political powers (see contributions to Comaroff and Comaroff 2018). In Botswana, by contrast, after independence, the state radically curtailed the powers of chiefs and headmen. At the same time, it sustained the symbolic aura and status of hereditary chiefs and headmen, enhancing it with extravagant public shows of respect and honour on ceremonial occasions. Chiefs and headmen were incorporated into the structure of government administration and received an income as low-level civil servants. Chiefship is thus something of a prize in small villages in Botswana.

The present chapter analyses the selection and installation of a new chief in Moremi village following the death of the previous incumbent. Although small, Moremi is the senior village among Tswapong with claims to longevity, centrality, and absolute authenticity; hence the office of chief is a symbolically elevated one, as we have already seen. This chapter highlights the vividness of memories of long-past political struggles with the state and local state outlined in Chapter 2. Although villagers engage in the factional politics associated with such encounters, they recently debated in the *kgotla* yet again the old ones, as though the past had all happened

DOI: 10.4324/9781003241881-5

just yesterday, instead of 40 years previously. In our account, we examine the pragmatics of appointment to office, and show the importance of claims to authenticity and legitimacy in the contest between protagonists for the vacated office. We extend a comparative analysis by reconsidering recent discussions of chiefship in Africa.

In anthropological debates up to the 1980s about chiefly succession, one strand stressed the rules of succession and, in particular, the extent to which a conflict in the rules, and their ambiguity, created the possibility of a 'cycle of rebellions'. This was the key theoretical point made by Max Gluckman in his reanalysis of Bemba succession to the *citimukulu*, the kingship (Gluckman 1963), although he admitted that the establishment of a British colonial order in Northern Rhodesia, with its preference for orderly promotion through chiefly posts, may have subverted this pattern by the mid-1940s. John Comaroff's analysis of Tswana chiefly succession among the Tshidi Barolong (Comaroff 1978) also stressed rule conflict. Although the primary rule that a chief, once ritually installed, cannot be removed, seemed to hold, secondary elaborations linked to ambiguity in the status of chiefly wives meant that once removed (which happened quite frequently), former chiefs could be defined *ex post facto* as regents. Comaroff recognised that chiefs were appointed in a mixture of ascription and practical political and administrative negotiation.

Neither Comaroff nor Gluckman, however, recognised the *process of decision-making* in public fora whereby tribal competitors and tribal rulers as well as administrative officials and judges dealt with claims and counter claims to succession. In response to Gluckman's original article, this is the point taken up by Richard Werbner (1997 [1969]), who argued that 'under British rule the traditional constitution and modes of succession among the Bemba of Zambia were modified in legal disputes' (1997: 246). Moving beyond a focus on rules, he argued further that alien administrators, like tribal rulers and tribal claimants,

> reason from a mixture of premises, administrative and tribal, and hold that only a decision shown to be in accord with earlier precedents is just. Each decision is not isolated but is linked to past decisions ... The claimants' manipulation of precedents can be seen as depending on the 'flexibility' (Gluckman 1955: 293–294, 311) of their legal concepts; their rights and qualifications for succession have multiple, competing, and shifting references.
>
> (Werbner 1997: 245)

In other words, in chiefly succession disputes, the struggle among contestants before a colonial administrator was not a mere trivial interlude but a critical juncture in which facts and rules were intertwined, re-evaluated, denied, or reiterated.

Postcolonial states have – sometimes with interruptions during which traditional chiefship was temporarily 'abolished' – continued to be involved in negotiations, at once bureaucratic and tribal, over the chiefship. As the editors and contributors to *The State and the Paradox of Customary Law in Africa* (Zenker and Hoehne 2018) show, the postcolonial encounters between local state bureaucrats and African traditional leaders over what is customary law continuously produce new, often unexpected, hybrids and precedents. In Botswana where chiefship was never abolished, chiefs accepted the curtailing of their considerable powers at independence in 1966. Unlike in neighbouring South Africa (see contributions to Zenker and Hoehne 2018 and Comaroff and Comaroff 2018), in Botswana mineral rights were nationalised from the start and, in time, the administration of land was devolved from chiefs to land boards in 1975. The House of Chiefs, *ntlo ya dikgosi*, has never had legislative powers, though it does debate and review new laws linked to customary law. At the same time, the number of customary courts of record has risen astronomically (see Fombad 2004), while chiefs and village chief have been incorporated into the lower echelons of the civil service.

The politics of memory: choosing a new village chief

In 2001, Moremi's village chief, Days Lengonapelo Mapulane, died. He had been the chief for the past 30 years, ever since the village split during the political turmoil of the government-inspired village 'centralisation' in the 1970s. After a very brief visit for reconnaissance in 1971, we began fieldwork in the village in August 1972. As Chapter 2 showed, it was a time of bitter dispute and factional politics, including confrontations with the paramount chief in the tribal capital Serowe, and an appeal to the nation's leader, Seretse Khama, *via* a close minister. Since those dark days, however, the village had been peaceful, but the competition over the succession to the chiefship, after Days' death in 2001 summoned painful memories which we, the ethnographers, assumed had long been suppressed, perhaps even forgotten. For our ethnography to be reflexive, we have to make plain our own shortfall in consciousness. We were really very surprised at the succession hearing by the passionate intensity of the politics of memory in assertions and counter assertions of oppression and chiefly mobilised resistance or grievous submission to resettlement. Despite our long and continuing fieldwork in both Moremi and Matolwane, we somehow remained in the dark or at least unattentive to what, under the apparently smooth surface of social life, was festering, awaiting a crisis to be openly fought over.

Although in the course of the public hearing over succession to Days as chief, villagers did rake up the past, many bitter disputes were left unmentioned, while still defining present alliances. In August 1972, we found the village in turmoil over recent events, with many of the huts in ruins. At that time Days was already installed as chief. His son Tshito was just a schoolboy. The villagers' struggles with the tribal authorities in Serowe and the endless conflicts within the Mapulane chiefly family consumed the chief and his close followers (see Chapter 2 and R.Werbner 1977).

Several key elements came together to create the original village split. Initially, the village was located by the hills and the permanent Mannonye spring, where hoe cultivation was used in the deep black soils there. As they began using oxen-driven ploughs, villagers shifted for the rainy seasons to the lighter soils a few miles north of the Lotsane river, living there at the 'lands' after the first rains for some seven months. A later shift occurring during the dry season was from Mannonye to the hill overlooking the river where a shop had been built. Water for drinking and cooking came from Mothodi, another permanent spring about a mile away. But not all the villagers shifted to the new village site on the hill.

Several members of the chiefly family stayed permanently in the lands. They were said to be living 'like jackals' (*phokoje*) in the bush. These were mainly men in the senior line of Mapulane, Moremi apical ancestor, who had been acting as chiefs or headmen in Leso's absence for the lengthy periods of his labour migration, and they were the ones who resented his choice of Days as Deputy Chief. Since their lands were located near Matolwane, they were also the ones who encouraged Leso to consent to the move there.

When Leso appointed Days to be the Deputy Chief, some people had said: 'This Days is a small person. He's the son of our father's younger brother. How can he grasp the works of the court'? Leso had said:

> It's true he's younger, but though he's young he's not a foreigner. He was born by us here, at home. As you have seen the Ngwato in Serowe may take the young ones as helpers. They don't bother with those who come [immediately] after them for those who come after them are fighting for the chiefship. That's what taught me to take the last one to help me in the works.
>
> (Interview, R. Werbner with Days, 2 October 1972)

Whereas Days was a wealthy diviner with a national reputation, Leso was a poor man, 'without even a chicken'. He even stole tax money, though he was pardoned later in Serowe. The Lesenepole people at Matolwane who wanted village centralisation were thus able to allegedly bribe him with beer to agree to shifting the village. He consulted no-one from Moremi. He was said to have just 'signed away the village'. He was also threatened by the authorities, saying that, since he had requested a borehole (he claimed only for the 'lands, his fields'), he would be charged for it, if he did not agree to move. Once there in Matolwane, he soon discovered he would not to be made the chief, and so returned to Moremi as an ordinary man. Those resisting the move were aware that, finally, a new era had dawned, of independence and democracy. In an interview, Days explained:

> I was astonished. What fault have we? We didn't go and sign for it (the new village). Can a man be arrested for what he hasn't done? Leso said: 'May I be forgiven?' Rasebolai (the senior tribal authority at Serowe) did not heed this. This was oppression, which Seretse (the President) had said: 'a person should not be troubled where he is. Let the works of government follow him to where he is.'
>
> (Interview with Days, 2 October 1972)

This is when Moremi village decided to write a letter to the president and travel to Gaborone to present it, and eventually they won the right to remain at Moremi at the site of their choice.

If disputes surrounding chiefly succession prove anything, they prove that the past is not a foreign country. As the chiefly hearing proceeded to decide the succession, after Days' death, it seemed inevitable that someone would push home the point of the presence of the past with very painful memories, bearing on vital issues well beyond the immediate matter of the succession. Someone had to continue to rehearse the past factional struggles within the village and the early threats from tribal and district authorities.

There was also the revelation of violent intimidation. It was a failure of peace and deliberation in the political struggles from the past to the present for public dominance over the newly formed community of four small villages united as one called Matolwane. There had been a very costly battle for Moremi people in Matolwane to resist losing what they cherish as their identity – their name. At the time of the succession hearing, much of the battle had already been lost under the successful drive by Lesenepole villagers to re-name the joint village as theirs, Lesenepole, not Matolwane. In Chapter 6, we foreground and analyse more of this ongoing battle, but here it is background in good measure, taken for granted by the people themselves.

The hearing for succession after Day's death took place on 30 March 2003, with a court bench of five senior chiefs of the Central District. One candidate was Days Lengonapelo's first-born son, Tshito Days, at the time still a serving major in the army; he was not present at the hearing. Standing against him was Pelonome Baloganye, the paternal granddaughter of the previous chief, Leso Maifala. Leso was, by general consent, the most senior Tswapong chief in the direct agnatic line of succession from Mapulane, the founding ancestor of all Bapedi in Tswapong Hills. Both Leso and Days were of the senior ruling ward, Moremi ward. Leso had formally relinquished the chiefship to Days, who was his assistant chief, during the dispute over the removal of the village to a centralised village, Matolwane, as documented in Chapter 2.

Figure 5.1 Shakey Bodilenyane, Chair of the VDC, welcoming chiefs from Serowe and Palapye.

The hearing over the succession took place in Moremi village court. Chairing it was Mothusi Seretse, Deputy Chief in the Central District; his fellow judges were another Serowe chief and chiefs from nearby Palapye, Mauntlala nearby and Matolwane. Civil servants, two clerks, and police officers accompanied the chiefly delegation. The speakers and audience included senior members of Moremi ward living in the neighbouring village of Matolwane along with Moremi's acting chief and other members of the village. The formal ceremonial nature of the occasion was evident from the start in formal introductions and greetings. First, the Chairwoman of Moremi Village Development Committee introduced 12 prominent elders, 'parents' from Moremi and also from Matolwane, starting with the seniors among Leso's agnates. As if to justify having introduced Leso's granddaughter, Pelonome, last, she offered a flattering proverb, perhaps with some ironic intent, '*moja morago ke kgosi*', 'Eating last is the chief'. She then turned to the Maunatlala Court Clerk, who introduced the delegation of five chiefs, including their presiding judge.

Moremi's acting chief Digapilwe then welcomed the delegation on behalf of the whole village, saying he had to stop short for lack of words. Immediately, however, he conveyed in proverbial terms that the matters at issue were such as to call for a whole day in court, necessary to delve into matters apparently tied up but actually still present. He reminded the court of the Tswana proverbial wisdom on issues seemingly tied up yet which may still be there, 'If there, they are tied up, but if (indeed) there, they will be opened out'. (*Ga ele gore di teng, di golegilwe, mme ga di le teng di tla a bulelwa*).

DIGAPILWE: Parents, my Masters (*beng ba me*). Let me start first by greeting you, my Masters, the chiefs from Serowe, from Palapye, from Maunatlala, from Matolwane, civil servants (*badirela puso*), police officers, all civil servants at large.

My masters, I do not have words, my part is to welcome you in your *kgotla*; to listen to what you have brought to us, my Masters. I will just stop with these short welcoming words. My people, my Masters. I won't go further. I will stop with those words, my Masters. Let us all stay the whole day long in the *kgotla*. We long heard about this visit. It has been said 'If there, they are tied up' (*ga ele gore di teng, di golegilwe*). 'But if there, they will be released' (*mme ga di le teng di tla a bulelwa*). I mean that my words are that. My Masters, I greet you with Pula!

Pula!

In his response, the presiding chief, Seretse recognised the need for succession to the vacant chiefship; he acknowledged that the people of Moremi had the best knowledge of the birth rights of their past chiefs' sons and daughters; and he promised the assembled villagers to report to the government their choice of one to shepherd the village, in this way highlighting the need for someone able to look after it, or as he later stressed, 'protect' it.

CHIEF SERETSE: I was sent by the Bangwato Tribal Authority, by Chief Sediegeng Kgamane, to come and talk to you as villagers of Moremi about

> the chiefship of this village. It would appear that for some years there has been no chief in the village. Now what we want is to ask you to say and give the name of the person you want to head this village. You are the ones who know how you were born, you know your chiefs, the sons and daughters of the chiefship. We will hear from you talking, with your words written and taken to the government that the people of Moremi say who it is we want to shepherd the village.

From this opening, the hearing allowed the first speeches to be made by the previous late chief Leso's supporters and close relatives, who claimed the birth rights of their family. Their aim was to obscure the long chiefship that his successor Days held in Moremi. Leso's oldest, and now frail and disabled son, Mokenti, bore witness first. Appearing confused, contradictory, and not a credible witness, he claimed that after his father's death, he had appointed his brother, then the brother's daughter, to the chiefship. Cross-examined by Chief Seretse, he contradicted himself, and had to admit that actually Days had long been holding the chiefship until, after his death, an acting chief, Digapilwe, was given his current temporary appointment. Chief Seretse hit on the witness's contradictions and cast doubt on his claim, 'You speak opposing yourself' (in contradiction); he then excused this frail elder's confusion, 'He is an old man' (*monnamogolo*).

Against that doubt, the next speaker, Ditlhonamo, regarded as an uncle of Leso, first accepted the mandate to speak under the authority of Chief Seretse and the duty to respond accordingly: 'It is true we received the chief's words as the mandate (*thomo*) has come and an obligation (*tshwanelo*) is that I have to tell him whom we want to be appointed in this *kgotla*, Leso's'. He went on to argue for common knowledge of the very essence of the nature of the village, that everyone knows that the village is Leso's: 'The village itself has its nature (*tlholego*, origins, essence), created being Leso's'. 'Are we to say', he went on to ask, 'that these disabled and sick persons should not be given what belongs to them, because of their disability?'

Continuing the defence of Leso's family rights, Ditlhonamo brought more of the history of the dispute to bear. First, he recalled the moot properly made in preparation for this hearing, then he went on to rehearse the moot's account of common knowledge, namely the genealogy of the named ancestors and past chiefs in Moremi's senior line. Even further, he made a point of praising the judiciousness of Leso, his capacity to run a straight hearing in consensual resolution of quarrels. This praise had an acutely negative undertone, nicely raking up things of common knowledge without saying them, with an implied contrast that discredited the controversial and sometimes conflicted Days. It seemed to be a covered barb, as if to convey that, should the family of Days succeed, it might live up to his past history of involvement in village quarrels.

> We had to meet for the *morero* (moot) according to the law (*ka molaong*) even though we all know that this land (*lefatshe le*) is Mapulane's who begot Senwedi, the first-born son, our great grandfather. This Senwedi is the one

> who begot Maifala and Ikalafeng, and just so he, Maifala, begot a child, namely Leso, being from Moremi, the one for whom we are talking about. The one who was convening a moot in the way that is straight (*ka fa tlhamalalong*) with his younger brothers and sisters, without conflicts.

This speaker on behalf of Leso's family himself had a challenge. Despite being an uncle of a previous chief, he had to assert his very right to speak and decide on the succession, coming as he did, along with many others present, as a resident not of Moremi village itself but in nearby Matolwane. His speech resonated with understandings of the resettlement conflict and the move to Matolwane that tore the village apart in the 1970s. He insisted he had the ***right*** to choose Moremi chief because he was actually still of the village. Matolwane is really Moremi.

> Even we know that if there are problems in this village, while we are in Matolwane, w*e have a right to this village to appoint a chief*. This Matolwane is Moremi; it's just an area, our fields are here, even if we meet there [at Matolwane] in development, our village is this one, Moremi. When my father here said he is Mokenti Leso in Moremi, he was telling the truth.

Ditlhonamo admitted that the chief from Serowe who had consulted them had told them he wanted names given only by the residents of Moremi. Nevertheless, in defence of his claim of still belonging to Moremi and thus entitled to have a say in the succession, he went on to rehearse more history. In his view, all the public developments at Matolwane, including the school and the *kgotla,* were made, for the common good of different villages, by Moremi village:

> In Matolwane we were doing development so that villages can join. Before Leso moved in here [back to Moremi]. Leso is the one who appointed (*tlhomileng*) the *kgotla,* when the government was saying small villages should join and help each other so that developments can be brought to them.

CHIEF SERESTSE: Oh! Leso being there at the Matolwane *kgotla?*
DITLHONAMO: Yes, Sir. Leso being there at the Matolwane *kgotla.*
CHIEF SERETSE: After that he came back here? Who did he leave at the *kgotla*?
DITLHONAMO: He left Rebammu at the *kgotla*. Rebammu, the younger brother (Leso's brother's son).

Ditlhonamo here obscured the dominant role of another village, Lesenepole, in the newly centralised village of Matolwane. Only reluctantly did he admit that Leso appointed Days to be chief of Moremi, even after he returned. But offering this admission gave him the opportunity to insist that the time had come for restoration, the birth right belongs to Leso's family and so it should return to his children, and in particular his granddaughter living in Moremi:

> I am standing here right now, being Ditlhonamo Mothabani, Leso's uncle, saying the chiefship should go back to Leso's children. It is [to be] taken by Pelonome Baloganye. Chiefship means to be born into it (*bogosi bo a tsalelwa*). It is never given easily, otherwise it will jump over (*tlola*) us. … I say the chiefship will go back to the owners, to Pelonome Baloganye. That's all.

Following Ditlhonamo, Moreetsi, the son of an elder brother of Days, took his turn as another prominent and senior Moremi ward member resident in Matolwane (see Genealogy 1, Chapter 2). He carried forward the politics of memory by recalling duress. It was not as if he and others had moved from living in Moremi of their own free will and could thus rightfully be excluded from the vote for the new chief. No, the very chair of the hearing, Chief Seretse had to realise that his own grandfather was responsible for forcing resettlement under threat of prison. It was a moral challenge from the past to the rule (*puso*) of the present tribal authorities:

> The village you hear is called Matolwane, I never went there by myself [voluntarily]. I was taken [by force] by the rulers (*puso*). The grandfather to Chief Mothusi Seretse [the hearing's chair] is the one who took me there, promising (*ntsholefetsa*, i.e., threatening) me with six months' imprisonment. It was his rule (*puso*), to leave this village.

CHIEF SERETSE: I wanted to ask, sir. Do you mean that you were moved out of this village by the Ngwato chiefship? Was it Rasebolai [the Acting Chief at Serowe]? Moreetsi reported that initially he refused to move, to abandon Moremi's spring and sweet water, and that he, like Days, gave in to the threat and moved:

I was saying I will not leave this river of my grandfather Mapulane, the one flowing [referring to the permanent spring where Moremi village was first located]. I said I do not want borehole water, but I moved there. Days also moved to Matolwane as we were threatened ('promised') with imprisonment together.

CHIEF SERETSE: This Days also once went to stay in Matolwane?

MOREETSI: Your honour, too much. We moved at the same time, started building at the same time and hired people to make huts there. They are still there, even the ruins of the huts are still there. That is when Leso absconded from Matolwane to Moremi, while we were still building. I appealed to elders asking Leso, who had he left me with there? '

Addressing Chief Seretse directly, he turned the question back to the presiding chief and the Ngwato at Serowe:

> You took us there. Now what is the problem? What makes you say we should go back to Moremi?'

Moreetsi then brought up more of the dubious history of chiefship in Moremi. He reminded the judges of an earlier complaint he had lodged contesting the very legitimacy of Days' appointment to be chief. There were six other candidates more senior than Days was, Moreetsi had claimed, including Moreetsi himself as the son of Days' older brother, in their line junior to Leso's for the chiefship. To make matters even more dubious, contrary to birth right, the acting chief at Moremi, appointed apparently by Day's son, Tshito, is not even from the chiefly ward, but from a sister ward, Mogoma.

Genealogical rules *versus* other moral arguments

So far in the hearing, the rules of succession, defined in terms of agnatic seniority, had not been challenged, nor were the basic facts of birth order and succession. But at this point, supporters of Days' family and his rightful successor, Tshito, took their turn. They introduced alternative and telling moral arguments. Their basis was the remarkable and unmistakable fulfilment by Days of the chief's duty to build up his village, and without any dispute over his rule, during Leso's lifetime and even after Leso's death. Thus Ramokoro, a Moremi elder and an uncle of candidate Baloganye's daughter, asserted the rightful succession by her rival, Tshito:

> I am standing here to say that the chiefship is for Tshito Days Lengonapelo. What is the reason? The reason is that all the buildings in this village were built by Days Lengonapelo.

SERETSE: Which things?

RAMOKORO: I am talking about this *leobo* (brick shelter at the *kgotla)*, I am talking about the village at large, even the primary school itself. They were done by Days. Now what I am saying is: a law is like a knife (*molao ke tipa*). When it is before you, you won't jump over it. That is, you should stop us so that we do not have questions. I heard my fellows saying, Leso gave Days the chiefship without them knowing but being there. It's been many years of Days ruling as you can see how big the village is. However, they [those complaining] were there during Days' life until Leso passed away. Leso did not die ruling. The chiefship was Days', but there was never a dispute or complaint (*kgang ya ngongorego*). As for what one man said claiming there was a complaint, I do not know where his complaint ended. Now we clarify that 'the inheritance of the baboon is eaten by its baby'. We are not saying that Leso was not a chief. Leso in *tlholego* is Mapulane's sibling, but he gave away the chiefship. About his giving away of the chiefship, there has never been anyone who complained. .... Now, that is why I concluded saying: I am standing here with all Days' works, while alive. After passing away, it teaches me that, as he was the chief, I relied on his legacy, and it should be taken by his son Tshito Days Lengonapelo. With all the works he did, I do not know whether I can give a person something which is not coming out of

> my pocket. I am talking about the chair of the chief. If I give a child a chair to sit on, should it not be the chair I was sitting on? My child can sit there so that people see. I finish there.

The next speaker from Moremi was Baleufi, a prominent elder and the wife of Bishop Olefile, who spoke later. She echoed Ramokoro's argument, when she told of the threat coming from Serowe to those like herself who insisted on remaining behind in the old village:

> There was Mokgatsha Mokgadi [a Serowe chief]. Being there myself, I was asked my aims and objectives (*maikaelelo le maikemisetso*), why are we not going there [to Matolwane] but staying here [at Moremi], what is the problem?

CHIEF SERETSE: Being asked?

BALEUFI: I was being asked.

CHIEF SERETSE: How did you answer?

BALEUFI: I said, here there is plenty of water. I won't suffer the shortage of water here, which comes from under the ground and never dries up. But a question was asked, what would it be if a borehole is drilled? I said drilled water would never be the same as water coming from the ground. However, it was said that those who delayed in Moremi, *you will never see anything, even any developments you won't have*. We said, it's alright if we do not see anything. At that time there was no primary school. Other children were schooling in Kgagodi and others in Choole. But they attended until finishing their standard seven and passed (the exams). Now, after being released to come back home (by the government), we came back [to the Moremi village site].

CHIEF SERETSE: Is it to come back or to stay?

BALEUFI: I mean to stay here. I am in the health committee. The health committee grouped themselves as we were told we won't have anything. We asked for a clinic with the LG17 programme and the government agreed with us. When agreeing with us, preparing ourselves to build the clinic, the Council brought the clinic. Men grouped themselves so that each man brought a cow to build the school, the Mapulane school, but while grouping themselves to bring the heads of cattle, the council brought the school. When we were drinking the Mothodi water, because we were fetching it from there [a mile from the village site], the government brought standpipes [into the village]. We were with Chief Days.

However, what hurts is talk during the absence of those people (Days and Leso) that we are talking about. Being dead. That is the most painful. I feel a pain because if we were talking while Days was still alive, and we were raising the alarm (*mokgosi*), it would be better. But here I will be pleading, pleading but asking a question that who is better between a person who is herding and the one who is not herding? I have finished.

NTEBELE: The herder is better with the owner of the cattle being there.

In other words, the government threatened Moremi remainers with never being granted 'development' but in the end, under Days' chiefship, it provided a clinic, a school, and standpipes for water to the village. Ending with a flourish of moral certainty in a rhetorical question of familiar moral wisdom, Baleufi asked: 'Who is better between a person who is herding (*disana*) or the one who is not herding?' It was Days who shepherded the village to its present state of development. His moral claims to leadership were vindicated by the developments he achieved.

At this point came a fresh challenge to the succession of Days' son Tshito. It was raised by Mothanka, a man living in Matolwane but who claimed to belong to Moremi. Mothanaka, was himself a diviner like Days but also a church leader, ready to call on the Bible for support. After establishing his mandate, as one who had once built a house in the village and, like a relisher of its goodness, 'eats its honeycomb', this challenger, Mothanka, began by criticising the government for waste. It was a criticism much liked by villagers from their frustrating experience of bureaucratic paperwork, of filling ever more forms in applications to government. Why waste more paper on getting names of successors, despite the fact that a preliminary enquiry by the government had already taken the names?

MOTHANKA: Let me come near you (*tla ke go atamele*) so that you see me perfectly. I am Isaac Mothanka Kgosiyarona in this village of Moremi. I have built in this village, the land of my grandfather, I am eating its honeycomb (*ke ja mana a lone*). I am disappointed because I was expecting (*ke ne ke solofetse*) that, as more government paper has been wasted already, you have come with papers to take names. I do not know where you take the papers with names, why you could not tell us that you have failed. You have been taking names here. Why is it that there is no conclusion of how it ended? Which names do you want because they are the ones we had been giving you?

Chief Seretse interjected with the demand that Mothanka should get to the point, and irritated, Mothanka threw the demand back, immediately and boldly, while he complained further to the point of calling into question due process in the procedure of the hearing.

MOTHANKA: Do not interfere with me, it is said that you should not interfere with a person when speaking. Even the Bible is refusing (*e a gana*, doesn't allow interference). I want the truth on why is it that now it is as if the information we are giving is collected in small quantities like drips of water (*re a kotlopisiwa*). That is the thing which makes me complain. I am investigating (*ke a tlhotlhomisa*), I want evidence.

Another elder, Ntebele, who was much respected as a senior member of Moremi's esoteric and secret cult of the *Komana*, demanded immediately that Mothanka reveal which side he was on.

NTEBELE: When talking of names, tell us the name you have given us.

In reply, Mothanka made it plain that he had a special mandate to speak about Moremi's court and its chief, because he was in the same line of descent as Leso, though a junior member

MOTHANKA: I am speaking as Kgosiyarona's son, the grandson of Senwedi, Mothabani and Maifala. This *kgotla* is of my grandfather and the kraal. Now, your honours, this day I have no mere chatter (*ga kena dipalabalo*). The name I am giving is the one which, when my grandfather Makwesa died, I said Pelonome Baloganyi is taking over. She is the one we are giving this chiefship of her grandfather to take it and rule. I am not saying because that one has made scatterings (*magasagasi*). I built for myself, not any other person. It is hurting very badly, this school was built when Leso was around, he was not in Matolwane. He passed away leaving all these things being in Moremi. Even his grave is here in the village, not Matolwane. The inheritance (*boswa*) of a person is eaten up by his child. It is never eaten by someone from there, saying he is the heir (*moja boswa*). The inheritance should be taken by Leso's descendants; they should rule. If our grandfather failed let it come back or for us to rule and to make things straightforward (*re tlhamalatse dilo*), we do not want what is being hidden (*ga re batle mo go itiketswang*). Ladies and gentlemen, that is all.

In rebuttal of Mothanka's argument, the next to speak was Mashate, a Moremi villager and well-regarded former teacher and leader in the Village Development Committee. He framed his remarks in deference. He drew attention to the facts of his paying due respect during the hearing: that he was a commoner in a ward, not of Leso's chiefly line; that he had waited to listen to his seniors of that line before intervening in the hearing, when he invited those from Moremi ward in Matolwane to come back and live in Moremi, if they wished to influence decisions about the chiefship.

Here, given this essential appearance of presenting due respect, the hearing came to a climax in troublesome matters morally of the greatest delicacy. It was towards the end of a long day of argument and counter argument, full of painful memories and bitter pleading. To raise troublesome matters, by someone not of the chiefly family, was to have to be more than merely civil. A commoner wise to village ways and village opinion, as well as the risk of being in contempt of the court and its members' care for chiefly dignity, had to be circuitous. Accordingly, Mashate took care to be seen to be reluctant to stir and expose, from long ago, chiefly family dirt, a shameful betrayal of trust in dishonourable conduct. Although actually an elder, he characterised himself as being 'too young' to be one to tell all, as he hinted at suspicion. This put in question the marriage of Pelonome's mother to her father, Baloganye, the son of Chief Leso. Was her mother merely a mistress, left unmarried when Pelonome's father, in breach of trust, took up with another woman and had a child with her? And was Pelonome thus exposed as not a legitimate heir to the chiefship? Hence the exposure answering these concerns came out as if extracted under cross-examination by the Serowe Chief from the embarrassing hint of a suspicion mentioned somewhat obliquely by Mashate. Nevertheless, for all the politesse, it was dangerous, and not at all tolerated by Pelonome herself. It was a terrible insult, she threatened to sue, but it was as if her complaint fell on deaf ears, left hanging, never decided one way or the other. The presiding chief Seretse simply moved the hearing to a decision by majority vote of the assembled Moremi villagers.

MASHATE: (After he made his preliminary and deferential remarks on Leso's agnates at Matolwane.) People, we are moving in a difficult discussion of the chiefship. I hope each and everyone knows that when talking about the chiefship, we talk of a serious problem, and we enter the holes that are hot (*re tsena diphatlha tse di bothito*). But this one, I wanted to leave it to elders as to how it can suit my cousins (the chiefly agnates) here and how it could not suit them. The elders know these matters, I do not want to enter them properly.

SERETSE: Sir, forgive me first, I am asking you. You have said Leso's people are at Matolwane; now the one (of his people) who has been shown here (Pelonome as the heir) does not stay here? Is she not staying here?

MASHATE: She has built here, my Master. You could have heard me saying there are some words, very remote (*a a kwa tennyanateng*), the ones I am too young to touch, to explain them.

CHIEF SERETSE: Speak.

Here, rather than spell out his meaning by reference to the case at hand, Mashate tried to illustrate his argument indirectly and hypothetically. If he were a sister's son reared among the chief's people, the descendants of Mapulane, he would have difficulty claiming to head his own people in the ward of Busang, their forefather. The presiding chief found this indirection and its surprising bearing on the case so questionable that he demanded an explanation and kept on asking the same question to get the issue clarified.

MASHATE: For example, if I was born and lived as a sister's son to the chief's side among the Mapulane people, and I went and pleaded (*seka*) for the chiefship of the Busangs it would be difficult. This is because I stay with my grandparents on my mother's side (*betsho-mogolo*). It won't be fitting to me (*go sa ntebagana*) to plead for Busang's chiefship. Those are my words.

CHIEF SERETSE: Yes, we have to talk, just explain with this one.

MASHATE: If talking about my sister Pelonome, she is Baloganye's daughter who was born at Mogoma (her mother's ward). Let me finish properly, because you wanted me to explain it. Even now, she is in her mother's brother's compound. If we were talking with her being at the chief's compound, at Mapulane's, we could have said it is proper for her to be appointed the heir.

CHIEF SERETSE: Her mother was not made to arrive (*goroswa*)? Speak.

.

.:

MASHATE: Chief, when talking about a person, when talking about an heir, we talk about someone whose mother was taken and made to arrive (*a tsholwa, a goroswa*). If talking about my sister Pelonome, she is Baloganye's daughter who was born at Mogoma (her mother's ward). Let me finish properly because you wanted me to explain it. Even now, she is living at her maternal uncle's compound. If we were talking being at the chiefship compound, at Mapulane, we could have said it is proper for her to be appointed a successor/heir.

CHIEF SERETSE: Her mother was not taken to arrive (*goroswa*)? Speak.

MASHATE: No, your honour, according to our knowledge, when we grew up, we found that her mother never went to the in-laws (*go o ra matsalaagwe*).

CHIEF SERETSE: She was never taken to arrive (*goroswa*)?

MASHATE: No. She was never taken.

CHIEF SERETSE: That is why you say, because her mother was never taken, she does not belong to the chief's side? She belongs there at her mother's side. Write, write those words (to the clerk).

In response to further probing from one of the other chiefs on whether her elders still had the right and the capacity to allow her to inherit the chair, Mashate resorted to expanding the earlier argument of residence:

MASHATE: Our suspicion (*pelaelo*) here is, Chief, that Mokenti the son of Leso, who spoke at the start of the hearing, and lives in Matolwane) cannot take the chiefship and give it to Pelonome, if he is staying elsewhere, not here in the village. That is our suspicion. It is that: How can you give away a chair not at home, (while) being at Matolwane?

Repeatedly, the chiefly genealogy of Moremi, starting with Mapulane, had been rehearsed. Now the need was to confront the question of Pelonome's mother's status. Under further questioning, Moreetsi as the proposer of Pelonome admitted, after some prevarication, that 'She was never brought home (*goroswa*).'

CHIEF SERETSE: Now you agree she was born at the mother's side (*o tsweletswe kwa ga bone mogolo*)?

MOREETSI: She was born at the mother's side.

CHIEF SERETSE: Ladies and gentlemen, I want elder men (men of authority as elders). I am talking about a person who is to be given the chiefship.

Accordingly, the question of legitimate birth was debated, and one chief said:

> In Tswana culture and Tswapong, *patlo* (the seeking of a bride) is whereby people would go to the *kgotla* or to any family compound to request that

their son should be allowed to marry the other family's daughter. But even in Setswana (the way of Batswana), *patlo* is the wedding (*nyalo*); it is not being made to arrive (*e sena kgoroso*). [i.e., among Tswapong the marriage agreement is sealed by the wedding and the move to the bridegroom's residence. On this difference between Tswapong and other Tswana in their district, see the adultery case in Chapter 7].

This speaker's secondary elaboration, that allowing for the public request (*patlo*) to be the wedding (*nyalo)*, could not be safe. There was an all too well-known precedent to the contrary. Importantly for its citation by the presiding chief, above all, is the fact that, in response to this chief, he had to cite what was then the outstanding case of modern succession to paramount chiefship among their very own Ngwato tribe, the famous case of Seretse Khama. It is worth noting the exceptional importance of citing such a precedent. The fact is that it has been rare in many tribal courts in Africa for judges to cite cases as precedents; there was not an elaborate body of case law (Werbner 2020: 201).

CHIEF SERETSE: Wait! Seretse Khama was the paramount chief of Ngwato. He was the youngest son of Sekgoma. He had his elder brother by the name of Gasetshwarwe, the biological son of Sekgoma, begotten with the daughter of Kgamane. There is no-one who does not know this. It came to happen that, after Seretse returned from England, 12 cattle were taken to give them to his brother. Now, he had even been the chief of the Ngwato. After Sekgoma, the father of Seretse died, other people from Ditlharapa ward said Gasetshwarwe, the brother of Seretse, is the one who is supposed to be the chief. Tshekedi (the regent and uncle of Seretse) refused, saying Gasetshwarwe's mother was not formally requested by his parents. He grew up at Mokwena, the biological son of Sekgoma, but because his mother was not formally requested by the parents and was never taken to arrive (*goroswa,* brought home), that is when I say you should take care of that issue (*le tlhokomele go lo foo*). If the son of Sekgoma Khama, Seretse's elder brother, was denied the chiefship just because the mother was not formally requested by parents, take care of that issue. But this one, there should be a proof. Now you see that they are denying, even Moreetsi said her mother was not made to arrive (*goroswa*). Now I become weak in my bones (*ke kgobega marapo*) with the fact of hearing that her mother was never taken to arrive in marriage; that is when I relate it to that one of ours (*ya gaetsho*). The problem comes here.

Later more was said about the illegitimacy of Pelonome. First came the answer to an even more telling question, posed by the rewriting of history in praise of Leso as a judicious chief, whose hearings were straight. What kind of chief actually was Leso, and how did he come to give up the chiefship to Days? To answer that bluntly called for a speech not by a commoner like Mashate but by a man of chiefly descent. Pifelo, one of Days' younger brothers, told a well-known and unchallengable truth frankly:

> Leso is our brother in the eldest family, [but] about the chiefship, it was failing (*ka bogosi go ne go relela*) ... He was failing to lead people (*goga batho*). He did not understand the way of chiefship. He was failing to lead the tribe (*sechaba*). The way of chiefship was hard.

CHIEF SERETSE: To whom?
PIFELO: It was hard to our brother Leso.

In response, Pifelo spelled out the turmoil of the past, remembered in much circumstantial detail. He recalled vividly and at length the coming together of four small villages. There were trips back and forth to Serowe. The upshot was, and without public and rightful consultation, that Leso consented to the village centralisation and left Days to rule in Moremi. Pifelo drove his point home further by attacking a sore spot for the Matolwane people with pretensions to still be in Moremi while residing in Matolwane. There they had already lost out on Moremi leadership. Originally, Leso had been asked to point to the man who would sit on his chair, i.e., the chiefship, in Matolwane. Pifelo stressed that the chiefship in Matolwane was taken away by the head of the biggest village, Lesenepole.

CHIEF SERETSE: Now there, the one who was pointed to be given Leso's chair [at Matolwane] was Rebammu, pointed at by Mokgatsha?
PIFELO: They were the Ngwato people (the tribal authorities). To say Mokgatsha, we do not know, they took the one given Leso's chair and made him a ward headman, a small chief (*kgosanyana*).

Pifelo then went on to cite a well-known Tswana proverb regarding chiefship:

> If they have desire (*keletso*) of the chiefship, what is that really for? Is it possible for the chiefship to be twice on a head of the same person? (*bogosi bote bon ne ga bedi mo tlhogong ya motho a le mongwe fela*)? It was then, when they moved, going to Matolwane and left (the person who) was the youngest son of my brother being Sekhanjane (Tshotelego Rebammu). Leso went there and Days just built some house but never went there. I am the one who told him that if he goes there, he will be a baby elephant (*tlotswana*) in this village (i.e., Matolwane), invoking a Tswana saying, 'if the elephant crosses the river, it becomes a baby elephant', '*tlou ga e tlola molapo e nna tlotswana*'). An elbow (*se kgono*, or *segokgola*, a term used by Pifelo) is never bitten. You will come and find me sitting on your chair.

For Chief Seretse, the legitimacy of Pelonome's claim to inherit the chiefship was still subject to testimony, an open matter, about which Pelonome's brother, Ralebante, was called upon to testify:

RALEBANTE: I am Ralebante Baloganye, who is the son of Leso. This person Titholwa [mother of Pelonome] is the daughter-in-law (*ngwetse*) of Leso. Dithola Magee is the daughter-in-law of the chief's side. She did everything there, being there as I was still young until I grew up. … she can kneel down and tell them. She is a lawful daughter-in-law, the one I grew up with at my grandfather's place.

Another close member of the family also tried to defend the legality of the marriage. But Olefile, another speaker from Moremi, brought the focus back to hardships in the very struggle for survival of the village and memories of Days' leadership in that historic village struggle. A renowned preacher and healer, Olefile spoke with much public authority as the influential bishop of a popular, well-established Zionist church, a highly respected elder and ward head in Moremi.

A trip to the capital to see the President

BISHOP OLEFILE: For all of us Baremi (Moremi villagers), Days was appointed by his grandfather and became the chief. When the time came for the village to move, going to Matolwane, Days was reigning, his grandfather Leso still being alive. Days agreed with the resettlement (*khuduga*) according to the words, which have been spoken by my peers (*mokaulengwe*), that you will be thrown in jail if you do not go to Matolwane. 'Truth never needed eating an amulet' (*Boammuaruri ga bo jelwe pheko*). When Days arrived in Matolwane … he found written somewhere [it was said on a tree] PASSOP! (Afrikaans for 'beware') (*tshaba*) of the rifle (*thobolo*). Truth is needed. He told us that he was not well [implicitly, that he was afflicted by sorcery] and we departed from there. [I was with] Days and other villagers who have [since] died, Blackie, Keitsile, and Tapologo being some of those who accompanied Days for that matter. Others said the person who said the words was not supposed (did not have the right) to do that. He is [trying] to sit on top of us [referring to the villagers from Lesenepole]. … As far as I know [since] the village of Matolwane was put there by Leso, and we ourselves. we could point to where we wanted to stay [choose sites in the new village]. We left there Days with a decision that he is returning from there to his home. We sat down, Days saying that he returned from there, and that he is crossing to the deserted homestead at Mannonye [the old site of the village near the spring]. We spent the day there [in Mannonye] to see exactly where the *kgotla* could be, where his family could live, and also us people, where we could live. We returned afterwards, after finishing that. We returned home [to Moremi]. As we were still proceeding [thinking] that now we are getting ready to migrate to that side [Mannonye], then other persons came back [from Matolwane] visiting us as if they were foreigners but being visitors (*baeng*). '*Mothusa motho ke mothodi wa tsa gagwe*' ('Who helps someone is his belongings'). They told us not to abandon the [current] village [site on the hill] but to rebuild it. 'There [at the spring], you would be gone [located] too far. Build where you would find the government programme funds nearby'. We agreed with them. Words which were said by a certain woman (Olefile's wife Baleufi] that you are never going to have a school, water, clinic, or even any development, are true. We were [treated] just like dissidents (*diganana*) but we were with Days, Leso being in Matolwane. After settling in here, we came together united (*ra kitlana*) to fulfil our aims, our understanding being that we had to go to Gaborone as the instruction (*taolo*) [to move] had come from Serowe. Days had a car, we filled it, he being the one paying for petrol and paying for our meals. We arrived in Gaborone and met the member of Parliament, Mr Moitaakgola Ngwako. He recognised (*lemoga*) that things were going badly as we wanted to see the President. He sent us back here with the instruction that he will go to the President. We said we would not return back because of [the threat of] jail. Ngwako arrived unexpectedly (*solofela*) and instructed us to go to Serowe. We went to Serowe. Rasbolai shouted at us. However, as there were some words from Gaborone, even he – being an elder and also a parent – he agreed with the words that *a person is never forced* (to do something). 'Go and stay' said Rasbolai. We came and stayed. The Land Board officers came to allocate plots to the villagers. … When the Land Board officers came, we had our rights and they had their rights, too, in Matolwane.

He then went on to discuss the events after Days died. The matter of the legitimacy of Pelonome, the second candidate had not, however, been settled.

Painful words

One of the candidates for the chiefship, Days's oldest son Tshito, had absented himself from the hearing. That left the moment for Pelonome, the granddaughter of Leso, to speak. She was about 50 years old and lived most of the time in Gaborone. Among Moremi and Matolwane villagers working in Gaborone, she had a good reputation as a businesswoman, marketing soap products door-to-door. She spoke passionately, angrily, and in distress.

PELONOME: I am Pelonome Leso Maifala. I never knew I wasn't Baloganye's daughter. It means there are people [here] who know that I am not Baloganye's daughter. For 50 years I have lived knowing that I am Baloganye's daughter. You are saying that I shouldn't be a chief, because I am child of a mistress (*ke ngwana wa nyatsi*). You used a polite manner of speaking (*setla se anya*) but in proper Setswana it is child of a mistress. I want to know more, because most of you know my father. I have [lived for] 50 years knowing I am Baloganye's daughter. I beg you not to insult my mother, when talking about the chiefship, because tomorrow you could find yourselves in trouble (*mathata*). It is said, 'You should not trample on someone's rights in life (*gatwe o seka wa gataka ditshwanelo tsa mongwe mo botshelong*).' Do not trample on my rights. I know that I am Pelonome

Baloganye. Now that you know well, there will be a day you will tell me who my father is. I know that I am Pelonome Baloganye, the one about whom there is a word saying, 'where have you been'? We couldn't fight with Days, because the chiefship was given to him by an old man (Leso) the way it happened. But at this moment, because Days has passed away, we are saying, '*Let the chiefship go back to the owners*'. I will call myself Leso, because I do not know any other person who is my father. Where have you been before messing with my names, my identities? Right now, I am called daughter of a mistress. My mother is even insulted by younger persons. Do not sweeten (*natetsha*) the chiefship with my mother. It is the fourth time telling you that God is Love (*Modimo o lorato*). Jesus knows how to plead for a foolish person (*sekema*). I beg you from now to mind your words. I do not want to talk. I thank my parents, the Lesos, the way they have handled this matter, because words are too much which we can talk about Days and also Pifelo [his younger brother]. We do not have the time to come and disappoint each other here (*tontololana*), insulting parents. Chiefs, I am saying that for 50 years I have lived knowing that I am Baloganye's daughter, the one I buried, and even Leso too. But I am being told at this moment that I am a child of a mistress. I do not know whether the chiefs hear this? You should find the way to this matter.

Pelonome had the last word. It evoked no further support. The time had come in the view of the presiding chief, Seretse, to have a vote.

Democracy rules

Seretse, a forceful character who had interrogated witnesses and dominated the proceedings, asked for a show of hands. In each case residence was checked – Moremi or Matolwane. The senior judges retired to the inner sanctum of the court room along with Digapilwe, Moremi's acting chief, who gave his opinion and then left. When they returned, Seretse as the Deputy Tribal Authority, complained about the inordinate length of time the case had taken. He announced that the delegation favoured Tshito, based on the fact that he had majority support among the villagers resident in Moremi. Ironically, then, those who had obeyed the tribal authorities and moved to Matolwane were now excluded from the chiefship of Moremi.

CHIEF SERETSE: When I started, I said I came to be given the name of the person you see to be someone who can protect the village. I wanted it from you, the owners of this village. But we have spent a day here, we started at 10 o'clock, now the time is 14.45. Starting from the time we began until 14.30 pm, each and every one talked the way they liked. I saw exactly that we would go back without the matter we came here for [settled]; then I saw that I have come for what I came for. However, you heard yourselves, you heard what the people of this village wanted. You heard whom they want. I cannot

> be asked to ignore him. The Europeans say majority rule. There came the decision from many people. Now there is nothing we can do to try to avoid that. We cannot take the decision from one person and throw away the decisions of many people. Now more people in Moremi want Days' son. I will go and send these words to the Minister of Lands in Gaborone. He will read the words from the start to the end to hear the reasons. The Minister does not have the power to change the one the people of Moremi have voted for. It is said that it [democracy] is the government of the people by the people (*puso ya batho ka batho*). Even Kgamane, the one who sent me [the Acting Chief of the Bamangwato], does not have the power to change what has been said.

Chief Seretse's decision to give access to the vote only to residents must have made the outcome well expected among many of Moremi villagers. Pelonome's vocal support had come, apart from the seemingly senile elderly son of Leso, only from her own immediate family in Moremi along with elders from Leso's family resident in Matolwane. No-one disputed Leso's seniority; and no one had to. No villager questioned the right of a woman to be a chief, and this was not raised by the high-ranking tribal authorities either. What seemed to have mattered in rallying the vote were the arguments put by Moremi elders in the light of protection – the survival and then development of the village under their late chief Days. As his successor, his son could be said to be 'born to the chiefship', and thus the rightful heir to office by birth right under the rule of hereditary succession, not an exception to the rule

Several further points are worth reviewing. The first is that, as Chief Seretse declared, everyone was given the chance to express their opinion, and listened to patiently, even though some rambled on. Secondly, the rules of succession were not disputed, but other moral bases for the chiefship were repeatedly invoked. It is significant that in making the appointment, Chief Seretse repeated that he had said he had come for the choice of a chief who would protect the village. That implied suitability from past example, not succession by birth right alone. This in itself opened out the question of Leso's failure and Days' success, and the importance of that for a successor, after the right moral and protective history. Who had actually been the one who made the village? Some past events were remembered in great detail. Many were glossed over as we spell out below.

What was never explicitly declared was the *personal suitability of either candidate for the office*. That was left implicit, and perhaps already gossiped about among supporters. One may surmise, however, that the grounds for seeing Tshito Days to be the better candidate were well-known. Wise in the ways of administration and government, he was literate, then an army major with proven leadership qualities and, moreover, said to be favoured by the then Vice-President, who had been his commander. In 2005, Tshito was still due to serve in the army for another two years. He was, in other words, a big man in a very small village, where his father had been the reigning village chief for over 35 years.

To maintain harmony and the appearance of equity, the chiefly delegation invoked democracy based on actual residence, which excluded from the vote members of the senior chiefly family living in the neighbouring village. As Chief Seretse insisted, no-one could dispute democracy, not even the Tribal Authority Acting Chief in Serowe.

In a later installation ceremony, on 17 June 2005, Tshito accepted the nomination, saying, 'I will be handing in my uniform. If sand is eaten here, we will eat it together'. Chief Seretse responded, summing up earlier discussions: 'You heard him for yourself, your child. I agree that he is a person, and you gave him this work, *knowing that his father made this village*'. He cited another village, Seolwane, where people voted for the son of a man who had stayed in the village and 'protected' it, rather than abandoning it like the original chief, and praised Tshito for being willing to give up his army salary.

> You [Moremi villagers] did not see who is the elder, you were looking to the person who has been holding the village, who gathered the people of the village. It is Days, given the power by Leso, Mokenti's father. I thank you Tshito for such big love. You are now a chief. That is why you can see your father managing to gather such people. *You were born the chief, really, truly.* I thank you for having accepted your people's request.

Given our account with its detailed documentation and close analysis, we want to raise a point for broader comparison of processual form in hearings. Looking back on the course of the argumentation, we find a remarkable contrast between the tendency towards absolute reasoning and narrower pleading by one side, and by the other, the tendency towards the conditional and more open pleading. It is not a matter simply of each side manipulating rules by self-interested selection. Rather, given the fact that consensus prevails about a primary rule, one side insists on sticking to that as straightforwardly as possible, almost as if the primary rule were an absolute. Against that, the other side pleads for the greater expansion of relevance, for one rule conditional on others and for a wider series of salient considerations of morality and performance of duty. The processual form of the hearing thus emerges, in good measure, through the advocacy of one tendency against the other.

In good measure, also, this working of argumentation through opposed tendencies is advanced, in the hearing as a customary forum, through proverbs and other sayings of common wisdom, and not only statements of legal rules. To illustrate this, we offer the following list of some of the cited proverbs and sayings.

On the side of Leso, his family, and Pelonome, their candidate for succession:

> Chieftainship means to be born into it (*Bogosi bo a tsalelwa*).
>
> Let the chiefship go back to the owners.
>
> Trample not on someone else's rights in life (O *seka wa gataka ditshwanelo tsa mongwe mo botshelong*).
>
> On the side of Days, his family, and Tshito, their candidate for succession:
>
> The inheritance of the baboon is eaten by its baby (*Boswa jwa tshwene bo jewa ke tshwenyana*).

If the elephant crosses the river, it becomes a baby elephant (*tlou ga e tlola molapo e nna tlotswana*).

Who helps someone is his belongings (*mothusa motho ke mothodi wa tsa gagwe*).

Truth never needed eating an amulet (*boammuaruri ga bo jelwe pheko*).

The one who eats last is the chief (*moja morago ke kgosi*).

A person is never forced.

Conclusion

A chief is both born a chief and achieves chiefship. These are not conflicting but linked aspects of the same mode of succession, as this case has shown. Both aspects relate to the very nature of a village or chiefdom (its *tlholego*) and hence its destiny. Both are respected, yet achievement trumps genealogy – within limits. After all, Days *was* a descendant of Mapulane, the source of authenticity and 'nature'. He connected past and present both genealogically and in terms of his works in (re)building the village anew and expanding it. Tshito was his first-born son, and he also had the support of the majority in the village under the democratic dispensation of the new Botswana. His legitimacy was thus twofold: genealogical and democratic. He may have had the best personal qualities for the job, but this was never part of the public argument for his appointment. Chiefship was a 'traditional' status within 'customary' law, which followed customary rules.

To push our argument further, for purposes of wider comparison in legal anthropology, it is important to keep in mind another point about the quest for customary justice. It is the value of the nonlegal in a working misunderstanding between the outsider and the insider in that quest. Coming from the tribal capital to a distant, hinterland community with its claim to ethnic difference in customary law, the outsider as presiding judge has to suffer seemingly endless tale telling about the past – for him, archaic and arcane, and he pronounces it a waste of time. Not so for the insider: the fine memory work, or rather reworking and *reprise*, is precious (on such postcolonial memory work, see R. Werbner 1998). It richly redefines the past not as past but as current in the present and thus reclaimed as it is expected to be current in the future. The stories, being full of many implicit understandings of good governance and chiefly shepherding or failure to shepherd the village, are exemplary. This rehearsal is not merely for nomination, for saying who should succeed, but for how the village ought to be well kept under good chiefship. In other words, it is through such deliberation with far-reaching memory work that villagers sustain and advance their public sphere as a reality defined specifically by and for themselves. Thus is their *kgotla* itself upheld to be traditional, according to their customs, and fair.

6 What's in a name?

The struggle for identity in the statutory courts

Introduction

Driving towards Moremi village in May 2018, we saw that the road signs had changed: instead of Matolwane and Moremi, the signs now directed us towards Lesenepole and Moremi. As seen in Chapter 2, from the very first firing of the gun carved on a tree in Days' intended homestead in Matolwane, Lesenepole villagers had been fighting for dominance and control of the chiefship and village court. What added insult to injury, this chapter shows, was that Moremi village had not only retained its name but had prospered, whereas their name, so the Lesenepole people felt, had been obliterated. The hostility evident in that early arboreal desecration and in the driving away of Moremi's chief was evident throughout the dispute and in the occasional open confrontations it provoked over the ensuing 50 years.

In Chapter 2, we saw that a community as a collectivity can challenge policy decisions, especially those taken by tribal authorities. It can escalate its challenge even beyond the tribal courts themselves, reach to a national level, and win an ambiguous victory, in a process akin to judicial review. As this book argues throughout, however, the prohibitive costs of suing in statutory courts (see, for example, Chapters 7 and 8) are an important consideration in attempting to achieve justice through judicial review in state courts. This became evident in the struggle of Moremi ward people settled in Matolwane, along with the wards of Matoposane and Raphiri, to retain the name of their village and its court against manifestly false claims by the people of Lesenepole who were escalating their challenge to a national level. The current chapter pursues the politics of memory, articulated repeatedly, as we saw, in earlier cases in village customary courts and assemblies, as these politics moved to Botswana's national courts – the High Court and the Court of Appeal. Here, we look at the huge costs at stake that led to the mobilisation of villagers across town and country. We consider how, not only for rural dwellers but even for urban villagers settled in the capital of Botswana, this escalated mobilisation reflects on the huge value vested in name as identity and in chiefship associated with a court and rule over a whole community. To name a village was to affect its governance, through the identification and appointment of a chief; hence capturing the name, itself a shorthand for

DOI: 10.4324/9781003241881-6

communal loyalty with primordial sentiment, even 'inherent right', was politically highly significant for command of land and access to many other goods, benefits, and amenities.

This case was clearly a matter of 'lawfare', the use of law as a weapon of war, a term recently popularised by Colonel Charles Dunlap (2001), often used in its negative sense to imply the misuse of legal systems and principles against an 'enemy', by damaging or delegitimising them, tying up their time or winning a public relations victory.[1] The fight with Lesenepole over the name of Matolwane through the statutory courts was a classic case of negative warfare. We trace the phases of this fight up to the present.

Lawfare 1: The first High Court case and the fallacy of judicial anachronism

For those who had witnessed, as we had, the struggles over the unification of the four villages in 1972 – the passionate politics, the confrontations, the political-cum-judicial threats, the chicanery, the ultimate coercion by those in power – the judicial considerations of the first of several High Court and Court of Appeal hearings about the name of the village of Matolwane[2] seemed patently presentist[3] – that is, oddly out-of-touch with the reality as it then was in 1971, at the time Matolwane was founded. Marumo J., a Lobatse High Court judge, heard the first of the judicial appeals regarding the village name in 1997 (cf. High Court, Lobatse 2006 – the judgement was given in 2006). From the sophisticated perspective of another age, in a later case that took place after the Marumo judgement, an official in the Ministry of Local Government, Lands, and Housing defined the cause cited by the three villages, Matolwane, Raphiri and Moremi, against Lesenepole in terms of social scientific terms:

> This is a 'cultural relativism' argument. The appellants (i.e., the three villages) want to assert their right to self-determination. *A name defines a people.* They are a minority. Having determined that they have a cause, what are the elements of the cause? That they would be injured by a change of name, and a probability/likelihood [of a change of name] exists. A vote prejudices them. They are a minority by virtue of their totem. They are Pedi. The others (Lesenepole) are Tswana stock. That Tswanas want Lesenepole and they (the three villages) want Matolwane [the name of the hill] … because ancestral worship has a lot to do with going to the hills to pray for rain. They would

1 Comaroff and Comaroff express their legal scepticism about the increased use of 'lawfare' in postcolonial nations, which they argue serves as a mere smokescreen for the pervasive rise in violence and corruption, though they also admit that law can be a "weapon of the weak" (2007: 144, 145).

2 see the full list in the bibliography.

3 On judicial anachronism, see Nurse (2014), and on presentism, Lynn (2002).

> be prejudiced and the probability/likelihood of a change of name should a vote proceed is prejudice in itself.

But this is to anticipate the judgement. In the crucial case that defined all the succeeding cases, Mosebi, representing himself and 319 others from Lesenepole, sued the Attorney General, the Bamangwato Tribal Authority, and Kgosi Mokgobelelo (the Matolwane chief), arguing that the proper name for the village also known as Matolwane was Lesenepole and the change of name to Matolwane was 'improper, wrongful, undemocratic, null, and void'. Moreover, the applicants claimed that it was 'their inherent right as the indigenous residents of the village to decide the village's name' (item 1). Against that, the defendants argued that the change of name had followed 'consultation and agreement' between the four *kgotlas* that make up the village of Matolwane (item 3.2), following their 'request that the wards be combined into one village known as Matolwane' (item 3.3). It was a 'popular choice' of the people.

Marumo J. immersed himself, with an expressed sense of troubling bafflement, made all the more acute by his mistaken assumption that naming was a matter for a vote, simply a majority decision. As he says (4),

> Much of the evidence turned out to be unnecessary details (much of it disputed) relating to the community ties and history of some of the principal players ... previous occupations and uses of the land ... and other similar issues. To make matters worse it became apparent in the course of the evidence of many of the witnesses that the issues they were called to testify on were not within their personal knowledge but were information passed on to them by their forebears.

Sifting through the information 'has not been easy', he said. Although Marumo J. did not say so in his judgement, the case was seriously compromised by the total absence of residents from the other three villages. This became the subject of future litigation, as we shall see. For example, the applicants claimed that Matoposane and Raphiri had not been villages but only 'wards' of Lesenepole (5). This supported their claim that the name of the village was changed illegally.

The court went on a tour to inspect Matolwane, the ruins of the three villages, and Moremi village, noting that Matolwane/Lesenepole was much larger than Moremi (7/6).

On the naming, the court heard from a former Assistant Minister of Local Government, Lands, and Housing (9). He said (10) that 'four agencies would [normally] be involved in the establishing and naming of the village' – the Land Board, the Department of Tribal Administration (for identification and appointment of a chief), the local district council (for amenities), and the district administration authorities, representing the government in the districts. The broader significance of naming in association with land, chiefship, amenities, such as a school, and district administration was authoritatively established in court, having already been constituted in practice.

According to Marumo J.'s judgement, the official 'acknowledged' (11) that in 1990 – note that this was well *after* Matolwane had been established, in 1972:

> there was a dispute between its inhabitants concerning both the names of the village and of the primary school. In his official capacity, he addressed *kgotla* meetings in the area on the subject. He says the matter was eventually resolved on the basis that the village would be called Matolwane and the school would be called Lesenepole Primary School.

In an affidavit prepared by the three villages to a later case, this narrative is located in real time.[4] It opens with the following statement:

> The people of the village of Moremi and the people of Matoposane, when they asked to have a school for each of them, were told that it would be quicker if they came together so it could be built as one, since their number would be suitable for a school to include up to standard VII. This was said by the MP Mr. A.M. Dambe and Councillor Mr. Tsenolo Sekwati in 1967–1968. …
>
> [somewhat later] After the meeting in Maunatlala, Kgosi Ofentse Bathobakae of Raphiri village came to ask us to come into the gathering together (*kopana*) of Moremi and Matoposane. Kgosi Letshositse Pipedi of Lesenepole [also] asked to join the coming-together and it was agreed and they called the councillor, and they met at Batlang Motshabi in Matoposane, and even at Kgosi (Leso) Mapulane, and all the chiefs were there, even their uncles (*borrangwane*) and the councillor. They were told that Kgosi Leapetswe [the tribal authority in Serowe] said that the villages will resettle after a well (borehole) has been dug. This was said by the councillor, T. Sekwati in 1968.
>
> [Not long after this] the Ipelegeng [relief work] programme came and it was said that the duties should be performed where they can benefit the people and the government. It was agreed that the duties should go on in the place of their coming-together under the little hill of Matolwane at Kgosi Motsabe in Matoposane. It was agreed that the village would be named according to one of the four names of the villages which came together, being Moremi, Matoposane, Raphiri, and Lesenepole. Two names were suggested, being Matolwane after the hill which was there, and Boipopo, being because the villages came together. And they agreed to the name of Matolwane, to be the one for the four villages that came together. It was agreed that the villagers should build separately and it was indicated how (in wards).

4 This document is titled 'FACT SHEET ON THE HISTORY OF THE MATOLWANE DISPUTE'.

This division into wards meant a division not only in residence but a separation in areas of fields; hence to rename the whole village after one part, Leselepole, would be to over-ride that separation, eventually subject to the land board, but with a claim to access to the land of the whole village, rightfully under the Leselepole chief and his court. The later assertion by the Leselepole people was that they were the rightful owners of the village as a whole: hence it had to have their name.

The affidavit then goes on to report on the threatening of Days with the gun carved on the tree and his return to Moremi 'ruins' followed by Leso, who moved back for lack of water. Hence, the affidavit continues:

> The school started working in Matolwane in 1971, even the well was dug, and the school was officially opened in 1979. *A long time after the official opening of the school* Basenepole complained about the name that they don't know Matolwane but they themselves know Lesenepole, and even the chieftaincy, they know Lesenepole rules and they don't know Tsotego Rebamu [of Moremi village], who was left by Kgosi Leso in that village [Matolwane] where he comes from.
>
> (emphasis added).

Complaining about the name meant for Lesenepole people complaining against submission to someone who was not their own known chief, and to strangers' rules. At this point, the non-cooperation by the people of Lesenepole was clearly evident:

> The people of Lesenepole totally refused the programme of chieftaincy of the village to be implemented and it ended up showing that, can't we be given someone to come and rule in the village, since the village cannot stay without a chief? In 1982 the customary court was built in Matolwane and it failed because no-one from the village was appointed to be the chief. It failed because of the backtracking of Lesenepole and that is when Kgosi Mokgadi [of Serowe] investigated and sent Kgosi Kebobatile Bareki to come and rule in Matolwane from 1982 to 1989.

The affidavit then mentions the intervention of the [deputy] Minister of Local Government and Lands, concluding by requesting that the name of the school be given in memory of Lesenepole. As we saw in the Marumo J. case, this was in 1990. The affidavit then continues with a narrative of Lesenepole violence and intransigence:

> After the death of Kgosi Kgobatile Bareki, the village failed to come together to seek a chief again and Kgosi Gabolekane Mogobelelo was sent [by Serowe] to rule. Basenepole people tore apart (*gagautlha*, i.e., criticised strongly) Kgosi Sediegeng Kgamane [the Serowe tribal authority] when he came to install Rre Kgosi Mokgobelela in the Matolwane court (*kgotla*). They told

> him to go back with his luggage since they have their own chief and they don't know who can sue them. The village is theirs. Rre Gaothobogwe Mosebe [of Lesenepole, the named plaintiff in the 2006 Marumo High Court case judgement] said unpleasant words in the *kgotla* before Kgosi Sediegeng Kgamani and his delegates, saying that he himself cannot bear children, he does not come like a cowpat (*sebi*) [?]. Basenepole [people of Lesenepole] continued, and took down all the road signs to the village. The matter led to the investigations by the police, and it was criticised (*kgalemelwa*) by Kgosi Kgamane and the delegates of the Serowe chieftaincy, all 14 of them.

We see here the repeated tendency of people from Lesenepole to use insults and take illegal action to defend their identity, their ownership of the village, and the precedence of their court and chief. These aggressive tactics, as we shall see, have continued right up to the present. The key point, however, which is made evident in the affidavit is that the question of the name came up on several occasions, but all these occasions were conflated into one in the court hearing. This becomes evident in the second part of Marumo J.'s ruling when arguably he commits the *fallacy of presentism* or *judicial anachronism* by passing what may be termed an 'anachronistic judgement'.

In Section 12 of the judgement, the learned judge begins by stating that the 1990 evidence created 'considerable doubt in my mind that the name of the village in issue, either as Matolwane or Lesenepole, was done procedurally'. Indeed, 'at no stage throughout the evolution of this dispute was the issue of the village name ever put to *democratic vote*'. 'It seems fairly obvious', he says, 'that it is not easy to ascertain the will of an entire population of a sizeable settlement on an emotive and potentially divisive issue such as that present without putting it to a vote'.

Many Batswana are great believers in procedure (*tsamaiso*). In this case, however, the application by the Honourable Justice, *post-hoc*, of voting as a procedure to achieve equity would appear to have been misplaced. This is because, as we saw, the original unification of the village was a fraught process initiated from above, and in order to secure it, the unity and equality of the four villages was promised by the tribal authorities in Serowe, although, even then, Lesenepole was known to be larger than Matoposane or Raphiri, while Leso Maifala of Moremi was recognised as genealogically the senior agnate among all Tswapong, and was expected to be the first chief. The way towards village unification at that time (circa 1970) proceeded by first consulting the four chiefs and their senior advisors, and later bringing the decision to be ratified in public *kgotla* assemblies. *This was the accepted procedure at the time.* The unification *would not have gone ahead* had the three other villages believed they were merely being asked to join Lesenepole. Indeed, the land on which the unified village was to be built belonged to Matoposane. The question is whether – almost 40 years after Matolwane village had been established, with a whole new generation born into the village, its identity could be contested by one village faction? The issue is not simply a matter of a struggle for dominance within a village and control of its resources, its court and chiefship, but of the very identity of the village itself, and thus of its inhabitants. Arguably, a vote could not rectify that.

Notwithstanding the fact that the signage on roads leading to the village had for many years directed travellers to 'Matolwane', that most identity cards noted the bearer as born in Matolwane, or that the customary court was officially named Matolwane, the judge claimed that the government had never 'made any decisions regarding the names of the settlements' (15). Hence, his final verdict to call for a vote within 90 days, noting (18) this had been a 'remarkably successful' strategy for settling hereditary chief disputes (clearly quite a different issue).

Lawfare 2 and 3: Appealing the verdict and the prohibitive cost of litigation

The judgement hit the headlines in Botswana, with the case of the 'nameless village' raised by Mmegi newspaper in May 2006. The Minister of Local Government at the time, Margaret Nasha, assured the villagers that services would be delivered as usual (Gaotlhobogwe 2006).

The Marumo J. case was followed by an initial appeal in the High Court in Lobatse before Newman J., six weeks later. The applicants, representatives of three villages (Raphiri, Matoposane and Moremi wards), wished to 'rescind' the judgement of Marumo J. and 'stay' the proposed vote for the village name on the grounds that the judgement was 'improper, unprocedural and inadequate' (5); above all, the appeal argued, they had not been 'parties' to the earlier case and 'only heard about the order of Marumo J. through radio broadcasts in early May 2006' (6). The judge accepted that the applicants had acted as promptly as possible (7). He thus granted, ***subject to acceptable affidavits being presented***, that the three villages had 'a real and substantial interest' in the matter and had not been party to the earlier judgement – hence the argument raised by the defendants of *res judicata* (i.e., the principle that a cause of action may not be relitigated once it has been judged) did not apply (9) and the plaintiffs had indeed been 'deprived of an opportunity to be heard [and thus] cannot now be bound by that decision' (11). In support of his judgement, the learned judge cited a range of precedents from Botswana and South Africa.

Here was an opportunity for the Matolwane residents to challenge the Marumo J. judgement. It was not, however, taken up – for lack of funds, we were told, although no explicit deadline for depositing the affidavits appears to have been given by Newman J. By July 2015, however, nine years later, the government had decided to hold a vote and a case was heard in Lobatse High Court on voting procedures. In it, the Lesenepole attorney argued that 'the applicants had previously failed to challenge the court order that was issued in 2006 by Judge Moatlhodi Marumo, stating that a name would be chosen through a voting process' (Mokwapi 2015, cited in Mmegi newspaper). The vote was duly held later in 2015, and was won by Lesenepole. The Matolwane people complained that Lesenepole had brought in people to vote from all the surrounding villagers to augment their numbers. In a letter by their legal team, challenging the outcome, the lawyers point out (item 8):

> We are also instructed that the position on the ground has always been that residents of Lesenepole village are more in number than the combined number of residents of Raphiri, Moremi, and Matoposane villages. In this way, by ordering that the determination of the name of the combined village be put to a vote, the order of 28 April 2006 effectively presented our clients with a *fait accompli*. The elections were lost even before they started.
>
> (Ramalepha Attorneys, 11 August 2015, stamped by Attorney General Chambers and Ministry of Local Government on 12 August 2015)

Despite this challenge, by 2016, driving to Moremi village, we found that the signs to Matolwane had been replaced by signs to Lesenepole on the main Palapye–Selibe Pikwe road. By this point, too, the people of Matolwane were mobilising to challenge the decision yet again in the High Court, this time with funding contributed by all the villagers.

Lawfare 4: Challenging Lesenepole in the High Court

We arrived in Botswana on 1 May 2017, just in time for a fund-raising meeting in Gaborone before the court case, due to take place at the High Court in Lobatse two days later. What was noticeable was that the men and women gathered together that day were all second-, third- and even fourth-generation descendants of the original founders of Matolwane, coming from all three villages.

The person negotiating with the advocate and lawyers, Molefhe Gabanakgosi, had been a youth when we lived on his grandfather's homestead in 1973, and was now a man in his sixties, a respected elder and a sophisticated man-about-town. Over the years, he had been our research assistant, and continues to be our good friend. We acknowledge our great debt to his knowledge, understanding, and devotion to the progress of our study, in which he and his wife also took leading parts in Moremi and Gaborone videos (R. Werbner 2005, 2007, 2015). We recognise also his reasonable influence on our account, and we have taken considerable care to document the matters in which he was an interested party, and to provide the court records, given here in detail, as substantial evidence for our own arguments.

The meeting took place in a house quite near his house in Gaborone West. When we arrived, just before 3 pm, there was no-one there, except the owner. Later, a few people trickled in, including the secretary of the fund-raising committee. They were expecting 50 people, we were told, but very few came. Those assembled had little to contribute – we contributed 1500 pula on behalf of Molefhe and altogether about 3200 pula were collected on that occasion. A man arrived in Gaborone from Matolwane bearing 33,000 pula collected there, and someone promised 30,000 to be delivered on 14 May.

The cost of the cases so far had been astronomical, over 200,000 pula, Molefhe said, in total close to 300,000 pula (some £20–25,000). Now they were owing about 75,000 pula just to the advocate, Pilane, but there were also sums owed to the lawyers' office. Pilane had said he would not appear at court without the money being there.

According to Molefhe, after the Marumo J. case, there had been two cases in Francistown, at the High Court, the records of which are missing mysteriously, with only the judgements available. In the end, the decision was to have an entirely new case with none of the original witnesses, etc. Instead, they were presenting affidavits from the three ward heads including from Ikalafeng, the senior agnate and *kgosana* in Moremi ward. This time, they were suing the Ministry, the Attorney General, and Lesenepole. The tribal authority was not disputing the three village wards' right to reclaim the name of Matolwane. The District Council was not involved and Sekwati, the original councillor who had negotiated the unification, was, according to Molefhe, never mentioned.

During the meeting, as the enormity of the task of collecting the money became apparent, participants appeared very downhearted. They passed around the accounts presented by the lawyer. Molefhe said fund-raising had got harder in Gaborone because people had started rumours of the money being pocketed, given the mounting costs. Was it all worth it?

When we asked those present why they were doing it, given the expenses, they said it was because of 'identity'; they could not afford to lose their identity. They all agreed on this. Molefhe told me that Moremi's chief was supporting them one hundred per cent but the trouble was, people at Moremi were not interested and simply told them – why don't you just move back here?! Hence, they wouldn't contribute to the costs of the case. Why indeed did they stay in Matolwane? Molefhe said it was because people had 'invested' there. He himself was thinking of building, but he hadn't yet decided if to build at Matolwane or Moremi.

As the legal costs mounted, the price of 'identity' became almost insurmountable. But as Molefhe said, optimistically, 'we are almost there'. He believed the village would win and the other side would then need to pay the legal costs. It was a big gamble because, if they lost, they might be told to bear the defendants' legal costs.

At the High Court in Lobatse, 3 May 2017

We went with Molefhe and Ikalafeng, the head of Moremi ward at Matolwane, to Lobatse. The case was set to start at 9 am but in the event, it was left last, and started just after 11 am. Ikalafeng had arrived from Matolwane the previous day as had the *kgosana* (ward head) of Matoposane ward. Ikalafeng had first worked in the mines in South Africa before working in construction in Gaborone for many years.

Sydney Pilane, the advocate hired by the village's lawyers, opened the proceedings. He argued that, in the 1997 case before Marumo J. brought by Lesenepole, the other residents of Matolwane were not 'cited', nor did they appear in the

Figure 6.1 Litigants from Matolwane at the Lobatse High Court.

judgement, nor were they notified in any way. He also argued that the decision of the Ministry to change the name was consequent to the Marumo J. judgement in favour of Lesenepole. The main argument presented by Lesenepole was that they were 'resident' of a place and were entitled as residents to determine the name of the place. But, Pilane argued, by the same token, the other villagers too were also resident with a similar entitlement.

Citing cases in Nigeria, the UK and South Africa, including English and Dutch-Roman law, Pilane argued that as a result of not citing the relevant party the original Marumo J. case was null and void. Because it was null, it was also not possible for the applicants (Matolwane) to be accused of 'delay' (which apparently was one argument of the respondents). There were four respondents – the Ministry, the Attorney General (represented by two lawyers) and Lesenepole (represented by a young man). One defendant was absent.

The case was replete with legal technicalities. The lawyers from the attorney general's office tried to argue, first, that you could not move from one high court judge to another, you had to go from a high court judge to the court of appeal. Second, that you couldn't challenge government to change or revoke a decision. Third, submission of an affidavit asked for in earlier cases had been delayed. The lawyer for Lesenepole tried to show, with numerous individual examples, that people were aware of the 2006 Marumo J. case and the name change, that some were in a list that challenged it in 2006 before Newman J. (where, as we saw, the judge had granted possible rescindment but the Matolwane people hadn't managed to follow through; they did not at the time have the money and were not mobilised yet, so ultimately the Marumo J. decision stood). He also showed that, of the three *kgosana* from Matolwane, one (from Raphiri) had been witness in the Marumo case and, further, that the decision was 'public' and had even been announced on the radio. The young advocate argued against granting costs for a case in June 2016 (on voting procedures) which Pilane had argued should have involved costs.

The case had been brought as an entirely 'new' case since one of the judges had decreed that it couldn't be reopened. The fact that some of the applicants had appeared in earlier cases on lists of appellants could have implied that the case wasn't new.

In his response Pilane dismissed the arguments. With regard to the attorney general's arguments, he first said that courts were constantly telling government to change decisions. He also explained, citing different laws, that it was right to move sideways to another high court judge, and that Marumo J. had in the meanwhile died, otherwise they could go back to him.

Regarding the arguments of the Lesenepole lawyer he said, first, that all the individual names he cited were not in the heads of arguments submitted or he might have been able to look up some of them. In any case, those appearing as witnesses in the original case were appearing in their individual capacity, had known nothing in advance, were not cited or notified, and were surprised to hear what was decided. He dismissed the argument that not everyone appeared among the applicants and thus the original judgement could not be nullified, saying that what was to be nullified was the judgement, not this or that individual. In so far as the affidavit had been delayed and not met the deadline for submission, Pilane argued that since the court had not dismissed it, apparently according to rule 33, it had *de facto* been accepted. He also argued again for granting the legal costs of the 2016 case.

During the debate, Judge Tebogo Tau mostly took notes at great speed but now and then intervened to repeat arguments, showing that she was following the points made by the advocate.

There were about 15 people from Matolwane and a somewhat smaller number from Lesenepole in the courtroom's audience. They sat patiently through the whole case which went on for three hours, until almost 2 pm. Afterwards, they gathered outside to talk to the lawyers. Molefhe was exultant – he said that Pilane was 'brilliant' and that he had easily rebutted the young (and he thought cheap) lawyer for Lesenepole. They, Lesenepole, were unhappy and humiliated, he said.

Altogether, the various cases so far had cost 300,000 pula and the committee still owed the lawyers 60,000. They had tried to get legal aid but had been refused, and had even gone to Ditshwanelo, the human rights organisation. They had tried to suggest splitting the village into two as a solution but to no avail. Molefhe had managed to collect about 70,000 pula before the case, with the promise of 33,000 from their 'benefactor' who could only pay up on 14 May. There was 5,000 pula remaining but nevertheless Pilane had agreed to come to court.

Advocate Pilane argued to us that so far the case hadn't raised any issues of natural justice, the fact that villagers had been forced to unite. He said, if they win the case, they will go to court again and this time those issues will be raised. But

Molefhe believed optimistically that with victory – after the judgement is delivered at the end of July – they can sort everything out, perhaps without another court case.

According to Pilane, Lesenepole had been forced at the time (in 1970) to move, threatened, their school shifted and their borehole stopped. They did not have a permanent spring like Moremi. So they moved to Matolwane reluctantly. What motivated them in the case, Molefhe thought, was a shortage of land. They were only given land by Moremi and Matoposane. Two of their main leaders were living at Lethakane as well as a man, originally from Moremi, who generations back was appointed by Sinwedi, an earlier Moremi chief from the ancestral ruling ward, or perhaps someone else, to look after the spring/borehole at Lesenepole. Anyway, the point was that they had connections in high places, claimed Molefhe. Slumber Tsogwane, Minister of Local Government and Rural Development at the time, was allegedly a Lesenepole friend, and had refused the Matolwane approaches to him. Molefhe said the chiefs in Serowe were entirely on their (Matolwane) side.

We waited many months for the judgement to be delivered. When it finally was delivered by the learned judge, it was simply to say that it was not possible for her, a high court judge, to make the decision already made by another high court judge, so the case would have to be taken by the court of appeal.

Here, the case can be considered in terms of the politics of memory and the emotion invested in the past. The intensely aroused emotion invested in the village name is clearly reflected in the money mobilised, even though the court case was technical and arcane, as is usual in statutory courts, apparently considered in deliberation free of any human emotion.

As a passionate and interested party, Molefhe insisted that Lesenepole was 'not really a village and had never been one'. It was fragmented with no real chiefly lineage, and was not predominantly Tswapong. Many are MaZezuru (in origin from Zimbabwe), he said. Many lived mainly in cattle posts, away from a village residence, and only slowly drifted into village residences at Matolwane. His cousin living in Matolwane said that now they were even pushing their interest in village ownership by claiming to own the land around Moremi lodge, an absurdity given the long historical connection of the spring with Moremi village. This cousin, very against the name change to Lesenepole, strongly urged on the battle to restore the name of Matolwane.

Lawfare 5: Confrontations

A series of confrontations between Matolwane and Lesenepole, especially over village resources and public occasions, also took place outside the court. One such confrontation arose over 'cluster fencing'. In a national policy decision, the Ministry of Agriculture wished to fence the combined fields of villages to prevent cattle invasions. Matolwane villagers, however, who objected to being fenced together with Lesenepole, were suspicious that this would be a prelude to land-grabbing. In a meeting that took place towards the end of May 2017, attended by Moremi village chief and two *kgosanas*, the chief told the gathering that the matter was straightforward – Moremi, Matoposane, and Raphiri wards in Matolwane wanted their fields to be part of Moremi village for cluster fencing purposes; Lesenepole could fence their part.

As it turned out, matters were a little more complicated. The village chief told us of a meeting due to take place later that day which would be chaired by the Agricultural Officer (AO). We arrived early, at 8 am, and had a chat with the AO. He claimed that, although the Land Board controlled land allocation, the chiefs still had to authorise these claims, so they were still important actors. He implied initially that the meeting would be in his office with four chiefs (Lesenepole, Matoposane, Raphiri, and Moremi) so we couldn't attend. In the upshot, the meeting was quite large, with about 50 persons present. First, there was the cluster committee of about eight, as far as we could tell mainly from Lesenepole, of whom many were women, including the secretary. The Raphiri chief did not attend but the Matoposane woman *kgosana* and Ikalafeng, the *kgosana* of Moremi ward, were there, as well as Kgosi Tshito, Moremi village chief. In addition, there were large numbers from Moremi.

At the beginning of the meeting there was a discussion about whether we should be allowed to attend. A couple of men from Lesenepole objected, and then a man from Moremi pointed out that it was not a secret meeting. Moremi village chief defended us being there, saying we had a permit from the Ministry of Presidential Affairs, and we were with him. After quite a long discussion, we were allowed to remain.

The Agricultural Officer explained that he had received two letters. One, a joint letter from Moremi village chief, Tshito Days, and the *kgosana* ward chiefs of Matolwane, claiming their fields should be in Moremi. The second letter came from Serowe (unspecified location), saying that the current cluster committee's constitution was fine, but the committee had no 'legal force' (in English) before it was ratified/recognised (possibly by the Land Board). It emerged that originally this had been a constitution for Matolwane and the name had been changed unilaterally to Lesenepole without consulting anyone.

The secretary of the committee explained that originally the cluster fencing was meant to include Moremi village but they were told not to include Moremi. The Lesenepole argument was that the fields were 'mixed' (*thakathakano*) and thus it would be impossible to demarcate between them. Second, one should think of the fencing only in terms of protection of the fields from animals and wildlife, not as a 'boundary'. Moremi village chief said that they 'respect' those people from Lesenepole who were ploughing in Moremi area but that should not stop the demarcation.

A Moremi ward villager from Matolwane pointed out that originally the constitution was called Matolwane and there had been a change of names. But in any case, from here to there it is Moremi, there is no mix-up. Oabile, the *kgosana* of Matoposane, said that when Lesenepole cluster committee members changed the constitution, it meant they wanted to fence their own lands, not Matoposane and Moremi. A villager from Moremi/Matolwane said that when they first made the (original) fence, with the agreement of chiefs who are no longer here, it followed a 1937 map. This was a map used by the electoral commission, which he had worked on.

The committee secretary said she was confused, she thought Lesenepole included Matoposane and Moremi wards. Another man from Lesenepole said – let us protect our fields (*sireletsa*) but not make the boundaries. The land is controlled by the government, not as before when it was said to be controlled by the chiefs. I can now build in Malaka (another village to the west of Moremi). The agricultural officer said they should start from the Maunatlala old road but each side would have to have their own committee. The secretary of the Lesenepole cluster committee said they had initially included Moremi and she asked where do Moremi fields start?

The village chief of Moremi, Tshito Days, responded that you are talking about a constitution that does not include me (i.e., Moremi village). The Lesenepole people said they included Moremi, there are two Moremis, aren't there? Another person said he was disappointed that a person can call himself a person of Moremi even though they are from Lesenepole. Tshito said that we have our own management plan (constitution)

The argument went on in this vein and, in fact, the matter was never settled. Confrontations between the two sides were endemic. We witnessed a violent confrontation which occurred during the Independence Day celebrations. The Lesenepole villagers tried (and failed) to 'capture' the roving torch of Independence from the Acting Chief in the main Matolwane *kgotla*. They also stole the meat intended for the assembled dignitaries, and only with some difficulty was the celebration feast recovered from the grab. Following on from the torch, the Lesenepole women's choir invaded the *kgotla* at Moremi, uninvited. Such confrontations occurred repeatedly, so much so that a Mmegi article in 2010 reported that the two sides never socialised; at *kgotla* meetings 'they sit opposite each other' (Modikwa 2010).

Lawfare 6: Victory for Lesenepole in the Court of Appeal

The verdict of the final challenge at the Court of Appeal on 26 October 2018, could hardly have come as a surprise. Summing up the events and court proceedings from 1997 onwards, the court of appeal judgement cited the fact that Nyamazabo J.'s rejection of Newman J.'s allowance for rescission was never taken by the three villages until 2013 (19). Tau's judgement in favour of Lesenepole cited (31), among other things, that the chief from Raphiri village, had been a witness in the Marumo J. case. The judgement added a key point not raised previously that this had always been a communal rather than an individual dispute, which required only representatives of the three villages to be informed. Two out of three had been informed early on (one bore witness and two had been called by the Palapye sub-chief in 2001). In other words, the judge concurred with the Marumo J. judgement. Like its predecessors in the High Court, the Court of

Appeal was unsympathetic to the villages' lack of funds and did not accept the legitimacy of delays. It dismissed the appeal 'with costs'.

Tlholego and dignity: the politics of identity

Having lost in the final Court of Appeal, leaders of the three village of Matolwane decided to abandon the courts, escalate the complaint, and pursue a political struggle. On 15 November 2018, they wrote a letter to the Minister of Local Government and Rural Development, Botlogile M. Tshireletso, in Gaborone. Having summarised the history of the dispute, the letter, written in English, sets out poignantly the case for keeping the name of Matolwane:

> We have always wanted it to be known that we cannot afford to lose our identity. Matolwane is our birth right and even generations to come will exist as the community of Matolwane. … It is highly unlikely that we will live harmoniously with residents of Lesenepole as we believe their numbers, which is what was used to decide the name of the village, will remain a curse to us even though we know factually our village is Matolwane. …Voting … being applied in a matter of cultural and identity significance will leave a permanent negative result as the communities will continue to be split rather than live in peace with one another. It is not right for voting/elections to have such an impact on a human being as denying their identity and cultural worth.

The letter was signed by the *kgosanas* of the three Matolwane wards. They were planning to continue their battle, during the period leading to and after the 2019 elections.

Conclusion

Our account of the struggle for *tlholego* and dignity, described in the first half of this book, represents an extended case study of events taking place over 50 years, and more. During this period, the factional politics of a small village in eastern Botswana were shown to lead villagers first to attempts to win justice in the tribal courts and then, one and even two generations later, through the statutory courts. In both kinds of attempt, the entanglement of law and politics made the possibility of winning a fair and equitable court resolution of the dispute almost impossible, we have seen. At one point, crucial decisions were made by fiat by powerful tribal rulers. Later on, they were made by powerful judges who ignored the earlier circumstances. This meant that for much of the time, villagers in Matolwane could only resist and manoeuvre, not win encounters conclusively. Apparently conclusive hearings turned indecisive or dubious, and the outcome was an escalation of conflict and contention, with an attempt to seek redress at a national level. By contrast, during the same period Moremi village has prospered beyond the imagination of those who early on had resisted the powerful forces of Ngwato chiefs and central government.

Part II

Legal subjectivities, ethics, and pluralism

7 Divorce as process, Botswana style

Customary courts, gender activism, and legal pluralism in historical perspective

Divorce, gender activism, and property settlement in Botswana

According to a well-known Tswana saying, *O tsaa hempe le borokgwe fela*, whoever initiates a divorce will be sent away with 'only their shirt and trousers'. As recently as 2012, when we discussed a case of marital conflict in Moremi village with a Botswana High Court judge, he invoked this saying. It implied that nothing much had changed in the past 50 years; that in Botswana's customary courts, adultery by a husband is not regarded as justifiable grounds for divorce (Werbner 2018b). If true, this would also mean that in apparent disregard of the new amendments to the (statutory) marriage law,[1] Tswana customary law would permit polygamy, although it is not practised nowadays. A 1988 report commissioned by the Botswana Women Affairs' Department, '*Laws affecting the status of women in Botswana*' (henceforth WAD 1988), based on a nationwide survey jointly prepared by several distinguished members of the Law Department at the University of Botswana, found that

> women are reluctant to institute divorce proceedings, and keep hoping that the husband will return. Another deterrent is the fact that ... most customary courts penalise the spouse who institutes divorce proceedings by giving him or her a less favourable property settlement.
>
> (WAD 1988: 69)

Furthermore, citing Isaac Schapera and Simon Roberts, the report argues that

> What a woman is entitled to following a divorce under Customary Law is as uncertain as her rights during marriage, and has been said to depend on whether or not she is responsible for the break-up of the marriage. The general rule appears to be that the party at fault is penalised by being deprived of

1 See the Abolition of Marital Power Act 2004, 2005, and the Matrimonial Causes Act 1973, Amended 2008.

DOI: 10.4324/9781003241881-7

> property (Schapera 1938; Roberts 1970). … women were often 'sent back' [only] with their separate cattle (if they had any) and household utensils, especially where they were at fault.
>
> (ibid.: 71)

This chapter aims to unravel the complex negotiations surrounding property settlements and custody in cases of divorce in customary courts today in the light of this earlier legacy of penalising divorce initiators. It argues that attempts to get the *other* party to institute divorce proceedings can entangle women in particular in lengthy manoeuvrings and sometimes frustrate the aim of achieving a divorce. Repeated court hearings can last for years, as we show later in some detail in extended cases. At the same time, in Botswana's statutory courts today, an equal division of property *irrespective of the causes of marital breakdown*, has become established practice.

This raises a general question, given a widely accepted premise. The premise is that customary law is to be grasped as 'living law', that is, responsive to changing circumstances, as argued most recently for Southern Africa by Fombad (2004: 183, 191) and Button et al. (2016: 301; see also Himonga et al. 2015). What needs to be asked is this: is such legal responsiveness to be constructed in historical terms, as a historical *trajectory*? A different option may be simply to argue that customary law is situational – that is, sensitive to particular circumstances in each case, while remaining constant. Against that, we make the point elsewhere, following Schapera (1970), that the existence of a historical trajectory in customary law stems from the 'possibility that customary court decisions are embedded in considerations of equity that also inform wider ideological, critical movements, and processes of judicial innovation and legal reform' (Werbner 2014: 485; see also Griffiths 1997). In the present chapter, we aim to show that customary laws regarding property settlement in divorce have indeed changed, gradually becoming responsive to notions of equity in women's rights in marriage, in response to a 'wider ideological, critical movement', despite the fact that this is not always explicitly acknowledged by customary chiefs or headmen presiding over customary courts.

Three intertwined issues raised here – first, the tendency of women initiating divorce in court to be penalised in the subsequent property settlement, often linked to, secondly, the ambiguity of their status as wives, and, thirdly, the reluctance of customary courts to acknowledge that relationships have broken down irretrievably – have been the basis for much feminist legal activism and progressive reforms of the law in Botswana. In this chapter, we attempt to show that these legal reforms, while in many ways enhancing the status of married women, often come at a price or lead to new anomalies and conundrums.

Marriage as process

Social anthropologists discussing marriage in Botswana, as in most of southern Africa, have stressed that marriage is a 'process' gradually completed over many years during which time the *bogadi*, the bride wealth payments, are transferred from wife-receivers to wife-givers. The processual nature of marriage, it is argued, makes the very existence of a marriage often highly ambiguous (Comaroff 1980; Comaroff and Roberts 1981). In these early accounts, virtually no stress was placed on the legal and symbolic significance of the *wedding*, the public ceremonial ritual feast known as *nyalo*, *gorosa*, or *dikobo* (blankets). In this ceremony, as celebrated by Tswapong villagers in Moremi and its vicinity in Botswana's Central District, who are the subjects of the present chapter, the groom is first escorted to the bride's compound by a large entourage of his kinsmen and women, bearing gifts, blankets, and cattle. These are displayed, before the united couple is ultimately moved back, amidst ululations, in the opposite direction, to the groom's compound, following feasting, ritual blessing, and public speeches. The omission of the wedding from these early analyses is significant, and we return to it below.[2]

Many conjugal disputes brought to customary courts in Botswana, as both Comaroff and Roberts (1981) and Griffiths (1997) show, involve long-term relationships with a *nyatsi*, 'concubine'. These relationships, while to all intents and purposes *de facto* marriages, often involving shared children and joint property, are not contracted formally, consecrated either by bride wealth or by a ceremonial ritual event, and this informality often becomes evident when and if the couple separate (ibid.).

A second feature associated with marital disputes that is repeatedly raised by socio-legal scholars relates to the advice commonly given by customary court judges for the couple to 'return' to the marriage and attempt to live harmoniously. As Griffiths (1997) says,

> the customary court ruling, that both parties should go and 'live together in peace and harmony' is very common in such disputes. It is something of a set text along the lines of a preordained homily. The social pressures of the *kgotla* [customary court] are mobilised, but at the end of the day it is left to the parties themselves to make the relationship work.
>
> (1997: 141)

Legal domains

In Botswana, customary courts are arranged in a hierarchy, from lower courts of record located in select villages to recognised courts of appeal above them, culminating in the Court of Appeal of the whole tribe, based at the tribal capital. Beyond that, appeals can be made to the national Customary Court of Appeal, of which there are currently two in Botswana (one in the north, the other in the south). From these, appeals are to Botswana's High Court. The court of Moremi

2 Recent studies, by contrast, have focused almost exclusively on the Tswana wedding (see for example van Dijk (2017), Solway (2016), and other contributors to the special issue of *Anthropology Southern Africa* 2016-17).

village, where many of the cases discussed in this chapter were heard, is under the Ngwato tribal authority. This court only became a court of record in 2009. Above it, appeal courts have been based, variably, in Matolwane, Palapye, and later Maunatlala, with the tribal Court of Appeal located in Serowe, the tribal capital. Under village courts of record are more informal wards and family moots in which many family disputes are initially heard, and often settled. Throughout the tribal customary court system, hearings are free and are held without lawyers. The customary court system in Botswana is at present a robust institution, with hundreds of courts of record in which thousands of cases are heard every year (see Fombad 2004).

Athalia Molokomme (1991) and Anne Griffiths (1997) both show the mutual influence of different legal domains in Botswana, with state legislation later gradually adopted in customary courts, whereas magistrate's courts often take on the mediatory role normally assumed by customary courts or, alternatively, often turn to customary courts to settle the marital household's familial disputes or division of property. Molokomme also contends that despite attempts to guard against 'forum shopping', women do endeavour to maximise their chances of redress by moving from one legal forum to another.[3] She makes the point, in relation to Roman-Dutch law, that 'the Botswana state legal system has become a true hybrid of what were traditionally referred to as civilian legal systems on the one hand and common law legal systems on the other'(1990: 263).

Molokomme was, from the start, one of the leading legal feminist activists in Botswana, first from her position as lecturer in the Law Department at the University of Botswana, and then as the first director of Emang Basadi, the women's association founded in 1986 and based in the capital.[4] The organisation's lobbying helped lead to the 'Abolition of Marital Power Act 34' of 2004, which aimed to give equal powers to spouses married in a (civil) community of property (all customary marriages are deemed by default to be in community of property, but the law did not apply to them). The Act also allowed for equality in initiating divorce, and an equal division of marital joint property.[5]

Emang Basadi campaigned widely, nationwide, for women to enter civil marriages, solemnised and registered at the District Commissioner's Office, and it advised women to marry outside of community of property, while acknowledging

3 On this tendency among women seeking divorce in Malawi see Johnson (2018: 59-60), where court hierarchies are far more complex and intersecting. Nonetheless, the tendency for magistrates to refer back cases to village courts has its parallel in Malawi. There are no Victim Support Units in Botswana villages and violence is not necessarily the main issue in divorce cases.

4 For some years she was Botswana's Attorney General, after periods in SADC and as a High Court judge. Most recently (2018) she has been Ambassador and Permanent Representative of Botswana to the UN in Geneva.

5 On this very progressive Act in detail see Quansah (2005). The author points out that there was opposition to the Act evident in the debate in Parliament where some members of Parliament argued it was out of step with Tswana tradition. So too, there were objections in the House of Chiefs, as reported in the local Mmegi newspaper at the time (Piet 2005).

that wives could possibly suffer from this arrangement, since husbands were likely to accumulate more property than their spouses over their lifetime. As early as 1973, the Matrimonial Causes Act, amended 2008, which emulated UK law, stated that no matrimonial offence need be proven in cases of civil divorces. The sole ground for divorce was deemed to be the irretrievable breakdown of the marriage. This law did not, however, apply to customary marriages, at least not formally, though customary courts continued to be turned to by civil courts to negotiate marital disputes or divide property, hence the entanglement of the different legal domains continues.

One obvious issue not attended to initially by feminist legal activists was the fact that civil marriages can only be dissolved in the High Court and require a lawyer and pre-court negotiations assisted by lawyers. Such marriages can thus be very expensive, logistically complex, and time-consuming for women, whereas customary divorce – if achievable – is free.[6]

In the cases discussed below, we trace what appear to have been changes in customary law as it has responded to historically changing statutory law. None of the cases we describe, it should be noted, ultimately hinged on the ambiguity of the marriage or uncertainty about the status of wives. In all the cases, even the first one that appeared superficially to reflect such uncertainty, judges and litigants in the customary court were more concerned with *blame*. Only much later, in a contemporary case, did the customary court adopt the no-guilt principle.

A case of rotting meat: Mori's suit

The final outcome of this case made it legendary in Moremi village. The plaintiff was the husband-to-be, Mori, who sued his promised wife, Timelo, for splitting up with him (*kgaogana*, a word also used for divorce, or for ceasing to live together) for the *third* time. The couple had been living together for nine years. This time, the break-up was more serious than before because Mori, a migrant labourer to South Africa, had bought the food, gifts, and blankets for a major wedding feast. He was fulfilling an agreement reached at a family moot (*morero*) between wife-givers and wife-takers in which Timelo, having been 'promised', was 'permitted' to be his wife "among people"', that is, publicly. Leaving the meat for the feast behind her to rot, Timelo went to Palapye where her parents were living. She did so without consulting her two village marriage go-betweens, the *sebaga* (known also as *maditsela*). To add insult to injury, her father then wrote a letter to one of the go-betweens outlining his daughter's allegations against her husband. In response, the go-between told the court that 'I don't talk with a letter!' and the father was summoned to a court hearing.

At the time, in 1972, Moremi village *kgotla* (court) was an arbitration court, not a court of record. The case was, however, recorded by one of the authors and transcribed and translated by his research assistant. In her defence, Timelo argued

6 The recent establishment of legal aid in Botswana may have changed this.

that Mori was consorting with another woman, he had 'married' her, though, when questioned, she admitted to having no evidence to prove this allegation. Mori himself reported that she had claimed their young baby was not his, again without proof, while at the same time she expected him to take care of the child's needs.

When asked, Timelo confirmed to the court that she was still 'married' to Mori. But she also insisted, on further questioning, that she was merely a *nyatsi*, a concubine or mistress, since according to her, Mori was living with another woman. The interrogation reveals her strategic jockeying at this point with regard to who was initiating the 'divorce' or even whether it had really happened:

Village Chief (to husband): You are not complaining against her that she is divorcing you in just any way? You are only complaining against each other about not treating each other positively (in good 'spirit').

Mori: Yes.

Village Chief: Did you hear him, woman?

Timelo: He says I have divorced [him].

Village Chief: How do you see yourself?

Timelo: No.

Village Chief: Do you see your husband as what, a husband or what? Is he no longer your husband?

Timelo: He is my husband.

Village Chief: He is your husband. Ahh … You regard him as your husband?

Timelo: Yes.

Village Chief: Do you look at him very, very well that he is your husband?

Timelo: Yes.

Village Chief: Do you understand him now that he says he too regards you as his wife? What are you complaining against him?

Timelo: He complains that *I* am divorcing him.

Village Chief: He is complaining that you are divorcing him. Hmm, do you say so, Mr. Mori?

Mori: I say we do not treat each other well.

Timelo: Yes, he says so.

(Chief then goes on to address the court regarding the need to sort out exactly what the offence is, since the case had been referred to Moremi by the customary court of record in Palapye, a railway town 60 km away).

Clearly, the defendant is denying that she is seeking a divorce. At the same time, she is claiming the child was born out of wedlock, which, as we shall see, will allow her to retain custody. The court then questions her as to why, if she had a complaint, she had run off to Palapye instead of consulting the go-betweens, living locally. Her father too was condemned by the assembled elders for writing a letter to the go-betweens when he lived nearby, in a neighbouring town. After all, he was not in Johannesburg. He was accused of 'spoiling the works' and the 'food' (of the wedding feast) and going back on his agreement. Mori, the fiancé, was asked how he knew his wife-to-be was 'divorcing' him? He said he had gone to Palapye but when he visited Timelo's parental compound, she did not talk to him and refused to serve him fresh food. He was just given leftovers. One of the judges reprimanded Timelo, saying she should have gone through with the wedding. Then, if she had complaints against her husband, she could discipline him:

Elder 1 (to Timelo): Isn't it about these matters of the blankets (i.e., wedding feast), about how you ought to have been decided upon (agreed) – isn't it that you were being given to Mori and given all the power and all the instructions (*taolo*) that you can hold on to Mori with a belt and rebuke him (*kgalemela*) day and night?

The defendant had, in other words, acted out of order, in advance of her right to claim absolute fidelity after the wedding celebrations. The interrogation thus compels the defendant to recognise that her conduct was not reasonable for a wife, given the significance of the 'blankets', the wedding feast, and gifting, in establishing mutual conjugal rights in the marriage. One of the elders commented on how her conduct could have put them too in trouble and in the wrong as wife-givers:

Elder 2: If we had already eaten the things of Mori, having worn overcoats also (given as gifts to chosen wedding guests), we would be in very great difficulty. The overcoats now cost about £20 each, so where would we get them, the blankets, worth so much money? Therefore what would we do? It would only be to die.

Timelo's father confessed his shame at his role in allowing the break-up of the marriage:

Father: Court, though you see me standing up, there is nothing I am standing up for. I am ashamed. That is, even though I stand up, I do not know what I can say. I have been shamed by my child, Timelo, especially. I had hoped that as my child had a complaint about her husband and O. (his alleged lover), there was love in her towards her husband, … towards this child, Mori, who wanted to marry my child. But now, there is nothing I can say. … I am ashamed. … But I have been killed by my child whom I bore. I am dead, really, that I cannot manage to raise my head … With me, I don't see how God can help me.

The father admits his fault under interrogation, while Timelo, the defendant, fails to convince the court that she is the one who has been wronged. The case was a lengthy one, and the elders repeatedly went over the same facts again and again. Did she or did she not regard herself as married? Had Mori supported her during their nine years together? The couple appeared to have accumulated very little property. Clearly, the wedding feast, blankets and gifts represented a huge expense for Mori, a poor labour migrant.

The final judgement by the village chief, when it came, insisted that there had been a marriage, invoked the paramount value of parental authority, and recognised the principle of patrilineal descent.

Village Chief: As we asked the child (Timelo) and she stated that Mori can even take the child (their baby) [her statement was not recorded]. We cannot investigate (*olatisisa*) further about it. That would be up to her, and her people. They are the ones to know what she is now inclined to do. … But the work that they (the couple) did is a child; the child who was made while the marriage was there. … Yes, the seeking was there at the time. I also agree with that: *Let the sister of Mori take the child.* She should wipe her tears with her. A child is not bought, with anything. … If her parents are not fit to lay down the law to her (their daughter, Timelo) and to rebuke her from crooked ways while living at their compound (*lwapa*) and if she is fond of her parents, when she does this sort of thing, they laugh, then I find that *she has released Mori in a white way* (a clean release). … the child is not like a cow to be kept apart (from its parent). … (in these nine years) the great work is a child, a child they made together while saying they were marrying.

Parental law hinges on parental responsibility and filial duty. This is a key legal premise of the court.

(Village Chief to Timelo): From this day you should cry for yourself and not for anyone else until you get a husband. But you, Mma (turning to the husband's older sister), you should wipe your tears. RaTimelo (the grandfather) should get her (i.e., the baby) ready for you and give her to you. But if he comes to see his child's child who was born by his foolish child (i.e., Timelo), do not show him disrespect. Even Timelo. … There will be no painful wounds. … She (the baby) is a child of those of Mogoma (ward) and those of Moremi (ward). …

(Chief now addressing the mother of Timelo): She (Timelo) says she is divorcing Mori because he is the one who delayed her, delayed the marriage. Is it not so?

MaTimelo: Yes.

Village Chief: Then we said, since you've got a child whom you bore while wanting to marry, what can be done about her? She said it doesn't matter. The child can even go with him (Mori). These are the words of your child (i.e., Timelo).

MaTimelo: What can we do? *She is throwing away her own child!* We cannot manage this. What else can we do?

Mori's sister: Whether this woman has been worked on (charmed, bewitched) or what else, I ask, for, if she had been worked on with medicines, it could be said that maybe she is being caused to reject another. *I have never seen a fully grown person like her, whose friends now send their children on errands, who yet casts away her own child that she has just got.*

Village Chief: That is all.

In an evolving relationship in which the couple appear to have accumulated very little property, when the court finally reaches the conclusion that the wife is indeed to blame for the separation, it is the child the couple had produced together that is transferred to the father's sister due to the mother's irrationality, her unreasonable, even unnatural behaviour. There is no discussion of *bogadi*, bride wealth. The focus is on the ceremonial 'blankets' and feasting that had been deliberately disrupted by the wife-to-be's actions, apparently supported by her parents. That the wife, Timelo, is willing to give up her baby, though earlier she had tried to argue that Mori was not the father, is seen by her own mother and by the baby's aunt as unnatural, leading to their almost Shakespearean, tragic pronouncements as the case concludes. In the event, the child grew up in Moremi to be an intelligent, attractive, highly responsible woman. Both her parents later married other partners.

One fact highlighted by the case was that divorce too, like marriage, is a *process, often a long drawn-out process.* The couple was said to have 'divorced' three times. The issues at stake do not merely concern the ambiguity of the marriage, but the price to be paid in divorce emotionally and materially. In the case of many women – divorce in customary courts can only be achieved by sheer grit and determination.

Assembly-line divorce

Unlike divorce cases in customary courts, divorce in the High Court has become a matter of establishing some basic facts: the irretrievable breakdown of the marriage, the jurisdiction of the parties (whether or not they are residents of Botswana), the authenticity of documents presented in court, the division-of-property settlement (usually negotiated and agreed upon before the hearing), the financial circumstances of each of the parties, the number of children, custody, visitation, and maintenance awarded. In most cases, the hearings take less than 5 minutes! Unlike in the customary courts, the issue of who is suing whom for divorce does not arise.

Although some cases in the High Court involve technical complications (in one case witnessed in 2005, the defendant was domiciled abroad; in another, the defendant had not responded; in a third, the settlement documents had vanished), in our observation, hearings averaged no more than 15 minutes per case. It was noteworthy, however, that whereas initially the judge presiding over the High Court in the morning session that we observed, said he was not interested 'in history', as time went on he seemed to get increasingly curious about each individual case. He dominated the cross-examination and the advocates representing the parties either kept quiet or repeated the judge's questions to their client. Judges were said, by the Emang Basadi lawyer we accompanied, to vary somewhat in the speed in which they judge cases, as well as in their 'humanity', informality, and generosity.

In the Lobatse High Court, in 2005, divorce cases were heard only on Mondays. On the one Monday we attended, there were 14 cases but there could be as many as 28, we were told. There was a long waiting list of couples wishing to finalise their divorce. Litigation was expensive. A minimum charge for a divorce case in 2005 was 3,000 pula (£200) but costs could easily rise to 30,000 pula (£2000). A day in court cost 1,500 pula (£100). Most negotiations between the parties took place before the court hearing and involved paying large sums to the lawyers representing each of the parties.

It is thus evident that civil divorces stand in stark contrast to customary law divorces in almost every respect, but they present their own kinds of challenges, as the next case illustrates. The following case shows the high expenses and huge obstacles involved in breaking up a civil marriage.

Breaking up a civil marriage: Mary's case

Mary, a good-looking, vivacious woman in her thirties, who was raised in Moremi village, was working as a messenger in Princess Marina hospital in Gaborone. We report the divorce case as Mary told it to us during many conversations, over a lengthy period. At the time we first met her, Mary was married to a man from a neighbouring Tswapong village; he had a government job in the capital as a mechanic. They had married in 2000 and had one daughter. She also had an older daughter from an earlier relationship, while her husband had a son as well. They had married at the District Commissioner's Office in a civil marriage, in community of property, but in fact, she said, her husband never told her his salary or shared it with her, and when he bought a car, it was for his use alone. Now, she said, he had started an affair with a 20-year-old girl (born 1985). He wanted to divorce Mary and take the house and also the new plot in a Gaborone suburb on which they had agreed to build a home. The house in Gaborone in which they were currently living was his before they married but he claims that even the new plot is his, she said. When we first knew Mary, she was trying to organise the digging of a pit latrine at the plot. Her husband had taken a lawyer.

During 2005, Mary took her husband and his much-younger girlfriend to the Gaborone customary court three times. In the first court hearing, she sued the girl for breaking up the marriage, and was awarded 10,000 pula (£670) in compensation, but the girl failed to pay her. On the second occasion she attended court without the girl. On the third occasion, the customary court judge decreed that if the girlfriend, who was unemployed, did not pay up, she would go to jail. The court also ordered her husband to hand over all his bank statements and financial affairs to his wife, on the grounds that she was remaining behind looking after the children. The husband had not objected, she said, saying, I'm still married. She claimed to be happy that he had gone off to a new job in Francistown.

Although petite in stature, Mary was a woman who clearly knew her rights. When one of us asked her if she would seriously consider sending the girlfriend to jail, she insisted that 'Yes!' For how long? 'Ten years' (perhaps … she said, maybe reduced by three). Would her husband pay the fine? No, he couldn't, 'I have all the accounts' (this is when she explained about going back to the court). She said that the girl had vanished but they would find her, definitely, since she is known and comes from another Tswapong village. Maybe the girl will have to pay ten cattle.

When asked whether she would take her husband back if he changed his mind, Mary said: Absolutely not. She wanted the divorce. He just sleeps around, she said, and she doesn't want to get infected (by HIV). She was tested and is negative, which she regarded as something of a miracle given his behaviour. If she slept with him occasionally, she insisted that he wear a condom. She just wanted to separate from him, to build a brick house on her plot and a house in her natal village. She said mud huts caused too many problems.

Initially, Mary had tried to consult Emang Basadi, the women's NGO, about her case. The limitations to the voluntary association's capacity were revealed, however, when she and her husband attended a scheduled appointment for reconciliation three times, only to find on each occasion that the person who was supposed to be dealing with their case wasn't there. Finally, she contacted the social welfare department and the social worker came/invited them, and sorted out the dispute. She said the social worker had even come again to visit the husband. In the end, however, despite this, the marriage broke down irretrievably.

Once she decided to divorce, she said, she gave up on Emang Basadi because they were 'too slow'. She had gone to another firm, Lesegi, who were representing her at the High Court. She will have to pay them 49 pula (about £3) a month for the rest of her life. She was definitely divorcing her husband, she said. She said she had been thrown out of the house she had been sharing with him by her mother-in-law, her husband's mother. He now had a new woman (not the original girlfriend) in Francistown. He had come to Gaborone and removed all the furniture and belongings, some of which she herself had bought – her TV, etc. She was now living at her new Gaborone plot, allocated to her by the local land board after several applications. She had had a theft from her plot of 7,000-pula worth of cement bags and other materials (£330), and her shelter there was destroyed. She reported the theft to the police but suspects her husband is the culprit. Ultimately, she managed to get the sole title to the plot and built two brick houses on it over time, from her relatively low salary supplemented by government loans.

In 2005, she was still working as a messenger at the hospital in Gaborone where she had worked for the past 13 years. Later, she was transferred to Palapye, the railway town further north and let out one of her houses. Her daughter and niece occupied the second house.

Mary was young and could remarry, we suggested, but she said, no way, who could she marry when everyone was infected (with HIV) and she couldn't trust men? In any case, she had children, one daughter was grown up and doing a secretarial course, the other had a baby; it was their turn now. They would complain if she started to go out with another man. She never wanted to have another man.

Mary had married in a civil marriage but this did not make the couple's divorce easier, and it certainly made it more expensive. Divorce was a lengthy process, with several attempts at mediation that ultimately failed. Parents seemed unable or unwilling to help from a distance; indeed, the husband's mother sided with her son. The courts seemed unable to ensure an equitable division of the property or (in the case of the customary court) payment of compensation for 'breaking' the marriage. In the final outcome, however, Mary was granted one of the plots (possibly by default, since she began to build on it) and her husband took the other plot. To this extent equity prevailed.

Moving back from divorce in civil marriages to divorce in customary marriages, it is true that customary divorce incurs no legal costs. However, gaining a fair share of a couple's joint property may prove an almost insurmountable barrier, as the next case illustrates. If Mary's divorce took several years, the following case, of Segametse, proves that divorce may ultimately fail.

Divorce as a never-ending process: Segametse

This next case, Segametse's unattainable divorce, shows the course of a complex dispute drawn out over a period of 15 years, from roughly 2000 to 2015. The documentation is primarily from the viewpoint of Segametse as an aggrieved wife. At the very start of the dispute, the couple were already long married; they had seven children, and Segametse herself was in her early forties, an attractive-looking, elegant, and usually smartly dressed woman, ready and able to fight for her rights, as sensibly as possible. Throughout the 15-year period, in a good number of hearings, petitions for appeal, shopping from venue to venue, delays, referrals, out-of-court consultations, and family gossip, Segametse was struggling tenaciously with her husband for the rightful safeguarding of family and marital property. Some of the complexity comes from the entanglement in her husband's extra-marital affairs, including the customary court's initial award, in 2001, to his mistress of exorbitant damages in payment for the mistress's first-born child. Segametse's cause was, in certain respects, a lost cause, for much of the time, although her marriage persisted; it even culminated, surprisingly, by the end of the period, in reconciliation with her long-estranged husband, in a working partnership with him very much under her dominant control.

As part of the context for Segametse's case, we report briefly popular shifts in expectations of marriage, from polygamy to monogamy, and in customary legal norms: these now require a husband to be faithful and no longer favour past sexual inequality which gave a husband the right to have liaisons or to take mistresses, subject to due respect for the maintenance of his wife and family. Very recently, also, customary law has come to relate to 2005 national legislation which secures an equal property division between husband and wife, irrespective of who brings the divorce suit. Hence, our approach takes into account a very recent turning point through legislation in regard to the property risk in divorce – seeking it no longer usually means losing any share of marital assets. We also clarify a problematic feature of legal uncertainty with which Segametse had to contend: namely, the extent to which a customary court judge would keep up-to-date or sympathise with certain national shifts in marital norms and expectations.

To set the case in the long-term context of legal change, it is worth recalling that in research in the 1930s, Schapera reported that, by contrast to his wife, a husband

> is not required to be faithful to her. Even if he has no other wives with whom she must share his attentions, he frequently has concubines, and normally she can take no action against them in court. … Usually, however, a wife does not complain about her husband's love-affairs, so long as he cohabits with her regularly.
>
> (1940b: 106)

In Moremi, too, in the 1970s, polygamy and concubinage were the norm for prosperous men. This is not true in twenty-first century Moremi village; monogamy prevails, and suits are brought by women who dispute that a husband is wrong to have a mistress and waste marital assets on her.

At the start of Segametse's efforts to seek legal protection against such wrongs by her husband, in 2001, the head of the customary court in Moremi village was himself an elderly polygamist. Personally, he was sympathetic to the idea that a husband ought to still be able to have liaisons, and he was himself notorious for his penchant for liaisons and girlfriends. In our discussion with him about whether a wife might sue her husband for divorce, he suggested she could sue him on the grounds that he was shaming her, that everyone was gossiping about her, laughing at her. In that case, the court could send her to her natal home with some property settlement. His opinion was hypothetical, a matter of the logic of parental law, but without a case for an example. When we discussed if there was any way that a woman could actually initiate divorce and still get a property settlement, he was evasive, talking about procedure in reply to a simple question: If a man was bad, beat his wife, and neglected the family, could she sue for divorce? The village chief insisted he could not act on hearsay, rumour, or gossip, but she had to bring witnesses, she had to come with parents, elders, and uncles. Members of both families should come, not just the husband's parents. They should get together and discuss things, and try to reach an agreement, before coming to court. If they had done all that and it had failed then the court had the right to transfer the property to the wife's name – the cattle and other things. This would put pressure on the husband himself to sue for divorce. In the end, in the face of our persistent questioning, he said that if the man was really bad, and there was proof, the court could compel him to divorce his wife, which would then entitle her to a property settlement. The village chief thus had real difficulty in coming out with a clear statement that a wife could herself successfully initiate a divorce, and come away with a good property settlement.

The village chief's stress on procedure, on mobilising witnesses, on consulting parents, elders, and uncles in family hearings, and mobilising them to appear in the customary court registers a resource in the maintenance of marriage. It is time not as of the essence but as the resource of delay in conflict resolution, which wears a complainant down, leading to an abandoned suit, and thus no decisive legal end to a marriage, whatever might be their practical domestic or conjugal relationship. This is not to say that the procedural hurdles, delays, and drawn-out referrals are deliberate devices but that they work against the making of an actual decision for a divorce; and our impression is that divorce had actually been rare in the village over a long period.

In the following detailed account of Segametse's case, we present it in three phases, for purposes of analysis and to demonstrate the major moves: *first,* to suing for divorce in 2001, *second,* to the perception of being abandoned, blocked, and bewitched in 2005, and *third,* to the moment when circumstances turned, and a new working partnership emerged from 2013 to 2016.

Phase 1: suing for divorce, 2001

Since her parents were dead, Segametse was represented in court by her mother's brother but she also presented her case independently. Two sessions of Moremi customary court, first late in 2000 and then early in 2001 started the long course of Segametse's dispute. In the first, the court awarded her husband's mistress substantial damages of 1,200 pula or six head of cattle on the grounds that the husband had impregnated her. No-one in the court expected him to pay the amount as such, but it was seen as a debt that meant the mistress could siphon off his earnings from driving his van back and forth to the town of Palapye, while he supplied her tuck shop, or small store selling food, sweets, and some personal items. In the second case, once Segametse's complaints about her husband's bad behaviour were heard in 2001, she and her husband were urged to reconcile and to save their marriage. Dissatisfied, and seeing her husband continuing with his liaison, she turned for a proper remedy to the court of record in the nearby town of Palapye.

A series of steps back and forth followed, from venue to venue, trying Segametse's patience, feeding her anger and grievance, and proving her determination to get rightful legal redress despite the hurdles in her way. The path to a customary court settlement was not easy. First, she tried unsuccessfully to have the hearing at the town venue of her choice, Palapye, because it was more accessible than Moremi village for her own relatives living in her natal village of Malaka, closer to the town. She was relying on the fact that her relatives, and her children also, took her side, and that their support would carry all the more weight because of their shared kinship with her husband, who is her first cousin (mother's sister's son). By the end of January 2001, the case was referred back to Moremi village customary court by the Palapye chief. His court is for appeals, but a referral following the hearing at the lower court of Moremi was not surprising, given the appeal court's tendency to send matters back in the face of entanglements and intricacies better handled at the lower level. There was also a technical fault in that Segametse had come without a letter from the Moremi village chief forwarding her case.

Once again at her primary venue, Segametse endured more of a run-around. In response to the Palapye referral, Moremi headman held a session, which he said was not a *tsheko*, a court case, but which he then conducted as if it were a court case. Over a couple of hours, he and other elders of the court did their best to make peace and reconcile the couple. But, as if bent on having his wife and his mistress, the husband left the court, walking off hand in hand with the latter. Afterwards, finding that her husband continued to spend all his time and money with his mistress, Segomatse secured a letter of referral, at the direction of the Moremi village chief, to an intermediate court of appeal at the nearby village of Matolwane, a customary court of record and appeal.

In Matolwane, at the next hearing, Segametse managed to convince the head of the local appeal court, after he heard the details of her case, that Palapye was a better place for her appeal because it was more accessible for her relatives. This judge then gave her a letter respectfully asking the Moremi village chief to write directly to the Palapye court in support of Segametse's appeal there.

On the way home from court in our car, K., a prominent village elder and the right-hand man of Moremi headman, asked Segametse if her husband ever sleeps with her. She said that no, she is alone, no one comes into her blankets. K. said that she should tell the court that she is thirsty, and her husband refuses to give her water. Everyone in our car laughed, including Segametse herself. She said that she does not want him if he comes to her satisfied already. She was so angry, she said she wanted a divorce, or better still, for her husband to come back to her.

On receiving the letter from the Matolwane judge, Moremi's village chief wrote a second referral letter, this time to the Palapye customary court. Segametse then delivered it in vain – the Palapye customary court insisted she had to proceed through the hierarchy, and go back to the intermediate level and the Matolwane customary court. There she ran into an *impasse*. Although the head of the court reviewed her second referral letter, questioned Segametse again about her case, and discussed it seriously with a local policewoman, he had to postpone the case, for lack of a court clerk, who was on maternity leave. The policewoman explained to us that the Moremi village chief had 'mixed things up' (*kopa kopana*) and had delayed too long (*thaka thakana*). At this point, having failed to reach her preferred venue in Palapye where her relatives would come to her support, Segametse gave up seeking a remedy in court.

By September 2001, she was saying that she no longer came into the village from her place by her fields and tuck shop, since whenever she came there, she became ill because of witchcraft inflicted upon her by her husband and his girlfriend.

Phase 2: abandoned, blocked, and bewitched, 2005

When we saw Segametse again, in March 2005, she was looking well. She said that her court case had failed and that now she was just ignoring her husband's adultery, even though she was feeling pain, because it seemed he and his girlfriend were now married – they were acting like a married couple and had three children. But she wasn't going to give him an excuse to say *she* had divorced *him*. Being nowadays poor, she was afraid that if she divorced him she would be even poorer. The trouble with the property they had owned jointly, she said, was that they depended too much on cattle and goats, and now only ten goats were left. Her husband had sold the cattle to spend everything on his girlfriend. Her husband's van was Segametse's as well. She had borrowed money and sold cattle to buy it. But, he never gave her money. She operated a tuck shop, and he came to collect the earnings once a month but she was not sure where or whether he was banking the money or how much there was.

At first (after the affair began), she ran the tuck shop on her own, she said, and deposited the money in a post office account. When she had unexpected expenses, she used some of the money. But later he demanded that he should run the tuck shop. Now he continues to supply the shop but takes all the profits. She didn't want to quarrel with him, even though it pained her.

We asked her if she was aware that there was now a new national law, giving equal marital power to husbands and wives, though it was not meant to cover customary law. Ever since her court case, she explained, she had been thinking that there may be organisations that could help her. Going through the customary courts was too upsetting; it made her feel tired. Worse still, she suffered illness caused by her husband and his girlfriend. They had *romelela boloi* (sent witchcraft). Her husband was pretending to love her still, even though he knew that she disapproved of him. His feelings were not genuine. He was still dangerous, she thought. If she started making a case against him, she would have ill health or accidents. She had gone to a prophet in Palapye about her illness. He helped her to be strong and to protect her. She recalled that, during the long dispute, her husband's parents, brothers, and sisters all met in their village to interrogate him. They were against him and supported her. Her husband just refused to budge. His younger brother asked him the question: if you go on like this, do we not have the right and the power to cut whatever we wish into two and even take all the property and give it to Segametse? Her husband begged them not to do that and promised to stop. But, she said, he has no connection with their children. He just shouts at them and says they are rude even when they are well-behaved and innocent. Now she thought the family could really take away his property and have a separation, since the relationship with the mistress hadn't stopped. They could instruct *him* to divorce *her*. What she really wanted was not just a divorce from her husband, but to get all the property that was left, because he had destroyed so much of it that she had worked for. If they divide it half-and-half, it would be unfair because some of it would go to his girlfriend.

Phase 3: the tables turned, 2013–2016

By 2013, customary law was clearly changing, to 'harmonise' with statutory law passed in 2005. When we visited the court of appeal in Maunatlala in June 2005, to ask about Segametse's case, the Chief and customary court judge there claimed that if all else failed – if a woman could show that she had made several genuine attempts to reform her husband but he still persisted – then the court would grant her a divorce with an equitable division of the property. He contended that this was customary law as it always had been, not that it had changed. Indeed, he said, *the feminists had learnt from us and borrowed these understandings from customary law!*

Even beyond the legal shift, personal circumstances finally turned in Segametse's favour. In 2013, her husband was rejected by his girlfriend, now pregnant by another married man. We were told that he was expelled unceremoniously from their joint residence. In retaliation, so it was alleged by a local Moremi policeman, Segametse's jilted husband had burned down the girlfriend's tuck shop, but this was never proved. He and Segametse then came back together again, running a joint (Tswana) chicken breeding enterprise.

In 2016, we met Segametse at her fields where she and her daughter, now an adult with her own child, were breeding superior supermarket chickens for sale. She explained that after the girlfriend kicked him out, she saw that her husband had changed. He now involves her and the children in constant *merero* (moots, meetings, consultations), on 'everything'; that means, he consults her every time he wants to do something, and, indeed, she had told him about the house in Palapye, built by her daughter. There had been a big family consultation with all their relatives – especially on her husband's side. They persuaded her not to divorce. Another brother, a highly placed civil servant, told her they would support her and the children because they knew she was her husband's back-up. Without her, he cannot do anything, he'd be lost. They advised her to buy her own cattle brand, and brand all the cattle that were hers.

Her husband had had the bad 'habit' (*mokgwa*) of selling everything even if it wasn't his, without consulting her, but he had come to recognise this weakness in himself – he told her to change the plot in Moremi to her name, and the field too, so he wouldn't be able to sell them.

They were not living together, because he is taking care of the cattle, while she is looking after some town house-building in Palapye. But they often check on each other. She still seemed a bit hesitant. She watches him all the time. She doesn't really trust him. He is the man of 'women's spirit'. She knows he is trying to change. When he came to her and suggested they should renew their wedding vows, she refused, knowing his tendency to be tempted by women. After years of struggle, Segametse had gained control over all the joint marital property, with her husband's agreement, supported by their extended family.

Segametse's case highlights the limitations of customary courts and parental law in contemporary Botswana. There is little the extended family can do in the face of the intransigence of one of the parties to a marriage. At times, as in the above case of Mary and the breaking of a civil marriage, parents collude with their child. At other times, as in Segametse's case, they encourage one party to take control over the joint property. Courts may be sympathetic to one of the parties while remaining indecisive, hoping for reconciliation against the odds.

Conclusion: the paradox of changing customary divorce law in Botswana

Ironically, as Segametse was struggling to get her husband to divorce her, customary law was gradually changing in Botswana, as confirmed by the presiding judge of the customary appeal court in Maunatlala. Phineas Makepe, then a judge on the national Customary Court of Appeal, told us that 'the customary court of appeal has accepted the principle of division of the property (in the case of divorce); in 1997, it was there and was confirmed by the High Court' (interview 17 August 2005). And yet earlier, in 2001, Makepe had also confirmed that according to customary law, if a woman sues for divorce, she will walk away without any property, even if she has cogent grounds for divorce.

Although the tendency to send divorce cases back to the family for further discussion persists, leading, as this chapter has highlighted, to endless delays, in recent cases in Moremi village customary court, now a court of record headed by the son of the previous village chief, the court has settled for equal division of the property or even, in one case, for the wife to receive most of the property with her ex-husband's consent. He was divorcing her, somewhat against her wishes, in order to put an end to her accusations of infidelity, which he said he could no longer bear. He had never been caught *in flagrante delicto* but everyone we spoke to who knew the couple insisted the accusations were true. A much respected, older couple in their sixties, after the divorce and following a period of deep emotional crisis for the wife, the couple continued to work their fields together, to eat together, and to behave like a married couple, much to local bemusement. The second recent case was of the marriage of relatively short duration of a mature couple. The court decreed that there was clearly no communication or understanding in the marriage and divided their property half-and-half: the joint compound was to be sold and the proceedings divided equally; the debt of over 6,000 pula was to be divided; a detailed inventory of the livestock and household utensils was allocated to each person, while the wife was to receive the van (which she had paid for). Such changes prove that not only is customary law *living law*, responsive to changing circumstances and wider processes of critical reform, but that it follows a clear historical trajectory.

This is not widely recognised in the literature. In a recent paper (Chiepe et al. 2016: 222) the authors suggest that in Botswana, 'customary law may be contrary to basic human rights of women' but that 'abolishing *bogosi* [chiefship] would still seem to be impossible given that Batswana still cherish the institution, no matter how weak it may be' (ibid.: 230). Against this view, we have argued in this chapter that, given the apparent changes leading to harmonisation of customary law relating to divorce, and given that feminists themselves are increasingly uncertain whether marriage in or out of community of property is the preferable mode, we suggest there is a need to recognise that, surprisingly, customary marriage, allowing for customary divorce, has now become more advantageous than divorce through the High Court. Divorce in customary courts is, after all, free, and can be – if customary courts follow the new interpretation of the law and don't penalise the party that sues for divorce – fast and convenient. The principle of gender equity is gradually becoming the 'living' norm in customary courts, as increasingly more cases are settled equitably, challenging prevailing feminist advice to marry in civil marriage.

8 Adultery redefined

Changing decisions of equity in customary law as 'living law' in Botswana

Adultery compared

Adultery has a violent history in the annals of European tradition and law.[1] Proprietary relations of power over persons, usually of a man (or lineage) over his wives and their progeny, are exposed as bogus in adultery. Thus, where marriages are arranged, the transgressive sexuality of a wife not only challenges the institution of marriage but proves her hitherto hidden agency and autonomy over her own body (Carnelly 2013: 187). This is what often leads to violent retribution.

Although adultery is still the subject of scandalous gossip, the legal history of adultery in the West, as in southern Africa, has been towards a shift, first, from being a criminal to being a civil offence, and, more recently as we shall see, to being dropped altogether as an offence in the statutory courts.[2] In the USA, exceptionally, adultery is still treated as a criminal offence in 21 states, though the statute is seldom enforced (Rhode 2016: 60). In customary – but not statutory – courts in Botswana, 'breaking the yard', as adultery is labelled, continues at the time of writing to be tried as an indictable offence, punishable by compensatory damages.

What explains the uneven but apparently inexorable shift in the judicial definition of adultery in so many different jurisdictions across the globe? Arguably, the rise of feminism and gender activism, including in the global south, has challenged patriarchal domination and alongside it laws on divorce and adultery: if women and men are regarded as equal and autonomous, the property presumptions of adultery as a crime akin to theft – of men being deprived of their ownership of their wives and children – is no longer valid. But equally important, as we shall see, has been *judicial activism* to abolish adultery even as a civil offence

1 See Marita Carnelley on this history in which women, regarded as male property, could be put to death for adultery, while men too were subject to torture and violent punishment (2013: 187).

2 Most recently, as part of this global trend, on 27 September, 2018, the Indian Supreme Court struck down a colonial-era law known as Section 497 criminalizing extramarital sex. https://www.indiatoday.in/india/story/adultery-verdict-supreme-court-section-497-1350477-2018-09-27 Accessed 28/09/18.

DOI: 10.4324/9781003241881-8

in the face of changing morés of everyday life. The incidence of adultery is so high,[3] and legal costs so prohibitive, that the judiciary itself in many countries has moved to abolish adultery, first as a crime and then as a civil offence. In her recent book, Deborah Rhode, a reformist legal scholar, defines the aim of her book as being to

> argue that the United States should repeal its civil and criminal penalties for adultery. These penalties are now infrequently and inconsistently enforced, and they ill serve societal values. Such sanctions remain on the books because American attitudes reflect a fundamental ambivalence. Disapproval of marital infidelity has increased at the same time that support for criminal prohibitions of adultery has declined.
>
> (Rhode 2016: 1–2)

Similarly, the prevalence of double standards in court judgements, in which mitigating circumstances are accepted in many countries for so-called crimes of passion – that is, of the murder of an adulterous spouse or lover – are no longer deemed valid by feminists and activists. As we argue in this chapter, changing morés have also affected customary law in Botswana's village courts, and we trace these changes as they are evident in exemplary case hearings.

A brief history of adultery in southern Africa

Roman-Dutch law, introduced into South Africa in the seventeenth century and later modified by English law, still defined adultery as a crime, although husbands could also claim damages. In 1914, however, the *crime* of adultery was abolished (Carnelley 2013: 199) so that adultery became a civil delict punishable with damages. The right of adulterers to marry each other was confirmed in 1919 (ibid.). In 1950, damage claims became gender-neutral (ibid.).

The legal framework, as it was extended into the Bechuanaland Protectorate in the 1891 and 1909 Proclamations, was a mix of the original Roman-Dutch law, brought to South Africa by the Dutch in 1652, English law that was progressively introduced by the British from 1806, and principles developed by local courts. According to Fombad (2011: 6), because of this Civil Law (Roman-Dutch) and Common Law (English) mix, some writers have suggested that it is probably more accurate to refer to what was received as Cape Colonial law or South African Common law. So too, sources of the law since 1966, in independent Botswana's legally plural system, include the Constitution, Customary law, Common law (shared with South Africa), state legislation, and judicial precedent (ibid.). Botswana, like Namibia, continues to be part of the southern African legal universe so that judicial decisions and precedents established in South Africa

3 Rhode (2016: 8) reports that in a Kinsey Institute survey in the USA in 2011, 23 percent of men and 19 percent of women admitted to having had an extra-marital relationship.

are regularly cited in Botswana's courts, while South African legal advocates are frequently brought over to argue important cases (see, for example, P. Werbner 2014a).

In Bechuanaland, paralleling developments in South Africa, adultery shifted early in the twentieth century from being a criminal offence to becoming a civil offence, defined as a delict in the statutory courts, which involved (a) a loss of *consortium* (the company of a spouse) and (b) *contumelia* (an insult, an offence to a person's dignity). In Botswana's *customary* law, these two delicts, which stress *individual* offence, are paralleled by the offence in customary law of 'breaking the *lelwapa*' – home wrecking, which implies a more communal dimension, since marriage among Tswana and other ethnic groups in Botswana is conceived of as a contract between families. Over time, the gendered dimensions of adultery as an offence have come to the fore, both in the statutory and in the customary courts. Customary courts in Botswana are not obliged to follow state courts, but there is an expectation that their verdicts should not be *incompatible with the provisions of any written law or contrary to morality, humanity, or natural justice*' (Customary Courts Act 2006, Section 2, (1)(b)). In modern Botswana this has come to include gender equality, a principle certainly upheld in the statutory courts, and increasingly, we find, in customary courts as well.[4]

Media reports: the national and international impact of landmark cases

Cases of adultery are continuously reported in the press in Botswana, as they occur both in statutory and customary courts. Such reports contribute to much public debate about changing attitudes towards extra-marital relations. The very culpability in adultery seems questionable – entangled in other marital problems.

Awareness of change, particularly in South Africa, has also been a factor in stimulating public interest and judicial reasoning in Botswana. In a landmark case in 2014, the Supreme Court of Appeal of South Africa passed a judgement rendering adultery no longer a culpable action in court. The Court's decision followed and reflected changes that had occurred in laws that abolished adultery even as a civil offence in the United Kingdom, other European countries, New Zealand, Australia, and the USA. In its decision, the South African Supreme Court argued for the need to recognise, above all, 'the clear anomaly that the action is available against the third party only and not against the adulterous spouse, although a clearer case of a co-perpetrator is difficult to conceive' (The Supreme Court of Appeal of South Africa Judgment 2014: 18). Indeed, if anything, 'the behaviour of the guilty spouse is patently more reprehensible than that of the third party and more hurtful to the innocent spouse. It is, after all, the guilty spouse, not the third party, who solemnly undertook to remain faithful and who is bound by a relationship of trust' (ibid.). Furthermore, citing a German

4 See Chapters 5 and 7.

Senate Court, 'highly personal relations should not be regulated by law, which is at least compatible with constitutional law and corresponds to modern ethics' (2014: 15). Whereas the Court acknowledges that the Adultery law is intended to protect the institution of marriage 'which our society holds dear' (2014: 20), against that, it argues that 'if the parties to the marriage have lost that moral commitment, the marriage will fail and punishment meted out to a third party is unlikely to change that' (ibid.); hence the law no longer has a deterrent effect.

More controversially, in our view, certainly when applied to the continued significance of values of honour (*tlotlo*) and dignity (*seriti*) in Botswana, the South African Supreme Court also argues with regard to the delict of *contumelia* in adultery, i.e., insult to the honour of the deceived party, that 'in this day and age, the reasonable observer would rarely think that the innocent spouse was humiliated or insulted by the adultery of his or her spouse' (2014: 22). More to the point, 'an action for wounded feelings as such has not as yet been specifically recognised by our law ... In addition, if the law is to be extended to protect wounded feelings, where would we draw the line?' (ibid.).[5]

In the end, the South African Supreme Court of Appeal concludes, 'the history of the delictual action for adultery reveals its archaic origin. On the one hand, it stems from the concept in old English law that the husband has some proprietary interest in the person and services of his wife. That is why in common law the action for criminal conversation was always confined to the husband of an adulterous wife' (2014: 23). Once no-fault divorce was introduced in South Africa, adultery (previously grounds for divorce) seemed redundant. Namibia and Botswana soon followed the South African lead regarding adultery.

The demise of adultery in Botswana, 2018

In August 2016, Namibia's Supreme Court cited a South African ruling for ending adultery as an offence in Nambia (Namibia High Court 2016). Two years later, on 2 May 2018, a Botswana High Court judge declared the termination of adultery as a common-law legal delict in Botswana, ending claims for *contumelia*, loss of dignity, or *consortium*, loss of companionship. High Court Justice Lot Moroka's key argument was that claims for adultery 'offend(s) against the constitutional principle of equality before the law' (p. 42).

The verdict created a flood of press reports throughout Botswana: 'A Victory for Cheats', a local tabloid headline screamed for a decision that shocked many of its Christian readers (*The Voice,* Friday May 4 2018, p. 7). The pros and cons were debated in cafes, living rooms, and around campfires in the countryside.

Apparently following the South African and Namibian precedents, the judgement in Botswana seemed to confirm a shared legal universe of modified Roman-Dutch common law. From a purely legal point of view, however, each court

5 See Chapter 8.

verdict was independent of the others as the various justices stressed. In South Africa, the judges emphasised that it is

> the Constitution which imposes the duty on the courts to develop the common law so as to promote the spirit, purport, and objectives of the Bill of Rights. Secondly, by the acceptance that the courts can and should adapt the common law to reflect the changing social, moral, and economic fabric of society.
>
> (p. 10, Clause 17, 2014)

The Namibian judge, reviewing this precedent, found such a duty not explicit but merely implied in the Namibian Constitution (p. 10, clause 26, 2016). Nevertheless, he argued,

> it is in any event well established that it has always been open to the courts to develop the common law.
>
> (ibid., p. 10, Clause 17, 2014)

Similarly, in Botswana, having surveyed the shared origins of Botswana and South Africa's common laws on adultery, Justice Moroka cited the recent abandonment of adultery as a legal delict in South Africa's Supreme and Constitutional Courts, and in the Appeal court of Namibia, before going on to stress Botswana's legal independence:

> Botswana is a sovereign state with its own peculiar norms and values. The law must answer to the peculiar *boni mores* [good morals] of this society. The question will therefore be answered purely from the perspective of Botswana.
>
> (p. 20, Clause 49, 2018)

Hence, 'the temptation to follow trends in other jurisdictions without careful regard to the peculiar legal convictions of the society that is Botswana should be resisted' (ibid., p. 21, Clause 51).

In his 1994 account of courts in Botswana, Otlhogile Bojosi, an eminent socio-legal scholar and legal historian, cites a judgement by then-Chief Justice Dendy Young, in which the latter argued that the decisions of foreign countries:

> are not binding on the courts in Botswana, but such decisions may have *very substantial persuasive value, especially those of South Africa*, where the common law is also Roman-Dutch law, and those of the United Kingdom, because of the very great influence of English law on all branches of law in this country.
>
> (1968–70 BLR 100 104; cited in Bojosi 1994: 52; emphasis added)

Striking in Justice Moroka's long judgement was the extent to which it echoes the South African and Namibian judgements. All survey the historical movement of adultery from criminal to civil offence, the radical change in women's status in the home, and the range of countries that have abolished adultery as a legal offence since the 1970s. All cite the exemplary German court verdict. The grounds for abolishing adultery's legal status are also similar, although Justice Moroka adds a somewhat flamboyant touch, for example, when arguing that, since the guilty spouse stands to benefit from damages paid to the innocent spouse, adultery 'could become a lucrative fund raiser for the family' (p. 43, Clause 95). He also elaborates on the consequences of digital 'affairs', sexting, pornography, and the like.

Finally, an important point raised by the high court judges in all three southern African countries is relevant to the broader argument put forward here about customary law as 'living' law. It seems the concept of 'living law' is not only applied to customary law but to common law as well. Justice Moroka cites an earlier 1990 case in which the judge is reported to have said:

> Law in a developing country cannot afford to remain static. It must undoubtedly be stable, because otherwise reliance upon it would be rendered impossible. But at the same time, *if the law is to be a living force, it must be dynamic* and accommodating to change.
>
> (p. 40, Clause 90; emphasis added)

In the South African Supreme Court judgement it was merely stressed that 'courts are more sensitive to have regard to the dynamic and changing nature of the norms of our society' (p. 10 Clause 19), a sentence cited in the Namibian Court of Appeal.

We see here how international jurisprudence impacts on substantive legal issues such as adultery, although there is still the possibility of a high court appeal in Botswana, and some litigants could be expected to turn to customary courts for delictual damages. This, in itself, however, cannot guarantee the continuation of adultery as a customary offence of 'breaking the *lelwapa*', since presiding customary court headmen and chiefs, too, are divided on the fairness of damages awarded against only one of the two offending parties, as Moremi case we discuss below highlights. Customary judges, too, read newspapers and are attuned to the prevailing normative assumptions in society.

In November 2019, a fellow judge in the Francistown High Court, Judge Moesi, disagreed with Moroka J.'s 2018 judgement in the same court, that adultery was no longer a delictual offence on the grounds that Botswana differs from South Africa in recognising the 'inviolability' of marriage which is not merely private but a 'social institution' (High Court Francistown, 2019, Clauses 39, 43). Disattending to most of Moroka J.'s detailed argument, Moesi J. also strongly rejected the appeal to the constitution (42). The judge thus awarded damages to the plaintiff of 100,000 pula ($9,280) for *contumelia* and 50,000 pula ($4,640) for loss of *consortium* (49). *The Voice* newspaper reported on the decision with the headline 'End of Honeymoon for Adulterers' (Dipholo 2019). Until such a time as a case of adultery is brought before the Botswana Court of

Appeal, the matter of whether adultery is or is not an indictable offence will not be settled.

The decline of polygamy and changing customary rights: wives against mistresses

When we first arrived in Moremi village in 1972, several, mainly wealthy, men had polygamous marriages. As in Moremi, elsewhere too it was taken-for-granted to describe women as mistresses (*nyetse*) in the twentieth-century cases reported by Comaroff and Roberts (1977, 1981) and Griffiths (1997). Early in the twenty-first century, in the higher-ranked customary courts, some judges still seemed to try to take rearguard actions against women prosecuting other women for 'breaking the yard', perhaps attempting to stem the gender-equality tide, but to no avail. In 2000, the then-Commissioner of Customary Law made a revisional judgement instructing customary courts 'not to entertain matters in which married women were suing others for damages for having adulterous relationships with their husbands, [which] brought custom and tradition into sharp conflict with the received law and internal standards regarding equality of men and women' (Lebotse 2005: 116–117).

This instruction followed a judgement to award a woman from southern Botswana, among Kwena, eight head of cattle as damages in a lawsuit brought against another woman for having an adulterous relationship with her husband (ibid.). In his revisional judgement, the Commissioner cited Isaac Schapera (1938: 156–7), whose authoritative handbook of law in the colonial period had documented that 'adultery on the part of the wife was held to be a more serious offence and the husband has a right to claim damages against her paramour – *a right which she cannot exercise against her husband's concubine*' (Lebotse 2005: 118, emphasis in the original).[6] Nyamnjoh, who also mentions the ruling by the Commissioner, says that 'Women and women's organizations [in Botswana] were reportedly "highly offended" by the ruling' (2012: 6). A critical public debate about marital equity and the rights of wives was emerging and already challenging past assumptions about extra-marital liaisons as a privilege of husbands.

Whether or not the Commissioner's 'instruction' ever reached the customary courts, it is evident that it was not heeded. In 2003, the Commissioner's judicial role, until then considered as being similar to that of a customary court *sui generis,* was abolished (Fombad 2004: 174). His post was replaced by that of Director of Tribal Administration. The current Director professed, in 2016, to

6 See also Schapera (1940b: 203–212) for an extensive discussion of polygamy and infidelity among the Kgatla in the 1920s and early 1930s. Even then, polygamy was on the wane, but men commonly had concubines whereas many women had extra-marital affairs. On the increase in pre-marital pregnancies and children borne out of wedlock, see Comaroff and Roberts 1977.

be unaware that Mr. Showa (the previous Commissioner) had ever made such a ruling. The Director was quoted (in a personal email) as saying that,

> What apparently has been happening is that a number of adultery cases against cheating husbands' lovers have been heard and damages awarded against the lover. However, this has not been practised uniformly. There have been some instances, particularly in the northern part of the country, where such cases have been dismissed. But in the south, they have been systematically heard and rulings against the lovers made.
>
> (3 October, 2016, email in authors' possession)

Lesedi Leepile, Research Director in the Ministry of Local Government and Rural Development, commented on this:

> I guess it is all about patriarchal tendencies that seem to be more prevalent in the north than in the south. Also, I am sure you are aware that customary law is not written anywhere and consequently, customary practices are also not written anywhere. Anyone can do whatever they like so long as it is not against the Constitution. Also, I think it all depends on whether people are married according to customary law or common law. I mean, according to common law, the laws are clear and written.
>
> (3 October, 2016, email in authors' possession)

The only other well-known challenge to the award of compensatory damages for adultery, this time to a cuckolded husband, was by Chief Sebele, acting as the President of the Customary Court of Appeal in 2008. He argued, appealing to a 'long standing' tradition 'over centuries', that compensatory damages could only be awarded if the wife was caught committing adultery in the marital bed. Other customary court judges, however, continued to award such damages in many other circumstances and ignored this judgement. Chief Sebele's decision overturned a case in the Gaborone urban customary court awarding a husband 10,000 pula in damages on the grounds that his wife's mobile phone call list cannot be used as evidence of adultery.

In a 2015 article, '*Dikgotla* (customary courts) Ignoring 2008 Customary Court of Appeal Judgement', a local newspaper reported this 2008 case in which Chief Sebele laid out in very extensive detail

> an elaborate process undertaken by Batswana *over centuries* to prove cases of adultery. The judgment refers to the culprit as a 'thief'. When a man finds his wife *in flagrante delicto*, he is not supposed to fight the thief or make any kind of scene. The victim (the husband) does that in order to protect his family and his wife's dignity and honor. 'The thief is also not supposed to make a scene,' Sebele's judgment reveals.

> What is of paramount importance at this stage is for the married couple to reconcile and for the thief to be punished for his kind of stealing. Sebele said that both tasks are supposed to be undertaken with the utmost secrecy.
> (Sunday Standard, 15 March 2015, emphasis added)

The newspaper article comments ironically that 'By this standard, customary courts would be guilty of said culpability because, even in 2015, "thieves" are still being fined for adultery that was committed far away from the marital bedroom' (ibid.). The attempt to freeze customary law in archaic tradition 'over centuries' is thus ineffective; customary courts respond to present-day understandings of culpability despite conservative pressures from the highest, national customary court.

We turn now to the detailed analysis of several adultery cases that took place in Moremi village customary court of record since 2010.

Adultery in a village customary court

In March 2016, Mosadi, a young 30-year-old woman, mother of three, sued her husband's female lover, eight months pregnant, at Moremi village customary court for 'breaking the yard (*lelwapa*)', home wrecking. The couple had been married for six years, since 2010, when the husband's family passed *bogadi* (bride wealth) of 12,000 pula (over £1000) to the bride's family. Their three children were born earlier, prior to the marriage, when the couple had cohabited in a traditional hut just outside her parental compound. The case was more radical than it appeared on the surface, even to the various protagonists in court; it confirmed transformations in gendered customary rights in relation to marriage and adultery in Botswana. The boldness of Mosadi's move also defied family consultation procedures.

Hence, the village chief hearing the case confirmed to Mosadi: 'You have the right (to sue); even your age [as an adult] allows you to take a complaint to court, to sue Lorato (the husband's lover)'.[7]

Customary courts pride themselves on their superior justice *vis-à-vis* magistrates' courts, arising from their careful consideration of *all* relevant facts, based on wide-ranging consultation. Once again, the village chief drew the contrast:

> At the magistrate's court they just 'cut', there is no fault. Now in the villages we always do all the procedures and rights. Everyone who has a stake in this matter, we pass through them. At the magistrate's, an axe (*selepe*) will just chop there. In the villages, we give each and every one the right opportunity. So that when we arrive ahead, it shouldn't be said, you have not given another one his/her right. If it means we will listen all day long or two days, each and every one should have a comment and the right (to speak). When

7 All names are pseudonyms.

> we finish, all the people should know when a person is married, what her/his rights are, where they stop, where they start. What right does she have in her husband and the husband too, what right does he have in his wife? If a blemish (*selabi*) enters between them, in what way will it be fought against?

During repeated hearings at the court, the demand by the village chief and various elders that the family should first hold a family '*morero*' (a closed consultation) was repeatedly given as the grounds for delay, for calling another court hearing. Thus, although it was agreed that a young woman like Mosadi had the 'right' to bring the case to court, the general feeling was, nevertheless, that she had acted with undue haste, circumventing the usual procedure. She should have turned, first, to Robert, her marriage go-between (*sebaga*). Nowadays, young people think they can just take matters into their own hands, Robert's mother complained, but, in the old days, families would settle the couple's troubles; the family disliked the way Mosadi had taken Lorato, her husband's lover, to court. That should have been done by her husband's family since the bride wealth was paid. Even more, Mosadi had gone away, her husband's family was having to wait for her to come home to her husband, before they did anything.[8]

During a series of customary court hearings interested parties – the accuser's parents, her go-betweens, other members of the family, repeatedly denied that they 'knew anything', to convey that they had no proper knowledge, as from a consultation. The go-between's sister told the headman, 'You are telling the truth. When you see me here, I am shocked to see these children, and now I am asking myself, what is happening? Myself, I do not know anything!'

Even the accuser's father professed ignorance. 'The way it is, we do not know anything. That is, this child (his daughter), if there was a ward headman (*kgosana*) [dutiful in consultation] would all these things have been said in the court? Later he added, 'it is shameful'. The accuser's mother spelled out the fault further, complaining that even the wife of the go-between should have seen the need to take the troubles back to Mosadi's parents, 'We are supposed to hear from her according to our custom'. Only the court clerk defended the accuser's decision to come to court and blamed her husband's family for neglecting and not taking due care of her: 'They did not take action. If all her in-laws neglect her, it is the cause for a wife to go back home (to her parents' home)'.

Several customary legal strands are hinted at in these brief comments. First is the tendency of customary courts, commented on by Anne Griffiths, to seek reconciliation between couples, even in the face of serious marital breakdown and the absence of the wider family's goodwill. As Griffith says, the customary court 'ruling, that both parties should go and "live together in peace and harmony" is very common in such disputes. It is something of a set text along the lines of a preordained homily. The social pressures of the *kgotla* are mobilised, but at the end of the day

8 For videos and documentaries about this court case and the role of the *sebaga* see R. Werbner (2016, 2018).

it is left to the parties themselves to make the relationship work' (1997: 141). The case she cites was similar to Moremi cases in which a wife raises the question of her husband's infidelity in public, subjecting him to public humiliation.

Griffiths also comments that 'women are powerless to prevent a man entering another relationship', which is seen as a 'sheer matter of concubinage' (ibid.). By 2016, in Moremi village and elsewhere in Botswana, this was no longer simply an accepted truth. Women everywhere were suing their husbands' lovers in both statutory and customary courts, demanding damages, asserting their rights to have a monogamous marriage, yet often finding implementation impossible, even when winning their cases.

Mosadi's case: silences in winning and losing against a mistress

As observers, we were struck by the fact that so much was left unsaid by the court. In a small community like Moremi, where people know each other intimately through day-to-day interactions and gossip, there is what Richard Werbner calls, in another context, a 'superabundance of understanding'. Neighbours and other villagers had long been aware, more in casual gossip than open discussion, that all was not well with Mosadi and her husband (see R. Werbner 2016, 2018b). She had gone off to the nearby town, Palapye, some 60 km away, three years earlier to train to be a constable, expecting ultimately to attend the national police academy and qualify as a policewoman. She had left her three children to be cared for by her mother, having moved back to her natal home from her husband's compound even earlier, complaining of mistreatment by her mother-in-law. It was said that Mosadi's move to Palapye was opposed by her husband, and even by his sisters, despite the fact they themselves were working in distant towns. He was determined to stay in the village, herd the largely inherited combined family herd, and not take a town job. The extent of marital cohabitation and other mitigating circumstances all have implications for the amount of damages courts award since damages for loss of '*consortium*' depend on the existence of ongoing marital relations.[9]

9 For example, in the High Court in Lobatse (2005), it was said that factors to be considered in determining damages were, *inter alia*, the duration of the marriage, the stability of the marriage, the outlook of the community amongst whom the spouses lived, their social standing, the plaintiff's moral character, the age of the plaintiff, and the likelihood of his or her remarrying. Justice Molokomme found that 'As for *consortium*, I have already indicated that the wife's case is weakened by the fact that cohabitation had ceased by the time the adultery was committed' (2005: 11). In another case, this time at the High Court at Lobatse in 1999, Justice J.A. Steyn said that 'Taking the South African decisions on damages and the Lesotho case, one can see that an award of damages for *contumelia* must entirely depend on the circumstances of each case, on the positions of the parties in society, on their characters, on the general view on adultery in the society in which the parties live, and on the ridicule, ill-will, and opprobrium suffered by the plaintiff as a result'.

After the first hearing in the village court, Mosadi said she was 'angry' with her husband, but asked if she wanted to divorce him, she insisted: 'Oh no, we still love each other'. What, then, was she expecting from the court since she didn't want to divorce her husband? She wanted him to 'pay', for the court to punish him. She could forgive her husband, but not his lover. She was suing his lover, not her husband, since she knew damage payments from a husband or wife are impossible for couples married in community of property. It made no sense to expect a husband to pay damages, she well realised.

Another silence in court was the silence of the two respondents, the husband and his lover, Lorato. When the headman asked her to plead, Lorato dodged answering, but seemed to plead not guilty. In the upshot, the court treated both respondents as pleading guilty and did not press Lorato, who was, after all, eight months pregnant. Following court procedures, according to the headman and the court clerk, since the two respondents had pleaded guilty, they could not be cross-examined. They themselves could ask questions of others, though in fact, they remained silent. According to Lorato's uncle, she could claim to be innocent, having been misled by Monna into believing he no longer loved his wife and they had parted. The headman, as Lorato's relative, no doubt was aware of this claim.

The view of the village chief and presiding judge, in personal comments, was that *both* the pregnant girl and the husband were guilty – the husband, according to Tswana custom and law *and* according to God, for betraying his marriage (in other words, the chief regarded adultery as a sin), and she for 'undermining the yard'. Hence, the husband should pay his wife and also pay damages for the girl herself and maintenance payments for her soon-to-be-born child. In the chief's view, a family consultation (*morero*) was needed to rescue the marriage through parental agreement, to make sure the couple did not divorce, and that the husband never did this again. When we commented that, for a man, having an affair had not been against Tswana law, at least in the past, the village chief objected. He insisted it definitely is, and always was, against the law. Even further, he seemed unwilling to conceive of the case as a single-issue matter, simply against the pregnant girl. The consideration had to include a move to reconcile husband and wife by the parental generation and ensure such acts of betrayal did not recur.

A further silence never raised during the court proceedings (which extended over four hearings, without a definite conclusion, while we were in the village) was the fact that the village chief was the lover's uncle, in Tswana terms; she was his father's brother's daughter's daughter. The girl was said to be an 'orphan' with no means of payment. These facts, too, were widely known. Indeed, a former judge on the national Customary Court of Appeal told us that the chief should have recused himself; that if such a case was considered in appeal, it would be nullified.[10] In Moremi village, however, the chief was a close relative of many

10 In Botswana, customary courts are arranged in a hierarchy, from lower courts of record located in select villages to recognised courts of appeal above them, culminating in the Customary Court of Appeal of the whole tribe, based at the tribal capital. Beyond that, appeals

of the litigants at court cases. When we questioned villagers about this, they told us that his relationship was irrelevant since, they claimed, he always followed customary law.

Due care for morality: parental responsibility and affinal suspicions

As the hearings progressed, with Mosadi's affines and even her go-between mostly absent, the village chief berated people at the court:

> Right now, we are talking about people who are still growing up (i.e., the couple), who are supposed to go forward with guidance. What does guidance mean in Setswana? … They (the couple) are still going to encounter serious problems (in their lives) and this needs parents so that, when it happens like this, they will stand up … for them to hold on to each other. We are counting on parents. If these parents are joined together, they will be the ones building the home of these children. If they pull back, it will mean that they have a part in wrecking the children's home … Isn't it, you hear?

Challenging the non-attendance of close relatives of the husband at the hearings, he continued:

> You will never know someone's responsibility (*maikarabelo*) and feelings (*maikutlo*) (when they don't turn up) … even if you do not comment, you should at least come so that you hear what is being said.

Mosadi's father had repeatedly – along with his wife – complained that he had not been informed by his affines or the go-between about the pregnant lover. Finding them still absent, he raised dark suspicions:

> The way I see it, the way the matter is, it means that those people who married my daughter have a problem and do not wish her to have a family. You mean to say the whole ward [the smallest section of a village] that came to

can be made to the national Customary Court of Appeal, of which there are currently two in Botswana (one in the north, the other in the south). From these, appeals are to Botswana's High Court. The court of Moremi village, where the cases discussed in this chapter were heard, is under the Ngwato tribal authority. This court only became a court of record in 2009. Above it, appeal courts have been based, variably, in various bigger villages, with the tribal Court of Appeal located in Serowe, the tribal capital. Under village courts of record are more informal ward and family moots in which many family disputes are initially heard, and often settled. Throughout the tribal customary court system, hearings are free and are held without lawyers. The customary court system in Botswana is at present a robust institution, with hundreds of courts of record in which thousands of cases are heard every year (see Fombad 2004).

> ask for the wife … all of them could not show up? … Or (is it that) they despise my family and myself? Myself, I see that they are the ones that tell their child (Mosadi's husband) to cause a problem in this child's home. They are the ones that separate the children! They cannot fail to hold a consultation. Yet, even when they are called to the court, they do not come. … I do not think that they will want this to be a proper marriage. … These children's home can be built by the two of us [both families]. … I was going to tell them that I do need Monna (my son-in-law) and I have no problem with him. If they do not want Mosadi, my daughter, they have to say straight out that they do not want her. There is deception (*boferere*) here. … Maybe they want it to go to the magistrate's. What I know is, Baremi (people of Moremi) … will take it that the owner of the case [the complaining wife and her family] comes from [the town] Mahalapye. Here, there are only kinsmen (*losika hela*) of the husband. … Now if the parents are in the forefront to wreck the home, I do not know [what can be done].

The background to this speech is the ongoing marriage dispute between Mosadi's family and her in-laws regarding the latter's failure so far to fulfil their promise to hold a big, public wedding celebration (*nyalo*), along with a name-changing civil marriage registration ceremony. The marital transactions, *bogadi* (bride wealth) and *dikobo* ('blankets'), had been passed, but the wedding celebration had been delayed, with the in-laws claiming they still lacked the funds to finance all the expenses. In retaliation, Mosadi had gone back to her parental home nearby, and left from there to Palapye. She had not taken the 'blankets' (household utensils, etc.) from her mother-in-law's house with her. Her parents, who were Kalanga, ethnic outsiders in the village, originally from Sebina, had moved to Moremi from the town, Mahalapye, to join close church friends, and Mosadi had grown up partly in Moremi. Her father was, in fact, an affluent man by local standards, a healer and bishop in one of Moremi's long-established Zionist churches. Despite this, her parents suspected their affines and even the village chief, they told us, of discriminating (*tlhaola*) against them. The chief, after all, was of the same family and descent (*losika*) as Lorato.

Inconclusive hearings, consultations and the unrecoverable compensation

The court ended the second hearing by instructing the go-between to get an 'answer' from all the affines and to report to the court five days later. The go-between warned that this might be difficult because Monna's sisters were widely scattered in different towns, but his intent was to try to contact them today and 'tomorrow to bring back the answer of when they will be free'.

In the upshot, the following Monday, when the third hearing was held, neither the go-between, nor any of the affines, nor even Monna, the husband, turned up.

Following the second hearing, Mosadi announced that she wanted to shift the adultery case to the magistrate's court, although she never went through with this move. She said she had consented to a family consultation because she had wanted to do everything according to 'Tswana custom'. She also wanted the relatives to give the husband a real scolding. But now she no longer wanted the consultation. The village chief had agreed to write a letter on her behalf to the magistrate (this was yet to happen even after four hearings).

Hearing after hearing in the village customary court called for a family consultation and lamented the absence of affinal representatives. In the fourth hearing, virtually all the affines living in the village attended, including the mother-in-law, and all agreed that a consultation would be called by the family. After the last hearing at the court, with the consultation promised, Mosadi told us her intent. After the consultation, but before going to the District Commissioner to register the marriage and change her name, she would pursue the case of 'breaking the yard' either in Moremi court or in Palapye, at the magistrate's court. She had attended such a case at the magistrate's court in Palapye in 2015, in her capacity as a policewoman. Of course, in the statutory courts, adultery is defined in terms of *contumelia* and loss of *consortium,* but she seemed unaware of the distinction. She claimed that, in the magistrate's court, the female lover was ordered to pay damages of 300,000 pula. She knew, of course, that less money was awarded at village courts,[11] but even in Moremi, some years previously, Mmagorata, a local woman, had been awarded 12,000 pula damages from her husband's woman lover for breaking the yard.

In the fourth hearing, in which the family, present in some numbers, promised a proper consultation, Mosadi addressed the village chief: 'What if I'm not happy (with it)?' The chief responded, somewhat surprisingly, perhaps misunderstanding her, that if she liked he could recuse himself and let someone else judge the case. Her comment was clearly intended to warn the court that she still retained the option of taking the case to the magistrate's court in Palapye. Earlier on, during the second hearing, the chief had promised her to try the case with skill (*botswerere*), despite the hurdles posed by the delays.

In the end, the marriage breakdown was never repaired, and the couple separated. The final customary court hearing took place on 15 December 2017. Mosadi was awarded 15,000 pula in compensation from her husband's lover. Earlier, there had been a family consultation but, since it failed to discuss her husband's adultery, Mosadi told us, she took the case back to the court. In the final case, unlike earlier ones, Mosadi, her husband, and his lover were all interrogated extensively by court members. After repeating her claim that she was told by Monna that his marriage was over, Lerato confessed to knowing her lover was married. Monna, who admitted his guilt, blamed his wife for being away and not talking to him. The village chief, summing up his judgement, delivered a moral lecture to both husband and wife about marriage and the need for cooperation and communication. They were both to blame equally for not having 'the spirit

11 In fact, it seems that at the magistrate's court damages are limited to 40,000 pula. However, according to the Daily Mail, a customary court awarded a woman 60,000 pula damages for adultery in 2013 (Nolan 2013).

of oneness', not sharing information about their mutual incomes, not sleeping together, following the call of 'nature' (*tlholego*). The verdict was in many ways a pyrrhic victory for Mosadi: an award of 15,000 pula to be paid in 625 pula instalments over two years. But, because the defendant was destitute, the chief warned, 'If she doesn't pay, because there is nothing that can be repossessed from her, if you take her to prison, you will feed her, pay her accommodation and pay all the expenses of the prison'. Mosadi appealed the verdict to a higher customary court and failed. She had no intention of feeding her husband's lover in prison. The marriage was over. Monna, it was rumoured, had found a new girlfriend.

Eventually, Mosadi did take Lorato to debtor's prison but without having to pay for her, due to a change in the law. After three months in jail, her mother's brother borrowed 6,000 pula (approximately £450) to pay for her release. In the meantime, Mosadi herself had a baby with an urban lover.

What the series of court cases exposed, perhaps most problematically, was the fact that adultery cases intensify feelings of deep pain, offence, and humiliation, and provoke a desire to take revenge on culprits and expose them publicly. This is all the more true in customary courts, since litigation is free and the courts allow a wide leeway for extraneous matters to be raised, not 'chopping' as magistrates court are perceived to do.

Catching a thief in Moremi village

An earlier case of adultery in the village made clear that polygamy was no longer an option in customary law among Tswapong. Hence, adultery cases test the definition of marriage and extra-marital relations, while revealing areas of ambiguity, which the court attempts to control through penalties but in practice fails to wholly redefine.

Many adultery cases rely on circumstantial evidence to prove their claims of adultery. In Moremi in 2010 and 2011, two 'revenge' cases of 'breaking the yard' succeeded each other within a relatively short space of time. In the first, Modiri sued his wife's lover for wrecking his home. Having called witnesses, Modiri caught his wife Keletso with a young builder 'under the blankets'. He found the door of his house locked with the suspect culprits inside. First, Keletso hid in the cupboard but, when he threatened to call the police, she came out. At this point she and her lover confessed. In her defence, she said that she had gone with this 'child' (young man) because her husband had abandoned her and was living with his lover, and she too 'had feelings'. Her husband's affair was well-known in the village but, although Keletso had tried to bring witnesses to catch him in the act, she had failed thus far. The court found the adulterous young man guilty but reduced the fine from 6,000 to 3,000 pula.

Some months later, Keletso got her retribution. She waited until midnight and then mobilised seven witnesses, including her 21-year-old son, waking up her neighbours, who all congregated around Modiri's lover's house. While some called out to her to open the door, Modiri escaped through a window, witnessed by his son and two neighbours. He jumped over the fence and went into his hut, pretending to be asleep. The ward head and his wife were called and eventually, his lover opened the door. They searched for clothing items, especially Modiri's shoes, since he was said to have escaped the hut barefoot but found nothing. According to a witness in court, when they gathered the next morning at Modiri's parents' house, while still denying his guilt, Modiri said at one point: 'I am tired of this escaping through the window. I want to marry Thabu (his lover) (as a second wife). Keletso will be my first wife'.

It was decided to bring the case to the village court since earlier attempts to reconcile husband and wife had all failed. It was an 'ancient' case (*kgologolo*). On this occasion, the wife sued her husband's lover in court for 8,000 Pula for 'breaking the yard'. Witness after witness described the scandalous events of that night, with the lovers persisting in denying their guilt. The verdict, when it came, was a moral condemnation of their behaviour by the village chief presiding over the case. He first scolded the husband's lover, reminding her that, even when her own husband was still alive, a case was brought by him against the husband-lover. He then turned to the husband: 'You say, "I will marry both" (*pataganya,* join both women together). ... But polygamy is no longer there' (in Botswana) (*go nyala lefufa ga go tlhola go le teng* – a marriage 'of jealousy' is no longer practised). You should feel ashamed of yourself for not caring for your family and children and should return to living well with your wife'. The final verdict, against the husband's lover, was for 12,000 pula in compensatory damages for home wrecking, more than had originally been asked for.

Anomalies and entanglements in the quest for justice

Certain changes in the 'unwritten' customary law had by now been established: the right of women to take adulterous husbands' lovers to court, and the understanding that polygamy is no longer acceptable. Nevertheless, the outcomes of adultery cases reveal unresolved anomalies in the quest for justice. Asked what had happened following the decision in the revenge home-wrecking case, a village elder responded that 'nothing' had changed, there was no peace (*kagiso*), no consultation. Modiri and his wife did not share in dialogue with one another (*rerisana*). As far as the elder knew, Modiri stayed in his compound but not together with his wife. He was still the lover of Thabu. His wife seemed to be 'tired' of fighting any further cases. Modiri did not divorce his wife, probably because he feared, the elder guessed, that if he tried to divorce her, the court would let his wife get all his property. Things had not changed, because there was constant quarrelling.

The court decision had not resolved the entanglement between the wife, the husband, and his lover. After a funeral, people were invited by Modiri's wife to a wake, which turned out to be held at the mistress's house. The elder explained this by pointing out, first, that the two women were first cousins, their mothers were sisters; second, Thabu's late husband and Modisi were sons of the same father but different mothers; hence, traditionally, the extra-marital affair would have been a levirate had polygamy been allowed. Finally, the elder was sure that, when the case came to court and the offending lover was charged 12,000 pula in damages, the adulterous husband had, in fact, been the one to pay the fine from his earnings as a diviner.

The case of Mosadi highlighted significant difficulties contrary to the moral rhetoric the village chief in Moremi village expressed, regarding parental responsibility and the need for family consultation. Parental law, with its stress on the responsibility of the parental generation and the responsibility and responsiveness of children, had become highly problematic. Normative practices, assumptions, and values regarding gender, generation, and marriage had all undergone radical changes.

Conclusion

Cases of adultery in Botswana reflect changes in gendered and generational relations in different historic periods. Despite the moral homilies pronounced by the village chief in Moremi village customary court, regarding parental responsibility and the need for family consultations, the case of Mosadi points to the relative independence of the younger generation, and the inability of parents to fully control young people's decisions, however much they may desire to do so. Equally important, as we have seen, has been the change in gendered relations in marriage: customary law no longer condones men's philandering or polygamy; young women can take their husbands' girlfriends to court, and many do; feminist and human rights activism since 1990 has created a major thrust in Botswana towards gender equality.[12]

In this chapter we have tried to show how changes in customary law have been impacted by and impact on the *rhetoric* and *ethos* of judicial decision making. Certain changes in unwritten law have a clear trajectory, we argue, and in this sense Tswana customary law, as in the rest of southern Africa, is to be grasped as 'living law', responsive to changing circumstances (Fombad 2004: 183, 191; Himonga and Moore 2015): although largely unwritten, a corpus of more or less agreed Tswana customary law does exist for any particular time and place (Schapera 1983). This implies that judges are not simply dealing with an amorphous body of unwritten custom and law, *mekgwa le milao*. Unwritten law is affected, we have shown, through customary judicial deliberation in court, regarding notions of contemporary morality, of 'fairness', (*tshiamo*) and reasonableness in response to changing circumstances, as Gluckman too, for example, argued (1955, 1963). Such notions of equity, it seems evident, were implicitly reflected in the level of damages awarded in the different cases we reported here for ostensibly similar delicts.

Our argument may be contrasted with Comaroff and Roberts' (1981) 'processual' paradigm of Tswana judicial decision making that envisages customary law as consisting of an unsystematic 'loosely constructed repertoire' (1981: 18)

12 On this see Geisler (1995) and Griffiths (2011).

of rules, habits, and norms, often contradictory or ambiguous, which enables litigants to formulate multiple interpretations ('paradigms') in their defence, as they engage in negotiations, alliance making, and individual political manoeuvrings. The whole range of customary rules, norms, and values, they argue, is constantly being constructed and reconstituted (ibid.: 20). Against that, we have demonstrated that, in Botswana, customary law, like statutory law, is historically inflected so that any analysis of law must incorporate the current state of the legal system as a whole (see Griffiths 1997: 208; P. Werbner 2014b: 485–486).

Taking a legal realist, living-law approach, this chapter has shown that customary court decisions are embedded in considerations of equity that also inform wider ideological, critical movements and processes of judicial innovation and legal reform. Schapera (1970) proposes that Tswana tribal 'innovators' have historically had the capacity to introduce legal judgements in response to not only changing circumstances or norms but also changing notions of equity and fairness. Clearly, however, as this chapter has also shown, attempts to shape customary law from above, for example by the Law Commissioner or the national Customary Court of Appeal, *against* changing local understandings of gender equality or adultery practices, must equally fail.

9 A case of inheritance

From citizens' forum to magisterial justice in Botswana's customary courts

Introduction: the *Kgotla* as a consultative judicial forum

Botswana's customary courts were known in the past for their procedural openness to debate and public opinion making. The chief or headman presided over the court but allowed members of the court, usually in ascending order of seniority, to express their views on the case, before finally reaching a judgement. Most scholars of Tswana society, from Isaac Schapera onwards, agree that the chief's final judgement was responsive to public opinion as expressed during a hearing. It was this public debate that made Tswana customary law 'living law', reflecting current understandings and changing normative assumptions. Our chapter considers evolving customary law in Botswana and the challenges to its continuity as 'living law' in the present context of reforms to the Customary Law Act.

Although largely unwritten, a corpus of Tswana customary law does exist. It reflects current realities, as judges seek to apply notions of 'fairness' (*tshiamo*) and reasonableness to changing circumstances. A key development in recent times has been the huge rise in formally recognised customary courts of record (429 at the last count). Hence, Moremi village, the focus of our study, now has, despite its small size (circa 500 residents), a court clerk, a bailiff, two policemen and several deputies. Presiding judges are no longer experienced members of the court. Thus, unlike his father, the current headman spent most of his working life in the army, while the number of 'elders' (over the age of 40) living permanently in the village and attending the *kgotla* (customary court) regularly has greatly decreased, from around 20 to only four or five. Despite these changes, many continuities are still discernible along with unacknowledged radical change in the nature, shape, and function of the village *kgotla*.

Early on in the history of the Protectorate, customary courts, in 1933, and particularly their distinctive procedural form of consultation, were challenged by Sir Charles Rey, the first British Resident Commissioner to Bechuanaland, who issued two proclamations authorising *nominated court members only* (not necessarily chiefs) to act as judges. This challenge to open public participation in *kgotla* decision-making was never implemented *de facto,* even though the appeal lodged by two prominent Tswana chiefs against the ruling had failed in the colonial courts.

DOI: 10.4324/9781003241881-9

So, the matter rested for some 75 years until an amendment in Botswana's Customary Law Act, in 2013, granted chiefs or presiding court headmen, almost as an afterthought, sole decision-making authority, *without the need for consultation*. This new dispensation was evident in the chiefly conduct of a customary court case convened in 2017 to consider the inheritance of properties of a long-deceased man in Moremi village, analysed here.

It seems, however, that not all customary courts in the district were following the new edict and there was also some confusion among court participants regarding the chief's requirement to seek advice from his counsellors and village elders as in the past. This indicated that consultative citizens' courts were an entrenched feature of customary law, not easily overturned by a statutory ruling from above. Nor was it clear why the ruling had been made as it had, almost imperceptibly, in a definitional footnote, a matter we return to below. There appeared to be no discussion about the change in the gazette appended to the amendment (B185, 21/9/2012). In the present chapter we consider the implications of this radical legal reform from above for an understanding of legal pluralism and customary law as living law, both in Botswana and comparatively.

Legal mobilisation: the 1934 Bechuanaland Proclamation and its aftermath

Writing about problematic procedural reforms in the 1934 and 1935 Proclamations issued by Sir Charles Rey, Lord Malcolm Hailey recognises that at stake was 'Native justice', underpinned by 'strong support in popular sentiment':

> Tradition had continued to regard a trial as being a trial by the Kgotla [customary court], and though the Chief usually (though not invariably) presided, the fact that the case was heard in public and that the public had a voice in discussing the decision was itself some guarantee against arbitrary or unjust judgements.
>
> (Hailey 1953: 216)

'Trial by Kgotla', arguably a form of citizens' justice, has been repeatedly noted, as already mentioned, by anthropologists studying Tswana customary courts. In his detailed description of the composition of the customary court, Isaac Schapera lists, apart from the Chief who acts as president of the court, his senior brothers and paternal uncles, a range of recognised assessors known as *banna ba kgotla* (men of the court), ward headmen, and finally, 'Every adult man in the tribe ... has a right to be present at any case and to take part in the discussion' (Schapera 1938: 282; see also Gulbrandsen 2012: 70–71). Usually, they speak in order of seniority. Decisions made through such collective deliberation are more likely to be accepted by litigants, as Elizabeth Colson has argued, even when court hierarchies are relatively weak:

> The authority of the court, such as it was beyond that given by the colonial administration, derived largely from this involvement of the general public in a forum in which contenders faced an emerging consensus backed by public opinion.
>
> (Colson 1976: 21)

The 1934 proclamations were intended to address the 'practical autocracy' developed by some of the stronger chiefs during the initial colonial period (Hailey 1953: 211, 215). Gulbrandsen sums up the proclamations (Gulbrandsen 2012: 71–73) as, broadly speaking, having the aim to ensure 'legal-rational accountability' by (a) opening formal complaint channels against the chief for members of the tribe; (b) establishing rules for recognition and installation of chiefs; (c) reducing the hierarchy of courts to just Senior and Junior Tribal Tribunals; (d) ensuring written records of cases heard in these; and, most saliently, (e) establishing tribal councils comprising named members whom chiefs were obliged to consult. This was perceived by the chiefs to conflict both with

> the *kgosi's* customary privilege to consult whomever he wanted and with his commitment to give due importance to the views of his subjects as expressed in the public sphere of the *kgotla* where the 'entire *morafe*' (i.e., all adult men) were entitled to participate.
>
> (Gulbrandsen 2012: 70)

Even before they were issued, the Ngwato Acting Chief Tshekedi openly opposed the Proclamations in the Advisory Council in 1933, as an encroachment on native law and custom (Hailey 1953: 217). When they were nonetheless enacted, in 1935, the Acting Chief challenged the Resident Commissioner in the courts, where he was joined by the Ngwaketse Chief, Bathoen II (ibid.), on the grounds, among other things, that 'the Proclamations purport to make alterations in certain native laws and customs; that he [Rey] has no power to make such alterations because the Order in Council from which he derives his powers directs him, in the exercise of such powers, to respect native law and custom' (court records, Lobatse 29/11/1936, Reported as Tshekedi Khama & Ano v High Commissioner 1926-53 HCTLR 9).

The case, heard on the week starting 6 July 1936, in Lobatse, was the occasion of massive countrywide and regional legal mobilisation, anticipating future legal mobilisations in independent Botswana (see P. Werbner 2014). The events as they unfolded are recorded by Resident Commissioner Charles Rey in his diary (Rey 1988: 207–210). People travelled great distances for the trial, he tells us. The Attorney General, specially appointed for the trial, was, he complains, delayed in Johannesburg, too busy to read the voluminous file of trial papers. The judge arrived by train along with hundreds of participants, officials, and witnesses, who had to be accommodated and fed, some in specially refurbished railway carriages Rey had commissioned. Beyond that, 'two thousand natives have turned up, and the Court will hold [only] fifty' (ibid.: 207). To solve the problem, Tshekedi and Bathoen's South African counsel demanded that the case be tried in the open. 'This was too silly for words', says Rey. It took two days to bring in loudspeakers from Jo'burg, but these proved to be a great success – 'all remarks in the courthouse could be heard half a mile away', with the upshot that 'the two thousand natives sit in long lines and listen delightedly to the loudspeakers, which they do not understand' (ibid.:208). Rey is equally disdainful in his assessments of the various (white) advocates whom he describes as 'rotten', poor cross-examiners, 'weak' or 'poor' though the AG's closing speech, he concedes, was 'admirable' (ibid.). The Resident Commissioner returns home 'thoroughly tired out and sick to death of the whole business'. The whole case, he concludes, was a 'shocking waste of time and money' (ibid.: 208).

Six months later Rey is finally able to claim: 'My greatest triumph! ... *We win on all points, with costs!* ... The papers have great headlines, ... What a fight – nearly six years of argument, and now I am justified. My Proclamations stand, and Tshekedi is defeated' (ibid.: 218).

Rey spoke too soon, however. He clearly underestimated the capacity of the losing parties to stonewall, delay, obfuscate, and simply ignore the verdict despite apparently accepting it. Justifying the chiefs' objections, Hailey makes the point that the law had made radical changes which undermined a system of trial to which local people were 'as deeply attached to as a Briton to the procedure of trial by jury' (Hailey 1953: 222). By 1943, when the Proclamation of 1934 came under revision, it was admitted that the provisions could not be implemented. The revised law of 1943 no longer insisted that the Chief notify the Administration of the names of his Councillors and says nothing about the composition of the Kgotla. There are no Senior and Junior Tribunals. 'Trial by Kgotla' is effectively reinstated (ibid.: 226). The Resident Commissioner may have won the battle, but the chiefs had won the war.

So, matters stood until 2013 when an amendment to the 2006 Botswana Customary Law Act granted chiefs or presiding court headmen, almost as an afterthought, with no explanation, sole decision-making authority, *without the need for consultation*. In the amendment, a 'member of the court' is described *by definition/interpretation action* as 'a person who presides over a customary court or customary court of appeal'. This implies that the presiding officer is not obliged to seek the opinion of any other participants in the hearing and, indeed, no other participants have the right to express their views in court. No further explanation of this radical departure from entrenched Tswana custom is provided in the *Gazette* of 21 September 2012, signed by Peter Siele, Minister of Local Government at the time. In the debate in the House of Chiefs about the Amendment, the Parliamentary Council from the Attorney General's Chambers, Ms Morolong, explained the new definition purely in terms of rhetorical convenience:

> Moving on to the one on the use of the word, 'Member'. The Minister has explained that a member in this case is a presiding officer at Kgotla level. Tribesman means a member of a particular tribe; let us not confuse the use of the term member and tribesman because they are different. A member was used collectively to refer to *Kgosi*, *mothusa Kgosi*, *moemela Kgosi*, *Kgosana*, Court President, and Deputy Court President *to avoid the monotony of a long sentence having to be repeated in the Act* and eventually losing the meaning along the way.
>
> (House of Chiefs debate, January 2013, pp. 36–37, emphasis added).

It is not that attendants at court are precluded from *cross-examining* witnesses. The point is that, following this definitional amendment, *their advice on the case as a whole* is no longer sought in weighing up the rights and wrongs of the case or in suggesting a fair, equitable verdict. Decision-making is now, apparently by a sleight of hand, solely the prerogative of the presiding judge, the chief or village headman.

A case of inheritance

The problems inherent in the new chiefly prerogative of sole adjudication were reflected in a case held at the customary court in Moremi village, Tswapong North, in May–June 2017. Inheritance cases are, along with cases of insult, divorce, and adultery, among the most complex and painful cases routinely heard in customary courts. They have also been subject recently to review in the High Court: most famously, a customary court case heard on appeal in 2012 in the High Court by Justice Key Dingake allowed equal rights of homestead inheritance to women, citing Botswana's Constitution, while denying the right of the male last-born son (ultimogeniture) to exclusive inheritance of the family homestead (see case MAHLB-000836-10, heard at the High Court Gaborone, 12/10/2012). Although this appeal to the constitution was rejected in the Court of Appeal, the verdict to allow daughters to inherit the homestead was upheld (see below).

At stake in conflicts over inheritance are not just issues of property but the intricate social relations implied by ownership, debt, and rights built up over time. The complexity in the present case was even greater because the owner of the estate had died in 1989, 27 years (!) before the case was finally held in the *kgotla*. There were numerous items of property involved, reflecting the fact that at one time the family had been quite prosperous by local rural standards. Complicating matters further was the fact that, of the four siblings entitled to inherit from the deceased, two, a sister and brother, had died in the early 1970s (the claimants were their children) and one son was adopted at birth. The eldest son, trustee of the estate, was at the time of the hearing, in 2017, 96 years old. As emerged during the hearing, he had in fact over the years distributed or sold much of the property for a pittance, without consultation. Indeed, he insisted at the hearing for much of the time that legally, he was the sole heir.

He also insisted that the property was worthless, apparently not recognising the exponentially enhanced value of land, wells, and guns that had occurred in the past 20 years, as these types of property have been commodified in Botswana. Another complication related to the bureaucratic management of rural plots after the establishment of the Land Board in 1970. Before that, the chief was responsible for distributing land from a communal pool on the basis of use and need, without registration. After the creation of the Land Board, land governance was taken from the chiefs and different types of land and wells were all subject to registration and certification. This process was, however, somewhat patchy, with overlapping and sometimes multiple claims on plots, including multiple land certificates on the same plot, according to local informants. Neither registration nor certification had, by 2017, yet been as systematically implemented as originally planned.

As the case highlighted, inheritance cases rake up memories of past, long-buried insults, offences, and transgressions. At the same time, the very intricacies of these past events and the assorted bits of property forming the estate make it difficult for an outsider, in this case the chief or village headman sitting as judge, to follow. The advice of *kgotla* assessors, 'members of the court', more familiar with the protagonists and the plots or wells passed on as inheritance, is therefore crucial. Without such advice and public participation, the decision-making is unlikely to be seen to be safe or just, according to customary law; and this danger is all the more subversive of customary law when the presiding officer has little or no personal knowledge of all the protagonists. The chief of Moremi knew one of the litigants, Neil, nephew of RreMogolo, the original owner (all names are pseudonyms), well; they had been to school together and had remained friends. The chief had known the old man, RreMogolo, who was, during his lifetime, an important elder in village politics, but only as a youth, before inheriting the chiefship. RreMogolo's eldest son Martin, the brother accused of mishandling the estate, his younger (adopted) brother, Keith, and his nephew, Maurice, were barely known to the chief. He was even less familiar with Martin's children and grandchildren who had mainly grown up in the neighbouring village, Matolwane, where RreMogolo and his wife had relocated in the 1970s.

There had already been two recent lower-level hearings or moots (*merero*) trying to sort out the dispute. Both were recorded, though informally. The first took place at Martin's homestead in Matolwane and was presided over by his cousin, now an elder and headman of one of Moremi's wards, Molemo (a pseudonym). The second took place in Moremi village court and was presided over jointly by the *kgosana* (ward heads) of three of its wards, including Molemo. Both moots failed in the end because Martin, the 96-year-old eldest heir, persisted in refusing to acknowledge the rights of (a) his dead sister's son and daughter, (b) his dead brother's son, and (c) his adopted brother, to share in the inheritance.

When the first formal village court hearing finally took place, in May 2017, the village chief arrived several hours late and was not debriefed about the earlier hearings, beyond a warning that he should treat the defendant/respondent gently because of his age. Martin, a likeable, gentle, but spendthrift man, had spent most of his life, after his return from a stint in the mines, drinking *bojalwa* (sorghum beer) in the company of his exuberant wife, playing his one-string guitar (*segaba* or violin) and generally abjuring the normal expectation that he take on the role of responsible village elder. Despite having 'eaten' the inheritance, as the three complainants claimed, he and his wife, before her recent death had, it was generally agreed, lived in relative poverty, not owning a brick house like most other elders in the village did. Martin also no longer owned the herds of cattle and goats he used to have. Nevertheless, at 96, Martin, though frail, was still able to walk long distances and to speak cogently in court. If he digressed, this seemed a deliberate ploy to avoid discussing the details of the inheritance. By all accounts he continued to frequent the village beer parties, drawing on his pensioner's income, and was fed and looked after by his children.

Neil, the leading complainant, was a sophisticated, educated, man-about-town who lived in Gaborone, the capital. Yet he had deep roots in the village and was also leading the village's litigation in Botswana's High Court and Court of Appeal to sue the Ministry of Land and Local Government against the change to Matolwane's name. Neither he nor the other two complainants were wealthy. The court case was precipitated by a government initiative to register all property in Botswana with the ultimate aim of creating a national, digitised databank. This led to a village scramble to register plots, wells, and the like before the deadline, 31 December 2017, fearing that they would be returned to the common pool. Investigating the three wells left by his grandfather (mother's father), Neil found that two had been converted into boreholes and were owned by outsiders. The third well was apparently registered in the name of Martin's grandson. He also found that his grandfather's gun had been sold. His grandfather's large arable plot had never been formally divided.

The example of one of the wells included in the estate gives some idea of the magnitude of commodification that had occurred in Botswana in recent years. The well was allegedly sold by Martin for 2,000 pula to a woman in Palapye, who developed a borehole and then sold it further for 250,000 pula, a multiple of 125! Similarly, the gun, sold by Martin for 5,000 pula, was said to be worth 50,000 pula, mainly for the hunting licence attached to it (the gun was worth very little). Martin had sold these two items, and a second well, also converted into a borehole, without consulting any of the other heirs. When Neil was asked in court why the matter was not settled earlier, he said Martin kept telling him he needed to consult his mother's relatives in another village. One can only guess that for most of this time the heirs were not strongly motivated to divide the estate.

One legal issue not explicitly addressed during the court case was the status of suspect goods bought in good faith by a third party, who then either resells them or invests substantially in them. Could they be claimed back despite the investment or further sale? The basic rule in Botswana in such cases is that a person who does not have legal title to goods cannot pass on the title; the original owner (in the present case, joint heirs to the estate) is protected if the goods were not bought in good faith. The *kgotla* did not ask for 'certificates' of ownership until very late in the second hearing, a month later, and in fact, never got them despite repeated attempts. In the meanwhile, we ourselves checked the registration of the wells and the field in the sub-district and district Land Boards. Despite the fact that the information was scattered and incomplete, it emerged that the wells had all originally been registered by Martin: he had registered the well sold to the woman in Palapye (who later resold it) in 2005; one well was registered in Martin's name in 1993 and later, in 2012, was transferred to his daughter's eldest son; the third well had never been registered but the land board entered the borehole there as a 'new point' in 2007, granting it a certificate in 2009. In other words, all three sales had been entered into in good faith. The complainants argued trenchantly that Martin had no right to claim the wells as his, register them in his name alone, or sell them. As the eldest son, he was merely expected to act as a trustee until the inheritance was settled.

Procedures in the court during the hearing were tightly controlled by the court clerk. The three complainants and defendant were asked to state their case in turn and to interrogate selected witnesses, who could then be interrogated by members of the public. The three *dikgosana* (councillors, heads of wards) sat in the front, next to the chief, completely silent throughout the hearing. At no point were they consulted and neither their commentary nor their advice was sought at any point during the hearing. It was this silence that struck us as requiring explanation, and which led ultimately to our 'discovery' of the radical change that had occurred in customary court legislative procedures. The village chief asked the litigants or witnesses questions now and then, mainly trying to sort out the locations of the wells and other details which he seemed to find confusing, but strikingly, he did not elicit advice or consult either his *dikgosana* or any other members of the *kgotla*. He was merely seeking elucidation, not public opinion.

Figure 9.1 Moremi court inheritance hearing.

This was significant because some of his decisions seemed strange and, indeed, they were challenged by the complainants. We cite *verbatim* from the conclusion of the case as we recorded it:

KGOSI (VILLAGE CHIEF): That means, concerning the wells, let me not say the wells. I want to 'be honest and open with you', here, it is going to happen in relation to two wells. It is going to happen in relation to H. and J. (the two wells sold to outsiders who developed them). The third well, which was said that it is Martin's son; the old man (Martin) has the right (*tshwanelo*) to give it to him (his son) because he is his child. Whether he told you or did not tell you. We can get the old man for the other wells but not this one. Because he has the right to give it to him. (In fact, the well was registered as transferred to his grandson).

MAURICE: The well being RreMogolo's (the deceased) and not his (Martin's) well?

VILLAGE CHIEF: Yes, being RreMogolo's. I am talking about Martin. All, we should talk all these things but not forget that it was RreMogolo's.

MAURICE: Yes.

KGOSI: Martin is the eldest son. Now, concerning the two (other) wells, I think those ones are okay, you can make an 'evaluation'. And now the one he has given to his son, how can you deny him that? Give me an idea (*leano*), let us all pass through it. 'Let us clear it first' – to see how he (Martin) can deny (*rontsha*) his son.

Here the chief seems to be quoting a customary rule privileging the inheritance rights of an elder son. He is immediately confronted with dissent by the complainants:

NEIL: Kgosi (headman).

VILLAGE CHIEF: Yes.

NEIL: 'I want to be frank and fair', the well that we are talking about is not RreMartin's. We are talking about the well which was RreMogolo's. He (Martin) wasn't given it rightfully (*tshwalenong*), so that he could pass it on to his children. I'm not saying the one of RreMartin, he cannot pass (*fitisetsa*) on to his children, but at this 'point in time' he used his capacity to grab or seize (*bogagapa*) it (the well) to pass it to his son. At 'this point in time', now at this time, he passed the wells on by selling them and all these are benefitting him, though they did not go to him rightfully. 'Here is my argument'.

VILLAGE CHIEF: Yes, 'your argument is very clear'.

NEIL: Yes.

VILLAGE CHIEF: 'It's clear' (interruptions). No, that side you will have a chance to talk.

PERSON: The old man says you are using English, and he can't understand.

VILLAGE CHIEF: Wait first. The complaints and the comments (*dikakgelo*) we have been saying they are just straightforward.

NEIL: Okay.

VILLAGE CHIEF: It will be answered by the 'petition' (future appeal). It will answer it. When you take this matter concerning the old man forward but not here (unclear what he means). The one you are saying is going to answer concerning the matter concerning the old man (Martin), even his rights where they start and where they end in relation to RreMogolo.

NEIL: Yes

VILLAGE CHIEF: The old man. Don't you see? That side, in his parents' and his property (*dithoto*), now that one it will be answered when the matter goes further, that what (were) his (Martin's) 'limits'.

COURT CLERK: Seelo (border), *selekanyo.*

VILLAGE CHIEF: His limits, where it starts and where it ends.

KEITH (complainant, brother of Martin): Can I comment on something?

VILLAGE CHIEF: Yes, you can comment.

KEITH: Let me go back to the beginning concerning the well he has given to his children. The well he gave to his children – even myself I have had too many expenses regarding it – myself, I'm standing here. I pegged it with poles and blasted it with dynamite (*jaratinni*), which I brought with my bicycle from Palapye.

VILLAGE CHIEF: Sit down, RreKeith. When we started this matter, these are the things that you could have put before us, what you did with regard to the well, how you spent labour/money on it, with what kind of expectations (*tsholofelo*) you had. Now when you stood up you said you do not have anything to say but the words were from the first complainant (Neil).

KEITH: I thought you said the first statement (he thought he would be given another chance to talk).

VILLAGE CHIEF: You just explained that you don't have anything to say. The words are from the first complainant (Neil), which you are all together about them. Now how would we know that you had pegged the well when you did not say it? When a person loses, he loses (*jewa*) in this way. How would we know that you cut the poles and pegged the well?

KEITH: And sold the cattle.

VILLAGE CHIEF: And sold the cattle?

KEITH: Yes, I sold two cattle for that well. *My* cattle. The ones I bought with the money I got (earned) from (working in) the mine. They have dug that well.

COURT CLERK (ignoring these revelations): The chief is coming to his conclusion.

VILLAGE CHIEF: Listen.

COURT CLERK: When the chief comes to the conclusion, he will be at the end of the matter. *You cannot interrupt* unless it is him, like when he was asking and you are told that you are capable of how you are going to handle these things (regarding the wells that were sold), the matter, concerning all the expenses of the people who bought the wells. Now he is concluding.

This extract from the court recording we made reveals that the chief has allocated the only well still available without further litigation to Martin, presumably on grounds of primogeniture, to pass on to the latter's son. He now refuses to open up the verdict when further facts emerge, citing formal procedures. Further deliberation about more issues would have to be on appeal.

A second verdict reached by the village chief, this time regarding the field of the deceased, RreMogolo, was equally surprising. Having apparently verified that

Martin had a certificate for part of field (at the land board, we found that he had a certificate from 1992, although this was not produced in court), with the rest of the field registered in the name of his mother, RreMogolo's wife (we were unable to find any certificate in her name), he concludes that the *whole* field is now Martin's! We quote again from the court records:

VILLAGE CHIEF: The field is all yours. (The old lady) is no longer alive. If she might have had a certificate, and the other certificate is yours (Martin's); at this time, all of them (certificates), if there are questions about the field, you are going to answer yourself because the old man has long died. All right – the field is all yours!

MARTIN: Yes.

VILLAGE CHIEF: It is understandable. Now when it is like that, we are about to finish. Go and drink water for five minutes. We will finish when you come back.

As we shall see, these somewhat unfortunate decisions were ultimately overturned in later hearings. The village chief himself changed his mind, perhaps in the face of pressure from Neil, who was very angry, and threatened to appeal.

The silence of the kgotla

We were puzzled by the striking silence of members of the court, particularly the ward heads, and, indeed, by the absence of any attempt by the chief to seek council and advice from those present at the hearing. This seemed contrary to Tswana custom. At the time, we were unaware of the changes made to the Customary Law Act in the 2013 amendment. As it turned out, no-one in the village and neighbouring village had heard of these changes either. The end of 'trial by *Kgotla*' had come unheralded, unannounced, and mostly ignored. When the Moremi court clerk was asked why the chief hadn't consulted anyone, she saluted smartly, implying that this is what one can expect from an ex-army man. He liked to do things his own way and hardly ever listened to advice, she said (in reality, in our perception she powerfully influenced both the procedures in court and the general thrust of cases, and the Chief repeatedly consulted her).

When we asked the head of Molemo ward why he had not spoken, he said at first that there had been no judgement (the final outcome still awaited evaluations of the wells) but, when pressed that there had been a judgement over the remaining well that was said to have gone to Martin's son, John, he said that was not right. The well was not Martin's and, in any case, John was adopted but not formally, he said. Also, the well was actually registered in two names, he thought, John's and Martin's grandson, though they hid this at the kgotla hearing since it would have raised further questions (we found the well was registered only in the name of Martin's daughter's son).

We asked if the chief should not have consulted his advisors, the three *dikgosanas*, since they sat through the whole meeting without saying a word. He said he thought he himself couldn't give advice because he was part of the family but the other two should have been consulted. His son, an educated young man, disagreed, and said that the decision was the chief's. This pointed perhaps to a generation gap. They laughed when I responded that the chief was acting like a magistrate.

Another of the three *dikgosanas* also thought there should have been consultation. The most senior *dikgosana*'s response was, however, ambiguous. His view was that the chief should seek advice but in private. There should be a *morero* before the case. In the end, the chief had to make up his own mind on the merits of the case, what was true or false. He didn't seem to put much stock by people in the court expressing their views, interpreting the evidence. But wasn't the present inheritance case an example of the chief making a series of wrong decisions – about the well and the field? He agreed that the chief had been confused (*tsietsega*) in this particular case, but later the chief had thought about it and realised he was wrong, he said. The chief hadn't actually made a final judgement and, in the next round, he would reach the right decision. He seemed clearly to be informed about the current thinking of the chief, either from Neil or from the *kgosi* himself. How did the chief come to change his mind? He just thought about it. And anyway, if litigants felt the decision was wrong, they could always appeal. He clearly accepted that the chief should make the decision '*a le nosi*', alone.

The court clerk in the neighbouring village disagreed strongly with this view. She didn't really think that procedures in Botswana had changed. The chief(s) at Matolwane still sought advice, she said. When we explained about the silence of the *dikgosana* at Moremi, she commented that they were oppressing themselves (*ikgatelela*), which they should not do. She said '*banna ba le kgotla*' (people/men of the court) should express their views. Speaking about her experiences as a court clerk, she said some chiefs refused to take advice. Then they just made mistakes.

An example of an inheritance case heard in Matolwane in June 2015 *(after* the amendment to the Customary Law Act) is instructive. The case concerned a field claimed by George, the complainant, vis-à-vis his elder half-brother, T. It was heard by a chief sent from Palapye. George had ploughed the field with his mother until her death and had then written to the Land Board to change the registration to his name, but previously the field had no certificate.

The case proceeded through a series of witnesses who were interrogated by the complainant and defendant and by members of the court. Eventually, the chief presiding over the case asked for comments. There were seven commentators before the chief summed up and gave his verdict. The first appeared to side with the defendant, but all the others sided with George:

J.M.: According to me, it tells me that the field that was said, it is before Palapye, it was for T. (the defendant) and his younger siblings. Mr. P. (father of George, the complainant) followed a certain Setswana law when he saw that he has M. as the second wife, (that) he should go and request a field for her somewhere, to separate the fields when he was still alive. T. is an elder. He had a right to meet with George concerning the field. The Raphiri field is there (of the first wife). The chiefs of Raphiri are there. He could have explained how he knows about this field. I am thankful that the matter went well.

B. D.: In this matter I see that the field is rightfully M.'s (George's mother) children. Because we are encouraged that when the man loses a wife and marries another woman, he should build her a homestead somewhere. Mr P. left the field of the first family and went and requested a field in Moremi for the second wife. The witnesses explained that he said he is asking it for George's mother. The field is rightfully for George's mother's children.

S. M.: I see the field being George's. Because P. said he is clearing it for George's mother, to separate the children. In his absence we can't but listen to his request.

B. O.: Mr. P. asked for a field for a junior wife, and he made a homestead with the junior wife. We don't know the children of the senior family. We are just seeing them now.

O. S.: I'm opposing the words of T. who says the homestead in Mahalpye built the one here. We haven't come here to make mischief (*lotlhanya*). The witnesses of the complainant showed the truth that P. said he is asking for the field for the junior wife. I see the field is rightfully George's.

B. R.: The truth is, when George came to me, I told him that they should make a *morero* in my absence. I wasn't trying to make mischief.

S. M: Mr. P., according to the Setswana customs we know, he did it (acquired a field) when he was taking the second wife. He built for the second wife. T. is (should be) respecting his younger siblings. This matter is straightforward. George is the rightful heir of his mother. The field is not rightfully T.'s. It rightfully belongs to the junior family.

Having heard the opinions of the 'men of the court' the chief sums up his judgement:

KGOSI: I am giving an example of a certain man who was called Read Kgosiemang. He married the first wife and, when he married the second wife, he built for her somewhere. The first sibling wanted all the goods of his father and the younger siblings asked him to bring even his mother's (goods) so that they can combine and divide them. P. went to Mahalapye to work. He had children and the wife died. And he had children with the second wife. And he left the Raphiri field with the children of the first wife and went and asked for another field for his second wife. T. could have asked George. Maybe he might have listened to him. P. did this (acquired the field) for the second family but not the first one. It is said that someone said that he does not divide the chicken's eggs. These eggs were separated by P. I thank Kgosi Serogola Seretse to say that this matter should be heard again. This matter is old, and we took the evidence from the parents.

JUDGEMENT

We end by saying the field is for the second house. It goes to George Gasha.

Even in the Tribal Authorities Headquarters in Gaborone, there seemed to be some disagreement over the extent of the chief's decision-making powers. The (Administrative) Director of the Tribal Authority was clear that, once the cross-examination of the litigants and witnesses had taken place, the chief decides. There is no further consultation. In exceptional cases, he might announce in advance to the two litigants that a *kgosana* or advisor would cross-examine. There was no question of seeking advice. Indeed, later on in our interview, the Director said that the chief could be considered a 'magistrate 3 or 4'. She also said that most of the time, there was hardly any attendance from the public at customary court hearings. Sometimes they came out of curiosity, but they were prohibited from participating. Nevertheless, the tribal authorities handled 25,000 cases every quarter, she said. The Deputy Director made the point that the main person a chief consults, on points of law and procedure, is the court clerk. He can take a break and consult others if he likes, but privately, not in public.

By contrast, one of the Customary Court of Appeal judges told us that Rule 25 of the Customary Courts Act 1971/5 had *not* changed. This rule, which lays down procedures in civil cases, 25 (*f*) says:

> The Presiding Officer having heard the views of other members present shall proceed to judgement: the view of the majority of the members shall be the judgement of the Court: if the views of the members are equally divided, judgement shall be for the defendant.
>
> (Customary Courts Act *LRO 1*2003: 04:05 (S.I.) – p. 7)

In the published consolidated customary law act, the two acts (1971 and 2006) were consolidated along with the Amendment 2013. The consolidation repeats Section 20 of the 1971/75 earlier act in which in item (o) (p. 6), it states *inter alia* as follows:

> If the Court is constituted by more than one member, and the members cannot agree to the guilt or innocence of the defendant, the view of the majority of the members shall be a verdict of the Court.
>
> (ibid.: p. 6)

However, while the Customary Court (Procedure) (Amendment) Rules 2016 incorporates the earlier Acts, this item, reproduced *verbatim* in the Rules (Section 9 (iii), p. 834) is now inflected by the definition of 'member of the court' in the 2013 Amendment, meaning that only named, recognised 'members' with a government warrant are being referred to, no longer unnamed, ordinary tribesman.

Despite this, as we have seen, it is quite possible for the amendment to be ignored *de facto,* if not *de jure*, overlooked or flouted much like the 1934 Proclamation was, so that 'trial by kgotla' retains its viability and vitality in the long run.

The village chief changes his mind

By the time we met the village chief, a few days later, he had clearly changed his mind about his verdict reported above, pronounced midway through the hearing, though most observers agreed that, by the end of the case, there had been no definitive judgement. This was pending more information about the financial limits of a village headman's capacity to pass decisions regarding inheritance, and on the investigation of the whereabouts of the gun and the value of the developed wells. For the first time, the chief demanded that certificates of ownership of the wells be brought to court by the following week (they never were and were still pending in May 2018, nine months later). This second hearing consisted only of the judgement.

The village chief told us when he met us a few days later that the main principle he follows is of fairness and equity for all. When the court reconvened, his verdict this time was that the first well sold should be considered Martin's inheritance. As for the other two wells, they were to be divided between the three remaining heirs. The field too was to be divided among them in a *morero* held by the ward head, Martin's cousin. It was unclear whether Martin was to retain his share.

After the case concluded, we gave Martin and his son a lift back home. They said that they were very unhappy with the verdict which they understood to mean they would get no share of the field. The son said they would appeal. Martin said his heart was aching. His daughter accused Neil once again, in public, in the court, of lying (that the well was registered in her son's name). Later, Neil told us that in his understanding the field would be shared by all of them. He dismissed the problem of Martin supposedly having to pay compensation for the gun and the second well, now owned by the widow of the original owner who bought it from Martin, saying these were small sums. But it wasn't clear how they would get the well back from her since a borehole had been dug there. Indeed, in May 2018 she was challenging the decision and Neil had employed a lawyer to sue the Land Board (which had mistakenly awarded her a 'new' well) to evict her. The case would be heard before the High Court. Ultimately, in September 2019, the borehole owner relinquished her claim to ownership. The owner of the gun had still not been found by the time of the second trial but was later found. Still, the village chief was reluctant to demand the gun back.

Throughout the case, fears of occult attack, of witchcraft, or ancestral wrath, and accusations of lying, *lefufa* (jealousy), corruption, and bitter betrayal permeated discourses behind the scenes. Martin, the 96-year-old elder son, accused the complainants in court of treating him like a 'ghost' (*sepoko*). Close cousins condemned each other in private, and in some instances in public, in terms that made one doubt they could ever be friends again.

Although the final case seemed conclusive, matters dragged on. The accused appealed to a higher customary court (and lost). Certificates had yet to be produced. It would clearly take time to settle all the affairs the case raised. In May 2018, a *morero* took place to divide the property. Representatives of all Moremi wards were present, along with key relatives from Moremi and Matolwane.

Figure 9.2 Moremi inheritance moot following court verdict.

Only Martin and his family were absent, though they had been invited. The division of the property was surprising, though it was handled very amicably. Keith was awarded the dry well, which he intended to develop. Neil was awarded the home plot in Matolwane, the gun (still to be retrieved), and the whole field, excepting the part ploughed by Martin's son. The second, functioning well was awarded to Neil's sister and to the third litigant, the son of Martin's deceased brother. Neil was leading the litigation to expel the present owner/occupant, which was ultimately successful at the end of 2019.

Navigating through the property-related entanglements over a long period among the close kin and reaching towards a safe and fair decision posed a considerable challenge for the court and the village chief as judge. His judgement emerged, perhaps to the judge's own surprise; it was not a foregone conclusion. Following the forensic evidence, somehow puzzling for anyone, like the judge, who was not a close kinsman, demanded problematic judiciousness – being seen to be baffled, while also seen to be determined to get things straight. Our own understanding is that the final settlement was perceived to be equitable by most of the family, though not perhaps by Martin and his immediate descendants, who felt dispossessed. If, for most of the family, the customary court proved its merit as a court of equity, applying parental law, it could not adequately provide the kind of conflict resolution deemed ideal and much advocated in court rhetoric – reconciliation and truly accepted peace making among the litigants. Disputes over inheritance bring out deep-seated sentiments of jealousy and greed and invoke long-forgotten memories of past betrayal. With few exceptions, however, the village chief succeeded in maintaining an atmosphere of calm civility and rationality. He refused to be distracted by extraneous matters and was firm in demanding that litigants stick to the point. This was an achievement in itself.

But what about court hierarchy and the right of appeal? The village chief very explicitly met his duty of care; he alerted the litigants, according to proper procedure, of their right to go beyond his court to higher authority, as a matter of course. Serving with distinction as a major had undoubtedly heightened his respect for acting within a chain of command, as he confirmed in a very recent conversation. Even further, in the inheritance case, he could not help but be conscious of the mixed motives and inflamed passions that meant the matter would not end with his judgement and without a drawn-out battle by the losers and recourse to an appeal court. Perhaps predictably, on appeal, there was no reversal of the chief's judgement. That the matter actually dragged out until it came back to the village and a well-mobilised, highly representative moot reflected a familiar aspect of customary justice: it often proceeds as if time is not of the essence, it does not fly like an arrow. After all, reaching a settlement of property entangled in multiple relations over many decades embeds the public days in court, however many, in the precarious navigating of much more behind-the-scenes negotiations, about which, like at least some of the main litigants themselves, we as ethnographers can only wonder in the light of the outcome.

Customary 'living law' debated by the Botswana judiciary in statutory courts

Whether customary law is frozen or is understood as 'living law', responsive to changing circumstances, has become the topic of a significant debate not only among scholars of legal pluralism but among High Court judges in Botswana. As Justice Ian Kirby noted with regard to a customary inheritance case brought before the Botswana Court of Appeal, customary law 'constantly evolves over time in line with contemporary norms and standards' (Kirby Court of Appeal, Concurring Judgement, par 21). Note that this implies that the law is 'living' in the sense that it evolves and changes over time. A signal case in this regard was the inheritance case of *Ramantele v Mmusi*, carried on appeal from the Customary Court of Appeal to the High Court in 2012 and then further to the Court of Appeal in 2013. Mmusi, the chief defendant in the Court of Appeal, was an 80-year-old woman threatened by her nephew with dispossession and eviction from a house she herself had built and had lived in for 20 years in her father's compound.

Clearly, beyond the tribal courts of appeal, judgements in the statutory High Court and Court of Appeal citing 'living law' do not rely directly on the normative experiences and expectations of ordinary folk 'on the ground', as in the lower customary courts we have been considering so far. Instead, judges draw on the verdicts of higher customary courts of appeal and on research by anthropologists and other social scientists. This was made evident in the Mmusi case (on this see also Weinberg 2016).

We disagree with Charles Fombad's conclusion (2014: 476) regarding this case when he argues that 'The High Court judgment was subsequently reversed on appeal'. In fact, the High Court verdict in favour of Mmusi and her co-defendants was *upheld* by the Court of Appeal, and both hearings cited principles of equity. What was rejected in the Court of Appeal was the *mode of judicial reasoning* used by the High Court in reaching its verdict. Thus Justice Kirby, in a concurring judgement in the Customary court of Appeal, argued that the verdict reached by the *Customary* Court of Appeal (to eject Mmusi from her home) 'was, on any view of the facts, manifestly unjust, and this was the conclusion of both Dingake J. (the High Court Judge) and of Lesetedi JA (President of the Court of Appeal), *with which I agree*' (concurring judgement, par 6, emphasis added).

In rejecting the *method of judicial reasoning* used by Dingake J. in the High Court, the Court of Appeal challenged his recourse to the Constitution of Botswana with its explicit foundational legal principle of gender equality. This principle was cited by the High Court in order to revise the verdict of the Customary Court of Appeal which it based upon an alleged customary law of male ultimogeniture in cases of intestate inheritance of the familial homestead among (in this particular case) the Bangwaketse. In fact, *pacé* Fombad, both the High Court and the Court of Appeal rejected this verdict.

We also disagree with Fombad's view that women in Botswana do not participate in deciding judgements in customary courts (ibid.: 481). In reality, throughout Botswana, court clerks, almost universally women, are highly influential in advising customary court judges of both the right proceedings and the law. As many recent cases in Moremi village attest, the principle of gender equality is by now well established in village customary courts (indeed, in the RreMogolo inheritance case in Moremi village discussed above, no-one challenged Neil's right to equal inheritance *via* his mother, Martin's sister).

The basic objection to the High Court judicial reasoning in the Mmusi case was that 'a court should not be too quick to consider the constitutionality of a customary law' (Court of Appeal para 37), above all because judges should turn in the first instance to the Customary Law Act (CLA; Concurring Judgement, par 30).[1] The CLA states very clearly that a (customary) law should be followed only in so far as '*it is not incompatible with the provisions of any written law or contrary to morality, humanity, or natural justice*' (ibid. emphasis in the original.) [Cf. Customary Courts Act 2006, Section 2, (1)(b)]. Moreover, in the Mmusi case, the Appeal judges argued, no evidence was brought that the Bangwaketse indeed had a hard-and-fast rule of male ultimogeniture in cases of homestead

1 The imposition of constitutional principles on any customary law might lead, Fombad suggests, to 'a weak, disjointed and incoherent system with gaps in it' (Fombad 2015: 482). This is to assume a coherence in the corpus of customary law which is not clearly there in the first place.

intestate inheritance (and this ambiguity was evident in the different verdicts on the Mmusi case arrived at by different customary courts). Even beyond that, the judges in the Court of Appeal asserted that a key principle of Botswana legal pluralism is that customary law should be recognised as 'an *independent* source of norms within the legal system' (Concurring judgement, par 51, emphasis added). Justice Kirby of the Appeal Court goes on to say, citing various anthropological studies among others, that 'There are two outstanding characteristics of customary law, namely its evolutionary nature and its flexibility' (ibid.).[2]

To sum up the Appeal judges' argument so far, then, customary law is (a) flexible (i.e., 'living'), (b) independent, and (c) must be compatible with natural justice, or as Justice Kirby puts it, 'justice, equity, and good conscience' (ibid.: par 33). Principle (c) implies that there is no need to appeal to the constitution and indeed, this would strike at (b), the autonomy or independence of customary law. Hence, Justice Kirby concludes that

> essentially, the Customary Courts Act has confirmed by statute what had in any event become the norm in practice – namely that the customary courts operate by and large as *courts of equity.*
>
> **(ibid.: par 35, emphasis added)**[3]

There is no need to appeal to the Constitution since,

> It need hardly be said that any customary law or rule which discriminates in any case against a woman unfairly solely on the basis of her gender would not be in accordance with humanity, morality, or natural justice. Nor would it be in accordance with the principles of justice, equity, and good conscience.
>
> **(ibid., par 36)**

Or indeed, Kirby adds, of 'fairness' (par 37).[4]

2 Weinberg (2016) labels such citations as the use by lawyers and judges, as well as activists, of 'social science evidence'. She errs, however, in attributing to Schapera a hard-and-fast rule of male inheritance of the homestead. A key source in this regard for the Mmusi team was the work of Anne Griffiths (2011) which showed clearly the extent to which women had become owners of fields, homesteads and other properties following the Tribal Land Act (1973) and the Abolition of Marital Power Act (2004). Above all, Griffiths shows, inheritance was a negotiated matter among family members. In an otherwise insightful and illuminating article, Weinberg wrongly states the date of Botswana's independence (the correct date is 1966) and of the Tlokweng law (which is Batlokwa, not Ngwato).

3 Kirby's concurring judgement invoking fairness as laid out in the Customary Courts Act, is cited in a subsequent Court of Appeal inheritance case: Court of Appeal Civil Case No CACGB-045-13, 31 July, 2014.

4 Unlike in Botswana, in the Republic of South Africa customary law, while recognised and protected, is subject to the Constitution and violations are decided in the SA Constitutional Court.

The question is, then: why *object* to any appeal to the Constitution (as the High Court did) when, in any case, discrimination on the basis of gender cannot be tolerated on the grounds of 'humanity, morality, and natural justice'? Clearly, the justices of the Court of Appeal were determined to uphold the 'autonomy' and 'independence' of customary law in Botswana, to enable customary law as a body of law to exist independently, within a highly elaborate, hierarchical system of customary courts that hear thousands of cases every year throughout the country. Few cases ever reach the High Court and Court of Appeal, as did the Mmusi case. Ultimately, then, the decision in the Court of Appeal was *political* in the sense of enforcing the overriding interests of the state: customary law needed to be retained as a 'semi-autonomous field' within a legally plural system (see Moore 1973). In the case of customary law, the social context – the community in which the law operates, is abided by, upheld, or transgressed – determines current legal understandings of customary law as living law. It is in this sense, as we have argued above, that wide consultation in the *kgotla* is important in reaching a just and equitable verdict.

Whatever the views of the venerable judges themselves, or of legal scholars like Fombad, regarding the outcome of the Mmusi case,[5] the media and public interpreted the outcome in both courts as unequivocally establishing the principle of gender equality with regard to customary laws of inheritance in Botswana. This was true in the aftermath of the High Court judgement as reflected in *The Telegraph* headline that 'Women can inherit the earth rules Botswana judge'[6]. The message remained the same after the Court of Appeal judgement: 'Botswana women win landmark right to inherit under customary law' (Reuters).[7]

5 Fombad argues, mistakenly in our view, that the Court of Appeal did not reach a clear verdict and instead, referred the matter back to the family (2015: 485). In fact, as mentioned above, the Court of Appeal found, like the High Court, that the respondents (Mmusi and her sisters) should *retain the family homestead and that the appellant had lost his appeal and should bear the costs* (Court of Appeal, 2013, par 103, emphasis added), as confirmed also in the concurring judgement by Kirby J. cited above. It is true that, perhaps in order to retain a semblance of upholding the (semi)autonomy of customary law, Lesetedi JA orders that '(c) The decision of Kgosi Lotlaamoreng II (in the Higher Customary Court, prior to the Customary Court of Appeal) is confirmed save that the latter part thereof is varied to read: *If* the surviving children of the late Silabo and Thwesane Ramantele are unable to agree who amongst them is to take care of the property on behalf of the others, the matter is to be referred to the elders and uncles for resolution, and this failing, the respondents are to be assisted by a person appointed by Kgosi Malope II' (par 105).Given, however, that all four 'surviving children' are the respondents in the Court of Appeal case, this addition appears disingenuous and superfluous. The key order is: 'It is declared that the Ngwaketse Customary Law of inheritance does not prohibit the female or elder children from inheriting as intestate heirs to their deceased parents' family homestead' (ibid.), to be taken in conjunction with par. 103 (see above).

6 http://www.telegraph.co.uk/news/worldnews/africaandindianocean/botswana/9605346/Women-can-inherit-the-earth-rules-Botswana-judge.html Accessed 2 February, 2018.

7 http://news.trust.org//item/20130904043025-btl5h Accessed 2 February, 2018.

Was the definitional amendment 2013 a 'mistake'?

Matters did not end there, however. On our visit to Botswana in May 2018, we tried to ascertain how the definitional amendment of 'member of the court' to refer solely to the presiding judge had crept into the law. Opinions on this matter varied. The chairman of the House of Chiefs, Kgosi Gaborone, assured us that the House of Chiefs had debated this amendment with which he seemed to concur. Indeed, he defended the decision saying, 'Who are these "members of the court"?' Clearly, the fact that they were not named or approved was unacceptable to him. He is a youngish man (recently married, apparently), very smartly dressed, an ex-teacher, and his attitude was clearly that the customary courts (and indeed customary law) need to be modernised and properly managed bureaucratically. The chief or headman is given a 'warranty' by the ministry (a sort of framed certificate), he pointed out, which gives him or her the authority to judge and preside over the *kgotla*. He said decisions made in response to anyone else were not 'authentic'. Litigants could complain (and he implied did complain) – who are these people sitting in judgement? They may then appeal. It was clear that he had no notion that local villages or elders would 'know' customary law equally or even better than appointed judges. The notion seemed to be anathema to his modernist attitudes. He said the courts had changed. There were many more roles than in the past (conversation, 7 May 2018).

Having ascertained that in fact, there had been no real debate on the definitional amendment in the House of Chiefs, Ntlo ya Dikgosi, apart from the rhetorical explanation given by the Parliamentary Council quoted above, we sought advice from an ex-Member of Parliament. He in turn referred us to the Deputy Attorney General. Unlike the Chairman of the House of Chiefs, both the MP and the Deputy AG recognised immediately that the definitional amendment changed the tradition of consultation in customary courts with long-term radical implications. In the Attorney General's Chambers, the deputy AG looked through several volumes of relevant Acts before pronouncing very clearly – 'This is a mistake!' 'It needs to be changed!', the definition needs to be 'eliminated'.' She explained that, in Botswana, after the debates about any new law had taken place but before the law was ratified, the AG Chambers always scrutinises the legislation for 'unintended outcomes'. This was an instance in which the unintended outcome of the new law was not caught, and, since it made a radical change to the procedures at customary courts, it definitely needed to be rectified. The definitional amendment could simply be removed, she said, without consequences for the rest of the legislation. This could not be done, however, by the AG Chambers unilaterally. The suggestion for an amendment would need to come from the law makers. She thus suggested we write to the relevant Minister concerned and explain the issue, but without referring to her. As an afterthought, she said that perhaps one had to distinguish between civil and criminal cases. In criminal cases, it may be justified to have a named presiding officer, but not in civil cases.

Following our meeting with the AG, we managed to see the Minister briefly before leaving Botswana. Once we had explained about the implications of the definitional amendment (which she barely recalled), she immediately recognised that the change to customary court procedures would be radical. We await news of any revision of the law.

Conclusion

Discussions of customary law as living law stress that customary law is a 'process', that it is 'situational' and changes over time in response to changing circumstances. Missing in these debates, however, has been an analysis of the connection between the *judicial process*, that is, the mode of adjudication, and the responsiveness of the law. Without judicial consultation, we have argued in this chapter, the 'living' dimensions of customary law may be greatly attenuated or rendered unsafe. As we show in the chapter, a single judge may be unable to feel the pulse of changing customs and everyday moralities in the way a forum of local decision makers can.

When asked what the secret of Botswana's continuing democracy was after he delivered the Oppenheimer Lecture in London on April 18 2018, the new President, Mogweetsi Masisi, answered proudly and without hesitation that this was due to 'our *kgotla* system'. By this he meant the tradition of deliberation and consultation in customary courts. And it is this openness to deliberation which, we have argued here, makes Tswana customary law 'living law'.

For social anthropologists, the idea that customary law is 'living' law, situationally responsive to change, is hardly new. This responsiveness has long been understood as an intrinsic feature of customary law. Thus Diala (2017) is in our view mistaken when he argues for the need to recognise the 'emergence' of customary living law, implying thereby that in the pre-colonial and colonial past customary law was relatively fixed. As Gluckman early on pointed out, however, in his discussion of the 'reasonable man',

> At the moment, in particular, controversy rages between orthodox jurists who hold that law is certain, and a so-called sceptical or realist school of American lawyers, who hold that law is uncertain. … Law in the orthodox sense is a known code of moral principles and legal rules, many of which have endured for centuries and are known in most countries – in ancient Rome, in France and England, and in Barotseland. The body of rules is fairly certain; judges' decisions, in terms of those rules, on various disputes may be uncertain. But the decisions are given in those rules. They can be given thus because the rules are composed of flexible concepts which can be permeated by changing social presumptions and which can absorb the variety of life itself.
>
> (1963: 206)[8]

8 Gluckman who followed the Realist school, argued for law as 'process' early on in his book, aptly titled 'The Judicial Process among the Barotse of Northern Rhodesia".

In other words, the uncertainty of law, its flexibility and responsiveness to changing circumstances, is as much an intrinsic feature of it as its apparent certainty. As the inheritance case above has shown, whatever the statutory law, it seems clear that village chiefs (headman), deeply embedded in a local community, cannot escape the weight of public opinion in weighing evidence in particular circumstances. When a presiding judge in a customary court tries to do so, as the Moremi inheritance case discussed above illustrates, this creates confusion, suspicion of ulterior motives, and ultimately, a reversal of unsafe decisions made in haste. The same was true of the Mmusi case, which ultimately reached Botswana's Court of Appeal.

In a period of rapid change and commodification, with the value of wells and communal land soaring, much is at stake for litigants. But the basic principle of the right (these days) to (equal) inheritance by men and women has become a bedrock of customary as well as common law. Litigants – and the community at large – now recognise that these must be respected (see also Griffiths 2011). If a village chief is to retain legitimacy and the respect of his subjects, he clearly needs to seek their advice before reaching a judgement. This implies that, as in the earlier Proclamation of 1934, which ultimately was superseded by customary court practice, so too the present definitional Amendment is likely to be ignored by most chiefs and headmen, relegated to oblivion in the daily traditional procedural practices of the customary courts. It appears, then, in conclusion, that 'living law' requires dialogue and consultation if it is to keep up with and be alive to changing circumstances.

10 A case of insult

Emotion, law, and witchcraft accusations

Introduction: towards a legal anthropology of emotions

Legal anthropologists have been slow to join the tide of lawyers, philosophers, and socio-legal scholars responding to the somewhat counter-intuitive proposition that the law is 'imbued with emotion' (Bandes 1999: 2). This is despite the fact that anthropologists have long been cognisant of the emotional intensity and complexity of familial and political relationships – and the disputes that such charged emotional entanglements give rise to. Indeed, it was A.L. Epstein, a legal anthropologist, who was an early pioneering scholar of the emotional dimensions of customary law (Epstein 1992). Epstein comprehended the emotional quality of the law in his study of courts among the Tolai of Papua New Guinea. He showed how emotions (of anger, shame, resentment, pride) pervade the law, and especially so because relations between litigants are multiplex and long term. Most disputes are among close kin and often concern multiple and conflicting loyalties and obligations to wives, sisters, mothers, brothers, uncles, or fathers. Epstein made the important point that, while Tolai judges do appeal to 'reasonableness', a focus solely on reason would 'ignore the way in which many of the norms and values in question were powerfully cathected. … Ultimately, that is, the appeal was an emotional appeal' (Epstein 1992: 132; see also 219). 'Cathected' is here used in a Freudian sense to mean 'invested with emotional feeling or energy'. Rationality and emotion are thus dialectically at play in Tolai courts as litigants and judges strive to find an acceptable, amicable resolution to disputes so as to enable a return to harmonious relations.

More recently, a whole new field, law and emotion, though still fragmented, has emerged, aiming to show that for legal academics and 'those involved in the practice of law … the role of emotion can neither be avoided nor neglected' (Conway and Stannard 2016: 8). Adding an anthropological voice to the debate, Kamari Clarke speaks of 'affective justice' in the field of international law in Africa, arguing that the very notions of justice and injustice are imbued with emotion, expressed in attitudes to the International Court of Justice and other human rights forums (Clarke 2019).

As in the present chapter, in which we argue that expressions of emotions are constituted in moral terms, Bens and Zenker propose that '[s]entiment describes

DOI: 10.4324/9781003241881-10

an evaluative regime of meaning as embedded in and coloured by affective and emotional dynamics' (2019: 96). Even beyond that, however, the chapter demonstrates that insults as speech acts in customary courts in Botswana are understood as 'inchoate crimes'. Such inchoate crimes, as defined by Richard Wilson (2017: 21), are akin to hate crimes or, in Wilson's examples, of incitement speeches tried in international tribunals. Such speech acts (public incitements, hate speeches, insults), causing extreme emotional distress or fear, are inchoate in the sense that they do not require evidence that they caused a tangible crime directly (for example, genocide) to be indictable. In the present chapter, insults alleging witchcraft are understood as offences in themselves for which the perpetrator of the insult is punishable. The matter at issue is not an accusation which calls for proof or disproof that someone is a witch, who uses occult means of attack. In this respect, to study witchcraft-insults is to deviate from the usual focus on accusations in much of the literature on witchcraft and law in Africa. Rather than exposing so-called 'witches' or sorcerers, witchcraft-insults lead to attempts by customary courts or family courts to persuade accusers to undergo a change in their legal subjectivity to regain their good sense and decency. They are expected to once again become rational actors of the kind who reach a self-conscious emotional balance and spiritual calmness. This process of persuasion to achieve decent fellow-feeling is pursued in the form of a dialogue between members of the customary court, the defendant, and the plaintiff, the insulted victim, which is intended to do at least three things: to restore public peace; to elicit forgiveness from the plaintiff, the insulted victim; and to get the insulter to apologise or show public regret for his or her insult. It is a dialogical process acutely focused on the *feelings* of the litigants. In this respect, customary procedures that generate such dialogue resemble restorative justice practices discussed by criminologists and other socio-legal scholars.[1]Remarkably, although much has been written about the tendency of Tswana courts to promote reconciliation, for example in cases of marital disputes (Griffiths 1997: 141; Guldbrandsen 2012; Werbner and Werbner 2019), discussion of this type of restorative dialogue is rare, and our account below opens out this interest for ethnographic and comparative analysis.

Our discussion builds upon Martha Nussbaum's intervention on the subject of hate crimes. Nussbaum has expanded the debate on law and emotion to an engagement with broader, philosophical questions of how the law defends or promotes so-called 'decent society'. Her work on dignity and shame highlights contexts in which these are ignored, leading to the demonisation of certain marginal groups and the avoidance or exclusion of others, who are often associated with feelings of disgust (Nussbaum 2006).

At the heart of much of the debate on law and emotion is a presumed opposition between the rationality of the law and the emotion displayed both by

1 Restorative justice is contrasted by criminologists with retributive justice, and often uses conferencing and dialogue to achieve reconciliation (cf. Braithwaite 2002).

litigants and in the responses of judges or juries. In Euro-American socio-legal discussions of the topic, however, certain substantive fields have also begun to emerge where emotion is recognised as being intrinsic to the very fabric of the relationships being contested and judged. Family law, and particularly inheritance disputes, is one such field (see Conway 2016; Huntington 2016). Another is the medical field of extreme disability where sometimes hard choices, including whether to live or die, have to be made. Here, too, issues of dignity, autonomy, and feelings are entangled with the law (Neal 2016). One substantive field that appears to have been neglected so far in this expanding socio-legal debate on law and emotion has been the field of hurtful and emotionally painful insults, though it could perhaps be linked to Nussbaum's study of anti-hate crime legislation as defending the decent society. The study of insults, however, has its own legal genealogy, at least in the USA, and we offer a brief introduction to that as comparative background to our own account, in order for it to be better understood within a broader field of legal change, and not merely as another exotic study of witchcraft discourse and witchcraft accusations.

Emotions, insults, and the law

In a landmark article in the *Harvard Law Review*, 1936, Calvert Magruder surveyed an extensive series of court cases. In these, compensation was awarded for 'mortification and outraged feelings', *even though no pecuniary reputational damage was at stake* (Magruder 1936: 1035, our italics). Again and again, in piecemeal, scattered judgements, he showed, American courts had recognised that 'the law gives the plaintiff redress for mental distress and humiliation caused by the defendant's conduct' (ibid.: 1052). This meant, Magruder reasoned, that one was witnessing the 'gradual emergence of a broad principle' according to which 'one who, without just cause or excuse, and beyond all the bounds of decency, purposively causes a disturbance of another's mental and emotional tranquillity of so acute a nature ... is subject to liability' even without further 'demonstrable' consequences (ibid.: 1058). In other words, 'the law will give damages for mental distress of an aggravated sort, resulting from an outrageous aggression by the defendant upon the plaintiff's peace of mind' (ibid.: 1064). Thus, he concluded, the law is in 'a process of growth' and it is clear that it is 'no longer even approximately true that the law does not pretend to redress mental pain and anguish' (ibid.: 1067). This includes insults causing 'mental anguish and humiliation' (ibid.: 1034).

Commenting on Magruder's contribution almost 50 years later, Daniel Givelber notes that, remarkably, it was

> Academics, rather than courts, (that) were the prime movers in the development of the tort of *intentional infliction of severe emotional distress by outrageous conduct*; the modern tort was introduced in the pages of law reviews, and then refined and finally defined by the American Law Institute in its Restatements.
>
> (Givelber 1982: 42, emphasis added)

'Outrageous' conduct, whether defined as defamation, libel, or slander, which causes extreme emotional distress, is thus recognised by American courts as indictable, not simply because it causes a loss of reputation measured in financial terms, but also because it attacks the *feelings* of victims. In the UK and Europe, bullying, harassment and attacks on personal dignity (Harthill 2008: 250, 260) fill a somewhat parallel legal function.

It is thus somewhat surprising that in their overview of 'Emotion and the Law', Blandes and Blumenthal (2012) fail to mention a whole body of scholarly legal and socio-legal work that discusses the established US common law of Intentional Infliction of Severe Emotional Distress (IISED); even more broadly, the authors ignore legal approaches to emotions inflicted by or associated with insults. As in the later review, so too in an earlier edited collection, *The Passions of Law* (Bandes 1999), whereas a whole range of emotions is surveyed, from disgust, shame and anger to humiliation, empathy, love, and grief, no mention is made of insult. The focus is mainly on the way that these emotions affect legislators, judges, and juries rather than, as in the case of insult, perpetrators and victims. Nonetheless, Bandes captures a deep truth that defines the whole field of law and emotion when she says that, despite the law's claim to be rational and cerebral, it

> is imbued with emotion. Not just the obvious emotions like mercy and the desire for vengeance but disgust, romantic love, bitterness, uneasiness, fear, resentment, cowardice, vindictiveness, forgiveness, contempt, remorse, sympathy, hatred, spite, malice, shame, respect, moral fervour, and the passion for justice.
>
> (Bandes 1999: 2)

Emotion, she says, 'pervades' not just criminal but civil and appellate courtrooms (ibid.).

Insult, *seriti*, and the law in Botswana

Insult in Botswana, unlike in the UK and many other western countries, is a penal offence. Sections 90–93 and 180–183 of the 2005 Penal Code of Botswana, concerned with the 'Use of Insulting Language', stipulate that

> Every person who uses insulting language or otherwise conducts himself in a manner likely to give such provocation to any person as to cause such person to break the peace or to commit any offence against the person is guilty of an offence and is liable to a fine not exceeding P50 or to imprisonment for a term not exceeding three months, or to both.[2]

2 Elsewhere, Section 90 of the Penal Code provides that 'any person who in a public place or at a public gathering uses threatening, abusive or insulting words or behaviour is guilty of an offence and is liable to imprisonment for a term not exceeding six months'.'

Further sections of the penal code involve the use of obscene or insulting language vis-à-vis symbols of the state, the president, members of the National Assembly and public officers. One section states that any person who utters any words or publishes any writing expressing or showing hatred, ridicule or contempt for any person or group of persons wholly or mainly because of his or their race, tribe, place of origin, colour, or creed is guilty of an offence and liable to a fine not exceeding 500 pula.

But insults among the subjects of our study, Tswapong villagers living in small villages in Botswana's Tswapong Hills, and especially extreme insults, also have occult dimensions. Insults are said to bear *botlhodi*, a bad omen that may herald the death of a person even in the absence of any direct sorcery accusation. Accusations or imputations of witchcraft (*boloi*), perhaps the most extreme, 'outrageous' kind of public insult, are prohibited by law and have been so in Botswana since 1927 (Witchcraft Act, Chapter 09-02: Sections 2 and 3, amended 1959). Accusers are liable for a fine and/or imprisonment. Despite the Act, Schapera reports in a 'short note' in *Man* that some 110 cases dealing with witchcraft were still being heard in customary courts between 1938 and 1940. Schapera found that

> The judgments show that chiefs have usually been much more cautious than their people about the kinds of evidence on which they will convict; and in several instances the accused, when found not guilty, has been awarded damages for the 'spoiling' of his name.
>
> (Schapera 1955: 72)

The demand in the customary court was for evidence of the administration of poison in most cases (ibid.). In statutory courts, the last witchcraft case recorded was in 1934.[3] Customary courts, in which the law is unwritten, were not

3 Personal communication, Otlhogile Bojosi. Cf. R v Dintwe Dithupe and Mpolokan Matsiboko, Criminal Case No. 20 of 1934 in BNA C/7/70. Professor Bojosi reports that:

> A similar observation was made by Justice Roper on his retirement from the Court of Appeal, that, in the period between 1939 and 1956, there were no cases of witchcraft and medicine murder [poisoning?] in Bechuanaland, but he was surprised when he rejoined the bench that such cases were now becoming common. This is what he said in part:
>
> The only hotel was the former railway refreshment room at the railway station, and the High Court sat in the District Commissioner's Court, where, if the court sat late, light was provided by hurricane lamps. We have advanced very far from those days. There were some notable trials in the High Court in those days, but it is interesting to recall that, during the whole eight years in which I held appointment of Attorney General, we never had a single medicine murder trial, or any case in which witchcraft was involved. I have never been able to form an opinion whether that form of crime did not occur at all in those days in Bechuanaland, or whether it took place but was not brought to light. It was, therefore, an unpleasant surprise to find on resuming my connection with Botswana in 1956 that this type of crime was, to some degree prevalent in the territory as it had been in other territories for years past. I am at a loss to understand the reason for this change in this respect.

apparently obliged initially to follow the Act but this was amended later so that in the Customary Courts Act in 2002, Clause 13 clearly states that 'no customary court shall have the jurisdiction to try (d) cases relating to witchcraft without the general or special consent of the Director of Public Prosecutions' (2006: p. 6).

Whether or not tried in public in court, allegations and gossip about sorcerers and witchcraft are not uncommon in Botswana generally, and Moremi village specifically, where our study took place. As in the case discussed below, beliefs surrounding witchcraft persist, even though no-one has been tried locally. *Botlhodi* and *boloi* can be recognised as extreme indications of the powerful and dangerous feelings 'cathecting' public insults.[4] Belief in witchcraft is treated as an extenuating circumstance in court in murder cases.[5]

But witchcraft-insults of the type discussed here differ *in principle* from witchcraft allegations of occult practice presented elsewhere in African courts as a mitigating circumstance for criminal activity. This is true even though they appear on the surface to be similar. Anthropological research on witchcraft allegations and the law has shown, for example, that persons accused of witchcraft have been jailed in Cameroon on the basis of diviners' 'evidence' (Geschiere 2006), and that lighter sentences have been given by 'liberal' colonial and postcolonial judges to attacks, including murder, of persons believed to be witches (e.g., Comaroff and Comaroff 2004; Kyed 2018; Leonardi 2018). By contrast, in the case of witchcraft-insults, the insulting language causes occult danger to the victims of the insults, rather than those accused of witchcraft being the cause of occult danger. In other words, the directionality of occult attack is reversed.

The hidden, occult dimensions of insults point to an underlying code of moral values, beyond legality, that is pervasive in Botswana, and even beyond it, as R. Werbner has argued for sub-Saharan Africa more generally: 'Care and respect for others – indeed, civility, is a precious and precarious condition of survival and as such is the object of recognised strategies for its conscious defence throughout the continent' (R.Werbner 2002: 20; for a further overview see also Klaits 2005). Public good manners, courtesy, respect, and decorum are highly valorised in Botswana, and this is evident in the present chapter in which we focus on a case of a public insult.

Cases of gossip, scandal, and loss of reputation are common in Moremi village. Since bringing a case to court is free, it is worth a try. Girls take other girls to court for calling them a 'slut'. Women sue adulterous husbands. In some cases the insults spoken involve shockingly offensive bodily images. Emotions are embedded in the body and can be 'invested with powerful affect' (Epstein 1992: 224). What is at stake for plaintiffs is often not merely winning the case, punishing the offender, or being awarded financial compensation, but the *seriti* of insulted plaintiffs, although the sense of anger and shame felt by them is not always enunciated publicly during court proceedings.

4 For a very early discussion of witchcraft among Tswana see Schapera (1934).

5 See, for example, State v Molapo 2007 (3) BLR 493 (HC).

Above all, plaintiffs want to redeem their dignity and reputation. *Seriti*, dignity or honour (*tlotlho*), is a highly valued quality of the person as a social being among Tswapong (R.Werbner 2015:2–3, 2018a: 321; P.Werbner 2009: 441-42).[6] *Seriti* combines spiritual dignity with embodied social capacity, and an active sense of mutual interdependency. It implies being 'shaded' by the ancestors, and being endowed with public respect and self-respect. The shades of the ancestors are said to create a canopy of protection of the living, and shade (*moriti*) is thus a central aspect of the notion of *seriti*. A person acquires *seriti* at birth and it is enhanced during his or her lifetime. It is thus a dialogical and relational term that depends on the social perception of and recognition by others.

The hearings about cases of hurtful insult that we recorded highlight an elaborate moral lexicon mobilised from everyday life by members of the court in their attempt, not simply to ascertain the forensic facts of what actually happened, but to advance the distinctive form of dialogue with its three-fold aims outlined above.

During our long-term research at Moremi village in the Tswapong Hills, we attended court hearings concerned with a whole range of insult cases. Some involved calling the police and were defined as prosecutions by the state; others were civil cases between villagers. Virtually all were among kin or neighbours. One of the cases, in which the accused, N., had allegedly called the claimant a dog, highlighted the occult dangers of insult.

The case of the dead chicken

This was a case heard in 2001. It illustrated the extent to which trivial matters may be regarded with deep suspicion and constructed as bad omens where prior animosities exist. It involved a dispute between two neighbouring families who used to be friendly in the past before a violent incident, in which A. intervened in the middle of the night when B. was beating his wife. B. then beat A., and accused him of desiring his wife. This was a case of domestic abuse in which, although the wife reported her husband for assaulting her to the court several times, she always withdrew her accusations and returned to him. From then onwards, the two families were constantly at loggerheads. In the present case, between A.'s daughter (the defendant, N.) and B.'s wife (the plaintiff, M.), the complaint was that the daughter had insulted B.'s wife, calling her a dog (*mpsa*) after the latter reported the existence of a/her dead chicken in the road, apparently run over by an NGO car the previous day. A.'s daughter (the defendant) had allegedly said she would beat B's wife and accused her of uttering a bad omen foreshadowing evil in reporting the chicken's death (*ke bothodi*). She also said she would chase her out of her compound. During cross-examination, the defendant denied she had called the plaintiff a dog, but she admitted to saying that reporting the dead chicken was a bad omen (*o abatlholela*).

6 It thus does not refer to the quality of an autonomous individual.

N.: I never called her a dog. She is the one who called me a dog. All I said was that by taking the case to court it is *bothodi* (a bad omen) (*o a batlholela*). M. (B.'s wife, the plaintiff) keeps on inventing nasty gossip about us.

Her father had told her to keep quiet but she responded that 'I cannot keep quiet because I feel burnt (hurt, *ke shwele*) by these long quarrels between the families'.' She hadn't bothered to report the dead chicken, which had died near their house, to B.'s wife (the plaintiff) because the latter had been gossiping about her. B.'s wife hadn't come to check on the hen, she said, because she was fearful of approaching the defendant's compound. At this point, there was a long and convoluted discussion in court about the hen: who owned it, what colour it was, whether it was still sitting on eggs or already had chicks. There seemed to be more than one hen, perhaps even three. No-one knew who the owner was and none of these issues was ever resolved. The case ended with the village chief presiding over the court admonishing both families to cooperate, to make peace, a sentiment echoed by other members of the court. In the upshot, no-one was found guilty or fined.

This case highlights the way long-term quarrelling between close relatives, neighbours, or friends generates mutual insults, hurt feelings (or 'burning'), and occult suspicions, amidst a spiral of seemingly trivial accusations that are, nonetheless, deeply painful and extend even into the next generation. The role of the court in such cases is to calm people down while apparently investigating the particulars of the dispute but, ultimately, appealing for peace and reconciliation.[7]

Insult, intimacy and gossip: the case of a sexual insult

It is worth noting that the same sort of judicial reasoning permeates the whole customary court hierarchy, from the lowest family hearings to the highest customary court of appeal in the tribal capital, and applies even in the deliberations in the national customary court of appeal. Insults threaten the fabric of social life at the most intimate, family level. Here, the family elders gather with junior members to try to persuade the insulter and the insulted to mend their relationship for the sake of the family. The following case, recorded in 1973, was a family moot or *morero* held inside the yard of an extended family of three brothers, living in adjacent homesteads with their mature children, mainly young women, who were still living at home at the time.

The three brothers between them had 14 daughters, most still unmarried, and several married sons. The case concerned a complaint about hearsay

7 Commenting sceptically on the tendency among scholars of African disputes to argue that courts attempt to seek 'harmony', Elizabeth Colson argues that 'Courts and courts cannot create a harmony that lasts outside their contexts, any more than rituals' (Colson 1995: 69). She shows that on return trips to the field many anthropologists found old disputes still churning. This issue is discussed elsewhere in greater depth.

gossip, brought by a daughter-in-law, P., against her husband's father's younger brother's daughter, N. N. was known through gossip, though not officially, to be pregnant from a liaison with a man who she ultimately married. At the time, however, she was still engaged to another man. P. sued N. for insulting language:

N.: These words came with M. [an older sister of P.'s husband] when I was in the bush with S. [another sister-in-law]. (It was said that) I said that 'the person who said that I am pregnant (referring to P.), I will pack her vagina with firewood'. I never said 'vagina'. I said I will pack firewood 'underneath'.

S. defended herself: When I told P., I never said her 'vagina' will be packed with firewood. She, P., told me that she heard this from C. (a younger sister) and C. was told by D. (another sister).

Evident here is the chain of gossip among sisters and sisters-in-law. Also expressed, as in the previous case, is the fear that insults can cause occult attacks and even death.

C.: Myself, I did not want to carry this dispute in my heart, because it hurts me. Our fight, me and N., when we hurt each other, it arouses the sleeping dogs, like some few days ago when this dispute was hard, a quarrel started. N. quarrelled, saying that she did not cause any omen (*tlhola*) and that she was not impregnated by a dog. I was impregnated just like you once were (she said).

It was reported that N.'s mother had said that the load N. was carrying (i.e., the foetus) 'should live'. 'She was not speaking a word of killing' (*lefoko la polao*).

Presiding over the moot were the patriarchal elders. P.'s father-in-law, uncle of N., warned:

> Insulting (*matlhapa*) is a big offence. If the customary court people come here, you will tell them who were insulting. It will not be right to insult someone. The charge for that is 50 Rand (£2.37, $3.39) and three months' imprisonment. I mean, if you don't know. Going around insulting people is R50.00 and three months' imprisonment.

The discussion went back and forth for some time, with N. denying she had insulted P., while P. said she had 'forgiven' them. The eldest patriarch summed up:

> I want you to tell her (P.) things that will build peace, not to collide with their chests (*thulana ka difufa* – hating each other). I agree with her. Myself, I don't see this matter ended, it is very difficult, because people of this land are liars, as you hear C. spreading lies without knowing anything. Now,

> when these words reach the ears of the parents of the one insulted, they will want to know what she had said to N. They will ask their child what she had said to N. that made her insult her like that. This child (S.) when she says this matter should end here, she is right. She sees where this issue is heading. Don't think she is a child and look down upon what she had said. Myself, I know that these words would be heard and spread by the liars of this land; they don't keep things in their jaws (*ga be tshwara ka tlhaa* – they don't know how to keep secrets). As you can see me here, I am a grown-up person, I am your father. … Here I am, I have aged, but I don't know why these things are spoken in this manner, and it is the first time by the children I have brought up, … , they had been there, but we never heard this kind of talk. … it is our first time to hear them from this youth (*bašu* – modern people). Never think that these words have ended. I am not saying I will spread the rumour myself. Myself, I am not a person who involves myself in other people's matters. This will be spread by these young ladies, they will tell their friends at the entertainment places, that these words were referred to by D., she is the one who will be packed by firewood in her private parts. I mean that these words will come out. Yes, like you heard how the words were spoken and C. came and changed what was said. Myself, I have finished speaking, I was just telling you young people's habits (*mokgwa*), that you have not finished talking about this matter, you are still going to sit for these words again.

The case ended with more warnings that if the gossip was spread, the case would be taken to the court.

Most insult cases we recorded were between women, many among young women. Men do occasionally insult other men but it may be that insults among men escalate to more serious offences of grievous bodily harm or affray, which may explain why so few men's insult cases come to court.

The final case, at the centre of the present chapter, was heard at a ward hearing presided over by the ward headman. It involved, among other things, witchcraft accusations. Indeed, much of the case consisted of attempts to persuade the defendant to drop her accusations, since the court considered that these would undoubtedly lead to her imprisonment if taken further, to the village court or the magistrate's court. It was widely recognised by attendants at the hearing that MmaLabadi, the accused, was unwell physically and mentally,[8] and thus not fully

8 Her (ex)boyfriend had just married his long-time fiancé in an expensive large-scale wedding with much public feasting and celebration. MmaLabadi had attended the first night's feast, and was said to have behaved scandalously, at one stage having an open fight with the wife and publicly smoking a cigarette given to her by the husband. She was banned from the rest of the wedding, the celebrations continuing for several days. MmaLabadi admitted to being HIV positive and had a child outside wedlock from her boyfriend. At the time she was not yet, apparently, taking anti-retroviral drugs but did attend the clinic in the neighbouring town for check-ups.

responsible for her utterances, however offensive, but it was nevertheless important for her to retract her accusations in order to restore public peace and prevent the case from going forward to the village court of record, which was likely to mete out severe punishment.

The case of witchcraft insult

The case of MmaLabadi is one that best exemplifies outrageous behaviour leading to intentional infliction of severe emotional distress.[9] Over long hours of discussion, the court reached the consensus that MmaLabadi had made an indictable grievous accusation of witchcraft (*boloi*) against MmaSiama, the mother of her close cousin (see Figure 10.1 Genealogy 2).[10] But, instead of a verdict or judgement, the conclusion was a dialogue leading to an expression of forgiveness and a humble apology.

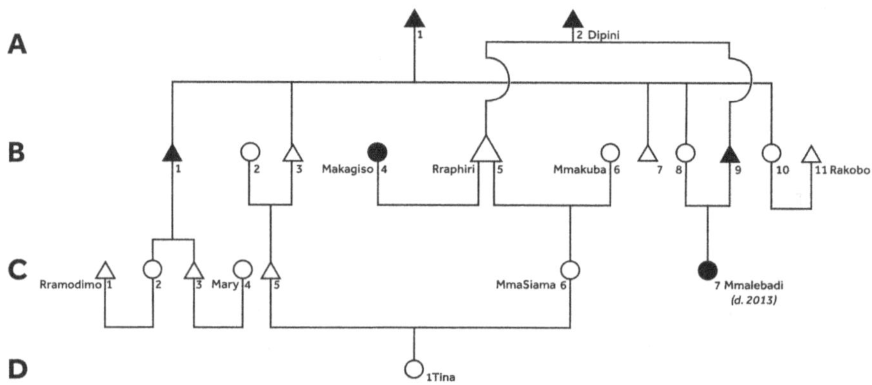

Figure 10.1 Genealogy 2: Mmalabadi.

The case brought into conjunction forensic, moral, and emotional discourses as court participants invoked everyday notions of the proper person, the moral subject, the gerontocratic authority of seniors or 'parents' over 'children', and the right, harmonious state of affairs in village life. An accusation of witchcraft disrupts all these, creating disorder that is public, turmoil within the person, and in many of that person's social relationships. To sum up the case briefly, it proceeded through a series of steps. First came the complaint by and on behalf of the insulted, presented with much fine circumstantial detail on the insult incident. Following this, the defendant responded asserting her innocence on various

9 All names throughout are pseudonyms.

10 She was her parallel cousin, father's brother's daughter, as well as her mother's brother's son's wife.

grounds while admitting she had been provoked into a wild fight in which she beat up the plaintiff's daughter for spreading slander against her. Next, the headman opened the cross-examination and the defendant made her first reply. The first witness, an elder present at the fight, testified to his inability to calm the defendant, and other witnesses spoke in the same vein, with dubious responses given by the defendant. A dialogue then ensued between the headman's wife and the defendant, who expressed her own painful feelings, called for sympathy, and began awkwardly to admit some fault in something of a half-apology. It was not judged a proper apology – it was not given face-to-face, and thus with respect and fear. Other members of the court pursued this, in turn, first with a rebuke demanding respectful feelings and a show of deference towards the court itself; second, a call for a retraction of the insult, and third, the defendant's avowal of her consciousness of how the defendant herself would have felt, and been wronged, had her own parents been insultingly accused of witchcraft. On this basis, the consensus of the court was expressed by the headman. He called for the defendant to reach an inner understanding of her own soul and thus for self-control; he asked her to beg for forgiveness, to offer a proof of her return to fellow-feeling, to sharing the human condition of being a person who was created, 'moulded' like clay, as everyone is. Below, we follow the steps of the case as they occurred.

The complaint by the plaintiff

The case was brought by MmaLabadi's cousin, MmaSiama, the plaitiff. She began her complaint by reporting her own surprise, when she heard of a fight. She had gone to visit her seriously ill mother, MmaKuba, in a neighbouring village. On her return, her daughter, Tina, told her she had been fighting with MmaLabadi, the defendant. MmaSiama told the court she was puzzled, wondering if her daughter might have got a beating for misbehaving towards an older person. When she questioned her daughter, however, she learned that Tina had gone to see her paternal grandmother to let her know MmaSiama was away, visiting her own sick mother. Tina's story was that, while she was informing her grandmother, MmaLabadi talked behind her back to say – 'Can a witch be sick? A witch is never going to die'.' Tina said, according to her mother: 'I looked at MmaLabadi and asked her whether she heard what she was saying? She said, "Yes, I heard myself"," and I (Mma Labadi) said, "MmaKuba (plaintiff's mother) killed MmaKagiso (her co-wife), the woman who was peaceful. MmaKagiso was not sick; she was killed by MmaKuba"."' MmaLabadi then said [according to Tina]: 'Do not talk to me or you'd rather shit [*nyela*, i.e., she would beat her]'.' Tina said: 'I said that to her also. MmaLabadi then stood up and beat me'.'

MmaSiama, the plaintiff, told the court that her daughter spoke of her fear of going out at night to parties where MmaLabadi, the defendant, would provoke her with 'remarks' [in English]; and Tina had admitted she had beaten

MmaLabadi and broken her grandmother's walking stick over MmaLabadi's head, but that eventually they had 'separated themselves'.

MmaSiama told the court that the others present were elderly and said they could do nothing, but when another woman came into the yard, MmaLabadi's words were reported to her. She said that her daughter and MmaLabadi, the defendant, had quarrelled at parties before, verbally, though she always admonished her daughter not to respond to provocations. Now the patience (*bopelotelele*) of Tina had reached its limits as MmaLabadi pursued Tina to her grandmother's. MmaSiama, the plaintiff, then put forward her complaint which was that MmaLabadi insulted MmaSiama's mother by saying she killed her senior co-wife, MmaKuba:

> But, my parents, I do not [want to] enter into MmaLabadi and Tina's [offensive] remarks. What I want [to ask, complain about] is the [alleged] witchcraft [*boloi*] of MmaKuba [i.e. MmaSiama's mother] –who did she kill? Right now, we do not have our grandmother [i.e., the senior wife of MmaKuba, MmaKagiso, who is deceased] because MmaKuba killed her [according to MmaLabadi]. Now I want MmaLabadi to tell me how MmaKuba killed my grandmother [i.e., the senior wife]? She should give us the herb [the actual evidence] which MmaKuba had used to kill MmaKagiso so that we can then kill her [MmaKuba] [spoken ironically]. That is, if MmaKuba could not let MmaKagiso live, how can we let *her* live? This [accusation] means MmaLabadi (the defendant) was there. She should tell everything. I want that only, not anything else. I end here.

The defendant's immediate response

MmaLabadi, the defendant, was a recidivist at the time, constantly insulting people and getting into fights. She was on probation for several earlier cases of insult or affray brought against her in the court of record at the nearby village of Matolwane.[11] This particular hearing, in 2005, was a court hearing held in the ward to which MmaSiama, the plaintiff, belonged. It was presided over by the ward headman and took place under a large tree, with about seven men and ten women attending, many of them relatives. MmaLabadi, had been through hard times recently, for which there was some measure of sympathy towards her in the court (see ftn. 7). Although she came from a respectable village family, she was, and often behaved like, a forsaken destitute.

At the beginning of the case, MmaLabadi, the defendant, first tried to argue that she was referring to the death in a neighbouring town of a man reputed to be a witch. It was on his death, she said, that she had commented, when she invoked the proverb, 'If one worm eats another, it never gets fat' (*ga se jele se sengwe,*

11 Moremi village court was not yet at the time a court of record.

ga se none. i.e., witches never die from their bewitching). She now claimed not even to know MmaSiama's mother, MmaKuba, or even her deceased co-wife. MmaLabadi told the headman:

> When exchanging words, I told her [Tina, the plaintiff's daughter] that you should not try to accuse me falsely [*pateletsa*]. I will soon make you shit [i.e., beat you until you shit]. That is when I beat her, hearing that she is bearing false witness against me [*o a nkgolega*] with words I did not say.

The opening cross-examination

The headman then tested MmaLabadi on whether she had taken care to report to elders and seek their peace making:

> Given that there were people there, did you not look to anyone to ask them to hear the person?

MmaLabadi gave a dubious answer:

> No, I did not look to anyone because I do not want petty talks (*ditontokwane* – gossip), and also, I did not take it as a big matter. Even people [elders] will be witnessing their things (giving wrong or misleading evidence).

The headman then turned to Rakobo, the sickly elder who had rebuked MmaLabadi without being able to stop the fight. Rakobo said he would not speak of matters of hatred *(letlho)*; that he regarded both women, Tina and MmaLabadi, as his children [hence he was not a biased witness]. He had reprimanded MmaLabadi: she had actually made her accusation against the grandmother, not the Palapye man. He had rebuked her, 'You know you are not saying good things.' He tried to calm her down and she said, 'I am just talking'.

Witnesses and victims then gave lengthy accounts of the events. In reply, MmaLabadi insisted,

> There is no way in which I could escape [the accusations] because they are making a clay cow of me [*ba mpopela kgomo ya mmopa*] [i.e., fabricating]. Myself, I do not have any relative here who could talk on my behalf.

In dialogue, the headman's wife expressed her own pained feelings. The defendant was being childish and not co-operating with the court, observed the headman's wife:

> You are playing. Do you know that you speak as if you do not want to answer people. You are supposed to tell the truth.

MmaLabadi appealed for sympathy for her own grieving heart:

> I am not playing. I did not say anything. I am telling the truth and also this heart of mine is painful.

The headman's wife rejected this appeal and demanded that MmaLabadi recognise that the testimony against her was coming from a responsible relative, her 'father' [as the husband of her close relative, see Figure 10.1 Genealogy 2]:

> Do you mean that Rakobo can accuse you falsely, being your father? I have been hearing you saying people have moulded you a clay cow but your parent there made this work [spoke his words] in patience [*botelele*]. 'What you are doing, you just do because you do not want to listen to people'.

At one point MmaLabadi admitted: 'I see myself at fault',' while also saying she doesn't know 'where it will finish' – a kind of half-apology.

The Court rebukes of the defendant

One member of the court demanded that MmaLabadi 'show respect', not turn her back away: 'You are supposed to [stand] apart from the people so that we can look you in the eye to ask you questions'.' Later, this same court member said that this matter showed that MmaLabadi was, 'undisciplined, totally; not being accountable to people'. He demanded, 'Answer people respectfully, knowing that this thing is [being discussed by] us, men and women. It is a full customary court. If you can play before us, we can abandon you'. The court member went on to appeal to the defendant to see the danger to herself if she failed to calm herself and put out what was, in effect, a 'fire', the witchcraft insult she had made, burning her, above all:

> This [matter] is fire [i.e., dangerous], it is in front; we will show it to you. We do not want to leave you just so. If you do not want to calm yourself [*kokobetsa* – shame yourself], but want to see that the fire is burning, you will see fire in this case of witchcraft, accusing a person of being a witch.

He concluded that her defence of talking about someone else's death was spurious,

> You never talked to anyone there about P.'s death [the man who supposedly was a witch who died in the neighbouring town]!

Another member of the court, a woman, tried to persuade MmaLabadi to withdraw her insult:

> Tell the people that this matter was a slip of the tongue [*e go fologile*, it tripped you up]. If you do not tell the people [that], this matter will torment [*sotla*]

> you. Right now, if you see these people, MmaSiama (the plaintiff) being the one who came to appeal, her heart is aching. Her [half-] sister's heart is also painful because of talking of the death of her mother [MmaKagiso, the senior wife]. Do you see that this matter is not okay? It is not good to play with someone who is dead. We have been thinking [all along] that MmaKagiso died the death of God; we did not know that she was killed by MmaKuba (the plaintiff's mother). You see that it is not good as it appears.

The woman court member continued by pointing out that MmaLabadi and the plaintiff, MmaSiama, were close relatives. 'I do not see the reason why you and MmaSiama should argue with unkind words in front of people. That is to insult/shame yourself [*itshotla*] and also your parents'.'

She went on:

> I always [*tlhola*] see you going around with MmaSiama and doing everything [together]. Today you are surprising me, being here and being the ones suing. When looking at you and MmaSiama, I can see that you are the same [close relatives]. If I were you, I could have asked people to go and ask forgiveness for me from Tina (the plaintiff's daughter) as I had sinned [*leofetse*] and talked to her badly. MmaSiama is a person and MmaKuba [her mother] is a person [with humanity]. They could have seen that you had made a mistake [i.e., forgiven you].

At this point emerged perhaps the most critical message of the court. *Adults, as sane, rational persons, must control themselves and their soul/spirit.* Only they can do so. The accused is a conscious being capable of achieving self-control in response to the words of the court. And if a person transgresses, as in the present case, they should listen to others, calm themselves, and ask forgiveness. Whoever sinned against relatives will be forgiven, if she manages herself as a social, human being. By contrast to the accused, the court here constructs itself as composed of rational, decent persons, and their arguments are thus presented as the outcome of rational reasoning.[12]

To bring the defendant to her senses, a visiting ward headman and the local ward headman presiding over the court both warned the defendant that her offence was so grievous she could risk going to jail if the case went forward to the village court of record or the magistrate's court. One of the most senior members of the court took on the role of speaker for the moral authority of the ward court and as the voice of everyday understandings of the human condition as shared by social beings living together; understandings which he warned the defendant, she

12 This is not simply an expression of western, liberal ideology or a Foucauldian call for care of the self. Notions of *seriti* among Tswapong imply interdependence and mutual recognition. They are dividualistic rather than individualistic (see P.Werbner, 2009; R.Werbner, 2015).

was wilfully breaching. She was admonished to 'turn back', stop being wilful, and stop inciting hate among her own kin.

The call for the defendant to reach consciousness

The case continued. A third court member, a woman and headman of another ward, cast doubt on MmaLabadi's claim not to have known MmaKuba, the plaintiff's mother, and tried to persuade her of the serious consequences of her insults. She asked MmaLabadi how she would feel if someone had insulted her own parents, now dead?

MmaLabadi admitted it would 'not be good' for her.

The court member then asked her to imagine how MmaSiama, the plaintiff, felt, with the two of them being close relatives?

The headman then appealed to the defendant to recognise the consensus of the court:

> My niece, enter in your soul [*moeng*] and control it [rule it – *laola*]. Ask forgiveness [*maitshwarelo*] of these people that you have sinned against and those related to them [*baba tshwalang nabo*]. … If you could have had obedience [*boikobo*], we could have dispersed [already] … I know their feelings [*maikuto*]. They are my younger sisters and, if you could have just come in and asked forgiveness, maybe even us, we were not going to find it [find you at fault]. Come back [from] where you are going. Come back to the fact that you are a person, you have been made or moulded yourself [*ipope*]. A person can manage his/herself; we cannot manage you.

The visiting headwoman went on to point out that the matter was very 'painful' and MmaLabadi would be put in jail. She would be asked to produce the herb that allegedly killed MmaKagiso, the co-wife of the plaintiff's mother. The local ward headman echoed her remarks, saying the dispute was very, very big [*tona tona*], as he summed up the case so far. Another senior member of the court, RraModimo, commented:

> MmaLabadi has so many things that offend her [*dilabenyana*]. Her feelings [*maikuto*] are totally different from those of my in-laws. She does not try to turn herself back [*ipusetsa*] to a human condition [*seemong sa batho*]. We do not know her intentions truly [*maikelelo tota*]. Looking at her as a young person, we ask, 'What is she going to end up doing [intending – *ikaelela*] or where will she end up?' That is, is it a matter of insults [*matlhapa*], stirring up [*lotlhanya*] small conflicts [*dikganyana*], and quarrels, that she enters too much into [*thata thata*]?

We see here the way that morality and emotions are intertwined with ideas about the person as a moral human being (see Figure 10.2). The speaker goes on:

Feelings (*maikuto*)	**Virtuous Personhood/ Selfhood**	**Occult attack**
Hatred *(letlho)*; This one is my enemy (*mmaba*), she hates me (*ntlhoetse*)	Patience (*bopelotelele)*	A bad omen (*ke bothodi)*
Hurt feelings (of 'burning'), which 'rise' (*ke shwele*)	Must be 'calmed', calm down (*busa moya*)	Witchcraft (*boloi*)
The heart is 'painful', 'painful' words, feel pain (*utwa botlhoko*)	Calm oneself (*kokobetsa*)	
Torment (*sotla*)	Ask forgiveness (*maitshwarelo*)	
They are dangerous, like fire (*kotsi* = danger)	Forgiveness, along with a demand to be shown respect (*boitshwarelo)*	
Insult (*nyatsa*) (You) insult yourself (*itshotla*)	Demand for humility, obedience (*boikobo*)	
Offend (*dilabenyana*)	'Bring your soul back' (*mowa*), calm down	
Bodily threats and insults (I will make you shit - *nyela*)	Enter in your soul (*moeng*) and control it (rule it – *laola*)	
Dispute causes family to quarrel and hate (*losa*) one another	Turn back (*ipusetsa*) to the human condition (*seemong sa batho)*	
	A person molds him/herself (*ipope*)	
	Understand each other (*utwana*), socialise (*utwana*) or respect (*totana*) each other	

Figure 10.2 Semantic grid of emotions.

> But I am speaking in the *kgotla* [court] that is to be respected, and we should try as we speak to MmaLabadi (the defendant) thus, [to] try to search herself [*ipatla*] and bring herself back [*ipusetsa*] to the human condition. … if her soul wants, she goes across, she crosses [causes conflict by insulting]. She does not look to see who the person is [young or old, whom she offends].

It is obvious, he said, that MmaLabadi would not be able to point to the herb or even its colour that supposedly had killed MmaKagiso, the plaintiff's mother, and yet she is 'destroying [*agolola*] families'. Hence the dispute is 'hurting', causing members of a single family to

> quarrel and hate [*losa*] one another, so that they do not understand each other [*utwana*], socialise together [*rerisana*] or respect each other [*totana*].

> They don't know each other [*itsana*]. The one saying, this one is my enemy [*mmaba*], she hates me [*ntlhoetse*] because she is saying, my mother killed her mother. It is not a good matter, a nice matter.

Here the speaker is spelling out the consequences of hateful feelings for family discord and non-cooperation. Such feelings, expressed in public, are deeply damaging and disruptive. He concludes that 'I mean that what you did this day, you, child of my father's sister, you hurt me [*nkamile*] beyond [*go feta*] hurting [*go nkama*].' As a consequence, he states his opinion that MmaLabadi should be beaten with a stick, since fining her will not stop her re-offending.

Witchcraft accusations and the competence of the court

In an effort to assuage the plaintiff, the ward headman acknowledged that the matter of a witchcraft insult went beyond his own jurisdiction, but perhaps the defendant's apparent admission could be accepted in a settlement. This was not acceptable to the plaintiff, who insisted that the defendant was appearing to make an admission but not meaning to stick by it with appropriate conduct once outside the court.

The idea of beating the defendant in punishment was rejected by the headman – he had never beaten a woman and never would – and the case seemed to have reached an *impasse*, but at this point the headman's wife appealed to the plaintiff to be appeased. The appeal evoked a very long speech from the plaintiff. She told in detail of her own goodwill and upright conduct towards the defendant as a relative and a neighbour, by contrast to the malicious nature of the insult, its offensive attack on her and her feelings, and the failure of the defendant even now to give her due respect. Seeking to assuage the plaintiff, several other women appealed to her to be consoled and forgiving, but the plaintiff remained adamant. She threatened to take the defendant to the village court, or even the magistrate's court, if she failed to make a true offering of respect in the ward court. Through repeated appeals by court members, the defendant failed to be humble and show fear and respect. All this time, she had not looked directly at the plaintiff. At last she did, and made a humble apology. The plaintiff expressed her disquiet and disbelief, but agreed to accept the apparent apology for the sake of the elders at the court. A senior elder warned the defendant again of her peril if she ever misbehaved and the case went to a village court of record or magistrate's court. Finally, the headman affirmed that, though he had no power to judge in a case of witchcraft accusation, the elders had reached a resolution so that peace between the litigants should be restored.

At this point in the case, the ward headman intervened but only to say that he was incapable of 'judging witchcraft':

> Now, truly this dispute, since [in] this dispute this child sees herself at fault, hence this dispute of witchcraft, people of God, I will listen to parents to hear what they say. Truly, I do not know how I could judge [*atlhola*] witchcraft. Now parents can help me with this dispute. To judge witchcraft is difficult,

> beyond my capacity truly, truly. You, parents [referring to members of the court], you will help me think how to judge it. MmaLabadi said, and I heard her saying, people of God, she finds herself at fault [*o ipona phoso*]. These are the words said. I mean that parents [the elders, *batsadi*] have to enter into this matter. As for myself, I do not know how to judge witchcraft. Only you parents can investigate [*seka seka*] it. I was telling the plaintiff that the dispute of your child is yours, you heard her saying she finds herself guilty.

In response to this appeal by the headman, MmaSiama, the plaintiff, stood up to say that MmaLabadi might *seem* to find herself guilty in front of the court but later she would deny her guilt. MmaLabadi had had a whole week to reflect before the court case took place but didn't apologise during that time, she just went on 'playing games'. Now MmaSiama wanted answers.

Another elder again reminded the court that, if the case was brought forward to higher court, MmaLabadi would go to jail. The only solution was to beat her. The ward headman then intervened to say that it was difficult for him to beat a woman. He had never been given that authority. He had never 'caused a woman to lie down on her stomach. These things are the ones that make a heavy load for me',' he said, 'when you both talk of sticks [of beating].' The matter would have to be taken forward, to the court of record.

By this time, the case had been going on for several hours and had reached an *impasse*. A reluctant admission of guilt by the accused was, it seemed, simply unacceptable to the plaintiff. The wife of the ward headman, now appealed to MmaSiama in the name of the lasting relationship she had with MmaLabadi, to 'bring back her soul [*mowa*]'. 'Won't you bring back your soul [i.e., calm down – *busa moya*]?' MmaSiama responded, reflecting on her closeness with MmaLabadi, her first cousin by marriage:

> I heard you [the previous speaker] when you were talking. Even the question you asked that how many matters [disputes] I and MmaLabadi have had [with one other]. As for myself, I do not have any matters with MmaLabadi – my home is MmaLabadi's whether I am around or not. The child you see her holding, when she runs short of milk she will come to me and I will give her some money. I also give her money for cigarettes, even if I am not the one who taught her how to smoke. The compound is hers, whether I am around or not. Even my neighbours can bear witness that, even if I am not around, she goes into my house and takes anything [she needs].

Insults: pain and respect

Court hearings, we have argued, reveal that insults are associated with hurt and deep pain, as well as disrespect. Thus MmaSiama, the plaintiff, continues:

> She hurts me with such big words today, and also she did not respect me after saying these words. She could have gone and reflected that the words

> about me were a slip of the tongue 'MmaSiama who is like this, that, what would she say when hearing these words?' Having respect.

MmaSiama then turns to address the contradictions implicit in the accusation of witchcraft, speaking ironically:

> Now, I do not know that as MmaLabadi knew MmaKuba (the plaintiff's mother) is a witch – a lion [i.e., a witch] gives birth to a baby lion cub [*tawana*], but even so, she just takes things in my compound knowing that I was given birth to by a lion [i.e., MmaSiama is the daughter of Mmakuba, allegedly a witch]. She [MmaSiama] also is a baby lion, she can eat me.

Finally, MmaSiama demands that she be treated with the respect she deserves:

> MmaLabadi did not show respect to me. If she had it [respect] she could have made me helpless [forgiving]. I thought that the way MmaLabadi takes everything [from my house], eating everything, even clothes also – I do not praise myself. People who are here can praise me about my compound and MmaLabadi. Today she hurt me and also … she did not humble herself when arriving here. I did not think MmaLabadi could be the one who could put hands on this child [Tina, her daughter]. Even wherever they go, MmaLabadi is always on her side, saying that this is my younger sister. If this girl is not behaving with MmaLabadi very well, MmaLabadi should come to me instead of waiting for her on the street. This old woman [Tina's paternal grandmother] is my mother. She is myself. If she [Tina] beat MmaLabadi, it is as though she beat her before me.

In response to MmaSiama speech, a woman elder, wife of the ward headman, intervenes, trying to placate the plaintiff:

> I hear you. That is why I asked you if you have had any matter with MmaLabadi [before]? I was saying bring back your soul [calm down]. I know that she is your child. No-one will come between you and MmaLabadi – only if she, MmaLabadi, does it to you as a trap [*meleko*]. This matter is hurting, you showed that when talking about it; we change faces [expressions, when hurt]. You are the one that it is said about your mother that she killed Mary's mother. Mary too came to listen [to find out] how her mother [MmaKagiso] was killed. Just as you heard her saying, when we talk about it, she does not feel well. Now facing you, do you see her, even if you take her [MmaLabadi] to another customary court, is she going to come out with the herb she claims MmaKuba used to kill the old woman with?

Another woman, speaking for the first time, also appeals to the plaintiff:

> MmaSiama, this matter is hurting [you], my elder sister. Now, you know we are talking to you as if we are pressing upon you. MmaLabadi is not telling the truth when she denies that she does not know your mother: MmaKuba breastfed her. Her surname is Diba [like MmaLabadi's] and also RraPhiri [MmaKuba's husband, see Genealogy 2 Figure 10.1], his surname was Dipini. Now, the thing hurting me is that the matter is hurting. Even when I heard that MmaLabadi was talking to you, I was puzzled, and also I did not think that I would find MmaLabadi not humble towards you here. We know as your neighbours everything MmaLabadi does in your compound. The love you give her and her children, we know it.

She then appeals to MmaLabadi: 'MmaLabadi, do you see that your misbehaving will end up putting you in jail?' Finally, appealing to MmaSiama:

> Now, I am bringing back your soul [calming you]. Even [if] she will go around praising herself, saying she is a winner in all things, God will stand by you on these painful words … which create a misunderstanding which won't end up here right now. Bring back your soul and see that the person is disabled.

The speaker points to the 'pain' which MmaLabadi's insults spread everywhere:

> All the time MmaLabadi's matters are hurting the people around her, or the ones she spoke about. Even if you think of them [these matters] you will see that they are painful. You will ask yourself what makes her do this, as young as she is.

The pressure of the Court towards reconciliation

Having listened to evidence and reprimanded MmaLabadi, demanding that she 'bring back her soul', the court is now attempting to reason with the plaintiff that *she* 'bring back her soul', on the grounds that MmaLabadi is disabled, disturbed, not fully in control of herself, not a whole person. The court makes clear that they appreciate MmaSiama's loving treatment of MmaLabadi over the years, her generosity, her caring attitude. They condemn MmaLabadi for not respecting her.

The headman's wife again appeals to MmaSiama to 'bring back her soul and see the people who are here [in the court]':

> Forgive them [for their sake] even if you do not [forgive] her. At least forgive the parents [the elders in the hearing]. I am begging you, child of my mother's niece, I am begging you, my sister. Even you, Mary, bring back

> your soul, my sister. Let it be back to the [original] position, do not disappoint yourselves. You just unite as you have been united.

Despite this plea MmaSiama, the plaintiff, insists:

> I hear you, but MmaLabadi should be compelled to show respect. MmaLabadi should totally admit her fault and, seeing that she is showing respect, saying from her own mouth [voluntarily], not being forced by people to show respect. I want MmaLabadi to show respect before these people, otherwise I am going further. She will go to jail. It does not matter – my aunt [MmaLabadi's mother] will take the child [MmaLabadi's child] and [let it] stay with her. Maybe my aunt will be relieved when arriving from there.

Now the demand made by the court that MmaLabadi truly 'show respect' gains momentum. The headman's wife insists:

> MmaLabadi, show contrition toward my niece. Say out your words in which you show humility to your sister. Take out your soul [calm down] and talk before the people.

MmaLabadi answers: 'I am saying [asking that] she should forgive me'.'
MmaSiama counters: There she is, looking down upon us. There is no respect from MmaLabadi. Do you really see her?
Headman's wife: 'Show respect, facing the people, my niece'.'
MmaSiama (repeats herself): If a person did something and humbled herself, even you, you will see this person is afraid and humble. If she could have done that [i.e., shown contrition], even if the words (she said) are hurting, you will see her that she is showing respect.

Her words are echoed by another court member, a woman who begs MmaLabadi to face the court and MmaSiama: 'Talk humbly to MmaSiama. Talk to MmaSiama in a free manner. Finish this matter and reconcile. From there, stop going around praising yourself'.'

After a lengthy further cross-examination, MmaLabadi finally seems to be apologising, admitting that she 'said the words by mistake'.' But she still will not face MmaSiama and she is warned that she has to apologise sincerely, facing her, showing respect. At last she says, 'I am asking for forgiveness'.

The final agreement

In her final speech, MmaSiama, the plaintiff, reminds people of the lies MmaLabadi has spoken and concludes:

> I will bring back my heart [calm down] only for your sake [the parents, elders sitting in the court]. I forgive MmaLabadi, but on the words of respect,

> really, MmaLabadi is not respecting. My compound should [will continue to] be hers as usual and should be my aunt's [MmaLabadi's mother] but she should show respect towards both of us. If MmaLabadi does not have respect, we will see, but if she is born anew [*a tsetswe sesha*], that will be seen. 'A good name is made by the owner'.' Now, if MmaLabadi is asking for forgiveness it should be a real forgiveness and it should even be seen that this is a real forgiveness. I am not like others who always excuse her [*rekolola*]. As for myself, if she does it again, I will take her to jail. My aunt [MmaLabadi's mother] will take the child and maybe will be relieved. I end there.

In a final warning to the defendant, the headman acknowledges the elders' consensus.

He warns MmaLabadi that 'our forefathers say, meat rots, but words never rot [i.e. the suit has no prescribed limit]. Do you hear?'. MmaLabadi agrees: 'Yes, Sir'. RraModimo persists:

> Do you understand that the headman should take a pen if she [the plaintiff, MmaSiama] hears [even] a whistle [of gossip]? She will come here [to me] and take the letter, then go straight [to the court of record]. … Please, I am begging you to change. Go back to the habits of your youth. You were good, good looking, I do not know what your problem is. … Try to go back to have human qualities.

The headman concludes with 'Parents, you fought [*le e lole,* struggled with] it, you finished it. I say they should reunite. They are children of the same person. You fought it. I do not have judgements on your matters'.'

Here the case ends, with an appearance of consensus, but without a verdict from the headman himself. We have presented extracts of the court dialogue between the litigants and with members of the court at length, in all their reasoning, passion, and pain, to illustrate vividly and forcefully the lengthy process of persuasion and restorative justice felt to be necessary in Tswapong village courts to restore amity and public peace in the face of offensive insults.

MmaLabadi died eight years after the case was heard, perhaps of a broken heart, since she refused to take the medication prescribed to her when her HIV count rose, despite MmaSiama and other relatives begging her to do so. Her child was said to be of the lover who jilted her. Beyond forgiveness, MmaSiama told me that she died in her arms in hospital.

Conclusion: judicial rationality *versus* out-of-control emotions

We have argued in this chapter that insults in Botswana are grasped as inchoate speech crimes that are tried in court as offences and, as witchcraft-insults, are thought to bear evil, occult danger for the victim of insult. We highlighted the relationship between pain/insult and forgiveness/apology as a way to restore public peace, kinship amity, and personal dignity in customary courts in Botswana.

In the newly revitalised field of law and emotion, Bandes and Blumenthal (2012: 162) suggest the need to avoid making a simplistic distinction between law as reasonable and emotion as irrational. As they say,

> Although the debate about the relationship between emotion and reason dates back to ancient times, there is a hardy folk knowledge portraying emotions as quick, hot, irrational bursts of feeling that short-circuit rational deliberation and that are impervious to study or correction (Maroney 2009). In the legal realm, the term has long functioned as a catchall category for much of what law aspires to avoid or counteract: that which is subjective, irrational, prejudicial, intangible, partial, and impervious to reason.
>
> (Bandes and Blumenthal 2012: 162)

A similar opposition seems to hold in customary village courts in Botswana, this chapter has argued. Members of the court judging cases of insult see themselves as rational and empathetic, and their role as one of bringing litigants' souls/spirits 'back' to reason and everyday good sense. With reason comes forgiveness and humble apology. Issues are aired at length but the aim is one of reconciliation and putting an end to hostilities. In Botswana witchcraft accusations are not only illegal but potentially life-threatening, recognised as being aroused by and arousing powerful emotions. In the main case discussed here, however, they are regarded less in occult terms and more as loose, irresponsible, insulting talk by an emotionally disturbed person acting irrationally. As such the solution is not to respond in retaliation, with counter-medicines or severe punishment but to reason with the offending person and to use all the court's means of persuasion, on the one hand, to 'bring back' her soul as a social being, and, on the other hand, to assuage the plaintiff.

Even beyond the emotion-rationality and legal-illegal oppositions, moreover, the cases reported here highlight the fact that for Tswapong villagers, expressions of emotions are constituted, during their hearings, in everyday moral terms within a known semantic field, as illustrated in Figure 10.2. Vindictiveness and aggressiveness, hurt and pain, are perceived to threaten the moral order as well as being defined as illegal. We may speak of the law in this case as imbued with affect: law and the judicial process itself are devoted to persuading litigants to change their emotions so as to recreate public civility and personal humanity. The legal anthropology of emotion, therefore, must capture terms reflecting upon the socio-moral order, personal humanity and legal conduct as intertwined within a single semantic field.

11 A moral economy of crime and the proportionality of punishment

Introduction: A moral economy of crime

The burden of criminal jurisdiction in customary courts is grave and controversial. To document and analyse it, as the actual extent of criminal jurisdiction in customary courts has changed, especially in relation to the statutory courts, is to enter into a minefield of social problems. Our argument in this chapter foregrounds controversy, in and beyond academic debate. The minefield before us runs through many troubling disagreements – about the public mood for serious punishment and long imprisonment of criminals, about the competence and proper jurisdiction of courts, about the unintended consequences of apparently popular legislation, about the right to representation and the subjective experience of justice and fairness in trial, and about the blinkered, modernist perceptions of customary courts as backward and failing, among other things.

We show that some of these social problems in the matter of rustling were made worse by Parliament legislating one harshly punitive solution after another. A basic law and its amendment increased the mandatory sentence with punishment in proportion not to the crime of stock theft but to something dubiously said 'to protect the people' and called 'the rule of law'. Other problems, we show also, are all the more intractable because of the mixing-up of petty and organised crime. Alongside stock theft as petty crime within a village or its neighbours has emerged large-scale organised crime across national borders, in particular across Botswana's borders with South Africa and Zimbabwe. One disturbing tendency in public discourse was to conflate petty crime with large-scale crime, apparently in response to popular pressure for public safety. Our approach in this chapter, as throughout most of this book, pays most attention, in the way of the new legal realism, to the examination of a whole set of actual cases, a good number of which form the main body of this chapter.

It would be a mistake, of course, to give the impression, even by way of a preliminary view, that the problems, while troublesome, are completely left without national control. In the face of increasing stock theft, including the theft of donkeys, goats and sheep, along with cattle, the Botswana police set up a nationwide operation named *Kgomokhumo* (cattle wealth). In August 2018, the Assistant Commissioner of Police announced that 69 persons had been arrested for stock

DOI: 10.4324/9781003241881-11

theft in one area, but with only nine so far convicted and sentenced to prison terms of between five and seven years; 169 head of cattle had been dealt with, many intended for the South African market. The thieves specialised, he said, in heifers, which were often unbranded.[1]

Nevertheless, and allowing for the reassuring value of such a nationwide operation, the conflation of petty and large-scale crime is evident in national legislation, we argue. Neither the Stock Theft Act, 1996, nor its revision in 2000 or its amendment in 2018, specifies the *level* or *circumstances* of the crime of stock theft. What is made clear are the *penalties*:

> Any person who steals any stock or produce, or receives any stock or produce knowing or having reason to believe it to be a stolen stock or produce, shall be guilty of an offence and, notwithstanding the provisions of any other written law, shall be sentenced for a first offence to a term of imprisonment for not less than five years or more than 10 years *without the option of a fine*, and for a second or subsequent offence to a term of imprisonment for not less than seven years or more than 14 years *without the option of a fine*.
>
> (Stock Theft Act 3, 1, 1996, emphasis added)

Of course, neither the Stock Theft Act, 1996 nor its successor, the amendment in 2018, specify the level or circumstances of the crime of livestock theft.[2] The 2018 amendment increased the minimum penalty to seven years and the maximum penalty to 12 years for a first offence and 15 for a second offence on the grounds that, as contended by the President Dr. Mogweetsi Masisi in Parliament, 'For us, livestock is a priceless resource and as a country that believes in the rule of law we should encourage people to observe the law and protect the people from cattle rustlers', (Botswana Government 2018).[3] Such sentiments seem to hark back to a time when, as Isaac Schapera had noted, beyond their utilitarian aspects, cattle in the 1930s were used for sacrifice, exchange, bride wealth, compensation payments, and communal celebration. Indeed, cattle were a key indicator of status and wealth (Schapera 1938: 213–214). They were a means of investment and saving for labour migrants. At the time of independence, before the discovery of diamonds, the Botswana economy relied heavily on cat-

1 *Botswana Daily News*, 'Botswana: Operation Kgomokhumo Breakthrough', 10 August 2018. Throughout sub-Saharan Africa stock theft is said to be increasing. Drawing on his research in Kenya, Bunei argues that 'agricultural crime is one of the biggest concerns affecting the rural communities and economies in the world' (Bunei 2017: 1). Stock theft is particularly prominent in South Africa where 'in recent decades, the frequency and intensity of the practice has reached an uncontrollable level' (ibid.: 3). Cattle rustling has now been taken over by organised crime (ibid.: 3).

2 It is worth noting that the Lesotho Stock Theft Act 2000 had lower penalties – three years for a first offence and a fine of 7,000 pula (Lesotho Stock Theft Act 2000).

3 12 December 2018. https://www.facebook.com/BotswanaGovernment/posts/masisi-calls-for-stringent-action-against-stock-theftparliament-the-state-should/1978029032279745/

tle export, with numbers peaking after independence, in 2002, at three million cattle in the country (Hillborn 2014). The industry had, however, gone through difficult times in the past 30–40 years (Solway 2016), and communal herds had declined.[4] Moreover, high numbers hide the fact that the distribution of cattle is extremely unequal, with many families owning no cattle at all. Nonetheless, even today among Tswapong villagers in Moremi, cattle are still used for sacrifice and communal celebration, for bride wealth payments in prestigious marriages, for exchange and gifting. To some extent, they remain an index of wealth and status.

Rather than being a matter of consensus, given a public mood of anxiety in the face of 'rampant stock theft' (Botswana Government 2018), the amendment itself, along with the appeal to the alleged countrywide belief and basic morality, became a bone of contention between the ruling party and the opposition. The only dissenting voice in the parliamentary debate was raised by an opposition politician, the member for Gaborone North, Mr Haskins Nkaigwa. He argued that MPs were

> using their emotions and personal interests in the matter, instead of looking at ways to rehabilitate offenders. 'We should not make laws based on our emotions or because we are interested parties with cattle ranches. Rather, we must rationally conduct research as to why people steal and address their condition. Some of those engaged in stock theft are poor people in the rural areas who have no source of livelihood. While there should be punitive measures for people engaged in crime, taking someone to jail for 12 or 15 years, separating them from their children, when an even more hardened criminal can be rehabilitated within three years, is harsh'.
>
> (ibid.)

Although in sympathy with the concerns raised about the consequences of stuffing prisons with young men, as first offenders, a senior magistrate at Serowe, the Central District capital, tried to get us to understand the challenge Parliament faced in the attempt to deter offences of high prevalence by increasing penalties and yet still to sustain the customary courts. We discussed the customary courts. He first read us the passages in law that define the special jurisdiction of the customary courts in a way that allows them to arrive at their own procedures. In his view, customary courts were 'kangaroo courts': they have no procedure and cases were just held 'free-style'. This is why customary courts find guilty 100 per cent of the criminal cases that come before them, he told us. He, on the other hand, acquits a large number of cases, mainly because of faulty police evidence (or the lack of it).

By contrast to the loose practice in the customary courts, the strict regulation in the statutory courts had to meet three requirements, he explained, for determining guilt in the case of 'possession' of stolen goods:

4 Solway gives a comprehensive account of the cattle industry, its development and decline.

1. The accused was in possession of the goods.
2. There was a reasonable suspicion that the apparently stolen goods had actually been stolen.
3. The accused had failed to give an account of how he came into possession of the goods.

If the prosecution failed to prove even one of the requirements, the accused would be acquitted and proof needed to be beyond reasonable doubt. Often, on the issue of reasonable suspicion, there was no proof. The police normally act on a tip-off, he said, and the informant does not become a witness. An informant could have various motives, even a grudge, and the policeman had to have tangible evidence that the magistrate him/herself could see. Informants are not called to the court in order to protect them. Often, the police abuse their power. They don't have the right to ask you without grounds about your property, he added.

This magistrate's perception of the unsafe customary courts is, of course, biased and misleading, though it shares modernist legal blinkers common even among academics who complain that the customary courts, lacking legally trained judges and lawyers, are not fit for purpose of criminal jurisdiction. Contrary to this blinkered perception, rules for customary court procedure are defined in great detail by legislation, most recently amended in 2016, cited as 'Customary Court (Procedures) (Amendment) Rules 2016'. According to the legislation, the hearing begins with the Presiding Officer explaining to the defendant the charge against him, followed by asking him whether there is anything to stop the case proceeding. Next, the Presiding Officer must ask whether the defendant admits committing the acts s/he is accused of. If admitted, the Presiding Officer records a plea of guilty; otherwise, the plea is not guilty. After the defendant has called witnesses s/he wishes to call, and they have been questioned, the Court must give the complainant and the defendant an opportunity to sum up their evidence and make any other relevant submissions they wish to make. Then the Court must consider all the evidence and pronounce judgement. Where the Court feels any real doubt about the guilt or innocence of the defendant, the Court has to acquit the defendant.

The actual facts of acquittal in customary courts are yet to be measured; evident only is the high number of sentenced prisoners in jail. In 2004, the legal scholar Charles Fombad reported an alarming trend in the growth of the urban prison population from customary court sentences:

> The common assumption that customary courts and customary law dispute-settlement institutions and processes are largely a rural phenomenon is no longer valid, for surveys carried out in prisons in the major towns in the country, such as in Gaborone and Francistown, have revealed, rather alarmingly, that almost 75% of those in prison today are serving sentences handed down in customary courts.
>
> (2004: 181)

Many prisoners were sentenced for stock theft, according to Fombad, without the option of a fine or of legal representation (ibid.: 188; see also Malila 2019: 129). Fombad saw the need to 'divest the customary courts even further of their criminal jurisdiction and in particular the six years prison term for stock theft should be reduced' (ibid.: 189). Prison terms are from five to 12 years, we note, however.

Fombad's criticism of the denial of legal representation was not in vain. In 2008, the Minister of Justice, Defence and Security, Mr. Phandu Skelemani, recommended that stock theft litigants should have the right, as enshrined in international law, to legal representation (Kumar 2009: 21); that is, they should have the right to opt for a hearing in a magistrate's court. There is still little in the 2018 Act, however, to distinguish the magnitude and seriousness of an alleged theft, or the circumstances and evidence of its occurrence, in deciding prison sentences.

In our view, it is no longer true to say, as Fombad recently does in writing with Baboki Dambe, (a) that few cases go to magistrates' courts, (b) that customary courts fail to follow procedures because of illiteracy and lack of education, and (c) that in the parliamentary debate in 1996 a key sentiment expressed by lawmakers was against 'lawyers' who manage to successfully defend cattle thieves on 'technicalities' (Dambe and Fombad 2020). Later we document our own view, the actual alternative in present-day customary courts or magistrates' courts.

The question of judicial discretion and clemency in customary courts clearly still needs to be seriously addressed, all the more so because of the blinding power of the blinkers, *against judicial and forensic skill*, all too easily taken for granted in certain modernist perceptions of customary courts. The criminologist Ikanyeng Malila, aware of the problematic implementation of state-made law and the skilful circumvention of top–down regulation, has offered an acute insight, with a better historical and realist perspective. He has illuminated current practice as it has actually developed under the impact of formal legal codification as well as in the complexity of legal pluralism, at once with obedient acceptance and also with avoidance and manipulative resistance:

> it should not be assumed that the changes brought about by codification and the universalisation of the criminal law have only made customary court sanctions harsher. There are a small number of offences for which penalties introduced under codified law are more lenient than they would have been under customary law. For instance, under customary law, cattle theft attracted [in the past] very heavy penalties, and the owner reserved the right to kill the thief if he was caught committing the crime (Schapera 1938: 48). This is no longer permissible under codified law (Malila 2015: 278).

No less important is Malila's recognition of instances of deliberate compassion in customary courts nowadays: that judges in customary courts sometimes use their discretion to minimise jail sentences. They try

> to circumvent the formal approach because they believe it can only result in offenders, especially young people, acquiring unnecessary criminal records (citing Gaotlhobogwe 2010).[5] As a result, some traditional leaders often attempt to push cases involving social disorder into the private domain. The family will normally be the arbiter. In some cases, 'offenders' will be punished extra-judicially, if the leaders think they can avoid alerting formal structures …
>
> (Malila 2010).

Some have openly defied the state and deployed traditional methods of dealing with low-level social disorder (ibid.: 278). As we shall show, however, once the police are alerted, this kind of diversion becomes almost impossible, resulting, Malila argues, in the 'criminalisation of minor conduct' (ibid.: 279). In general, and despite a good measure of semi-autonomy and traditional containment of low-level social disorder, Malila found that 'customary courts' punishments were harsher than those awarded by magistrate courts' (Malila 2012: 631), and that they tended to adopt multiple forms of punishment. They were also harsher on young people, claims Malila (ibid.). This may explain why those accused of stock theft often prefer to be tried in magistrates' courts, *even in the absence of a lawyer*, as several cases below illustrate.

The (dis)proportionality of punishment meted out according to the law and by courts in Botswana, as in many African countries, diverges from the trend in Western liberal democracies where the proportionality principle is perceived to protect the human rights of the accused (Malila 2019, esp. 126 *et passim*). Proportionality, Malila argues, 'in the mind of the ordinary person, is instinctively linked to fairness' (ibid.: 124). The liberalising effects of the proportionality principle seem to be, however, in Botswana, as in other African countries, 'in direct conflict with the general thrust of legislation which tends to emphasise harsh penalties and penal instrumentation' (ibid.: 125).

When we asked, in 2014, why there was the need for a police station in a small village like Moremi, we were told both by village residents and by the police stationed there that Moremi was a hotbed of stock theft. The police sergeant said that he had caught many cattle thieves but they had asked to have their case heard at the magistrate's court. This ensured a very long delay, he said – none of the alleged culprits are in jail, and, given the backlog in court, they are free to come and go as usual. The last case of cattle theft he knew of that was heard at the magistrate's court was, he said, in 2014. He explained that it was difficult to prove theft, since the cattle were usually eliminated (slaughtered and their skins thrown away). They were often sold to butchers in Palapye. In the 2014 case, they had caught the cattle and put them in a special kraal in the nearby village of Tamasane, but then they all died in the drought, so when the case went to court,

5 The article referred to mentions the advantages of traditional discipline such as flogging, which does not leave one's name dented with a criminal record. It does not discuss stock theft.

it was simply for the case to be dismissed. No-one has been jailed from Moremi, the policeman claimed. Later he changed his story. He said that, though the cattle had died, they'd kept the skins. The case had taken place and the culprits were awaiting judgement (interview 18 April 2016).

Criminal cases examined

In the following account, we examine in detail criminal cases, including theft, possession of allegedly stolen cattle, and the unlawful driving of cattle to a pen away from the owner's. Several of these criminal cases were tried in the first instance in the nearby villages of Moremi and Matolwane. Others began in the Palapye magistrate's court and went on appeal to the High Court of Appeal in Gaborone We document the regard for evidence and admission of guilt in a straightforward case brought by an owner, and on appeal, the complexity of restatements, revisions of applicable law, and reworked decision making in different customary courts.

All of the criminal cases in customary courts attest to the permeability of customary law within a legally plural context. Contrary to the magistrate's caricature of 'kangaroo courts', and his implicitly modernist blinkers, they are obviously responsive to statutory rules for police conduct, for their fair procedure in forensic investigation, and their reporting of material evidence, such as from the inspection of brands on cattle, and the tracing of owners, as well as the practice of having the judge and members of the court get first-hand knowledge of the material evidence and crime site, such as the pen in the case of theft. Serving as prosecutors on behalf of the state, local police follow standard regulations for introducing the complaint, on the basis of an account of their investigation and observed evidence. If a tip-off from an informer aroused their suspicion, they report going beyond that in their own collection of material evidence. For confirmation of material evidence, they do ask the court, represented by the presiding judge and his advisors, to gain first-hand knowledge by themselves inspecting the recovered cattle.

Even further, and perhaps more taken for granted than permeability in the forensics of policing, is the permeability in clerical practice. The renown of customary court clerks, mainly women, for being meticulous keepers of formal procedure, is hardly surprising. Often long-serving and sometimes more highly experienced than the chiefs they serve, they become influential, if often behind the scenes, in effecting the changing interlinkages under legal pluralism. They command permeable documentation. Realised in their clerical texts as transcripts is the documentary work of standardising the customary court hearing from what emerged in the making of the hearing, extracting, and simplifying it in a prescribed format, recording answers, while omitting the questions, leading up to the concluding judgement of the presiding chief. The outcome, introduced in the making of customary courts as courts of record, is the creation of court records that are commensurable to one another, or almost the same, despite the often disparate deliberations and leading questions in actuality.

In other words, if the hearings enact customary law as living law, their recordings obliterate any dialogue and cross-examination. This may be a shortcoming where such records are considered in higher customary courts of appeal, without usually taking in further evidence or cross-examining witnesses. Our citations from various customary court records show the extensive standardisation introduced into the documentation of due process in customary courts.

The first and most recent case we consider here, recorded in 2019 by the court clerk at Moremi, is one the Moremi village chief told us was an 'open-and-shut' case, with the twenty-two-year-old offender admitting his guilt, and the court mitigating his sentence to three years, allowing clemency, as against a harsh, prescribed sentence. The case is instructive in revealing how the proportionality principle may be skilfully manipulated as it is applied to different crimes of 'theft' in Botswana. Rather than being accused of stock theft, which carries a mandatory minimum five-year jail sentence, the defendant was accused of 'common theft' for stealing cattle bells, a crime which carries the lesser penalty of no more than three years' imprisonment. In fact, the accused had moved the cattle to another kraal, hoping to hide them. The village chief in his summary makes clear that 'the accused intended to steal the cattle. He removed the bells so the cattle could not be easily found'. In other words, the village chief reprimanded the accused for cattle theft, but sentenced him for the theft of cow bells, even while recognising that his intention was 'to kill the evidence with bells'.

In response to our query later, the village chief told us of his concern that too many young men were 'rotting away in prison' under long sentences. Against the unequivocal statutory law that required sentencing cattle thieves to a minimum of five years in jail, the customary court in this case sentenced the offender to only three years in jail, almost by a sleight of hand.

The second case of theft we report here was recorded in 2013 by the clerk of the nearby Matolwane village and then by other court clerks on appeal. It exemplifies current and standard practice in the sentencing of a young man, in the customary court of his home village, who confessed to guilt when accused of the theft and possession of cattle, and then amended his plea on appeal. We follow the course of litigation through the hierarchy of customary courts, first at Matolwane village, then to Maunatlala and then to the tribal headquarters in Serowe. We did not follow the appeal to the High Court in Francistown. In the next three cases we discuss here, the accused, as they are entitled, shifted the venue from the start to the magistrate's courts. The first of these cases highlights the hardship that a serious jail sentence inflicts on the families of the sentenced men. In the third criminal case, proceedings were appealed from the magistrate's court to the High Court, and then the Court of Appeal.

Following from these criminal cases, we turn to the contractual, to examine the consideration through a hierarchy of customary courts of the breach of cattle trust known as *mafisa*. *Mafisa* entails the giving out of cattle on a trust. It is beneficial for the owner, who is free of their care and who profits from any increase, and for the caring herder, who gains their use, for milking, ploughing, and hauling, with due care to the good condition of the cattle, and who is often given a calf or two in payment. It is a private contract, usually not a concern of the police, and commonly an expression of a good, moral, and well-valued relationship, such as friendship, between owner and herder.

The case of the stolen calves

In this case, heard at Matolwane Customary Court on 28 May 2013, and recorded by the court clerk, a 24-year-old man, Molomo Fala (pseudonym) was accused of stock theft. The presiding judge was a chief from Maunatlala, Mapena, standing in for the Matolwane village chief. Present also as a recognised member of the Court was Sinwedi Ikalafeng, a Moremi ward headman. On the record, the state was the complainant, and the complaint was for Count 1: Stealing stock (section 3 (1) of stock theft); and Count 2: Possession of suspected stolen property (318 of penal code CAP 0801 ARW 33 of the penal code). The court sentenced the defendant on Count 1 to five years' imprisonment, and for Count 2, an additional two years' imprisonment; the defendant was granted the right of appeal within 30 days.

For each count, in turn, a particular statement of the offence was given. Two calves were involved, one greyish without a known owner, and one brownish whose owner, TL, had been found, becoming a complainant along with the state. At first, the statements focused on TL's calf, alleged to be stolen from a cattle post, branded with JG/G4, the defendant's brand, and seen by police in a pen containing 11 calves, a number in itself arousing so much suspicion that the police at first arrested and questioned the pen owner. He informed the police that, to his knowledge, two double-branded calves belonged to MF, the defendant.

The record shows the Court following the prescribed procedure. We cite the record at length to show the documentation itself as well as the due process followed. It begins, according to rule, with the statement of the complaint, count by count, followed by asking the defendant, if he understands the crime. Given his admission of guilt, the record shows the case followed the prescribed procedure: the Presiding Chief checked that there was no obstruction to the case, and that the defendant agreed for the case to go ahead.

CHIEF: You, the defendant, you have been brought before this court to answer for the crime of stealing stock in May 15 2013. You stole a calf of TL in the cattle post of KBL, near Maunatlala. And you branded it using your branding iron (JG/G4). On the left, it had the brand with a sign for the sharpness of a knife. The branding iron of the complainant [the cattle owner] is JC/CY and the calf is brownish in the colour.
(CONTINUES): Do you understand the crime?
ACCUSED: I understand.
PRESIDING CHIEF: Do you find yourself guilty?
ACCUSED: I find myself guilty.

PRESIDING CHIEF: Is there anything that can obstruct the case from moving forward?
ACCUSED: The case can move forward.

On this basis, the policeman as prosecutor reported and 'unrolled the case', in detail, citing the law for each of the two counts in the case, giving an account of the cause and course of the investigation, the material evidence inspected, the history of loss of the stolen stock, the arrest of the defendant, and the alerting him of the law for the alleged crimes. The Court was then asked to view the evidence, directly.

PROSECUTOR (Police number 9709): Let us unload the case (*rola tsheko*). I am reporting before people [Count 1] the case of stealing of stock and also [Count 2] being found with a calf that is suspected to have been stolen, the one seen in the laws of the penal code section 318, Chapter 01.08. On 15 May 2013 the police were patrolling, and they entered into BK's kraal, in the fields area of Lekgale. And they found 11 calves. The police had a suspicion about those calves but they wanted the owner, and they arrested Mr. BK who is the owner of the pen, and questioned him about the calves. He showed that two of them are ML's. The police went and arrested ML and questioned him about the two calves, one being brownish, branded in the left ear. And the greyish one branded in the left ear. All of them are branded JG/G4. It was suspicious, chief, because the cattle were of one person but branded with different brands. The thing that made the police take and show them to people – the brownish was identified by PM that it belongs to TL, and TL was called to come and see it. TL proved that it is his – it got lost in December 2012. The greyish one the police could not find the owner and the defendant said he stole it, also he said he branded them with his own brand JG/G4 on top of the complainant's brand. We later told the defendant about the crime of stock theft – that it was a crime even to be found with the stolen stock. I'm taking out the brand certificate JG/G4 of ML and JC/C1 of TL who is the complainant, to be part of the evidence, even the cattle that went to the Tamasane (stray cattle) pen because we don't have transport, to show them to you now. As the defendant has already found himself guilty, I will close the evidence. The case will continue on 28 May 2013 after the cattle at the pen have been seen [by the judge and court] being part of the evidence.

Hence, the police report clarified that that there had been material evidence of the accused's brand superimposed on the owner's; their complaint was not based merely on a tip-off but on an actual investigation, and witness to ownership. The case continued on 28 May 2013, with the following on the record:

> The cattle were seen at the Tamasane kraal. The defendant ML before the court has been brought to answer for the crime of giving himself (*ipha*) a

calf. He branded it with his brand over the owner's brand. The court showed him the matter of denying the calf owner and he admitted that he was the one who had branded the brownish calf. The court agreed with him, because he pointed to it. This is straightforward and there is no way we can change it.

Under the heading 'Mitigation', the record shows the defendant's plea: 'I am left with the old woman and the cattle. The old man died a long time ago'. No recorded response appears, and the record continues with the following notes.

Previous convictions: nil

Sentence Count 1: Since the defendant has already pleaded guilty, the court sentences him to five years' imprisonment. In the second crime, ML was found with the greyish cow which was suspected to have been stolen. When the court asked him about it, he said it does not have an owner. According to the court's knowledge, each and every cow has its owner even if it can be a stray. Being in your pen [as a stray], you have to go to the chief and report it.

On Count 2, the court penalised ML with an additional two years' imprisonment.

From prison, the defendant wrote a letter of appeal against his sentence. In the presence of the court, inspecting the stolen animals and his brand, he had admitted branding the brownish calf himself with his own brand, the same as the brand on the greyish calf, which he claimed had no owner, although he failed to report the stray, as lawfully required, to the chief. For his appeal, he changed his story. He denied he himself had branded the calves, claimed the brand was not identical with his, but larger, and the police had failed to listen to him telling of a possible suspected brander, who had confessed to him. He had only admitted guilt because the brand appeared to be his, and the police had misled him into thinking the owner would not sue and he would be released. The police and the judges had acted too hastily, giving no time to deal with the other suspect.

The following document was placed on record as the defendant's letter of appeal, on 30 May:

> Serowe prison to Matolwane customary court, Appeal:
>
> I was accused and sentenced to seven years by the Setswana court in Lesenepole [Matolwane, under another name] concerning stock theft (section XX etc.). I found myself guilty. Reasons for appeal: (1) The first reason is that I explained to the police that I did not brand any cattle, even though the brand was mine. Truly, for to find myself guilty, it was that the truth is, the brand is written like mine. But the letters are bigger than my brand. (2) The investigators did not prove if truly the brand used is mine. They didn't measure the brand to see if they are identical since those brands are new. (3) The chief accused me twice even though I was accused on one day and on top of that, the 'charge sheet' combined the cattle. The calf which did not have a complainant, I was sentenced for it for two years while the one with a complainant, I was sentenced for five years. (4) At the end, someone told

me that they were the ones who branded those cattle and when I tried to explain to the police, even that they should follow that person, they told me that they don't waste their time with lies. The question is, wasn't it rightful for them to follow the person who said that matter (*kgang*) so that they can hear whether he will tell them what he told me? (5) The other thing is that the owner of the cow said he is not suing me, but the police told me that I should admit the crime and I would be released. The truth is that for me to find myself guilty, I found myself guilty since the brand is mine but not meaning that I am the one who branded the cattle. With humbleness, I'm asking the honourable court to examine these reasons, and to be aware whether the procedure has been followed with these reasons above. Further reasons: (1) To be forced by the police to admit the crime, saying I would be released. (2) That they are drawing their own conclusion by refusing to follow the person who told me they were the ones who branded the cattle. (3) Also, did the judges make investigations properly, because I've been accused even though they did not see me branding the cattle and no-one saw me? Even to prove that the brand that branded the cattle or whether a brand has been made similar to mine. (5) The matter started on 24 May 2013 and in that short period of a week I was sentenced. And it publicly showed I was sentenced by the police who refused to follow that person who said he had branded the cattle. The police and judges did not give themselves time to investigate the matter.

With humbleness

ML

The Appeal was heard on 19 August 2013 by Chief Gabosamang from Maunatlala. After reading the letter by ML, the chief made sure that the reasons given in the letter were the only ones for ML's appeal, and he listened to further points, and the rehearsal of ML's points in his letter, in response to court elders, questioning.

Chief: Are these your reasons for appealing?
Appellant: They are.
Chief: Are you adding to them?
Appellant: I am adding. I did not know the procedure because it was my first time to be sued so I admitted to the crime.

One court elder questioned, and TL responded:

(1) **I am telling this court the truth that I am not the one who branded the cattle.**
(2) **The brand which branded the cattle is mine [i.e. the letters]. I'm the only one who uses this brand.**
(3) **I'm not associated with the crime because the brand that branded the cattle is bigger than mine and the cattle were not found with me.**

(4) **I agreed to the crime because the police said I should agree because the brand [letters] is mine.**
(5) **The crime is mine because the brand is mine.**
(6) **If a person finds himself guilty, he is sentenced.**
(7) **I did not bring my brand to the court.**

ANOTHER ELDER: We've been listening to the appeal of ML in which he complains about the judgement of the Matolwane court on 28/5/2013, the one for seven years' imprisonment, and this court does not agree with what he is saying.

The court record then concluded with the *katholo*, the judgement:

> This court does not change anything in the judgement of the Matolwane court for seven years' imprisonment.
>
> Right of appeal: thirty days.

TL then again appealed, this time to the higher tribal court at Serowe, and his case was heard by Chief S. Seretse, the deputy tribal authority. TL rehearsed his defence in his prison letter, and his allegations against the police. In his questioning, the Chief reminded him that to brand someone else's cattle without permission is a crime, and TL insisted again that he was not the one who had branded the calf, and that he had found himself guilty, even though he did not commit the crime, because he was expecting to be freed. He admitted he was being bound by his own words, and that 'The court is not mistaken to sentence me'. Nevertheless, he pleaded with the court to allow his mitigating circumstances.

Summary by the chief:

> The court has been listening to the appeal of ML against the sentence of Chief Mapena of five years' imprisonment for cattle theft and two years' for being found with a stray cattle. The defendant found himself guilty and now he is challenging this court to release him from this crime because he's saying his brand was used by someone, he's not the one who used it. But when he was accused, he showed [pointed out] he was the one who stole all the cattle and also he's the one who branded them with his brand on top of the other brand. And he also agreed that he had committed a crime and what the crime was. This court finds he is making tricks to dodge the crime.
>
> Judgement: This court *otelela*, confirms, the judgements of the lower courts. It instructs the defendant to go and continue at the prison for seven years.
>
> Right of appeal: 30 days.

TL exercised his right of appeal to an even higher Customary Court of Appeal at Francistown, but here our knowledge of the case stopped. The records of the long-drawn out progress of the case through the customary courts, with a whole series of opportunities for appeal in a hierarchy, register the permeability of the courts and their highly formal attention to a framework of forensic procedure and criminal law. They also show the young defendant repeatedly expressing his respect for the courts, even in a hasty judgement, while tenaciously persisting in the hope that in mitigation he might at least get some clemency, if only for the sake of his old and needy mother.

The case of the destitute family

The implications for the offender's family, as the previous case showed, are not considered by the court. In the following case a well-respected Moremi man, Balebetse, bishop of a local Apostolic church, was charged with stealing the stray calf (*maTimelo*) of the daughter of the reputedly richest man in Moremi, owner of 200–400 head of cattle and of at least one borehole. The case was heard in the magistrate's court in Palapye, and Balebetse was sentenced to five years in jail. This left his wife and children destitute. We were told by his wife, who was about 50 at the time, that the village social welfare committee had refused to give her destitute funds. They said she was 'still young' and that she could find a job. The problem was that she still had several children in primary school, two of her daughters had three new-born babies and were not working. She said neither her husband's brother nor her own brother helped her. Later, her brother did raise cash for her, from friends. Her son, in Senior High School, needed toiletries, football shoes, and a list of other things which she could not afford. She had no goats or cattle to sell.

About the theft, the calf owner's daughter told us a somewhat garbled story. She said the case was not of a *maTimelo* but simply the theft of a calf. The cow that had given birth to the calf was in her care, it was not hers, and the calf vanished and was never found. She had called the police from Maunatlala. Balebetse was somehow implicated.

Having been rejected by the village welfare committee, Balebetse's wife tried her hand at various enterprises, from leather treatment to selling fruit and vegetables in a stall in Palapye. During this time, Balebetse tried to get the prison sentence overturned. The first lawyer he employed was barred from practising law for the offence of misuse of trust funds. The judge then ordered the government to get the accused a lawyer at government expense, and he was released in the meanwhile until the government had found him a lawyer. This never happened, and the case was never finally settled. He returned to the village some two years after first being imprisoned – and to cattle herding, along with his respected position in his growing church.

More than anything, the case highlighted the huge suffering caused by sentencing alleged cattle thieves to long prison terms, with no government or village agency taking responsibility for dependents left behind. Given the precarious existence of most rural dwellers, with only a small number being cattle owners or having salaried jobs, removing the main breadwinner in the family for a dubious or minor offence seems, we believe in our view, harsh, unsafe, and unjustified. If the stock man wails, must that take precedence over the wailing of whole families, including young children? The case also shows how matters in the magistrates' courts may be inconclusive, postponed almost indefinitely: if sometimes benign, then not always by deliberation.

The case of the stock theft 'syndicate'

One of the suspected ringleaders of a stock theft gang or, in police jargon, a 'syndicate', was Tsala, a young man from a prominent Moremi family, whose father had died quite recently. One of the cases against him and his brother was first heard at the Palapye magistrate's court. They were accused of stealing a heifer on 16 October 2015 and appealed to the Serowe magistrate's court (Case CMMSW-000134-15) where first, one of the accused was acquitted and dismissed, whereas Tsala, the other accused, was sentenced to five years' imprisonment. He kept reappearing before the court regarding this case,[6]which was ultimately transferred, first to the Francistown High Court and then to the Court of Appeal in Gaborone.

When we again renewed our contact with Tsala in 2018, his case had long been transferred from Palapye to Serowe. We witnessed the hearing, which was held in a dilapidated courtroom in need of repair, with ceiling plaster falling down in places. The magistrate was a young man who took his own notes on his laptop. The prisoners were all young and sat in a row, shackled to each other, though the shackles were removed when each one, in turn, stood up before the magistrate. Most did not appear to have lawyers and pleaded their lack of money. Tsala too stated he had no lawyer, though he told us his brother (at Moremi) said he had a car he was trying to sell. It was a conveyer belt, with court prosecutors taking turns (either a woman or a man or both), speaking fast and much of the discussion in Setswana, though the court clerk translated a bit.

Tsala's appeal before the High Court in Francistown was heard that very day. Having appeared before the magistrate in Serowe, he was taken in shackles to Francistown in a police car. He still had no lawyer. When the judgement finally came, the Francistown judge had increased his jail sentence to seven years, on the grounds of an indictment he had had more than ten years earlier.

The police at Maunatlala alleged that Tsala had a string of cases pending. They thought he would go to jail for many years. What was remarkable from our perspective was the poverty in which he seemed to be living in the village. He was far from being a rich cattle baron, even though his father had been a successful, apparently prosperous diviner.

In the meanwhile, at the end of April 2019, against police predictions, Tsala was acquitted at the magistrate's court in Serowe for possession of three head of cattle. Again, he defended himself. Although the court records were difficult to obtain, we spoke to the magistrate who had judged the case and he remembered it well. He said that the policeman in Tsala's case had not satisfied him that he

6 10/11/16, 7/11/16, 6/9/16, 30/8/16, 29/8/16, 10/8/16, 23/5/16

had seen the cattle and had evidence they were stolen. There was no evidence, no brand or anything else, such as tampering with ears, etc. Hence, the magistrate said that the defendant claimed 'these are mine' and he asked that the policeman prove to the court that they were stolen – 'they had my brand on it'. The policeman was just relying on his informer. There was no complainant, no-one claiming to be an owner. If there's no owner but cattle are shown to be stolen goods, they revert to the state, the magistrate told us, but in this case there was no proof the cattle were stolen, and Tsala was acquitted.

There remained only the final case of the stolen cow, first heard in Palapye in November 2016. Again, Tsala defended himself, though his defence was weaker than in the previous case. We witnessed his appearance in the Court of Appeal in Gaborone in 2019. The bench was made up of three Court of Appeal Judges: Lesetedi, who presided and was the main interrogator, Dambe, a female judge, and Letsididi, an older man with grey hair.

When his turn came, Tsala stood in the dock facing the judges. He was adept at finding his way through his notes, contained in a folder which included the grounds for his appeal, voluminous court records, accounts of his previous cases and various affidavits. Tsala had a list of 15 points he had presented in advance as the grounds for his appeal and the judges took care to go through each one of them. During the interrogation, the state prosecutor sat waiting her turn to respond. At some point in the proceedings, Lesetedi J. commented to Tsala on his facility in defending himself: 'You would put not a few lawyers to shame'. At the same time, he complained that Tsala was making tricky arguments, wasting the court's time and the Justice seemed somewhat biased against him. Lesetedi's remark seemed to us to have a double edge, on the positive side praise, and on the negative side, the suggestion of a suspicion that Tsala was a recidivist, too knowledgeable to be an innocent. It is as if his very competence meant a strike against his innocence. Lesetedi J. did concede, however, and compelled the prosecutor to concede, that procedures were not followed in the magistrate's court, and Tsala was not given forewarning of the evidence the prosecutors had in their possession.

Although he could speak English, Tsala insisted on conducting his defence in Setswana, which was translated into English for the record. He had graduated from Form V at Palapye Senior School. As mentioned, he had had an earlier conviction, 12 years before, and whereas the Serowe judge had sentenced him to five years on the basis that, after ten years, a person is considered to have no record ('the ten-year rule'), the judge in the Francistown High Court sentenced him to seven years. Tsala disputed this and the young woman state prosecutor – when challenged by Lesetedi – said she thought it might be a policy because she could find no law to that effect.[7]

7 In fact, the South African courts observe a ten-year rule after which a crime can be expunged, for most crimes. https://www.saps.gov.za/faqdetail.php?fid=57

At first the discussion revolved around the branding and the witnesses to the branding. The judge asked him if he had cross-examined or challenged the witnesses' statements and T. shuffled through the pages and found places where he had challenged them but not all. Watching him one had the sense that a person not used to documents and files had, nevertheless, to cope with documentary skill at speed, to leaf through several dozen pages under challenge. He was a defendant under unsafe pressure, having no advocate, while having to archive and respond by providing references that would support his view for the judges. Now and then, he would endure the judicial complaint that this was not relevant or he hadn't shown what he claimed. One witness was taken by the judge to be credible.

The judge asked Tsala about the number/digits and what it was in the bolus. He said there was a mistake. Was it the same throughout all the hearings? The judge commented – you're finding little errors and not looking at the whole picture. It leads me as a judge to think you are trying to eat up the time with technicalities and distractions from the main issue. You are being tricky. 'Is it your argument that the system has made an error and is wrong?' since the bolus showed an early date, before it came to Tsala.

Tsala's nitpicking of little errors (he had scrutinised the record for mistakes, even in typing or registering numbers from instance to instance) brought the judge to make his double-edged remark that he could 'put not a few lawyers to shame', the implication being perhaps also that while he was competent to stand up and argue his case, he might be a crooked lawyer. He was evidently 'not a stranger to the court' in need of his right to advance warning of the case against him. He was asked what he would have challenged had he been prepared in advance? To which he did not have a clear answer, perhaps because he was after all not prepared. Throughout the appeal the judges appeared determined to dismiss procedural errors as minor. Citing an earlier case, the learned justice argued that

> In my view, it is sufficient for the state to produce evidence by means of such high degree of probability is raised that the ordinary, reasonable man, after mature consideration, comes to the conclusion that an accused person committed the crime charged.
>
> (Court of Appeal, Gaborone, p.4)

Furthermore, the judges state that 'technicalities should not obscure real and substantial justice' (ibid.: p. 6). In particular, whereas the judges admitted that

> It is clear from the record of proceedings that the Appellant was not advised on his rights and options as required by law, ... the record clearly indicate (sic) that the appellant is not a stranger to the court and its processes. He was able to challenge the witnesses through cross-examination. It must be noted that an appellant who is familiar with court processes is not in the same position as an offender who is inept and unfamiliar with court processes.
>
> (p. 5)

In other words, the appellant loses his right because he is perceived to be in the position of an experienced criminal! In effect, a perversion of natural justice: he is presumed to be guilty until proven to be innocent. Minor discrepancies in witness accounts or in the bolus number are dismissed by the judges as inconsequential in the face of the weight of the evidence, and despite the denial of a fundamental right to advance preparation.

At the very end of the trial, Tsala was asked if he disputed anything. This puzzled him a great deal then and, in conversation with us, later in prison. He said he did not realise he was accepting the affidavits when he didn't object. He couldn't deny that Segametse's brand was on the cattle. At some point, he asked that the smear of dung should be removed, which it wasn't, but this request had not been put on record.

The prosecutor then cited 'customary law' as justification for the sentence of seven years. She said she could not find the 'ten-year rule'. The judge criticised her for not doing 'research' properly (she said she tried). The role of the other two judges seemed to be merely to clarify matters. As the end of the trial, the day of sentencing was announced, some three weeks later. The official final judgement handed out gave some of the details and background to the case but none of the pronouncements recorded above, perhaps most significantly none of the claims and the dismissal of the right to preparation and knowledge of the charges to be made. Nor were the judges inclined to use their discretion to minimise the sentence:

> A court faced with a statutory requirement to pass a mandatory minimum sentence has no discretion whatsoever to pass a lesser sentence than that prescribed, unless where there are 'exceptional circumstances' allowing the court to invoke the provisions of s.27(4) of the Penal Code.
>
> (Court of Appeal CLCGB-045-19, CLAUSE 21)

Tsala was devastated by the verdict. All the (intellectual) work he had invested in the appeal had come to nought. In our conversation with the prison officer in the Gaborone First Offenders prison, where Tsala was first incarcerated after the trial, the officer sensitively explained the difficulties faced by ex-prisoners that lead them to re-offend: having a criminal record which, as we saw, was never expunged, meant they could never be employed in government jobs, yet government was the biggest employer in the country. They often, he said, lived on their own and felt isolated; they'd left behind, in prison, all their friends. Without a job and a support community, it was not surprising that they re-offended. Tsala was lucky in this respect, since his brother and sister both supported him.

A week later, we went to visit Tsala again, this time in the Serowe prison where he would remain for the next two years. Although the atmosphere was more relaxed in this apparently more open prison away from the city, he admitted to being in 'shock', unable to really function. He looked miserable and seemed depressed. Of the judges, he said they were '*batho fela*', merely people like him. He did not look up to them with awe. We ourselves had felt that, were we in his position, we would have been overwhelmed by the dominance of the ominously black-robed justices high above while, below them, belittled in precarious self-defence without an advocate. He told us he had put together his appeal with the great help and careful advice of other prisoners who share law books and knowledge. He felt that seven years was very harsh. We asked him what he thought he would do when he came out, and he said he would go back into herding and farming, clearly a precarious subsistence occupation. Given the seriousness of the crime as defined by the weight of its punishment, the question we are failing to answer is: Why was no advocate appointed to represent him in his case and, indeed, in many similar cases?

A harsh punishment regime

The various cases documented so far in this chapter all bear witness to Botswana's harsh punishment regime, in particular for stock theft, and its instrumental nature (see Malila 2019: 127 *et passim*). It is true that cattle in Botswana are valued, but Botswana is not 'cattle country' in the sense once familiar in Africanist literature. In Botswana, the attachment to cattle cannot be compared to the identification and personification of cattle felt, say, by Nuer men towards their beasts (Evans-Pritchard 1940: 41 *et passim*). Tswana men do not compose poetry for their cattle, for example. Nor are cattle as crucially central to the transactional lifeworld of modern-day Batswana, as they were to Nuer in the 1930s and '40s, or even to Batswana in the same period. Although bride wealth is nominally passed from wife-takers to wife-givers in the form of cattle, in most cases a fixed monetary value is substituted. Most Tswana groups no longer sacrifice to the ancestors, though exceptionally, Tswapong still do. Cattle and goats are slaughtered at funerals and weddings to feed attendants, and relatives contribute cattle for this purpose, signalling their closeness to the convenors, but these are customs sustaining the honour and reputation of families, not critical ritual acts.

Malila makes the point that imprisonment in Botswana remains a standard or default punishment for almost all offences, and that moreover, a large body of legislation stipulates imprisonment as the mandatory minimum punishment (2019: 128). Botswana has one of the highest rates of imprisonment in Africa today (ibid.: 130), and the criminal justice system is 'excessively punitive' (ibid.). As we have seen, despite the evident sensitivity of some prison officers, respecting the human dignity of the people in their command, there is little effort devoted by prison authorities to training and rehabilitation, and no concern or provisions regarding the welfare of families, deprived of their main breadwinner.

Cattle in rural Botswana wander freely around without close supervision. They often die of natural causes, as the following case of *mafisa* illustrates. For young men, many of them herders on very low income, stealing a calf may seem a trivial matter, almost a game. Yet when caught, they are subjected to disproportionately high jail sentences, often without mitigation, though sometimes even arbitrarily with more or less reduction. This is equally true of statutory and customary courts. In the next section, we move from theft to possible breach of trust, and the precarity of cattle herding in Botswana.

The case of the dying *mafisa*: breach of cattle trust or act of God[8]

The following case was first heard in Moremi village in 1972 and, as in an earlier case reported above, was appealed *via* a higher customary court (at Palapye) all the way to the tribal court in Serowe. The 1972 case preceded a radical change in herding practices: in 1972, most cattle in Moremi were herded by teenage herd boys or men, whereas, in the 2000s, most cattle in the areas of villages wandered around the countryside freely, with occasional checks by the owners and, in some areas, confined by fencing to defined pastures. Some few cattle can even be seen wandering about in the outskirts of Gaborone. Ownership is proved by personal brands and bolus, which is why they are seen as such crucial evidence.

The difference between the criminal cases discussed so far and contractual cases is stark: the 1972 case was one of alleged breach of trust by a herder in which the judges actively considered the morality of sentencing, when it came to the death of cattle from 'God-given' natural causes. Striking in the 1972 case was the significant transformation in reasoning and argument as the accused moved through the court hierarchy. This transformation entailed a dual process: firstly, the cumulative education of the defendant; secondly, the reduction and narrowing of the issues. By the final appeal, the accused had mastered the arguments against him, and he dealt with them strongly and decisively. The final appeal was marked by the judicial care for a strictness of relevance, and it centred on a single issue: the liability for natural plant poisoning of cattle, when it is a universal hazard, and when the owner has the option of removing his or her cattle from an evidently incompetent herdsman.

In Moremi court, the case was brought by a woman who claimed the cattle she had lent as *mafisa* to a village herdsman, Mojako, had been abused by him. The cattle had eaten *Mogau*, a poisonous plant (*Dichapetalum cymosum*) particularly dangerous in the dry season when its green leaves attract livestock. The owner claimed that, rather than resting the cattle, Mojako secretly harnessed them during the night to bring water in his sled to the cattle post. One of the court participants pointed out that the owner had not gone to court after the first two cattle died. Mojako admitted he had not removed the cattle. The question was whether careful husbandry could prevent the cattle from grazing in the *Mogau* area. The same hearing also heard that Mojako had not been paid for his herding. One villager argued that this non-payment was the reason the owner had brought the case to court, perhaps implying that a judgement of bad herding would free her of any

8 The cases in the different courts were recorded by Richard Werbner, who revised the translation made by his research assistant, Ontlogetse Mafoko, who meticulously transcribed the cases.

liability to reward Mojako for his herding. Another villager said that he had urged the owner to take her cattle away from Mojako, but she had refused. It seems that the relationship between owner and herder had soured. The owner came to the village court with a reservoir of covert opinion and sentiment against Mojako, due to her campaign of bad-mouthing gossip, alleging he had worked the cattle while they were weak. Mojako denied this accusation in court, and she admitted to having no witnesses. Later, as the case proceeded, she seemed to battle against several others at Moremi and began to appear unreasonable and wild, so that opinion began to turn against her outside the court, and gradually swung in favour of Mojako. All of her support came from Palapye people, none of whom were witnesses.

The case was referred to the Palapye Tribal Sub-Chief. Defending Mojako in court, his father, the retired village chief, Leso, made the point that Mojako's labour had benefitted the cattle owner:

LESO: My masters, these people are cheating me. The cattle came into Mojako's hand in 1971 when the clouds were sounding [i.e. with thunder before the rainy season] just as you heard this man say. So, I say, the corn of 1972 belonging to this old lady (the cattle owner) has been ploughed by Mojako, by her cattle, this old lady's. The very corn that we are eating now, which is in the granaries, has been ploughed by Mojako.

The owner was then asked why she had refused the meat of the cow that had died. She said it was because Mojako had not moved the cattle as she had requested him to do. She said that, after the third head of cattle died, she took the cattle away, but Mojako came and took them back. In response to her allegations, Moremi's chief spoke at length, denying that the owner had ever taken steps to complain about Mojako. It was suggested that the dead cattle may have been given to him as payment since he had not been paid for his work as a herdsman. The owner claimed she had left the cattle with him waiting for the hearing. At some point in the trial, retired chief Leso was asked whether the dispute did not grieve him? He replied, in sorrow and in anger.

LESO: It grieves me because what they speak is of oppression and oppression. I mean that they are oppressing each other in this way: that one has given cattle to the other and after the second cow died and it was said that they should take the cattle, the owners of the cattle refused to do so, yet when the latest cow died, a lawsuit was started.

Another member of the court, N., defended the accuser, arguing that the cattle had died for 'lack of care'. Mojako, he said, was 'at fault'. Three cattle had died and a fourth had gone astray. He continued in this vein for some time, imputing that Mojako was known for his carelessness while, shamefully, he had nothing he could offer in compensation, being a poor man.

By this time the hearing had been going on for three days. Now, the chief in Palapye, presiding over the court, intervened to give his concluding judgement:

CHIEF: My home people. … I have been listening to this dispute for three days but there are my words of yesterday. I said, my home people, you should help me with this: Are these cattle the first ones to die of *Mogau*? And again, has *Mogau* ever been sued for?

The chief went on to argue that the cattle were given to Mojako, knowing 'there was a plant which is deadly'. Moreover, even after a cow had died, the cattle were left with him. Despite the knowledge that Mojako had no cattle of his own, the owner left her cattle with him. Hence, the chief asked his question rhetorically, sure of the answer.

CHIEF: Can he (Mojako) go to prison for a cow which he hasn't stabbed with a knife? Will he go to prison for a cow he took by agreement with its owner? These things, my home people, are difficult. I mean, as for me, I don't see Mojako at fault.

The chief thus concludes, offering to give the claimant a letter so she could appeal the case in Serowe.

In Serowe, about 20 men were present. The major difference with the earlier hearings was that the owner's personal vilification and in particular her allegation of fault in the herding were not accepted. Each cattle death was examined separately. It was established that, in one case, Mojako had been on an errand of the court. Retired Moremi chief Leso, Mojako's father, pointed out that all over the country cattle were dying of Mogau and none were prosecuted. In Moremi, there was great *lefufa* (jealousy).

LESO: We took a statement of this affair at Moremi, finding that many cattle had died and I wrote down a total of 47 cattle of Moremi.
CHIEF: That died of *Mogau*?
LESO: Yes, that died of *Mogau*. (After two beasts had died, people suggested to Mojako that he abandon the trust.) 'Return the cattle, (they said) but this one, the owner, refused. She said – you want to destroy the friendship between me and Mojako, let him keep them. That was said when only two beasts had died. … Now, when it came to the third beast, it was said – he should eat it. I said – you see now you have set a trap for my son; that is why I said some time ago at Moremi that you should have taken your cattle at once and released my son.

He then reminded the court that the chief of Palapye 'could not manage this dispute'.

LESO: Bamangwato, in the area we are talking about, there is no-one untouched by the death of cattle. There are twelve cattle posts there. From each of them there was a loss of two, one, two, one, due to *Mogau*. In all the cattle posts, no-one remains free of it. In the very place the old lady intended to bring her cattle, death was there. That is by those cattle posts where the people of Gotau are, and the chief knows the place, it's beyond the river. A man called Totego Molefi lost cattle – six of his cattle died. This is right where the old lady intended to have the cattle move to. … I say that in this year there was neither a good herder nor a bad herder, because the area has been made worse through the burning of the bush, for the country is female (*namagadi*) whose grass is so tall, so the cattle insist on going there. None of the Moremi people have ears that are pleased; there is only crying.

The figures were disputed by the owner's daughter, who said cattle had died when their owners were away and, in some herds, no cattle had died, because their owners had taken care of them. Even Leso's cattle had not died. Mojako explained that only one cow had died, while he was there. The rest fell ill or died when he had to go to Serowe on court business.

SEROWE CHIEF: I don't know what I can say because domestic animals are matters of grief for a person, and we cannot laugh at a person who cries like this. We have to look into this and say – Mojako himself is not the one who killed the cattle. Due to Mojako's care, there are still ten cattle alive. … [They died after]. He untied them on the sixth day because he was hurried by this child (son of the owner).

At this point, Mojako explained that he had ploughed four fields, three for the owner, her daughter and older sister, and one his own. They had not yet paid him. Finally, the presiding chief spoke, underlining the moral issues at stake:

CHIEF: Bangwato, this is the issue (*puo*) I have just been on. For if someone's cattle are dead he wails, he is like one whose child is dead, but he cannot sue God for this, that He killed the child. These cattle died of Mogau and were made by God. The *Mogau* too was made by God. This man was not there when the cattle died. He had brought the goats of the *maTimelo* (stray goats) here (to Serowe). This man was in the work of the government, bringing the *maTimelo* goats here, and to say that he is in the work of the government is to say no man should criticise him. For the women (owner and daughter) knew where he went … He is not the one who sowed *Mogau*. They must pay him for the tax.

The discussion in the court repeated the issues already raised, one speaker making the point that Mojako had actually 'saved' ten of the cattle. One speaker suggested the government attempt to fence the *Mogau*. Finally, it was the turn of the Acting Deputy Chief to sum up the debate.

CHIEF: As for these words, we have truly discussed them. The difficulty is that the words being tried are about *Mogau*. I see that the cow Mojako has to follow is the one that has gone astray. As for the *Mogau*, since all the people had a disaster on that side, it is a matter of wailing. The wailing of the stock man. And seeing Mojako's poverty, what can he do? He went to ask for (to borrow) the cattle when he found himself poor. I see that. I don't know either about this, because the plant is everywhere (wherever he tried to shift them). Truly in this affair you are eating him ravenously because of his poverty. … I cannot manage to find Mojako guilty for *Mogau* cattle, inasmuch as all the cattle are sometimes wiped out by it, because *Mogau* is like that and it is such a plant. Particularly now, when the cattle are scattered, eating the grass in the bush.

The case ended there with the accusers, still grumbling, informed they can appeal to the District Commissioner.

Conclusion: the wailing of the stockman

'The wailing of the stockman' – this phrase by the Acting Deputy Chief captures the emotional sentiment and moral attachment binding many Batswana to their cattle, and their sense of being at God's mercy: 'For if someone's cattle are dead, he wails, he is like one whose child is dead, but he cannot sue God for this, that He killed the child. These cattle died of *Mogau* and were made by God. The *Mogau*, too, was made by God'.

Our findings from our study of Moremi customary court do not confirm the view that these courts are more punitive than statutory courts or that they don't follow procedures laid out by the state (Malila 2019: 136). The disproportionate punishment of young men for stock theft lies in legislation passed by Parliament which customary courts, like statutory court, must uphold, especially under due regulation by the police. Whereas loss of cattle caused 'by God' is not seen to be justiciable by customary courts (or any court), in the case of cattle theft, customary courts can only circumvent the heavy sentences by redefining the offence. On the whole, customary judges' hands are tied and minimum jail sentences cannot be avoided. This is an area where legal pluralism has evidently led to a *convergence* between customary and statutory sentencing. This means that jail sentences, rather than being understood by judges as degrading and potentially harmful to individuals, usually young men, with tragic consequences for them and their families, are treated with too little clemency, as though serving a seven-year jail sentence is not a highly serious matter. The moral economy of stock theft is skewed in favour of a wealthy minority of cattle owners. The victims of this punitive legislative regime are mostly penniless young men and their families. Critical legal studies in Botswana, to which this chapter contributes, now call for long-needed reform, at least to make the punishment proportionate to the crime and to favour greater discretion for clemency and reduced sentencing.

Conclusion

This book relies heavily on actual cases described in ethnographic and comparative contexts to tell the story of customary law and the seeking of justice in customary courts in Botswana and, more widely, in Africa. This is so for at least two reasons, both of which are imperative for the attention we pay, as anthropologists, to fine particularities in our use of ethnographic cases as grounds for our more general theoretical arguments.

The first reason concerns the relation between forensic deliberations intended to be just and fair, on the one hand, and customary law as a folk concept whose *raison d'etre* – above all for the people themselves – is *traditional*, on the other. In accord with that, forensic deliberations in moots and courts are expected to have a popular source in received parental wisdom. Even further, such deliberations are explicitly valued as conservative, rooted over generations in the people's own ways with their likely pious claim that we have always done it this way. Participants thus naturalise customary law in their appropriation of the past. And yet their deliberations are implicitly for the present and the future, expected to be true to the times, to respect everyday life as it is lived now, and should be in the future. Hence, customary law is also recognised as *open* to new rule-making by traditional authorities, such as chiefs, with legislative powers to change the past for the sake of the future, powers conditional upon the consent of their people. It is the people who bring their understandings of everyday life to bear on disputes in their own courts and moots, and who expect their presiding members or judges to be seen to uphold public interests in amity, goodwill, and peace, as well as to protect the courts' responsibility for the fair and rightful settlement of the immediate matter at hand. Lawyers and professional judges are permitted to play no part directly: the customary courts are meant to be open forums under traditional authorities intended for, and only for, the people themselves. Obviously, in actual practice, all of that is time-consuming. Even more, it is likely to appear to an outsider as not at all straightforward but perhaps tortuous and involuted, especially in addressing the many cases involving multiplex relations between litigants.

Hence the first reason for our detailed presentation of cases in this book: we have to follow and enable our readers to grasp the somewhat paradoxical deliberations that take place in village customary courts, often back and forth over several hearings and sometimes with untimely, seemingly inconclusive delays. As we

DOI: 10.4324/9781003241881-12

have shown for cases of divorce, adultery, insult, and inheritance, the arguments are often superabundant in contentious details of misunderstandings; the issues emerge as entangled in contradictory personal circumstances, and the challenge is to follow the cross-examination, the more or less judicious disentanglement of claims and counter-claims, and the due process as it unfolds with expectations of *maitseo*, proper procedure. Rather than mere illustrative vignettes, we advocate the value of exploring forensic argumentation in cases, with participants tracking facts and reasons in deliberative practice. Only by thinking with and through cases documented and then analysed in depth can we, along with our readers, comprehend the complexities of the customary judicial process and the perceptions by the people themselves of safety, justice, and fairness in customary trials.

The complexity is a familiar one in the anthropological literature: the provision of detailed cases to study familial and neighbourly disputes in customary courts derives from the need to document and analyse the implicit as well as the explicit tensions emergent in the somewhat unpredictable course of such cases, as intimately sensitive to entanglements of familial multiplex relations while responsive to the changing understanding of everyday life and the navigation of appeals within and between court hierarchies, customary and statutory.

Our second reason for our exploration through a substantial case method is the importance, in the seeking of customary justice, of legal pluralism as it has to be understood historically: a development from the colonial past to the postcolonial present. A simple question, easy to ask in general terms, but needing case material to consider across salient variation, is this: how far and in which respects are customary courts actually autonomous, given the changing interrelation between the legal systems, statutory and customary, as these are recognised, sustained and administered distinctly by the state?

Some postcolonial African states increasingly marginalise or even try to suppress customary courts, whereas others invest customary courts with authority, permanence, and certain protected areas of jurisdiction. The latter is true for Botswana where customary courts are respected for having foundational authority, according to the Constitution and judgements by the highest Court of Appeal.

Multiplex relations, 'relational justice' and the long durée

In an obvious way, all court cases, and not merely cases in customary courts, are relational: all address a disturbance of relations between persons, groups, corporations, or the state. It might seem, however, that what is distinctive particularly in customary courts is inconclusive 'resolution', not actually coming to a decisive end. Yet even in customary or village courts, some cases, for example of small debts to a local store, once decided, are settled conclusively, soon forgotten. The cases examined in this book, however, neither begin nor end in court. These court cases may be grasped as temporary or even transitory interruptions in the flow of social life in which protagonists attempt to change the direction of the flow or its consequences. As long recognised by legal anthropologists, most relations considered in customary courts are, in Gluckman's terms, multiplex or multi-stranded, involving complex obligations, competing claims, and disparate interests; and while disputes may arise in terms of one strand of a relationship, the other relational strands may become implicated or sustain ongoing conflict, to the point of contentious escalation beyond past limits. Time often seems to turn back on itself, with events perceived to be instances once again of what was never finally settled, despite appearances of a desirably smooth surface of social life. As we have shown in the first part of this book, a conflict over village centralisation, chiefship, and naming continued for 50 years with details raked up, often bitterly, from one generation to the next. So too, the consequences of suing for divorce, adultery, insult, or inheritance continue beyond the court case itself, affecting many and diverse relations. This complexity and durability are what make many cases and the affording of justice in customary courts 'relational' in a distinctive way, even though, as stressed above, social relations are central to conflict resolution everywhere.[1]

Judicial developments

The definitions of legal offences in Botswana have been reworked and undergone radical changes in recent years, both in statutory and in customary courts. A consideration of recent customary court cases in Moremi village, central Botswana, thus needs to be understood, the present book has proposed, in the wider context of judicial developments in Botswana, in the Southern African region, and internationally. Examining the long durée of anthropological studies of familial and marital disputes in Botswana from the 1940s onwards,[2] as well as our own research on the rule of law, courts, and politics in Moremi village since 1972,[3] we have considered the transformations in contemporary customary courts' hearings. These have arisen, we argue, from inherent tensions, for example between parental law and changing everyday notions of equity in relations of gender and generation. It is a salient, though not unique, feature of parental law that it calls for judges to lecture about upright conduct, to rebuke moral faults, to chastise not only the protagonists, such as the complainant and the defendant, but also significant others, such as kin who fail in their duty of care or responsibility. The court's own responsibility is ideal: to speak to and for the good life, as a parent might to an errant child.

1 In this respect we diverge from Robbins (2009), for example, who wishes to draw a contrast with modern courts supposedly focused on the rights of the 'individual' or the 'group', but not rights and interests in relations.

2 See in particular Schapera (1940b, 1970), John Comaroff and Simon Roberts (1977, 1981), and Anne Griffiths (1997).

3 See R. Werbner (1977, 2016, 2018); P. Werbner and R. Werbner (2018, 2019, 2020a, 2020b).

In retrospect: the book in detail

Following our Introduction in Chapter 1, Chapter 2 recounted some aspects of the political conflict that preceded the split in Moremi village and led to it. The analysis traced a continuous course of political action through tribal courts, administrative tribunals, and other meetings with civil servants and elected officials from district councillor to Minister of Local Government and Lands. It distinguished different types of events – blind probes, confrontations, and encounters – in order to illuminate the power struggles advanced by a policy for the centralisation of small villages.

The chapter contrasted factional politics in small villages with the mobilisation for judicial review against top-down policy decisions. The sequence the chapter analysed shows how blind probes recur repeatedly under conditions of uncertainty, without necessarily leading to any decisive conclusion in an encounter. While it took account of bids for factional support based on transactions over goods and services, the chapter also tried to establish where the power of citizens *qua* citizens enters into the political equation. The aim was to comprehend the intersection of law and politics by following citizens' rights, claims, and accountability under the rule of law. Protection against misrule and oppression can never be automatic, a matter of necessary constitutional devices only. Hence the study of small-man politics in a developing nation, we argued, provides a much-needed approach to the understanding of political pluralism and, indeed, its opposite, the concentration or even monopolising of power.

As the rest of the book showed, the conflicts generated by the centralisation process did not end with the establishment of a new village named Matolwane, but continued for the next 50 years, recurring also in the non-justiciable dispute over the court of divinity, *Sedimo*, in Chapter 4, the politics of memory in the election of a new village chief (Chapter 5), and ultimately leading to the current conflict over the Matolwane village name as it has gone through the statutory courts (Chapter 6).

In Chapter 3 we considered the notion of *tlholego*, a Tswana concept encapsulating both nature and culture, and having broad meanings of history, ancestrality, and God's creations. These notions are intermeshed and inseparable, just as the lives of many of the villagers are, in multiplex relations, inextricably interlinked with each other, past and future. At the heart of *tlholego* are issues of *seriti*, dignity, reputation, and respect, which also underlie many customary court cases. These underpin not only the symbolic centrality of village chiefship but of Moremi village as the primary 'first' village among the villagers scattered around the Tswapong hills. Claims to cultural primacy and destiny have become a source of symbolic/cultural capital for the village, invoking an imagined reality, a moral universe. Despite its small size and relative poverty, the chapter showed, the village's glorified history has endowed villagers with the capacity to resist bullying by outsiders while readily taking subsidies from the same outsiders, in order to build a viable community. The symbolic authenticity and value of chiefship is promoted by the government, despite the curtailing of the actual effective power of chiefs and headman, and was signalled, the chapter showed, in the celebration of 50 years of Botswana's independence in 'the roving torch of unity' ceremonial which encompassed Moremi village, while highlighting the politics of authority and recognition. The village has also become the focus of 'development': it is the communal owner of Moremi Lodge and Moremi Gorge, a tourist attraction jointly managed with the Ministry of Tourism. The gorge, site of the sacred spring of the ancestors with its cascading pools, had now been made accessible to visitors, while Moremi village has become a publicly recognised centre of 'culture', held to be distinctive of Tswapong as a minority among Tswana.

Chapter 4, which focused on an unprecedented customary court case heard in Matolwane village near Moremi, explored the non-justiciable. The hearing addressed a cause beyond the rightful jurisdiction of any customary court, because the cause over-reached from court to court, from *kgotla* to *kgotla*, and into the sacred preserve of the court of divinity (*Kgotla ya Sedimo*, for short *Sedimo)*, the oracular proceedings for consulting the ancestors known as *badimo* (divinities of the dead). To contextualise the hearing, we situated the occasion historically with an account of the recent development of *Sedimo* and of changing leadership, that of both the chief and the *Sedimo* leader, 'the keeper of secrets'. The deeply held conviction was, and is, that a disturbance in the moral order was also a cosmic disturbance; above all, it held back the rain, a shared good vital for everyone. This meant that the ancestral wrath of *badimo*, aroused over public disorder, undermined nature, the original nature of chiefship, and the village itself – it could not work together as one, a single, whole community. What was delicate, risky, even unsafe, was that the bone of contention engaged the customary court in sorting out the quarrelsome, troubling affairs of another court so secretive and mysterious that customary deliberation had to be baffling. Questionable from the hearing's very beginning was the appropriate nature of the hearing itself. Was it to be an adversarial fight to the finish in a trial (*tsheko*)? The way forward, attending to the *kgang*, a debate and a matter of contention, and seeking to cleanse and clarify abusive words for the sake of reconciliation, had to be established against the complaining elder's opening outburst in rude, uncivil, and subversive anger. Everyone agreed eventually that a deliberate process was essential. Accordingly, the court and its presiding chief made much of reminding everyone of the values of reconciliation, consultation, cooperation, dialogue, and peace-making, which are the bedrock of customary law decision-making and the chiefly court ethos in Botswana. The chapter documented closely the contested rehearsal of past faults and the somewhat tortuous course of cross-examination. The sentiments of fear and awe for the court of divinity which grip many villagers informed our analysis of the politics of memory and the passions evoked in the case. We reported the presiding chief's final turn, first to long drawn-out moralising with a severe warning of the cosmic danger for everyone, and then to a reprimand – to wise up and chastise the adversaries, no one was simply in the right, everyone had to be better, for the sake of harmony with the wrathful *badimo*. In sum, we suggested that the outcome in reconciliation was momentary. The following chapters pursued further the politics of memory and the enduring, if intermittent, strife along with the negotiation of apparent conciliation.

The tendency to call for reconciliation in cases of marital dispute is a well-known feature of customary courts which, as we discussed in Chapter 7, has been repeatedly subject to feminist critique. In the case heard at Matolwane, we argued, reconciliation, peace, and unity take on *cosmic significance*, a matter of life and death for both individuals and the whole community. Recent transformations in the court of divinity have come alongside radical changes in the village's locational politics of place, which added to the endemic internal competition for leadership within the village's chiefly lineage. The politics of memory raised in the previous chapter and in the next chapter were here shown to be deeply embedded in the collective identity of the village.

Chapter 5 examined the *kgotla* as both a court of law and a space for deliberation, public ceremonial and spectacular display. The *kgotla* embodies the village as a community, and is thus also the site for struggles over its history and future destiny. The *kgosi*, village chief, presiding over the *kgotla*, epitomises the community in his (or her) authoritative capacity, but is also regarded as the current living representative in a chain of being from the distant past. The *kgotla* as a space of spectacle enhances this symbolic centrality of the chief.

The chapter analysed the selection and installation of a new village chief in Moremi village following the death of the previous incumbent. Although small, Moremi is, as mentioned, the senior village among Tswapong with claims to longevity, centrality, and absolute authenticity; hence the office of the village chief is, remarkably, a symbolically elevated one. The chapter highlighted the vividness of memories of the long-past political encounters with the state and local state, associated with the village split, and the factional village politics in those encounters, recently debated yet again in the *kgotla*, the village forum, as though it had all happened just yesterday, instead of 40 years previously. The chapter highlighted the pragmatics of appointment to office set against claims to authenticity and legitimacy in the contest between protagonists for the vacated office. It extended a comparative analysis by reconsidering recent discussions of chiefship in Africa.

The hearing is an example of the *kgotla* as a public deliberative forum, and the election was the occasion for a lengthy debate about the past that highlighted the way notions of public ethics, nature and culture, *tlholego*, underpin the village's politics of memory as these impact on hereditary chiefship and its symbolic centrality in the village.

Chapter 6, the final chapter of Part I, pursued the politics of memory from the village customary court to Botswana's statutory courts: the High Court and Court of Appeal. The central case concerned the change of the nearby centralised village's name from Matolwane to Lesenepola by a faction, within the newly created village, originating from the neighbouring village of Lesenepola. The chapter showed the huge expenses undertaken by the appellants, previously residents of Moremi village and two other villages, who challenged the decision of an earlier case in the High Court that recommended the change of name. It looked at the mobilisation of villagers across town and country, and considered the enormous value vested in name as identity even for urban villagers settled in the capital of Botswana.

Three intertwined issues were raised in Chapter 7: (i) the tendency of women initiating divorce in court to be penalised in the subsequent property settlement, often linked (ii) to the ambiguity of their status as wives, and (iii) the reluctance of customary courts to acknowledge that relations have broken down irretrievably. All three have been the basis for much feminist legal activism and progressive reforms of the law in Botswana. In this chapter we attempted to show that these legal reforms, while in many ways enhancing the status of married women, often come at a price or lead to new anomalies and conundrums.

Atalia Molokomme (1991), herself later a High Court Justice, and Anne Griffiths (1997) both show the mutual influence of different legal domains in Botswana, with state legislation later gradually adopted in customary courts, whereas magistrate's courts often take on the mediatory role normally assumed by customary courts or, alternatively, often turn to customary courts to settle the marital household's familial disputes or division of property. Molokomme makes the point, in relation to Dutch-Roman law, that 'the Botswana state legal system has become a true hybrid of what were traditionally referred to as civilian legal systems on the one hand and common law legal systems on the other' (1990: 263). The chapter surveyed a range of cases that came to the customary court from 1972 onwards. Although the tendency to send divorce cases back to the family for further discussion persists, and leads to endless delays, in recent cases in Moremi village customary court, the court has settled for equal division of the property.

Given these changes, and given that feminists themselves are increasingly uncertain whether marriage in or out of community of property is the preferable mode, the paradoxical question arises: has customary marriage, allowing for customary divorce, now become the more advantageous, preferred mode? Customary divorce is, after all, free, and can be – if customary courts follow the new interpretation of the law and do not penalise the party that sues for divorce – fast and convenient. The principle of gender equity is gradually becoming the 'living' norm in customary courts, as increasingly more cases are settled equitably. The challenge to prevailing feminist advice to marry in civil marriage is worth considering. The chapter examined at length the case of a woman who, after attempting to get a divorce with a property settlement, ultimately remained married but in control of all the marital property.

Chapter 8 was the second in a series of chapters considering gender and changing customary law. Cases of adultery reflect changes in the way that gendered and generational relations have been treated in different historic periods. Despite the moral lecture delivered by Moremi's village chief, in terms of parental law regarding responsibility and the need for family consultations, a case heard in 2016–2017 in the customary court pointed to the relative independence of the younger generation, and the inability of parents to fully control young people's decisions, however much they desired to do so. Equally important has been the change in gendered relations in marriage: customary law no longer condones men's philandering or polygamy. Young women can take their husbands' girlfriends to court, and many do so.

The chapter showed how changes in customary law have been impacted by and impact on the *rhetoric* and *ethos* of judicial decision-making. Tswana customary law, as in the rest of Southern Africa, is to be grasped as 'living law', responsive to changing circumstances (Fombad 2004: 183, 191; Himonga and Moore 2015). This implies that at any given time, although largely unwritten, a corpus of more or less agreed Tswana customary law does exist for any particular place (Schapera 1983) and judges are not simply dealing with an amorphous body of unwritten *mekgwa le milao* ('custom and law'). Admittedly, Moremi's village chief and court clerk in 2016 continually invoked this phrase in claiming that their reasoning was authoritative. The question is, however: how and to what extent are changes in unwritten law effected through customary judicial deliberation in court regarding notions of contemporary morality, of 'fairness' (*tshiamo*) and reasonableness in response to changing circumstances, as Gluckman, for example, argued (1955, 1963)? It is evident that such notions of equity were implicitly reflected in the level of damages awarded in different cases for ostensibly similar delicts.

Taking a legal realist (contextually responsive), living-law approach, this chapter showed that customary court decisions are embedded in considerations of equity that also inform wider ideological, critical movements and processes of judicial innovation and legal reform. Clearly, however, as this chapter also showed, attempts to shape customary law from above, for example by the national Customary Court of Appeal, *against* changing local understandings of gender equality or adultery practices, fail in the long run.

Chapter 9 started from the fact that Botswana's customary courts were known in the past for their procedural openness to debate and public opinion-making. The chief or headman presided over the court but allowed members of the court, usually in ascending order of seniority, to express their views on the case, before finally reaching a judgement. Most scholars of Tswana society, following Isaac Schapera's studies in the 1930s, agree that the chief's final judgement was responsive to public opinion as expressed during a hearing. It was this public debate that made Tswana customary law 'living law', reflecting current understandings and changing normative assumptions. But early on in the history of the Protectorate, this customary form of consultation was challenged by Sir Charles Rey, the first British Resident Commissioner to Bechuanaland, who issued a Proclamation authorising nominated court members only (not necessarily chiefs) to act as judges. Following a failed appeal by two prominent Tswana chiefs against the Proclamation, the judgement was undermined in practice and ultimately dropped in a revision of the Proclamation nine years later. So the matter rested for some 90 years until an amended redefinition in Botswana's Customary Law Act, in 2013, granted chiefs or presiding court headmen sole decision-making authority, *without the need for consultation*. This new dispensation was evident in the chiefly conduct of a customary court case convened in 2017 to consider the intestate inheritance of the properties of a long-deceased man in Moremi village.

In fact, however, not all customary courts in the district were following the new edict. Even more striking was the confusion among Moremi court participants regarding the chief's requirement to seek advice from his counsellors and village elders. This indicates that consultative citizens' courts were an entrenched feature of customary law, not easily overturned by a statutory ruling from above. Nor was it clear why the ruling had been made as it had, without any comment, as a definitional item. The chapter considered the implications of this radical legal redefinition from above for an understanding of legal pluralism and customary law as living law, both in Botswana and comparatively. It went on to show that the highest court in the land, the Court of Appeal, while stressing the flexible, 'living' nature of customary law, at the same stressed the need to preserve its independence within what has been defined by legal anthropologists as a semi-autonomous field.

Chapter 10 examined cases of insults, frequently heard in customary village courts. To show the continuing salience of these cases, we analysed in some depth one case of a family hearing or *morero* held in 1973. In this and other more recent cases what is at stake is often not merely the outcome or financial compensation for accusers, but even more, the public disciplining and shaming of a person or the redemptive demand by the dishonoured for remorse, recognition and dignity. Very often the cases are between women of different ages, young as well as old, and about insults, including witchcraft accusations; although we did not ourselves record insult cases between men, we were told of actions about abusive words between men, and their cases of physical violence and drunken brawls involving insults.

The chapter argued that legal anthropologists have been slow to join the socio-legal debate about law and emotion, a movement responding to the counter-intuitive proposition that the law is 'imbued with emotion'. As in the USA and Europe, in Botswana too, cases of public insults frequently heard in the village court are emotionally charged, and this is particularly so in witchcraft insult-accusations. These, the chapter argued, are to be grasped as inchoate crimes, akin to hate crimes, rather than allegations of literal occult practice. Insults threaten communal harmony and attack personal well-being. They are addressed through an elaborate moral lexicon, mobilised by members of a customary court in their attempt not simply to ascertain the forensic facts of what actually happened, but to elicit affective self-control. It is to persuade offenders to regain their rationality and reach with calmness of soul, a self-conscious emotional equilibrium. Ideally, if not always in practical accomplishment, the court tries to hold its hearing as a dialogue leading to the restoration of public peace and eliciting forgiveness from plaintiffs, the victims of insults.

The central case in this chapter was heard in a ward moot in which an attempt was made to persuade the accused to drop her accusations, since these would undoubtedly lead to her imprisonment if taken to the village court. It was widely recognised by the moot members that the accused was unwell physically and mentally, and thus not fully responsible for her utterances, however offensive, but it was nevertheless important to prevent the case from going forward to the (village) court, which was likely to mete out severe punishment. The chapter considered the significance of honour and dignity for villagers.

Insult cases are often heard at the lowest level of customary hearing, the *morero*, or family moot. Insults threaten the fabric of social life at the most intimate, family level. Here the family elders gather with junior members to try to persuade the insulter and the insulted to mend their relationship for the sake of the family. As has already been noted previously, insults often use offensive bodily images. Indeed, Epstein argued that emotions are embedded in the body and can be 'invested with powerful affect' (Epstein 1992: 224). One of the cases presented here was of a family moot or *morero* held inside the yard of an extended family of three brothers living in adjacent homesteads with their mature children, mainly young women, who were still living at home at the time, in 1973.

Chapter 11 focused on criminal offences and, in particular, on cases of stock theft. We followed one case through its progress to the High Court and Court of Appeal in order to illuminate the legal learning and changing legal subjectivity of an accused and imprisoned rustler. Although customary courts have been denied the right to judge many types of crime, from murder and rape to serious bodily injury, they still retain the right to judge cases of theft, burglary, and insult, as seen in the previous chapter, and in cases of stock theft, to sentence culprits to five years in jail or more. Chapter 11 critically examined customary court sentencing in cases of cattle theft or negligence in herding, recognising the huge symbolic value cattle are endowed with among Batswana. It drew comparison with magistrate court sentencing in order to reflect on the equity of such heavy penalties in cases often involving young, impoverished men or cases where imprisonment leads to the destitution of whole families. It also disclosed the vicissitudes of the appeal process from a magistrate's court to the Appeal Court and the construction of a subject, the accused, as a recidivist, 'incorrigible', and a repeated offender.

Three aporias

Adopting a perspective of the new legal realism, the emergence of which we elucidate in our Introduction, the cases in this book have disclosed three central aporias, apparently irresolvable dilemmas or contradictions, characterising the legal anthropological study of customary law and village politics today. These are (a) the aporia of customary law and chiefly politics, public ethics and cosmic morality as played out in courts; (b) the aporia of legal pluralism; and (c) the aporia of customary law as living law.

The aporia of customary law and chiefly politics, public ethics and cosmic morality

In the first half of this book, we explored the controversial, problematic, and, indeed, contradictory intersections of this aporia. Like the Athenian *agora* or the Roman forum, the *kgotla* is a place of assembly and the hub of public decision-making in Moremi village, as it is in virtually all small villages in Botswana. Court cases dealing with both interpersonal disputes and also with major, enduring, and sometimes intractable conflicts over chiefly succession, village centralisation, or the name and identity of a village, find their way into the *kgotla*, and from there they may be appealed to higher-level tribal and statutory courts. Although communal conflicts may sometimes seem to be focused on the ambitions of individual men or women, at a deeper level, we show in this book, they draw on a shared universe of values and ideas about public ethics. Such shared ethics are inextricably and intensely intertwined in problematic ways with politics. The *kgotla* is the centre of public deliberation, whether on legal, political, policy, or administrative matters, and invariably such deliberations draw, often contentiously, on this common pool of values and notions of morality, nature and destiny, of *tlholego*, held by villagers.

The duality of Moremi's *kgotla*, distinctive in Botswana though having the same or similar pairing elsewhere in Southern Africa, counterposes, uneasily and more or less in tension, state and non-state authority. The former is deployed along with the secular authority of hereditary chiefship in the customary court, whereas the latter, having its sacred source in ancestrality and Pediness, the *tlholego* of Tswapong, is invoked in the oracular consultations of the court of divinity, *Kgotla ya Sedimo*. Although two in many respects – in the priority of secular law versus that of ritual, with esoterica and communion in feasts and libations; in deliberate practice with exclusive, mysterious secrecy as against inclusive transparency; in peer as against executive leadership; in organisation within hierarchy; in somewhat overlapping membership, among other things – the pair are one, together being the *kgotla*.

Not surprisingly, at least for the people themselves if not always for the ethnographers, matters spill over between the pair. The court of divinity is not only a traditional check on chiefly conduct and new village development, but it is something of a gossip mill, from which leak personal confidences and pronouncements of moral fault with outstanding debt towards the ancestors. And yet there is the non-justiciable: it is a breach for matters of the court of divinity to become so politicised that they are taken for serious consideration by the customary court. Our account of such a breach, intensified by confrontational inter-village politics, examines the problematic, even baffling course of a case in an unprecedented customary court hearing. It was deliberately kept from becoming an adversarial trial instead of the peace-making deliberation needed for bringing together kin as sacred peers with responsibility for amity and thus cosmic morality; but it provided merely temporary relief, a show somewhat on the surface of social life, and the undercurrents of unsettled strife remained irresolvable – it is of course in the nature of an aporia to be contradictory and undecidable.

To pursue the aporetic intersections in and around the *kgotla*, further, we turn to considerations of democracy. Although the *kgotla* is conceived of in Botswana as being democratic, indeed *the* place of democracy *par excellence*, it is, in the final analysis, a democracy conceived of according to chiefship and brought forth under hereditary leadership by the village or tribal chief. At the same time, as we have seen, a simple one-man-one-vote democracy can distort or even subversively undermine both history and current values, as the struggle over the village name, chiefship and court at Matolwane illustrated. The 'democratic' vote held there effectively disenfranchised a large number of villagers, who felt denied of their very being, their Pediness, and deeply felt identity. This is the aporia at the heart of communal politics constituted by the irresolvable tension with ethics, law and morality.

As we have seen throughout this book, the legal sphere is often a sphere of emotions, all the more so in communal conflicts. Such conflicts are, invariably, passionate, a source of pain and of a shared sense of affliction. They draw on memories of past conflicts, often so vivid they seem to refer to events which happened just yesterday. There are no presentist politics. Politics are always enveloped in, and draw upon, past conflicts and humiliations. The micro-history of the village is constantly being rewritten with irreconcilable glosses on rights and wrongs in unfinished narratives and festering legacies. The aporetic is, of course, the passionately disturbing truth from the past to the present and for the future.

The aporia of legal pluralism

In the second half of the book domestic and familial cases have been repeatedly juxtaposed as they have been judged alternatively in customary and statutory courts, or have reached statutory courts on appeal. At times, villagers have turned directly to the statutory courts, and sometimes statutory courts have sent cases back to the village *kgotla*. Some key differences between the two types of court are evident: customary courts aim, if possible, to settle disputes by negotiated compromise while statutory courts are prohibitively expensive. A huge number of cases in Botswana are heard and decided in customary courts. The government supports these courts with paid subventions to village chiefs and their deputies, the ward headmen and women, with salaries also provided for police, bailiffs and court clerks, and with capital investments in offices, computers and new *kgotla* buildings.

Customary courts are, however, nonetheless the poor cousins of statutory courts in Botswana. The aporia surrounding customary courts in the context of legal pluralism in Botswana relates to their putative autonomy. On the whole, as we have seen, family law in customary courts tends to follow imperceptibly the lead of statutory courts when progressive legislation regarding marriage, divorce and inheritance is adopted over time by the statutory courts. Customary courts nevertheless retain their self-declared independence. The Court of Appeal in the Mmusi case, we saw, rejected the judgement by High Court judge Dingake that appealed to the Botswana Constitution, but then passed its own judgement based on a provision in the Customary Law Act that a (customary) law should be followed only in so far as '*it is not incompatible with the provisions of any written law or contrary to morality, humanity or natural justice*' (ibid. emphasis in the original, Mmusi case, citing. Customary Courts Act 2006, Section 2, (1)(b). This, in effect, reinstated the basic principles of equity, fairness and human rights central to the Constitution. More directly, even, in the case of crimes like stock theft, the law instructs customary courts on minimum prison sentences, with no room for discretion, clemency or consideration of mitigating and extenuating circumstances.

The *illusion* of autonomy is thus maintained in the interest of upholding the legitimacy of the *kgotla*. At best, customary courts may be grasped as occupying a semi-autonomous legal sphere (Moore 1973). We have moved, in effect, into a situation described by Sally Engle Merry as the 'new legal pluralism', or of 'plural normative orders' (Merry 1988: 873), indeed, of spiralling pluralities. These include bureaucratic ideas of accountability that have led most recently and perhaps temporarily, as we saw in Chapter 9, to customary court presidents becoming sole decision-makers. Disagreement and inconsistency exist even within the statutory sphere in Botswana, as we saw in relation to conflicting judgements on adultery in Chapter 8. The overlapping of jurisdictions is most problematic, as indeed Aninka Classens and Geoff Budlenger (2014) show, when it comes to communal rights; when the political is also legal, and the legal is imbued with ethical issues of identity and history, and with communal political interests.

The aporia of customary law as living law

Finally, we arrive at the central aporia animating this book. In a masterly article on living law in contemporary South Africa, Classens and Budlender (2014) highlight the aporia at the heart of customary law as 'living' law. It starts from the current rejection by statutory courts of reliance upon earlier official codifications of customary law. These are now recognised as distorted, based on biased informants, senior men, chiefs and colonial administrators. Instead, customary law is now understood by higher courts as law *in practice*, which changes over time, *in context*. If this is so, however, the question remains – how is a court to ascertain what these laws are at any given moment? The question is particularly acute when, in addition to finding what the law in practice is, customary law is scrutinised in the light of higher constitutional principles of equity. A further complication arises from the fact that South Africa's constitutional court is expected at the same time to 'respect' customary law as culturally autonomous. The result, as the authors show, is a series of ingenious compromises by the Constitutional Court of South Africa relating to chiefly succession, polygamy, and inheritance. The aporia lies in the fact that there is no clear, fixed, once-and-for-all resolution of what customary law is. Every effort at resolution elicits counter-interventions, gaming manoeuvres, and re-interpretations. The customary law is law ever on the horizon, if momentarily on record. A similar aporia is evident in the judicial consideration of contemporary land law in Kumasi, Ghana (Ubink 2011).

By contrast to South Africa or Ghana, in Botswana the aporia is not as stark. Changes in customary law happen all the time and historically, over time, but the 'livingness' of the law, in the absence of lawyers, is often not made explicit in village courts. Nonetheless, as we show in this book, there has been a clear trajectory in customary courts towards more progressive interpretations of the law. In Moremi, gender and generational equity are asserted and practised without judges declaring that the law has changed. Even if some conservative chiefs sitting on the national Customary Court of Appeal attempt to stem the tide of change, they ultimately fail, as we show. Unlike in South Africa where a prior Bantustan rural population, 17 million strong, is subjected exclusively to customary law courts dominated by conservative, unelected chiefs (cf. Claassens and Budlender 2014; Weeks and Classens 2011),[4] there is no geographical monopoly over the law by traditional authorities in Botswana. In Botswana, customary and statutory courts operate side by side in all the country's different districts, including its towns, and litigants may shop for a venue or opt for either type of court. Moreover, land is handled by land boards, open to everyone, if still somewhat influenced by considerations of respect for chiefs and their care for communal interest in once-tribal land.

Under these circumstances, customary law as living law is highly contextual and situational in Botswana in several important respects: first, it reflects the particular situation and circumstances of litigants; second, it reflects the biases of local judges, their personal biography and values; and third, it reflects the current values widely held in particular localities. Hence, Moremi may differ even from neighbouring Matolwane in the extent to which members of the court are consulted, as we saw in Chapter 9. We argued that the 'democratic' vote held in Matolwane effectively disenfranchised many villagers, While in the long run there may be legal harmonising as cases are appealed through the customary court hierarchy, both certainty and uncertainty remain intrinsic to customary law as living law at any given moment, with consequences for what justice actually means.

The problems involved in these aporias take us to the very frontier of debate about how the politics and authority of chiefs, so-called traditional or neotraditional leaders, prevail during democratisation in postcolonial Southern Africa (Baldwin 2016; Comaroff and Comaroff 2018; Fontein 2006; Gulbrandsen 2012; Hickel 2015; James 2007; van Kessel and Oomen 1997; Kramer 2016, 2020; LiPuma and Koelbe 2009; Meyers 2008; Ntsebeza 2005; Nyamnjoh 20; Oomen 2005; Williams 2010; Zenker and Hoehne 2018; R. Werbner 2002a, 2004). It is, of course, a vast debate, and despite the relabelling of chiefs in neotraditional terms, it is hardly a new one. As we have documented for Botswana, however, although chiefship was upheld symbolically, it has been stripped of much of its

4 Lower customary courts in South Africa exist in a hierarchy, as van der Waal documents (2004; see also Bennett 2004), somewhat like in Botswana, but the new Traditional Courts Bill (TBA 2017) approved 2019, does not appears to contain a formal 'opt-out' clause for litigants wishing to hear their case in a magistrate's court (see val Dalsen 2019; also Weeks 2011 on the earlier 2008 TBA) except after 'after exhausting all traditional court system appeal procedures' (van Dalsen 2019). While autocratic chiefs are rejected, Deborah James has observed that in South Africa, as in other parts of Africa, people faced with government failure to secure land access often turn to traditional authority even though formerly they may have opposed it. Chiefs appeared to present an alternative model of ownership and leadership (James 2007: 163).

power over land and resources. In this respect it differs from much of the rest of Southern Africa. Nonetheless, it is integral to our understanding of customary justice, which in itself now serves as the focus of a growing field of postcolonial studies.

Seeking customary justice is thus, to conclude, both a quest of the people themselves who go to the law to seek retribution, redress, and fair settlement through customary and statutory courts and moots, and also a scholarly quest to comprehend the dynamics of customary justice as a dialogical interplay of ethics and pragmatism, politics and morality, law and change. These dynamics are grounded in notions of legality and fairness, *under the circumstances.* There are no fixed, once-and-for-all legal truths but a continuous argument, a juggling of facts, norms, and values in order, if possible, to reach an agreement in court among litigants and, if at all possible, to recover communal harmony. This often involves interminable delays as cases are returned to litigants. In the final analysis, however, judges may, and do, assert the authority of the court to decide what is right or wrong.

Bibliography

Bailey, F.G. (1968) 'Parapolitical Systems,' in M.J. Schwartz (ed.) *Local-Level Politics: Social and Cultural Perspectives*. London: University of London Press, pp. 281–294.

Bailey, F.G. (1970) *Stratagems and Spoils: A Social Anthropology of Politics*. Oxford: Basil Blackwell.

Baldwin, Kate (2016) *The Paradox of Traditional Chiefs in Democratic Africa*. Cambridge: Cambridge University Press.

Bandes, Susan A. (1999) *The Passions of Law*. New York: New York University Press.

Bandes, Susan A. and Jeremy A. Blumenthal (2012) 'Emotion and the Law,' *The Annual Review of Law and Social Science* 8: 161–81.

Bennett, T.W. (2004) *Customary Law in South Africa*. Claremont: Juta.

Bens, Olaf and Jonas Zenker (2019) 'Sentiment,' in Jan Slaby and Christian von Scheve (eds.) *Affective Societies*. London: Routledge, pp. 96–106.

Bierschenk, Thomas (2014) *States at Work: Dynamics of African Bureaucracy*. Leiden: Brill Publishers.

Bohannan, Paul (1957) *Justice and Judgement Among the Tiv*. Oxford: The International African Institute for Oxford University Press.

Bohannan, Paul (1969) 'Ethnography and Comparison in Legal Anthropology,' in Laura Nader (ed.) *Law in Culture and Society*. London: University of California Press.

Bojosi, Otlhogile (1994) *A History of the Higher Courts of Botswana 1912–1990*. Gaborone: Mmegi Publishing House.

Booyens, J.H. (1985) 'Aetiology as Social Comment on Life Amongst Tswana-speaking Urbanites,' *African Studies* 44, 2: 137–157.

Botswana Democratic Party (1969) *Election Manifesto: Build Botswana*. Gaborone: BDP.

Botswana Government (December 12, 2018) 'Parliamentary Debate on Stock Theft,' https://www.facebook.com/BotswanaGovernment/posts/masisi-calls-for-stringent-action-against-stock-theftparliament-the-state-should/1978029032279745/

Botswana Women's Affairs Department (WAD) (1988) *Laws Affecting the Status of Women in Botswana*. Gaborone: Government of Botswana.

Braithwaite, John (2002) *Restorative Justice and Responsive Regulation*. Oxford: Oxford University Press.

Brunnegger, Sandra (ed.) (2019) *Everyday Justice: Law, Ethnography, Injustice*. Cambridge: Cambridge University Press.

Bunei, Emmanuel K. (2017) 'Keynote Address: Stock Theft in Africa: Current Challenges and Future Direction,' Conference on Rural Crime in Africa, Nairobi.

Button, Kirsty, Elena Moore, and Chuma Himonga (2016) 'South Africa's System of Dispute Resolution Forums: The Role of the Family and the State in Customary Marriage Dissolution,' *Journal of Southern African Studies* 42, 2: 299–316.

Cardozo, B. J. (1928). *Nature of the Judicial Process.* New Haven: Yale University Press.

Carnelley, Marita (2013). 'Laws on Adultery: Comparing the Historical Development of South-African Common Law Principles with Those in English Law,' *Fundamina* 19, 2: 185–272.

Chiepe, N.A., M.H. Roy, Q.D. Khama, and K.M. Merafhe (2016) 'Effects of Customary Laws on Basic Human Rights of Women in Botswana,' *International Journal of Law and Legal Studies* 4, 7: 222–231.

Claassens, Annika (2014) 'Denying Ownership and Equal Citizenship: Continuities in the State's Use of Law and "custom", 1913–2013,' *Journal of Southern African Studies* 40, 4: 761–79.

Claassens, Aninka and Geoff Budlender (2014) 'Transformative Constitutionalism and Customary Law,' *Constitutional Court Review* 9: 75–104.

Clarke, Kamari Maxime (2019) *Affective Justice: The International Criminal Court and the Pan-Africanist Pushback.* Durham: Duke University Press.

Colson, Elizabeth (1974) *Tradition and Contract: the Problem of Order.* Chicago, IL: Aldine.

Colson, Elizabeth (1976) 'From Chief's Court to Local Court,' in Myron J. Aronoff (ed.) *Freedom and Constraint: A Memorial Tribute to Max Gluckman.* Amsterdam: Van Gorcum, pp. 15–29.

Colson, Elizabeth (1995) 'The Contentiousness of Disputes,' in Pat Caplan (ed.) *Understanding Disputes: the Politics of Argument.* Oxford: Berg, pp. 65–82.

Comaroff, John L. (1978) 'Rules and Rulers: Political Processes in a Tswana Chiefdom.' *Man (NS)* 13, 1: 1–20.

Comaroff, John L. (1980) *The Meaning of Marriage Payments.* New York and London: Academic Press.

Comaroff, John L. and Jean Comaroff (2004) 'Criminal Justice, Cultural Justice: The Limits of Liberalism and the Pragmatics of Difference in the New South Africa,' *American Ethnologist* 31, 2: 188–204.

Comaroff, Jean and John Comaroff (2007) 'Law and Disorder in the Postcolony,' *Social Anthropology* 15, 2: 133–52.

Comaroff, John L. and Jean Comaroff (eds.) (2018) *The Politics of Custom: Chiefship. Capital and the State in Contemporary Africa.* Chicago, IL: University of Chicago Press.

Comaroff, John and Simon Roberts (1977) 'Marriage and Extra-Marital Sexuality,' *Journal of African Law* 21: 97–123.

Comaroff, John and Simon Roberts (1981) *Rules and Processes: The Cultural Logic of Dispute in an African Context.* Chicago, IL: The University of Chicago Press.

Conley, John M. and William M. O'Barr. 2004. 'A Classic in Spite of Itself: *The Cheyenne Way* and the Case Method in Legal Anthropology.' *Law & Inquiry* 29, 1: 179–217.

Conway, Heather (2016) 'Where there's a will...: Law and Emotion in Sibling Inheritance Disputes,' in Heather Conway and John Stannard (eds.) *The Emotional Dynamics of Law and Legal Discourse.* Oxford and Portland OR: Hart Publishing, pp. 35–57.

Conway, Heather and John Stannard (2016) 'Contextualising Law and Emotion: Past Narratives and Future Directions,' in Heather Conway and John Stannard (eds.) *The Emotional Dynamics of Law and Legal Discourse.* Oxford and Portland OR: Hart Publishing, pp. 1–8.

Cook, Susan (2018) 'Corporate Kings and South Africa's Traditional-Industrial Complex,' in John L. Comaroff and Jean Comaroff (eds.) *The Politics of Custom: Chiefship. Capital and the State in Contemporary Africa.* Chicago, IL: University of Chicago Press, pp. 211–230.

Cooper, Frederick (1996) *Decolonization and African Society: The Labor Question in French and British Africa.* Cambridge: Cambridge University Press.

Dagan, Hanoch (2005) *The Realist Conception of Law.* Tel Aviv University Law Faculty Papers, No. 21.

Dambe, Baboki Jonathan and Charles Manga Fombad (2020) 'The Stock Theft Act and Customary Courts in Botswana: Justice Sacrificed on the Altar of Expediency?' *The Journal of Legal Pluralism* 52, 1: 65–81.

Diala, Anthony C. (2017) 'The Concept of Living Customary Law: a Critique,' *The Journal of Legal Pluralism and Unofficial Law* 49, 2: 143–165.

Dipholo, Kabelo (2019) "End of Honeymoon for Adulterers," *The Voice,* 10 December, 2019. https://news.thevoicebw.com/end-of-honeymoon-for-adulterers/

Ditsheko, Enolo (2019) *Wrestling Botswana Back from Khama.* Gaborone: Yearbook Publications.

Dunlap, Colonel Charles J. (2001) 'Law and Military Interventions: Preserving Humanitarian Values in 21st Conflicts,' *Talk Given,* 29 November, 2001. https://people.duke.edu/~pfeaver/dunlap.pdf

Eckert, Julia M. (2021) *The Bureaucratic Production of Difference: Ethos and Ethics in Migration Administrations.* Bielefeld: Transcript Verlag.

Englund, Harri (2006) *Prisoners of Freedom: Human Rights and the African Poor.* Berkeley, CA: University of California Press.

Epstein, A.L. (1973) 'The Reasonable Man Revisited: Some Problems in the Anthropology of Law,' *Law & Society Review* 7, 4: 643–66.

Epstein, A.L. (1992) *In the Midst of Life: Affect and Ideation in the World of the Tolai.* Berkeley, CA: University of California Press.

Faulk, Karen and Sandra Brunnegger (2016) 'Introduction: Making Sense of Justice,' in Sandra Brunnegger and Karen Faulk (eds.) *A Sense of Justice: Legal Knowledge and Lived Experience in Latin America.* Stanford, CA: Stanford University Press, pp. 1–21.

Fallers, L.A. (1969) *Law without Precedent: Legal Ideas in Action in the Courts of Colonial Busoga.* Chicago, IL: University of Chicago Press.

Fallers, L.A. (1977) 'Administration and the Supremacy of Law in Colonial Busoga,' in Ian Hamnett (ed.) *Social Anthropology and Law.* London: Academic Press.

Fombad, Charles (2004) 'Customary Courts and Traditional Justice in Botswana,' *Stellenbosch Law Review* 15, 1: 166–192.

Fombad, Charles (2011) 'Botswana and the Dynamics of Legal Modernisation within a Dual English Common Law/Roman Dutch Law Legal Heritage,' *African Journal of International and Comparative Law* 13, 1: 7–24.

Fombad, Charles Manga (2014) 'Gender equality in African customary law: has the male ultimogeniture rule any future in Botswana?' *The Journal of Modern African Studies* 52, 3: 475–94.

Fontein, Joost (2006) *The Silence of Great Zimbabwe*. London: Routledge.

Fontein, Joost (2009) 'Anticipating the Tsunami: Rumour, Planning and the Arbitrary State in Zimbabwe,' *Africa* 79, 3: 369–398.

Frank, Jerome (1930) *Law and the Modern Mind*. New York: Brettano.

Gaotlhobogwe, M. (2010) February 8 "Kgafela Tears Molokomme's Riot Act to Pieces." *Mmegi Monitor* (Botswana). https://www.mmegi.bw/index.php?sid=1&aid=161&dir=2010/February/Monday8/

Gaotlhobogwe, Monkagedi (2006) 'Botswana: Residents to Decide on Tswapong Village Name,' *Mmegi Online*, 8 May. https://allafrica.com/stories/200605081301.html

Garth, Bryant and Elizabeth Mertz (2016) 'Introduction: New Legal Realism at Ten Years and Beyond,' *UC Irvine Law Review* 6, 2: 121–135.

Geertz, Clifford. (1983) 'Local Knowledge: Fact and Law in Comparative Perspective,' in *Local Knowledge*. New York: Fontana Press, pp. 167–234.

Geisler, Gisela (1995) 'Troubled Sisterhood: Women and Politics in Southern Africa: Case Studies from Zambia, Zimbabwe and Botswana,' *African Affairs* 94, 377: 545–578.

Geschiere, Peter (2006) 'Witchcraft and the Limits of the Law: Cameroon and South Africa,' in Jean Comaroff and John L. Comaroff (eds.) *Law and Disorder in the Postcolony*. Chicago, IL: University of Chicago Press, pp. 219–246.

Gillet, Simon (1973) 'The Survival of Chieftaincy in Botswana,' *African Affairs* 72, 287: 179–185.

Givelber, Daniel (1982) 'The Right to Minimum Social Decency and the Limits of Evenhandedness: Intentional Infliction of Emotional Distress by Outrageous Conduct,' *Columbia Law Review* 82, 1: 42–75.

Gluckman, Max (1960) *Custom and Conflict*. Oxford: Basil Blackwell.

Gluckman, Max (1963) 'The Reasonable Man in Barotse Law,' in Max Gluckman (ed.) *Order and Rebellion in Tribal Africa*. London: Cohen and West, pp. 178–206.

Gluckman, Max (1967[1955]) *The Judicial Process among the Barotse of Northern Rhodesia (Zambia)*. Manchester: Manchester University Press for the African Studies University of Zambia.

Gluckman, Max (1973) Limitations of the Case-Method in the Study of Tribal Law. *Law & Society Review* 7, 4: 611–642.

Griffiths, Anne M.O. (1997) *In the Shadow of Marriage: Gender and Justice in an African Community*. Chicago, IL: University of Chicago Press.

Griffiths, Anne (2011) 'Delivering Justice: The Changing Gendered Dynamics of Land Tenure in Botswana,' *The Journal of Legal Pluralism and Unofficial Law* 43, 63: 231–262.

Gulbrandsen, Ornulf (2012) *The State and the Social: State Formation in Botswana and its Precolonial and Colonial Genealogies*. Oxford: Berghahn Books.

Hailey, Lord Malcolm (1953) *Native Administration in the British African Territories, Part V. The High Commission Territories: Basutoland, The Bechuanaland Protectorate and Swaziland*. London: Her Majesty's Stationery Office.

Harthill, Susan (2008) 'Bullying in the Workplace: Lessons from the United Kingdom,' *Minnesota Journal of International Law* 17: 247–302.

Hickel, Jason (2015) *Democracy as Death: the Moral Order of Anti-Liberal Politics in South Africa*. Berkeley, CA: University of California Press.

Hillbom, Ellen (2014) 'Cattle, Diamonds and Institutions: Main Drivers of Botswana's Economic Development, 1850 to Present,' *Journal of International Development* 26, 2: 155–176.

Himonga, Chuma and Craig Bosch (2000) 'The Application of African Customary Law under the Constitution of South Africa: Problems Solved or Just Beginning,' *South African Legal Journal* 117: 306–341.

Himonga, Chuma and Elena Moore (2015) *Reform of Customary Marriage, Divorce and Succession in South Africa: Living Customary Law and Social Realities.* Claremont, South Africa: Juta and Co.

Horwitz, Morton J. (1992) *The Transformation of American Law 1870–1960: The Crisis of Legal Orthodoxy.* Oxford: Oxford University Press.

Hund, John (1998) '"Customary Law is What the People Say it is" - H.L.A. Hart's Contribution to Legal Anthropology,' *Archives for Philosophy of Law and Social Philosophy* 84, 3: 420–433.

Hunt, Alan (1986) 'A Theory of Critical Legal Studies,' *Oxford Journal of Legal Studies* 6, 1: 1–45.

Hunt, Lynn (2002) 'Against Presentism'. Presidential Address. *Perspective on History*, May 2002. https://www.historians.org/publications-and-directories/perspectives-on-history/may-2002/against-presentism

Huntington, Claire (2016) 'Affective Family Law,' in Heather Conway and John Stannard (eds.) *The Emotional Dynamics of Law and Legal Discourse.* Oxford and Portland OR: Hart Publishing, pp. 10–33.

James, Deborah (2007) *Gaining Grounds? Rights and Property and South Africa's Land Reform.* London: Routledge-Cavendish.

Janzen, John (1992) *Ngoma - Discourses of Healing in Central and Southern Africa.* Berkeley, CA: University of California Press.

Johnson, Jessica (2018) *In Search of Gender Justice: Rights and Relationships in Matrilineal Malawi.* International African Library. Cambridge: Cambridge University Press.

Johnson, Jessica and George Karekwaivanane (eds.) (2018) *Pursuing Justice in Africa: Competing Imaginaries and Contested Practices.* Athens, OH: Ohio University Press.

Kapferer, Bruce (1972) *Strategy and Transaction in an African Factory.* Manchester: University of Manchester Press.

Kapferer, Bruce (ed.) (1979) *Transaction and Meaning: Directions in the Anthropology of Exchange and Symbolic Behaviour.* ASA Essays in Social Anthropology Series, Vol. 1. Pennsylvania, PA: Institute for the Study of Human Issues.

Kaplow, Louis (1992) 'Rules versus Standards: An Economic Analysis,' *Duke Law Journal* 42, 3: 557–629.

Klaits, Fred (2005) 'Postcolonial Civility,' *Journal of Southern African Studies (JSAS)* 31, 3: 649–662.

Klaits, Fred (2010) *Death in a Church of Life.* Berkeley: University of California Press.

Krämer, Mario (2019) 'Violence, Autochthony, and Identity Politics in KwaZulu Natal (South Africa): A Processual Perspective on Local Processual Dynamics,' *African Studies Review* 63, 3: 1–20.

Krämer, Mario (2020) 'Neotraditional Authority Contested: The Corporatization of Tradition and the Quest for Democracy in the Topnaar Traditional Authority, Namibia,' *Africa* 90, 2: 318–338.

Korobkin, Russell B. (2000) 'Behavioral Analysis versus Legal Form: Rules vs. Standards Revisited,' *Oregon Law Review* 79: 23–60.

Kumar, R.A. (2009) 'Constitutional rights and judicial activism: Bridging the gaps in Botswana,' in E. Quansah and W. Binchy (eds.) *The Judicial Protection of Human Rights in Botswana*. Dublin: Clarus Press.

Kuper, Adam (1970) *Kalahari Village Politics: An African Democracy*. Cambridge: Cambridge University Press.

Kuper, Adam (1975a) 'Council Structure and Decision Making,' in A. Richards and A. Kuper (eds.) *Councils in Action*. Cambridge: Cambridge University Press.

Kuper, Adam (1975b) 'The Social Structure of the Sotho-Speaking People of Southern Africa (Part II),' *Africa* 45, 2: 139–149.

Kyed, Helena Maria (2018) 'State Police and Tradition in Post-war Mozambique: the Dilemmas of Claiming Sovereignty in Legal Pluralistic Contexts,' in Olaf Zenker and Markus Virgil Hoehne (eds.) *The State and the Paradox of Customary Law in Africa*. London: Routledge, pp. 64–86.

Laidlaw, James (2002) 'For an Anthropology of Ethics and Freedom,' *Journal of the Royal Anthropological Institute (N.S.)* 8: 311–32.

Lambek, Michael (2003) *The Weight of the Past: Living with History in Mahajanga*. London: Palgrave Macmillan.

Lebotse, K.K. (2005) 'Adultery and the Rights of Women under Botswana Customary Law,' *Lesotho Law Journal* 15, 2: 115–128.

Leonardi, Cherry (2018) 'Mixing Oil and Water? Colonial State Justice and the Challenge of Witchcraft Accusations in Central Equatoria, Southern Sudan,' in Olaf Zenker and Markus Virgil Hoehne (eds.) *The State and the Paradox of Customary Law in Africa*. London: Routledge, pp. 87–108.

Letsedidi, Bashi (2015) 'Dikgotla Ignoring 2008 Customary Court of Appeal Judgment.' *SundayStandard*, 15 March. http://www.sundaystandard.info/dikgotla-ignoring-2008-customary-court-appeal-judgment Accessed 14 October, 2016.

LiPuma, Edward and Thomas, A. Koelble (2009) 'Deliberative democracy and the politics of traditional leadership in South Africa: A case of despotic domination or democratic deliberation?' *Journal of Contemporary African Studies* 27, 2:201–223.

Magruder, Calvert (1936) 'Mental and Emotional Disturbance in the Law of Torts,' *Harvard Law Review* 49, 7: 1033–1067.

Mahmood, Saba (2005) *Politics of Piety: The Islamic Revival and the Feminist Subject*. Princeton, NJ: Princeton University Press.

Makgala, Christian John (2006) *Elite Conflict in Botswana: A History*. Pretoria: African Institute of South Africa.

Malila, Ikanyeng S. (2010) 'Reconciling Plural Legal Systems: Between Justice and Social Disorder in Botswana,' *Botswana Notes and Records* 42: 71–78.

Malila, Ikanyeng S. (2012) 'Severity of Multiple Punishments Deployed by Magistrate and Customary Courts Against Common Offences in Botswana: A Comparative Analysis,' *International Journal of Criminal Justice Sciences (IJCJS)* 7, 2: 618–634.

Malila, Ikanyeng S. (2015) 'Codified Law and the Changing Normative Context of Disputes in Traditional Settings in Botswana,' *Canadian Journal of African Studies* 49, 2: 267–283.

Malila, Ikanyeng S. (2019) 'Modulating and Limiting Punishment through the Application of the Proportionality Principle: A Perspective from Botswana,' *Nordic Journal of Human Rights* 37, 2: 123–142.

Maroney, T.A. (2009) Emotional common sense as constitutional law. *Vanderbilt Law Rev.* 62: 851–917.

Maurer, Bill (2005) 'Due Diligence and "Reasonable Man" Offshore,' *Cultural Anthropology*, 20, 4: 474–505.

Mbaiwa, Joseph E. (2011) 'Cultural Commodification and Tourism: The Goo-Moremi Community, Central Botswana,' *Tijdschrift voor Economische en Sociale Geografie* 102, 3: 290–301.

Merry, Sally Engle (1988) 'Legal Pluralism,' *Law & Society Review* 22, 5: 869–896.

Meyers, J. C. (2008) *Indirect Rule in South Africa: Tradition, Modernity, and the Costuming of Political Power*. University of Rochester Press.

Modikwa, Onalenna (2010) 'Lesenepole and Matolwane fight over village name,' *Mmegi Online*. https://www.mmegi.bw/index.php?sid=1&aid=2184&dir=2010/May/Friday7

Mogami, Gaamangwe (2017) 'Haven in the Hills,' in *Peolwane: The Inflight Magazine of Air Botswana*. Gaborone: Bupendra Taylor, pp. 14–22.

Mokwape, Mpho (2015) 'Lesenepole/Matolwane name to be put to vote,' *Mmegi Online* 28 July. http://www.mmegi.bw/index.php?aid=52887&dir=2015/july/28

Molokomme, Athaliah (1991) "*Children of the Fence*": *the maintenance of extra-marital children under law and practice in Botswana*. Leiden: African Studies Centre.

Molutsi, Patrick and John D. Holm (1990) 'Developing Democracy When Civil Society is Weak: The Case of Botswana,' *African Affairs* 89: 323–340.

Moore, Sally Falk (1973) 'Law and Social Change: The Semi-Autonomous Social Field as an Appropriate Subject of Study,' *Law & Society Review* 7, 4: 719–746.

Moore, Sally Falk (2001) 'Certainties Undone: Fifty Turbulent Years of Legal Anthropology, 1949–1999,' *Journal of the Royal Anthropological Institute* 7, 1: 95–116.

Motzafi-Haller, Pnina (2002) *Fragmented Worlds, Coherent Lives. The Politics of Difference in Botswana*. Westport, CT; London: Bergin and Garvey.

Neal, Mary (2016) 'Discovering Dignity: Unpacking the Emotional Content of "Killing Narratives",' in Heather Conway and John Stannard (eds.) *The Emotional Dynamics of Law and Legal Discourse*. Oxford and Portland Oregon: Hart Publishing, pp. 83–103.

Nhlapo, Thandabantu (2017) 'Customary Law in Post-apartheid South Africa: Constitutional Confrontations in Culture, Gender and "living law"', *South African Journal on Human Rights* 33, 1: 1–24.

Ntsebeza, Lungisile (2005) *Democracy Compromised: Chiefs and the Politics of the Land in South Africa*. Leiden: Brill.

Nurse, Andrew (2014) 'Judging the Past,' *Active History*, January 16. http://activehistory.ca/2014/01/judging-the-past/

Nussbaum, Martha (2006) *Hiding from Humanity: Disgust, Shame, and the Law*. Princeton, NJ: Princeton University Press.

Nyamnjoh, Francis B. (2012) 'Taking Africaness and African Law Seriously in South African Law Schools: Some Conceptual Challenges,' in Jon Abbink (ed.) *Fractures and Reconnections: Civic Action and the Redefinition of African Political and Economic Spaces: Studies in Honor of Piet J.J. Konings*. Berlin: LIT Verlag, pp. 113–132.

Nyamnjoh, Francis B. (2015) *Modernising Traditions and Traditionalising Modernity in Africa: Chieftaincy and Democracy in Cameroon and Botswana.* Mankon, Bamenda: Langaa.

Oomen, B. (2005) *Chiefs in South Africa: Law, Power and Culture in the Postapartheid Era.* Oxford, Pietermaritzburg and New York NY: James Currey, University of KwaZulu-Natal Press and Palgrave Macmillan.

Peters, E.A. and J.M. Ubink (2015) 'Restorative and Flexible Customary Procedures and their Gendered Impact: A Preliminary View on Namibia's Formalization of Traditional Courts,' *Journal of Legal Pluralism and Unofficial Law* 47, 2: 291–311.

Piet, Bame (2005) 'Govt erred on Marital Power Bill – Mfa,' *Mmegi Online*, Thursday 3 February 2005.

Prins, Gwyn (1980) *The Hidden Hippopotamous: Reappraisal in African History: the Early Colonial Experience in Western Zambia.* Cambridge: Cambridge University Press.

Quansah, E.K. (2005) 'Abolition of Marital Power in Botswana: A New Dimension in Marital Relationship?' *University of Botswana Law Journal* 5: 5–27.

Reis, Ria, Rijk van Dijk, and Marja Spierenburg (2000) *The Quest for Fruition through Ngoma: The Political Aspects of Healing in South Africa.* Oxford: James Currey.

Rey, Charles Sir (1988) *Monarch of All I Survey: Bechuanaland Diaries 1929–37.* Neil Parsons and Michael Crowder (eds.) Gaborone: The Botswana Society, London: James Currey.

Rhode, Deborah L. (2016) *Adultery: Infidelity and the Law.* Cambridge, MA: Harvard University Press.

Ricoeur, Paul (1992) *Oneself as Another.* Chicago: University of Chicago Press.

Robbins, Joel (2009) 'Recognition, Reciprocity, and Justice: Melanesian Reflections on the Rights of Relationships,' in Clarke Kamari Maxine and Goodale Mark (eds.) *Mirrors of Justice: Law and Power in the Post-Cold War Era.* Cambridge: Cambridge University Press, pp. 171–190.

Robbins, Joel (2013) Beyond the Suffering Subject: Toward an Anthropology of the Good. *Journal of the Royal Anthropological Institute (N.S.)* 19: 447–462.

Sapignoli, Maria (2018) *Hunting Justice: Displacement, Law and Activism in the Kalahari.* Cambridge: Cambridge University Press.

Schapera, Isaac (1934) 'Oral Sorcery among the Natives of Bechuanaland,' in E.E. Evans-Pritchard, Raymond Firth, Bronislaw Malinowski and Isaac Schapera (eds.) *Essays Presented to C.G. Seligman.* London: Kegan Paul, Trench & Co. Ltd, pp. 293–306.

Schapera, Isaac (1940a) 'The Political Organisation of the Ngwato of the Bechuanaland Protectorate,' in M. Fortes and E. E. Evans-Pritchard (eds.) *African Political Systems.* Oxford: Oxford University Press, pp. 56–82.

Schapera, Isaac (1940b) *Married Life in an African Tribe.* London:Faber and Faber Ltd.

Schapera, Isaac (1952) *The Ethnic Composition of Tswana Tribes.* Monographs on Social Anthropology 11. London: London School of Economics.

Schapera, Isaac (1955) 'Witchcraft Beyond Reasonable Doubt,' 'Shorter Notes' *Man* 55: 72.

Schapera, Isaac (1956) *Government and Politics in Tribal Society.* London: Watts.

Schapera, Isaac (1955[1938]). *A Handbook of Tswana Law and Custom.* Oxford: Oxford University Press.

Schapera, Isaac. 1970 *Tribal Innovators: Tswana Chiefs and Social Change 1795–1940*. London: The Athelone Press.

Schapera, Isaac (1971) *Rainmaking Rites of Tswana Tribes.* Leiden: Afrika-Studiecentrun.

Schapera, Isaac (1983) 'Tswana Concepts of Custom and Law,' *Journal of African Law* 27, 2: 141–149.

Schler, Lynn, Louise Bethlehem, and Galia Sabar (2009) 'Editorial: Rethinking Labor in Africa, Past and Present'. Special issue, Rethinking African Labor, Past and Present. *African Identities* 7, 3: 299–325.

Silverman, Sydel (1974) 'Bailey's Politics,' *Journal of Peasant Studies* 2, 1: 111–120.

Solway, Jacqueline (2016) '"Slow marriage," "Fast *bogadi*": Change and Continuity in Marriage in Botswana,' *Anthropology Southern Africa* 39, 4: 309–322.

Solway, Jaqueline (2016) 'The Sacred Cow: Botswana's Livestock Industry and Urban Bias,' Unpublished paper.

Subramanian, Ajantha (2009) *Shorelines: Space and Rights in South India*. Stanford, CA: Stanford University Press.

Tamanaha, Brian Z. (2008–9) 'Understanding Legal Realism,' *Texas Law Review* 87: 731–785.

Tamanaha, Brian Z. (2009) *Beyond the Formalist-Realist Divide: The Role of Politics in Judging*. Princeton, NJ: Princeton University Press.

Tomlins, Christopher (2007) 'How Autonomous is Law?' *Annual Review of Law and Social Sciences* 3: 45–68.

Tordoff, E. W. (1974) 'Local Administration in Botswana,' *Journal of Local Administration Overseas* 12: 303.

Ubink, J. (2008) *Traditional Authorities in Africa: Resurgence in an Era of Democratisation*. Leiden: Leiden University Press.

Ubink, Janine (2011) 'The Quest for Customary Law in African State Courts,' in Jeanmarie Fenrich, Paolo Galizzi, and Tracy E. Higgins (eds.) *The Future of African Customary Law*. Cambridge: Cambridge university Press, pp. 83–102.

van Dalsen, Anton (2019) 'The Traditional Courts Bill Will Enable Concentration of Power in One Individual – A Traditional Leader,' *The Daily Maverick*, 9 April 2019. file:///C:/Users/Toshiba/Documents/A/MISC%20ARTICLESpdf/Customary%20law%20and%20chiefship%20articles/2019-04-09-the-traditional-courts-bill-will-enable-concentration-of-power-in-one-individual-a-traditional-leader.htm#gsc.tab=0 Accessed 9 July, 2020.

van Dijk, Rijk (2017) 'The Tent versus *Lobola*: Marriage, Monetary Intimacies and the New Face of Responsibility in Botswana,' *Anthropology Southern Africa* 40, 1: 29–41.

van Kessel, Inek and Barbara Oomen (1997) 'One Chief, One Vote: The Revival of Traditional Authorities in Post-apartheid South Africa,' *African Affairs* 96, 561–585.

Van Niewaal, Adriaan van Rouveroy, and Rijk van Dijk (eds.) (1999) *African Chieftaaincy in a New Socio-Political Landscape.* Leiden: African Studies Centre.

van Velzen, H.U.E. Thoden (1973) 'Robinson Crusoe and Friday: Strength and Weakness of the Big Man Paradigm,' *Man* 8, 4: 592–612.

van der Waal, C.S. (2004) 'Formal and Informal Dispute Resolution in the Limpopo Province, South Africa,' *Anthropology Southern Africa* 27, 3–4: 111–121.

Vengroff, Richard (1974) 'Popular Participation and the Administration of Rural Development: The Case of Botswana,' *Human Organisation* 33, 3: 303–309.

von Benda-Beckman, Franz (2002) 'Who's Afraid of Legal Pluralism?' *The Journal of Legal Pluralism and Unofficial Law* 34, 47: 37–82.

Walter, Eugene V. (1969) *Terror and Resistance: A Study of Political Violence*. Oxford: Oxford University Press.

Wass, Peter (1972) 'The History of Community Development in Botswana in the 1960's,' *Botswana Notes and Records* 4: 81–93, reprinted from *International Review of Community Development*.

Watson, Alan (1993) *Legal Transplants: An Approach to Comparative Law*. Athens, GA: University of Georgia Press.

Weinberg, Tara (2016) 'Pushing the Boundaries of Customary Law Jurisprudence in Botswana: Social Science and the Law in the Case of *Ramantele vs. Mmusi*,' *The Journal of Legal Pluralism and Unofficial Law* 48, 2: 186–207.

Weeks, Sindiso Mnisi (2011) 'The Traditional Courts Bill: Controversy around Process, Substance and Implications,' *South Africa Crime Quarterly* 35, March: 3–10.

Weeks, Sindiso Mnisi and Aninka Claassens (2011) 'Tensions Between Vernacular Values That Prioritise Basic Needs and State Versions Of Customary Law That Contradict Them,' *Stellenboch Law Review* 3: 822–844.

Werbner, Pnina (2009) 'The Hidden Lion: Tswapong Girls Puberty Rituals and the Problem of History,' *American Ethnologist* 36, 3: 441–458.

Werbner, Pnina (2014) 'The Duty to Act Fairly": Ethics, Legal Anthropology, and Labor Justice in the Manual Workers Union of Botswana,' *Comparative Studies in Society and History* 56, 2: 479–507.

Werbner, Pnina (2014). *The Making of an African Working Class: Law, Politics and Cultural Protest in the Manual Workers Union of Botswana*. London: Pluto Press.

Werbner, Pnina and Richard Werbner (2018) 'Divorce as Process, Botswana Style: Customary Courts, Gender Activism and Legal Pluralism in Historical Perspective,' *Legal Anthropology* 2, 2: 1–23.

Werbner, Pnina and Richard Werbner (2019) 'A Case of Insult: Emotion, Honour and Witchcraft Accusations in a Botswana Village Customary Court,' *Social Analysis* 63, 3: 1–25.

Werbner, Pnina and Richard Werbner (2020a) 'A Case of Inheritance: From Citizens' Forum to Magisterial Justice in Botswana's Customary Courts,' *Anthropology Southern Africa* 42, 4: 10–20.

Werbner, Pnina and Richard Werbner (2020b) 'Adultery Redefined: Changing Decisions of Equity in Customary Law as "Living Law" in Botswana,' *PoLar: Political and Legal Anthropology Review* 43, 1: 136–152.

Werbner, Richard (1969) 'Constitutional Ambiguities and the British Administration of Royal Careers among the Bemba of Zambia,' in Laura Nader (ed.), *Law in Culture and Society*. Chicago, IL: Aldine Press, pp. 2. 245–272.

Werbner, Richard (1977) 'Small Man Politics and the Rule of Law: Centre-Periphery Relations in East-Central Botswana,' *Journal of African Law*, Essays in Honour of Isaac Schapera, 2, 1: 24–39.

Werbner, Richard (1980/1982) 'The Quasi-Judicial and the Experience of the Absurd: Remaking Land Law in North-Eastern Botswana,' in Richard P. Werbner (ed.) *Land Reform in the Making: Tradition, Public Policy and Ideology in Botswana*. London: Rex Collins. First published in 1977 as a special issue of the *Journal of African Law* 24, 1:131–150.

Werbner, Richard (ed.) (1980/1982) *Land Reform in the Making: Tradition, Public Policy and Ideology in Botswana.* London: Rex Collins. First published in 1977 (dated 19980) as a special issue of the *Journlal of African Law* 24, 1.

Werbner, Richard (1989) *Ritual Passage, Sacred Journey.* Washington, DC: Smithsonian Institution Press; Manchester: Manchester University Press.

Werbner, Richard (1997 [1969]) 'Constitutional Ambiguities and British Administration of Royal Careers Among the Bemba of Zambia,' in Laura Nader (ed.) *Law in Culture and Society*, 2nd edition. Berkeley, CA: University of California Press, pp. 245–272.

Werbner, Richard (2002a) 'Introduction: Challenging Minorities, Difference and Tribal Citizenship in Botswana,' *Journal of Southern African Studies* 28, 4: 671–684.

Werbner, Richard (2002b) 'Postcolonial Subjectivities: The Personal, the Political and the Moral,' in Richard Werbner (ed.) *Postcolonial Subjectivities in Africa.* London: Zed Books, pp. 1–21.

Werbner, Richard (2002c) 'Conclusion: Citizenship and the Politics of Recognition in Botswana,' in Isaac Mazonde (ed.) *Minorities in the Millenium: Perspectives from Botswana.* Gaborone: Lightbooks.

Werbner, Richard (2004) *Reasonable Radicals and Citizenship in Botswana.* Bloomington, IN: Indiana University Press.

Werbner, Richard (2005) *Séance Reflections with Richard Werbner*, Documentary film. International Centre for Contemporary Cultural Research; London: Royal Anthropological Institute.

Werbner, Richard (2007) *Shade Seekers and the Mixer*, Documentary film. International Centre for Contemporary Cultural Research; London: Royal Anthropological Institute.

Werbner, Richard (2009) 'Safe Passage for Well-being: Substances, Sacrifice and Oracle Supplicants,' *Cambridge Anthropology* 29, 3: 46–68.

Werbner, Richard (2015) *Divination's Grasp: African Encounters with the Almost Said.* Bloomington, IN: Indiana University Press.

Werbner, Richard (2016) *Caught In Between.* Documentary film, Ethnographic Video Online: Alexander Street Press, London: distributed by the Royal Anthropological Institute.

Werbner, Richard (2018a) 'Botswana's Ecumenical Funerals in the Making,' in Richard Werbner and Anthony Simpson (eds.) 'Special Issue: Grassroots Ecumenism in Conflict,' *Journal of Southern African Studies* 44, 2: 315–330.

Werbner, Richard (2018b) *Breaking the Yard.* Documentary film.Ethnographic Video Online: Alexander Street Press, London: distributed by the Royal Anthropological Institute.

Werbner, Richard (2020) *Anthropology After Gluckman.* Manchester: Manchester University Press.

Williams, J. Michael (2004) 'Leading from behind: Democratic Consolidation and the Chieftaincy in South Africa,' *The Journal of Modern African Studies* 42, 1: 113–136.

Wilson, Richard A. (2001) *The Politics of Truth and Reconciliation in South Africa: Legitimizing the Post-Apartheid State.* Cambridge: Cambridge University Press.

Wilson, Richard Ashby (2017) *Incitement on Trial: Prosecuting International Speech Crimes.* Cambridge: Cambridge University Press.

Zenker, Olaf and Markus Virgil Hoehne (eds.) (2018) *The State and the Paradox of Customary Law in Africa.* London: Routledge.

Court cases

Court of Appeal, Gaborone. 2013. Ramantele v Mmusi and Others, CACGB-104-12: Gaborone, 3 September 2013.

Court of Appeal, Gaborone. 2013. Concurring Judgement, Civil Appeal No.CACGB-104-12: Gaborone, 11 September 2013.

Court of Appeal, Gaborone. 2014. Civil Case No CACGB-045-13, 31 July, 2014.

Court of Appeal, Gaborone. 2018. Court of Appeal Civil Case No. CACGB-194-17. Ikalafeng Sinwedi and others vs. Ministry of Local Government and others. Heard by Letsededi J. and two others, 26 October, 2018.

High Court, Francistown. 2014. MAHFT-000088-11. Mosebi vs Dintwe, Ofentse and Moesi heard by B. Nyamadzabo, 6 August, 2014.

High Court, Francistown. 2018. Kgaje v Mhotsha. CVHFT-000237-17, Francistown, 2 May, 2018.

High Court, Francistown. 2019. Machangan v Botsho CVHFT-000869-16, 25 November, 2019.

High Court, Gaborone. 2012. Mmusi and Others v Ramantele and Another, Case No. MAHLB-000836-10, Gaborone, 11 October, 2012.

High Court, Lobatse. 1996. Medupe v. Baakanyang 1996 BLR 612 (HC).

High Court, Lobatse. 1999. Mabote and Another v. Mabote (1) BLR 386 (CA). July 23, 1999.

High Court, Lobatse. 2005. Madidmalo v Mamadidimalo and Another (2) BLR 102 (HC) Matrimonial Cause No 224 of 2001, July 14 2005.

High Court, Lobatse. 2006. Case No F568 of 1997, BLR 203 (HC) Gaotlhobogwe Mosebi vs. Attorney General, Bamangwato Tribal Authority and Kgosi G. Mokgobelelo, heard by M.B. Marumo, April 28, 2006.

High Court, Lobatse. 2007. MAHLB-000336-06. Keotsenye Ofentse and others vs. Attorney General, Gaotlhoboge Mosebi (and 319 others of Lesenepole Village, Bamangwato Tribal Authority and Kgosi G. Mokgobeleo. Case heard by D. Newman, 5 July 2007.

High Court, Lobatse. 2017. MAHGB-000733-15. Ikalafeng Senwedi and others vs. Ministry of Local Government and Rural Development, the Attorney General of Botswana, Bamangwato Tribal Authority and Mosebi and others, heard by T. Tau, 15 September, 2017.

Namibia Appeal Court (2016) Shivute CJ, Mainga JA and Smuts JA, JS v LC (SA77-14) [2016] NASC (19-August 2016).

R v Dintwe Dithupe and Mpolokan Matsiboko, Criminal Case No. 20 of 1934 in BNA C/7/70.

State v Molapo 2007 (3) BLR 493 (HC)

The Supreme Court of Appeal of South Africa Judgment. 2014. RH v DE (594/2013) [2014] ZASCA 133 (25 September 2014).

Parliamentary acts and amendments

Stock Theft (Amendment) Bill 2018 (Bill No. 30)

Customary Courts: Subsidiary Legislations (Chapter 04:05), 25 June 1971.
Customary Courts Act (consolidated) (Chapter 04:06), 2006.
Customary Courts (Amendment) Bill, No. 21 of 21st September, 2012.
Customary Courts (Amendment) Act, No. 22 of 2013.
Customary Courts Act (Procedure)(Amendments) Rules, 2016, Customary Courts Act (Cap 04:05), *Statutory Instrument 107of 2016.* 28 September 2016.
Abolition of Marital Power Act 2004, 2005.
Matrimonial Causes Act 1973, Amended 2008.
Stock Theft Act 1996 (Act 21).
Stock Theft (Amendment) Bill 2018 (Bill No. 30)
Witchcraft Act 2, Chapter 09:02. Proclamation (1927), 1959.
House of Chiefs Debates
Ntlo ya Dikgosi Debates, 11th Meeting of the 2nd Ntlo ya Dikgosi, 28 January-01 February 2013.

Other documents

'FACT SHEET ON THE HISTORY OF THE MATOLWANE DISPUTE'.

Lesotho Stock Theft Act 2000 (Act No. 4)
Mothlhabane, Dithonamo et al (2018) 'CONCERNS ON ISSUES AFFECTING OUR VILLAGE,' 15 November, 2018. Addressed to the Honourable Minister, Ministry of Local Government and Rural Development.

Author index

Subject index

For Product Safety Concerns and Information please contact our EU
representative GPSR@taylorandfrancis.com
Taylor & Francis Verlag GmbH, Kaufingerstraße 24, 80331 München, Germany

www.ingramcontent.com/pod-product-compliance
Lightning Source LLC
LaVergne TN
LVHW011117300926
849160LV00008B/413

9781032149462